# PORTRAITS

*of a*

# MERCHANT FAMILY

# PORTRAITS
*of a*
# MERCHANT FAMILY

## T.P. BENTHALL

*For All the Descendants of William Bentall and Dr. William Marshall*

MILL CITY PRESS

Mill City Press, Inc.
2301 Lucien Way #415
Maitland, FL 32751
407.339.4217
www.millcitypress.net

Printed in the United States of America

Library of Congress Control Number: 2020907813

ISBN-13: 978-1-6305-0260-7

# TABLE OF CONTENTS

# PREFACE

This book began in Shropshire, at Benthall Hall. My father and mother lived there as tenants of the National Trust, after his cousin Clementina had purchased the house in 1935, lived in it herself for 25 years, and donated it to the Trust before she died. As a college student I lived there too during vacations, and loved everything about it, including the many portraits of family members – some hung on display and others that sat in attics because they were too large or ugly to display – and the trunks of letters and documents that went back hundreds of years.

Only three of the people in the portraits had ever lived in that house. The branch of the Benthall family I am descended from had left Shropshire long, long ago, before the house now known as Benthall Hall was built. Two brothers went to Essex in around 1550, and dropped the 'h' from their name. Five generations later, one of their descendants, named William Bentall, moved to Devon. He became a grain merchant and then a banker, and founded a family that became politically influential in the town of Totnes. I went to Totnes a few years ago looking for monuments to him and the other Bentalls who had lived there, and found not only memorials to them in the church but also, in the Guildhall, a list of all the annually appointed mayors of Totnes. The list contained the names of William and of two of his sons (and one grandson), some several times over.

Those two sons married two sisters, daughters of a Dr. William Marshall, and two of their brothers also appeared on the mayoral list. Between 1801 and 1843 there were five marriages between the Bentall and Marshall families, and the portraits at Benthall Hall include several Marshalls as well as Bentalls.

I later discovered that Totnes politics were dominated for 30 years by a faction known to modern historians as the 'Adams–Bentall–Marshall interest'. William Adams, a member of parliament for Totnes for over 10 years, was a nephew of Dr. William Marshall. His younger brother married William Bentall's daughter. In a small way, the leading families of Totnes did what other prosperous merchant families did at that time – intermarried to maintain power and wealth.

These Marshalls and Bentalls from Totnes (and later on Benthalls, since in 1843 that family decided to put the 'h' back in the family name) were merchants, doctors and clerics, although some of their younger sons sought their fortune in other spheres. Some went to sea, some settled in the colonies, some worked in the government bureaucracy in Westminster, and one became Professor Alfred Marshall, the famous economist. Not all were successful – in fact, some were quite spectacular failures.

This is their story, and the story of how all those pictures and documents ended up at Benthall Hall. Having written it, I now understand better why, on my birth certificate, my father listed his occupation as "merchant" – an archaic term that is nowadays rarely heard except when qualified – as in, "wine...," "coal...," "...banker" or "...of Venice."

While researching the material, I became aware that the stories in the book provide source material for more serious historical studies. I have therefore tried to adhere to formal academic standards that will allow for such use.

# ACKNOWLEDGMENTS

This book could not have been written without help from many individuals and institutions.

My father, Paul Benthall, was very interested in genealogical research and wrote copiously – though not intended for wide publication – about himself, his family and his ancestors. I have used much of his research for this book, and I quote extensively from his work. My brother, James Benthall, has also done genealogical and historical research relating to our family, particularly about those who spent time in India, and his work has also been very important to me.

The National Trust in 1958 agreed to acquire Benthall Hall, then owned by Mary Clementina Benthall. They agreed to preserve it as a family residence, but open to the public for much of the year. Its furnishings include the family portraits that illustrate this book and images of those portraits are reproduced here with the Trust's permission.

Philip Morrell made contact with me by email in 2015. Philip had a pioneering and successful career in international tourism, and wanted to write a book about an Englishman named Thornton Benthall who moved to Norway in about 1847, changed his name to Thomas Bennett, founded one of the first international tourist agencies, invented the concept of a "traveller's cheque," and thus paved the way for the modern credit card. Thornton was a stockbroker and one of my many great great-uncles, who left London in a hurry after squandering his clients' investments. I agreed to help Philip, and in doing so found that I had my own book to write. Since then Philip has been an encouraging and steady source of valuable information.

The administrators of a website named The Genealogists' Forum[1] enthusiastically helped me with my early investigations, and gently trained me to become more self-sufficient in genealogical research. A distant cousin, Megan Stevens, descended from another Marshall-Bentall marriage, saw a post by me on that website and made contact by email. We both thought that the disparaging and error-filled accounts of our common relatives written by the biographers of Professor Alfred Marshall should be refuted. We had complementary research to share, specifically about the professor's grandfather and his uncle Charlie, her ancestor. Her paper correcting those factual errors is due to be published in 2020 in the journal *History of Political Economy*.[2] She has generously shared all of her research and helped me with mine in innumerable ways.

Another distant cousin, Ralph Ravestijn, has undertaken extensive research about his Marshall ancestors and has documented much of it on his website.[3] Ralph is descended from a Francis Ord Marshall, a grandson of Dr. William Marshall, and from his daughter by his Chinese mistress, with whom he lived for many years on the island of Java. We communicated via email, and discovered that I am his great-grandmother's fourth cousin, twice over. Ralph has also very kindly provided me with all his research relating to our shared relatives.

Other original sources of family material come from my 19th century relatives, Frank and Laura Benthall. Frank Benthall, another of my great-great-uncles, paid for the Royal Licence that restored the "h" to the family name, and conducted extensive research on his Shropshire ancestors. His sister Laura, a gifted artist (some of whose paintings are on display at Benthall Hall), wrote in 1871 an account of her family history titled *Annals of the Benthall Family*. Although incomplete and not always accurate – Laura left out anything that could be embarrassing, such as bankruptcies (of which there were several) – it is nonetheless of historical value and oft-quoted in this book.

A book by Professor Adam Kuper, entitled *Incest & Influence: the Private Life of Bourgeois England*, gave me helpful insights into the economic rationale behind the peculiar social norms to which these families subscribed.

Other acknowledgments are due to: my immediate family, who have been patient with my obsessive interest in this endeavour; Len Barnett, an expert on British Maritime History whose research helped fill in some critical gaps in the family historical record; Lucasta Miller, who discovered that one supposed family portrait is in fact a painting of a rather notorious poetess; Alan Burrage, who provided information about how Benthall Hall was saved from demolition; John Morton, who provided helpful information about Tom and Ruth Benthall; and Charles Campbell-Jones, who has been a very

effective editor, and who helped me organise and explain the material.

A general acknowledgment is also due to the many online resources that I have made use of in compiling the information presented here. These include foremost *Google Books*, through which many 19th-century texts are now available online. Others are the website of the National Archives at Kew, *The History of Parliament Online*, the many articles available on *Wikipedia*, and the genealogical websites *FamilySearch.org* and *Findmypast.co.uk*.

The UK census records from 1841 to 1911, frequently referenced here, are the property of the Public Record Office, and can be accessed online through the genealogical websites mentioned above, along with records of births, baptisms, marriages and deaths, wills, etc.

This book contains over 160 portraits of the people whose lives are described in it. About half of these come from portraits in the National Trust collection at Benthall Hall and most of the others from family archives there or owned by my family. Some images are from other sources, and the relevant licences to reproduce these are provided in the section entitled 'Illustration Sources' at the end of the book.

Many of the stories told here require a sense of the places where the protagonists lived. The maps that follow are taken from *Google Maps*, whose copyright they remain. I have added additional place names that are historically relevant.

# MAPS

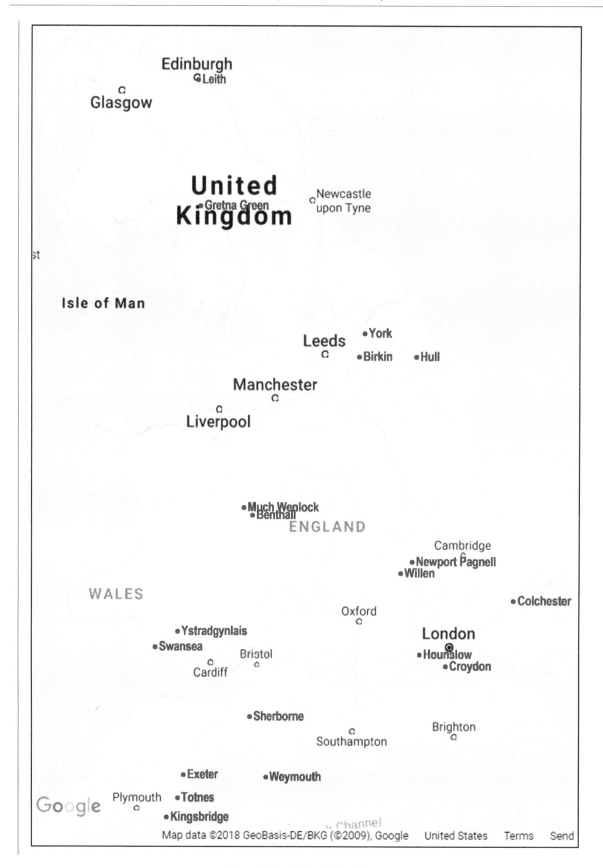

Map 1: The United Kingdom

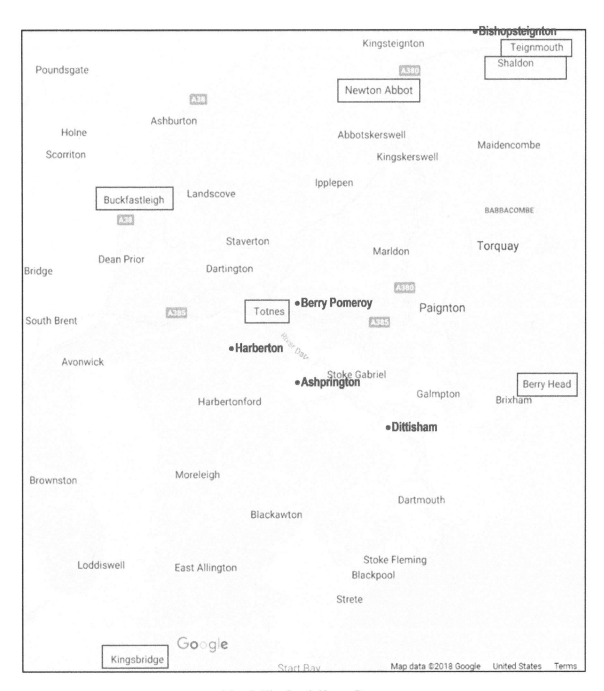

Map 2: The South Hams, Devon

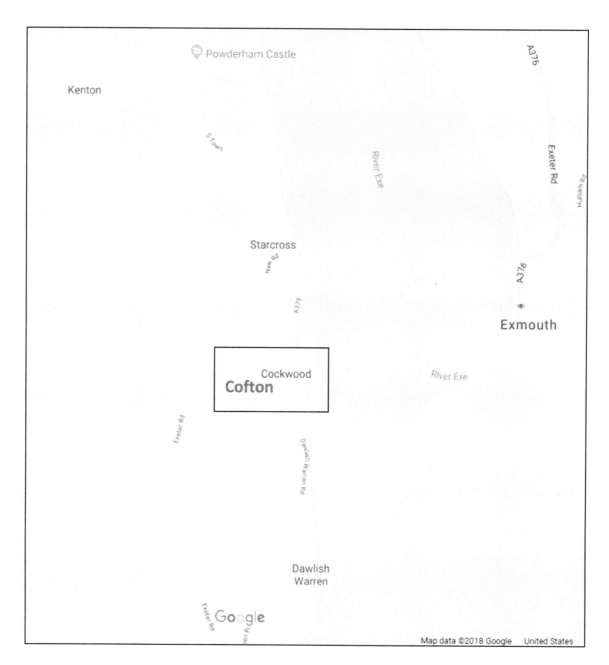

Map 3: The River Exe Estuary

# INTRODUCTION

John Bentall, a wine merchant at Colchester, in Essex, died in 1750 while visiting Portugal on business. His wife's brother, John Thornton (also a merchant who had lived in Portugal) had recently retired to the town of Kingsbridge, in South Devon, and offered to take charge of John's 14-year-old son, William Bentall, to launch him on a career as a merchant. A few years later, William met a young medical student his age, named William Marshall. The two became friends for life. William Bentall learnt much from his uncle, and became a successful grain merchant, with interests also in cider and other commodities, and later also a banker. In due course both Williams moved to Totnes, an ancient borough on the river Dart, a few miles north of Kingsbridge, Dr William Marshall to practise medicine and later William Bentall to operate his businesses out of warehouses adjacent to the wharves that lined the river. Portraits of both men are on display at Benthall Hall.

Both men married and had families, and became patriarchs of a merchant dynasty. William Bentall's wife Grace produced four boys and two girls, while Dr William Marshall's wife Dorothy had four boys and five girls. In due course, William Bentall's two older sons

Figure 1: Dr William Marshall (l) and William Bentall (r), ca. 1800

– William Searle and Thornton Bentall – married two of the doctor's daughters, and the two Bentall daughters married nephews of the doctor, Samuel Adams and another William Marshall. Thornton was childless, but these children of William Bentall children produced 34 grandchildren for him, of whom 31 lived past infancy. Fifteen of those could claim Dr William Marshall as their other grandfather, while the remaining 16 knew him as a great-uncle. Four of William and Dorothy Marshall's other children also married and produced 22 additional grandchildren, of whom 18 lived to adulthood.

This combined horde of 47 grandchildren remained very close, and it is not surprising, given the customs of the time, that two of the Bentall grandchildren married their Marshall first cousins. Edward Bentall married Clementina Marshall, and then later, Edward's sister Mary married another Marshall grandson, also named William. The chart in Figure 2 shows all five Bentall-Marshall intermarriages.

About a hundred years later, in 1935, another married couple, both grandchildren of Edward and Clementina and so also first cousins, decided romantically and on the spur of the moment to buy a manor house in Shropshire named Benthall Hall, in the village that their ancestors had left 400 years earlier (before that house was built). In 1959 the property was given to the National Trust, and under a lease agreement, the house still serves as a family residence.

The primary goal of this book is to tell the story of how the Benthall family that moved away from Shropshire to Essex and then to Devon reconnected to that house and arranged for the family portraits to become part of its museum collection, and also to provide an account of the lives of the people depicted in those portraits.

The second goal is to use their stories to illustrate the evolution of the English merchant class during and after the Industrial Revolution: its social history and its role in the expansion of the British Empire. Adam Kuper, in his book *Incest and Influence: The Private Life of Bourgeois England*, argues that this propensity for in-law and cousin marriages was in fact an effective strategy for prosperity, and so *"played a significant part in the making of the nineteenth century world."*[4] The stories here provide examples of how such marriages came about, how they were used to advance the family's political and financial interests, and how the extended family connections persisted when cousins met in unlikely places.

Associated with "incest" is the vexed topic of "influence," also part of Kuper's study: the way people in power found jobs and secured incomes for their relatives. Today such string-pulling is thought of as nepotism or corruption, but it was commonplace in the political system that prevailed during the early part of the 19th century, and continued in various forms for much longer than that. The involvement of the Marshalls, Benthalls and their close relatives in local and national politics – in the borough of Totnes as well as Westminster – provides good examples of how family influence played out, and how it became a source of political controversy. Indeed, in the 1830s and 1840s it could be said that the Marshall family ran the War Office, the Waterfield family (married to the Benthalls) ran the India Office, and the Adams family ran the Office of Woods, Forests, Land Revenues, Works, and Buildings, a primary source of government revenue.

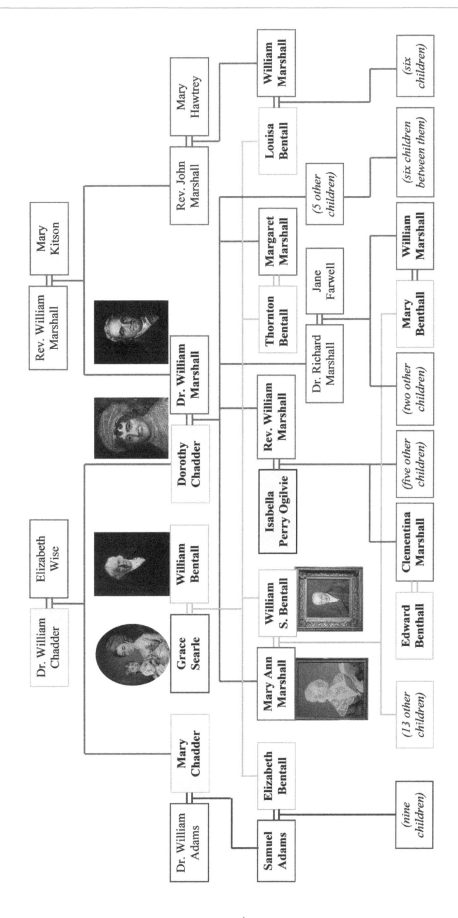

Figure 2: Bentall and Marshall intermarriages

There are difficult themes – specifically the institution of slavery, and then later the building of empire through colonial expansion – that play out in these stories. I am not qualified to do more than report that facts as I have found them. I hope that the stories documented here may be of some use to professional historians who address those topics. Other less difficult themes that crop up in the book are addressed in the last few chapters.

In addition to the topics of incest and influence, I have been intrigued by the Victorian obsession with the definition of what it meant to be a "gentleman." Did one qualify through ownership of land, high education, or good manners? The merchant class was never quite accepted by the landed gentry and aristocracy as qualifying, and this book includes several examples illustrative of the problems that ensued.

The lives described in this book are arranged more or less in chronological order, starting with the two patriarchs and their ancestors, and then later concentrating primarily on the descendants of Edward and Clementina who brought the portraits back to Benthall Hall, but digressing occasionally to give an account of other relatives.

Part I provides an account of the ancestry of the two patriarchs and their wives, their brothers and sisters, and some of the descendants of those siblings. Part II covers the lives and families of the many children of the two patriarchs and also gives brief accounts of some of the many descendants of those who did not share both Bentall and Marshall ancestors. Part III moves to the next generation and provides details of the lives and families of the 21 grandchildren who had both Bentall and Marshall parentage, and again provides brief details of the descendants of those who play only a limited role in the main story. Part IV is about the children of Edward and Clementina Benthall (née Marshall). Part V then moves on to the descendants of those children, who purchased Benthall Hall when it came onto the market and then arranged for its acquisition by the National Trust. Part VI picks up some loose ends in the narrative and addresses some of the themes outlined above.

Patient readers may enjoy the steady build-up of various narrative threads from their provincial roots. Others may prefer to jump to some of the more melodramatic sections, for which these previews are intended to provide a reading guide.

### The Perry-Ogilvie Affair

In 1791, a 25-year old apothecary named Richard Perry, living in Bristol, eloped with a wealthy 14-year-old schoolgirl named Clementina Clerk, raced at eight miles per hour by stagecoach to Gretna Green, Scotland,[i] where they were married, fled to the Continent to avoid his arrest on the capital charge of abduction and rape of a minor, but then returned to face justice in England when Clementina was expecting a child. A trial took place and he was acquitted. That child, a daughter named Isabella, married the eldest son of Dr William Marshall (also named William). Their eldest daughter, also named Clementina, married her first cousin, Edward Bentall (later Benthall). The story of the elopement and trial is told in Chapter 8.

### Rossetti's Landlord

Henry Benthall, a brother of Edward Benthall and serial bankrupt, became landlord

---

[i] At the time, it was illegal for anyone under the age of 21 to marry in England or Wales without their parents' consent; no such law existed in Scotland.

to the artist Dante Gabriel Rossetti and his wife and muse, Lizzie Siddal. In 1862 Henry was a member of the jury at the inquest into Lizzie's death, from a lethal mix of brandy and laudanum. His family story is told in Chapter 18.

## Deaths by Drowning

The deaths by drowning of Alfred and Octavius Benthall, two more brothers of Edward and Henry, are told in Chapter 19. Alfred at the age of 22 became the master of a merchant brig named *Permei*, and his first cargo was a diplomatic gift of horses from the British government to the Sultan of Turkey. He then sailed on two voyages to China and back, but succumbed in 1839 while trying to recover the cargo from his vessel after it struck rocks near a foggy Venice. Octavius drowned in 1846 while trying to bring help to the passengers and crew of a naval brig, H.M.S. *Osprey*, after it ran aground off the west coast of New Zealand.

## Inventor of the Credit Card?

As noted in the acknowledgments, Thornton Benthall, another brother of Edward, Henry, Alfred and Octavius, fled to Norway and changed his name to Thomas Bennett He became a 19th-century pioneer of the international tourism business. After arriving at Oslo, Thomas taught English to Henrik Ibsen, the playwright. George Bradshaw, creator of the first railway guide, went to visit him and died there, from cholera. Later Jules Verne also went to meet him, when he wanted to figure out how to travel *"around the world in eighty days."* That story is told in Chapter 20.

## Indian Business and Politics

Two brothers, Tom and Paul Benthall (respectively my uncle and father, both grandsons of Edward and Clementina) made their careers as managers of an agglomeration of businesses in India between 1920 and 1950, but also became deeply involved in political deliberations in the 15 years before, and the five years after India became independent. Both were honoured with knighthoods. Tom's story is told in Chapter 35, and Paul's in Chapter 37.

## Michael Benthall, Bobby Helpmann and Katharine Hepburn

Michael Benthall was Tom's son, a stage director who made his name directing opera at Covent Garden, Shakespeare's plays at Stratford-upon-Avon, and various productions in London, mainly at the Old Vic Theatre. His lifetime romantic and professional partner was Robert Helpmann, the Australian dancer, actor, choreographer and stage director, known to his friends as Bobby. Michael was also the stage director chosen by Katharine Hepburn, the American film star, when she decided to become a stage actress and perform in plays by Shakespeare and George Bernard Shaw, and who would use no other for 20 years. Michael, Bobby and Katherine became good friends. Michael's story is told in Chapter 39.

## Righteous Indignation and Family Pride

Professor Alfred Marshall was a great-grandson of William Bentall and a great-great-nephew of Dr. William Marshall. His entry in The Oxford Dictionary of National Biography states *"The work of R. H. Coase and*

*P. D. Groenewegen has revealed the truth of Marshall's parental heritage, which, if it lacks the social distinction felt by the Victorians to be so important, lends added weight to Marshall's achievements.*" The 'truth' revealed by these two biographers was based on research that contained serious errors and omissions. The paper by Stevens referred to in the acknowledgements sets the record straight.[5] See Chapters 13 and 23–28 for a summary of the lives of that branch of the Marshall family.

Those biographers (in a familial way) and contemporary sources (in a political way) published disparaging allegations about members of the Adams, Bentall and Marshall clan. Chapters 41 and 43 list some of those allegations, and provide my assessment of how far they are supported by facts.

# PART I.
## PATRIARCHAL AND MATRIARCHAL ORIGINS

As noted in the introduction, this book is about the origins and descendants of two couples – William and Dorothy Marshall, and William and Grace Bentall – who lived at Totnes, in Devon, at the end of the 18th and beginning of the 19th century. The first chapter provides an essential overview of the history of Totnes, and the next five chapters provide an account of origins of the Marshall and Bentall couples, and their roots in the clerical and merchant classes of their time.

# Chapter 1

## THE TOTNES CORPORATION

The small but ancient borough of Totnes plays a large role in the first two parts of this book. It was in the town's Guildhall that I first took an interest in learning about my ancestors who had lived there, when I saw a panelled wall listing the names of all the town's mayors. Remarkably, between 1799 and 1832 the surname Bentall appears eight times, and Marshall three times (see Figure 1.1). But understanding these families requires first some understanding of the topography and history of the town.

Totnes lies about 180 miles west-southwest of London, in a part of Devon known as South Hams (see maps 1 and 2) and situated at the head of the estuary of the River Dart. Fed by the peat bogs and mires of Dartmoor, the river has a total length of about 30 miles. For the last 10 miles it is tidal, passing through a deep and narrow drowned valley. Today the main road from Exeter to Plymouth (the two largest cities in Devon) runs further inland, but for centuries there was an important trackway at Totnes which crossed this river by a ford and then climbed a steep hill on the river's west bank.

The South Hams district contains rich farmland, and the hills further upstream around Buckfastleigh and Ashburton were for millennia mined, ever since the Bronze Age, for tin and copper. When the Romans came to that part of Britain they established a camp and a city at

Exeter, and a trading route from there as far as the River Tamar and Plymouth. A small town grew up at the site of the ford across the Dart, and was known as *Statio ad Durium Amnem* (literally, "outpost on a harsh river"). That became the town of Totnes, which, being at the head of the tidal section of the river, served as a small port. The tidal range at the town wharf is about nine feet; as a result, seagoing sailing vessels were able to reach Totnes by "riding" the tide up the river and then departing as it fell again.

Totnes and its environs have always been somewhat "apart" from England. Even while the Romans ruled much of Britain, their control over the region south and west of Exeter was tenuous. When they left, an independent Christian kingdom evolved to cover Somerset, Devon and Cornwall; it was known by the Anglo-Saxons as West Wales and by the indigenous Celtic Britons, influenced by centuries of contact with Roman culture, as Dumnonia. Although most of the country became united under the Saxon King Alfred, his rule did not extend into this part of the island, and it was not until the year 928 CE that Devon came under Anglo-Saxon rule. Later, after the Norman Conquest of England in 1066, it took a further two years for King William I (a.k.a. "the Conqueror") to travel to Exeter and compel its surrender. The king then granted a large estate south of Exeter to a Breton named

Judhael, who built the first castle at Totnes and founded a priory in the town. After William's death, his son and successor King William II seized Judhael's lands, for reasons that are not entirely clear, and exiled him to France. In the 12th century another Norman noble expanded the castle, which is nowadays considered "*one of the best-preserved examples of a Norman castle in England*."[6] Its ruins, high atop a mound, still dominate the townscape.

Easy accessibility by road and river, together with abundant local natural resources, soon established Totnes as an important regional market town. By the 14th century it had become one of the chief clothing manufacturing towns in England, and "*hose of fine Totnes*" was a term used to describe someone's dress as especially splendid. Buckfast Abbey, a Cistercian institution a few miles up the river from Totnes at Buckfastleigh, had become one of the wealthiest abbeys in the southwest of England thanks to its extensive development of a wool industry, herding sheep on Dartmoor and using water from the River Dart to power its mills. The resulting woollen cloth was exported by boat through Totnes.

In 1523 Totnes was assessed as the second richest town in Devon and the 16th richest in England, ahead of cathedral cities like Worcester and Gloucester. Even though Buckfast Abbey was in decline, the merchants of Totnes were by then trading with western France, Spain and Portugal.

Buckfast Abbey was destroyed in 1539, like so many others after Henry VIII broke with the Roman Catholic Church and ordered all the monasteries and abbeys to be dissolved and their land confiscated. Nonetheless, the local wool industry continued to grow. Around 1580, a weir was constructed from stone about half a mile upstream from the Totnes town wharf. This became the limit of the tidal flow. The weir improved navigation as well as providing water power; from the millpond or lake above it, a leat[i] supplied water to drive eight new mills, "*probably the largest milling complex in South Devon*."[7] But there were downsides too: the weir was costly to maintain and generated endless lawsuits between the town and upstream landowners when their fields were flooded.

Totnes is also graced by a fine church, built originally in the 10th century, rebuilt in the 13th, and rebuilt again in the 14th century. The south pinnacle of the tower was struck by lightning in 1634. Another major renovation of the interior was undertaken by the town in 1722. In 1799 the church sustained another lightning strike, this time to the southeast pinnacle, and was almost destroyed. These disasters further undermined the town's finances.

By about the year 1100, the townspeople had established a "town guild" which increasingly took charge of the management of the town's affairs. The borough became an official municipal entity when it received its first charter from King John in 1206. This made it a "free town," able to make local laws, and formalised the establishment of a "guild of merchants" to regulate trade and administer the borough. Members of the guild had the right to use the town's wharves without paying a fee, and so were known as "freemen." As people with local authority, they were also known as "burgesses" (synonymous with the French term *bourgeois*).

From the earliest days of the English Parliament, comprising an upper House of Lords and a lower House of Commons, the burgesses of Totnes had the right to elect two members to the lower house. By the 14th century the guild also ran the town, appointing a mayor in

---

[i] An artificial open watercourse.

charge of municipal affairs (including the local church), while the feudally designated "lord of the manor" merely collected "manorial dues" – i.e., annual rents. A second, revised charter was obtained from King Henry VII around 1500, and this again provided for a merchants' guild (officially named the "*Company of Merchant Adventurers of Totnes*") which controlled trade, and left the administration of the town under the control of the "*Mayor and burgesses*," who in practice were the same people. For much of the late 16th century the governor of the merchants' guild was John Wise the Elder, and in 1579 he arranged for a substantial overhaul of the guild's rules. He was also mayor in 1574 and 1587. (See Chapter 3 for more information on John Wise the Elder and his family.)

In 1596 Queen Elizabeth bestowed a new, third charter on the borough.[8] Under its terms, the role of the independent merchants' guild was taken over by a "Corporation," styled "*The Mayor and Burgesses of the Borough of Totnes, in the county of Devon.*"

The Corporation consisted of a mayor, a recorder, a town clerk, 14 "masters and counsellors" (also known as "aldermen") appointed for life, and an indefinite number of burgesses/freemen, not all of whom actually lived in the borough. The recorder was elected for life and organised Parliamentary elections. Each year in September one of the aldermen was elected mayor. The mayor presided over meetings of the aldermen, while most of the management of the town was in the hands of the town clerk. (It appears that in practice, the mayor's primary function was to throw an annual banquet for the townspeople.) When an alderman died or retired, his replacement was elected by the resident freemen. From time to time the aldermen would also appoint new freemen, often their relatives. According to one historian, "*some tradition of the old guild roll survived, as it appears that sons of freemen retained the right of enrolment.*"[9] Parliamentary candidates were officially nominated by the aldermen and voted upon by the freemen, both resident and non-resident.

At that time, and for most of the period covered by this book, there was a well-understood stratification of society. At the top was the aristocracy, who usually owned substantial estates and derived their income from their agricultural tenants. Below them were the lesser "landed gentry," who owned smaller estates but also lived off their rents. Below them were the commercial and professional families – merchants, clergy, doctors and lawyers – who were considered to be "gentlemen" but not "gentry". For centuries at Totnes, like other similarly ancient boroughs, the aldermen were generally respected local gentry and gentlemen; but when it came to nominating candidates for election to Parliament, the local aristocracy and landed gentry maintained effective control, and as a result, candidates were often not local people. However, in the mid–18th century Totnes merchants began to assert their independence by insisting on controlling the selection of at least one of their Parliamentarians. Furthermore, by the end of that century the Corporation, and thus the voter roll, was stacked with members of a few interrelated families. Many of the men named in this book were freemen of the borough; several became aldermen and took their turns as mayor, as shown in Figure 1.1 (overleaf).

The Corporation continued to be managed in this self-perpetuating fashion until the passage of the Great Reform Act of 1832. The politics of the period from 1770 up to 1832 will be discussed in more detail in Chapter 10.

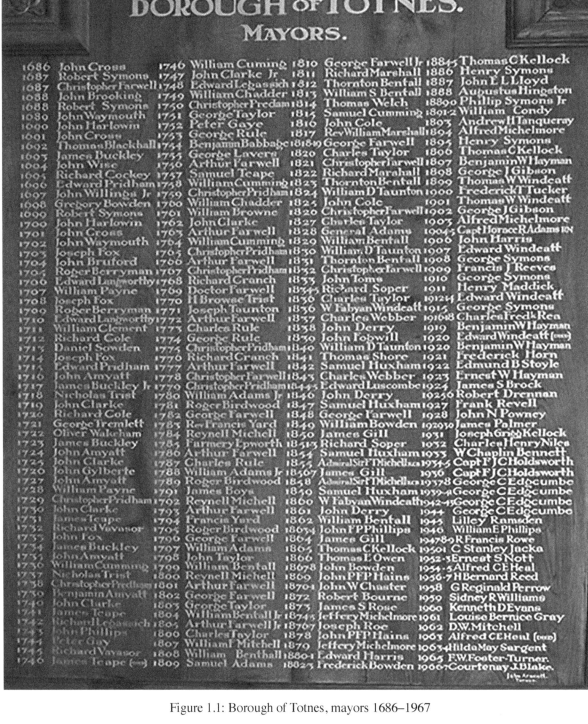

Figure 1.1: Borough of Totnes, mayors 1686–1967

## Chapter 2

# THE MARSHALLS:
# A CLERICAL FAMILY OF THE WEST

Our two patriarchs were born less than a year apart. William Marshall was younger, but was a Devon native, and ancestor twice over to the later Benthalls, so he is the first to be accounted for here. The oil painting of him in the Benthall Hall portrait collection has been displayed in the introduction in Figure 1 and another younger silhouette is also in the collection (see Figure 2.1).

He was the youngest son of the Rev. William Marshall, rector of Ashprington, a village about four miles southeast of Totnes (see Map 2). The economist, John Maynard Keynes, in an obituary for his tutor and later friend Professor Alfred Marshall,[i] described these Marshalls as *"a clerical family of the West"* and the Rev. William Marshall as *"the half-legendary herculean parson of Devonshire, who, by twisting horseshoes with his hands, frightened local blacksmiths into fearing that they blew their bellows for the devil."*[10] There are many stories about the Reverend's great strength which have been retold for 200 years by his many descendants, including Professor Alfred. One of several told by Laura Benthall[ii] was this:

> *A party of farmers had come together to pay their tithe of corn, and while waiting for Mr Marshall who was out, they amused themselves with trying who could swing a sack of corn onto his shoulder (a favourite test of strength). The parson returned just as one of them with great pride accomplished the feat,*

Figure 2.1: Dr William Marshall

---

i  As noted in the introduction, Professor Alfred Marshall was a great-great-nephew of Dr William Marshall and a great-grandson of patriarch William Bentall.

ii  As noted in the introduction, Laura Benthall, granddaughter of both patriarchal couples, wrote a history of her family from which I have taken many quotations.

and rather astonished them by swinging both man and sack onto his shoulder and walking round the kitchen with them.

This is her version of the blacksmith story:

*On another occasion the Rector was riding at some distance from home, where he was not so well known, and, his horse having cast a shoe, he stopped at a wayside Blacksmith's to have it renewed. The smith made a shoe, and was about to put it on, when his customer asked to look at it. Taking it in his hands with the knuckles together, he bent it back till the smaller joints of his fingers met. He then told the man that it was very good iron, but not well made, and desired him to hammer it out better. This was accordingly done, and, the horse being shod to his master's satisfaction, the blacksmith was asked what there was to pay. 'Nothing', was his decided reply, 'I'll never touch the devil's money'.*

This super-strong clergyman was born in 1677 at Poundstock, a village in the north of Cornwall. He probably obtained his education at Wadham College, Oxford. He became a curate at Ashprington in about 1702, in due course was appointed rector, and lived there for 54 years. He was married three times. He married his first wife, Susannah Nosworthy, in 1706, but she died in 1709. Their two sons died in infancy. One daughter, also named Susannah, lived to adulthood and married John Michell of Exminster.[11]

The Rev. William's second wife was Mary Kelland, née Ford. She gave birth three times, but only one daughter (also named Mary) lived to adulthood, and married John Clarke. This John Clarke and his elder brother Richard were sons of another John Clarke, a wealthy merchant in Totnes, who built and lived in a grand house next to the River Dart which later became the home of William and Grace Bentall and was then bequeathed to their son and grandson. The elder John Clarke was mayor of Totnes four times between 1719 and 1740. His son, the younger John Clarke, was also mayor in 1747 and again in 1762. Laura wrote: "*It was from great-uncle Clarke's elder brother Richard that our grandfather bought the house on The Plains, when he moved from Kingsbridge to Totnes. In one of the windows of the house there is still (Sept. 14th, 1875) a pane of glass with 'John Clarke, 1737', scratched on it.*"

The Reverend's second wife died in 1720, and his third was named Mary Kitson, whom he married in 1722. There is a family story that she was the first child he baptised when he came to Ashprington as a curate, and that he said as a joke that "*she should be his little wife.*"[iii] Mary Kitson had a younger sister, named Margaret, whom the elder John Clarke, being a widower, married. Laura mentions that in later years, Margaret was known as "*Great Aunt Clarke,*" while Margaret's step-niece (and also step-daughter-in-law), being short in stature, was known as "*Little Aunt Clarke.*" The Reverend's third marriage lasted twice as long as the first two combined, until his death in 1756. The couple had eight children, of whom four sons and two daughters lived to adulthood.

The three elder sons all attended Oxford University and became clergymen. But the Reverend died before his youngest son, William, our patriarch, could follow in the family footsteps. Instead, William moved to the town of Kingsbridge, Devon, to study medicine under a respected doctor named Tripe, and there met

---

iii This anecdote was also mentioned by Keynes.

and started a lifelong friendship with William Bentall. In due course Dr William moved to Totnes, established a medical practice there, and married Dorothy Chadder in 1771. She was the daughter of another doctor, named William Chadder, and had grown up at Totnes (see Chapter 3). As noted in the introduction, Dr William and Dorothy Marshall produced nine children, all of whom lived to adulthood. Two of Dr William and Dorothy's daughters married sons of William Bentall. Figure 2.2 is a pedigree showing those of the Rev. William's descendants who are important to this family saga.

The family of Dr William Marshall's eldest brother, John, is included in the pedigree because it is significant to this history. John Marshall

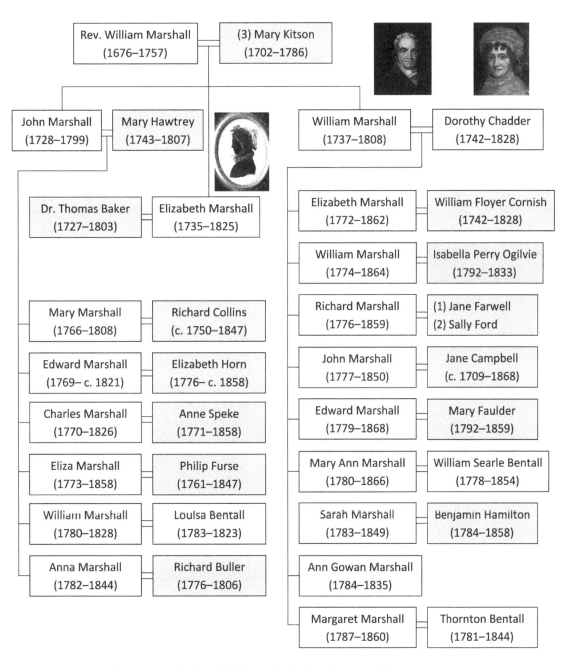

Figure 2.2: The Rev. William Marshall and some of his descendants

attended Exeter College, Oxford, later becoming rector of All Hallow's, Exeter, and then headmaster of the Exeter Grammar School.[12] He and his wife, Mary (née Hawtrey), had three sons and three daughters who survived to adulthood and marriage.

The eldest, the Reverend Edward Marshall, born at Exeter in 1769, was, like his uncle and cousin, elected to scholarships at Eton and at King's College, Cambridge, and took holy orders.[13] He moved to Jamaica, married, and spent most of his life there. Through his wife he inherited an estate named Mount Moses, including a number of slaves. One of their sons, another John Marshall, reappears briefly in Chapter 13.

The second, the Rev. Charles Marshall, born at Exeter in 1770, attended Exeter College, Oxford, and spent his life as rector of Lawhitton, Cornwall.

The third, yet another William Marshall, born and baptised in 1780, married Louisa Bentall,

Figure 2.3: Elizabeth Marshall, Mrs Thomas Baker

younger daughter of our second patriarch William Bentall, and was Professor Alfred Marshall's grandfather. Their story is also told in Chapter 13.

There were also three daughters who lived to adulthood. According to a book published in 1903:

> *...the three daughters were thus married: Mary to Mr [Richard] Collins, Eliza to Mr Furze [sic], and Anna to Mr Buller, son of the Bishop of Exeter. It is a well-known and accepted tradition of the family, I am told, that Eliza and Anna were models to Miss Austen, with whom they were acquainted, for her characters Elizabeth and Jane Bennett in 'Pride and Prejudice' but whether this was really the case I cannot say.*[14]

It *is* known that Anna's husband, the Rev. Richard Buller, had been a pupil of Jane Austen's father, and that in 1801 Jane Austen and her family paid a visit to the town of Sidmouth, where Richard was vicar and newly wed to Anna.[15]

Mary Collins died in 1808, but her husband Richard lived until 1847, acquired part-ownership of his brother-in-law Edward's estate in Jamaica, and was compensated financially for the emancipation of the slaves there. Meanwhile Eliza became the third wife of Philip Furse, an iron merchant and banker. She and her husband lived at Kenton Cottage, near Dawlish in Devon (see Map 3). He died there in 1847 and she died in 1858. Richard Collins, Eliza Furse and the house at Kenton will play brief but important roles in Chapter 25.

Dr William Marshall's sister Elizabeth married Dr Thomas Baker (a doctor of divinity, not medicine). There is a small portrait of her displayed at Benthall Hall (see Figure 2.3).

Elizabeth and her husband were both buried at Berry Pomeroy, a church a few miles from Totnes. The latter is named on a deed in the National Archives as *"Thomas Baker of Loventor D.D. and Prebendary of Exeter."*[16] His father, the Rev. George Baker, had been archdeacon of Totnes, and was also related by marriage to the Rev. John Marshall. Thomas Baker's brother, George, was the personal doctor to King George III and Queen Charlotte, and in due course became Sir George Baker, 1st Baronet. That connection is probably how Anna Maria Adams (wife of William Adams, MP for Totnes) became wet nurse to Princess Amelia, King George III's youngest and favourite daughter (see Chapter 7).

## DIGRESSION: THE HAWTREY FAMILY

John Marshall's wife, Mary, came from a family that had been closely associated with Eton College for several generations. Various members of the Hawtrey family make brief appearances in the lives of John and Mary's descendants. Mary's father was a canon and sub-dean of Exeter, and her mother was the sister of the provost of Eton College. Three of her four brothers attended Eton and then King's College, Cambridge. One of these, named Stephen, became a barrister, a registrar at Eton, and then Recorder of Exeter. The other three brothers became ordained ministers. Her elder unmarried sisters became "dames" at Eton – i.e., surrogate mothers or landladies for the boys who boarded there. Another brother, Edward, became a master at Eton and vicar of Burnham, a village not far from the college. His son, Edward Craven Hawtrey, also went to Eton and King's and became a master at Eton, eventually becoming headmaster in 1834 and provost in 1853. In about 1840 he provided a recommendation when Mary's grandson, Thornton Marshall, applied to become a medical student at Guy's Hospital (see Chapter 28).[17]

As headmaster, Edward Craven Hawtrey introduced the study of mathematics and hired his cousin the Rev. Stephen Hawtrey, a grandson of the eponymous barrister, to start up a mathematics department. Stephen had not been to school at Eton, but he did attend Trinity College Cambridge, where he read Classics and Mathematics and placed as "Eleventh Wrangler" (i.e., 11th in the Mathematics final exam). Stephen officiated at the wedding of another of Mary's grandchildren, Charles Henry Marshall and that couple named one of their children Hawtrey in honour of the family connection (see Chapter 26).

This Stephen's younger brother, John William Hawtrey, also became a master at Eton, and his grandson Sir Ralph Hawtrey (1879–1975) was another Cambridge mathematician and economist, and also a close friend of John Maynard Keynes.

# Chapter 3

## DOROTHY MARSHALL, NÉE CHADDER: TOTNES ROOTS

Dorothy Chadder, the wife of Dr William Marshall, was born in 1742, the second of three sisters. There is a silhouette and an oil painting of her at Benthall Hall, but neither does real justice to her as a subject (see Figure 3.1). The names of the artists are not on record.

Dorothy's father, William Chadder, was also a medical doctor at Totnes, where his father, another William, had been an engineer. The families of Dorothy's two sisters also play important roles in the stories that follow (see Figure 3.2).

Laura Benthall's account of the origins of the Chadder family at Totnes reads:

*Towards the end of the seventeenth century, three friends, namely, M. Chadder, M. Rule and M. ___ emigrated from France and settled at Totnes. The first of these, our great-great-grandfather* [the William

Figure 3.1: Dorothy Marshall, née Chadder

12

Chadder who died in 1727], *was a very clever man, and introduced many improvements and innovations on the ancient established usages of the place. This naturally drew in turn much indignation and jealousy from the old-fashioned inhabitants of the place, and after his death he was condemned by popular opinion to expend those talents which he had so greatly misused during his life on the* hopeless task of tying up the Dart with ropes. [This is a reference to the hopeless tasks that Greek mythology often assigned as punishment to characters in Hades.] *At the end of the town marsh was, within William's recollection* [another William Bentall, Laura's eldest brother] *what was called the 'Buttle Hole', having a sort of valve for preventing the water from flooding the marsh at high tide.*

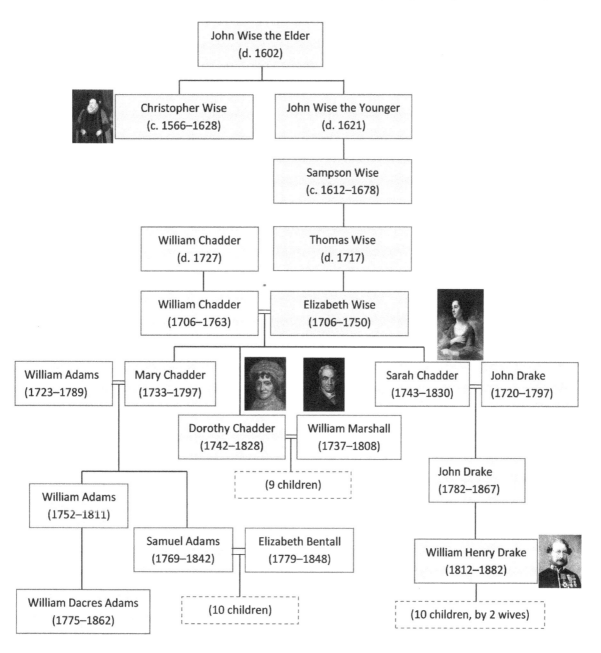

Figure 3.2: Dorothy Chadder's family and ancestry

*The pressure of air and water caused a loud roaring sound, which was clearly understood to be the troubled spirit of our defunct progenitor crying for 'More Ropes'.*

Other family records suggest that the three emigrés from France were Huguenot refugees, but Chadder was a relatively common name in Devon and Cornwall, and there is no independent evidence of any Huguenot ancestors.

Dorothy's mother, christened Elizabeth Wise, was descended from an influential Totnes merchant family. As noted in Chapter 1, John Wise the Elder was governor of the Totnes merchants' guild for many years and was the leading merchant in Totnes in the late 16th century. His eldest son, Christopher, was mayor in 1605 and again in 1621, and had his portrait painted by Nicholas Hilliard, one of the most famous miniaturists of his time. The "*scarlet gown with the tippet and velvet jacket*' he wore for the sitting had been bequeathed to him in his father's will.[18]

Christopher had a brother, John Wise the Younger, who was also mayor in 1609 and died in 1621. This John had a son named Sampson Wise, referred to in some records as "*Sampson Wise of Dittisham*" (Dittisham being a village downstream from Totnes on the River Dart – see Map 2). Sampson's son, Thomas, was Elizabeth's father, and lived at Harberton, another village close by.

William and Elizabeth Chadder produced nine children in all, but five died in infancy. An older brother became a doctor, but also died young. That left three sisters: Mary, Dorothy and Sarah. According to Laura Benthall, their father was "*popular among his own acquaintances, but too dissipated and extravagant to be a suitable guardian for his two unmarried daughters,*

*Dorothy and Sarah, commonly called Dolly and Sally.*" Whether because or in spite of his excesses, Dr William Chadder was a freeman of the borough and served as mayor in 1749 and again in 1760. Evidently Mary, the oldest of the sisters, before her father's drinking got out of hand, had safely married another medical doctor, William Adams, who had started his medical career abroad with the Honourable East India Company[19] but then settled back at Totnes. William and Mary Adams had a son, also of course named William (1752–1811), followed by three daughters and finally another son, Samuel (1770–1842), who married the elder of William Bentall's two daughters. (The Adams families play important roles in this history, but their stories are deferred until Chapter 7.) Sarah (Sally) Chadder also married a doctor, named John Drake.

Figure 3.3: Christopher Wise, mayor of Totnes in 1605 and 1621

Dr William and Dorothy Marshall seem to have lived uneventful lives, and almost no details are on record. William died in 1808, but Dorothy lived another 20 years. On the occasion of her 80th birthday, on 29 August 1822, a party was held in Totnes. The guests included her nine children, their six spouses (three being then unmarried), 25 grandchildren, her 87-year-old sister-in-law Elizabeth Baker, and about ten other relatives and friends. During the event an attendance register was drawn up and signed by everyone there (see Figure 3.4, overleaf).

The document's preamble states that the party took place "*in the house of William Searle Bentall, Mary Ann Bentall, Thornton Bentall and Margaret Bentall who have there resided as one family since the month of April 1810.*" The house in question was the mansion bought by William Bentall about 50 years before and then owned by his eldest son, William Searle Bentall. Below that preamble, Dorothy's children signed their names across the page in birth order, with their spouses and children signing or adding their marks below. Dorothy herself, Elizabeth Baker and nine other "witnesses" signed on the left-hand side, while one grandiloquent great-great-nephew took up more than his fair share of the page on the right.

Among the witnesses were two governesses and a couple of other servants (possibly caregivers for the two old ladies). Apart from them, everyone present at the party is accounted for later in this book.

Figure 3.4: Dorothy Marshall's birthday party register, 29 August 1822

## DIGRESSION: THE DRAKE FAMILY

Dorothy Marshall's younger sister, Sarah, married Dr John Drake and lived at Exmouth. Figure 3.5 reproduces a photograph of a portrait of her.[20]

John and Sarah Drake had five children. The eldest, a daughter also named Sarah, married Matthew White, who was Member of Parliament for Hythe from 1802–1806 and 1812–1818. A transcript of the family names inscribed in their family bible has been published on the internet.[21] Sarah White produced 17 children in total, of whom two died young. The godparents of these children included many Adams, Bentall and Marshall cousins. There were seven daughters who lived to adulthood. They lived at Brighton and none of them ever married. Possibly having watched their mother endure so many pregnancies, they decided that they wanted to have nothing to do with motherhood.

Sarah Drake produced two more daughters, then a son, William, who went to India and died at Madras aged 24, and lastly a son named John, who was born around 1782 and joined the Commissariat, a civilian department under the control of the Treasury which managed the supply chain for the British Army.[22] In 1805 John married Maria Story, and from 1809 until at least 1814 he was a Commissariat officer serving with the Duke of Wellington's army in Portugal and Spain, after which he was awarded a Peninsular War Medal with two clasps (for the battles of Coruna and Busaco). He also distinguished himself in 1814 by entering, at great risk, the French-held city of Santona under a flag of truce to buy back clothing taken from the British Army, and he was present at the Battle of Waterloo. He eventually rose to the rank of Commissary-General and died in London in 1867.

Figure 3.5: Sarah Chadder

In September 1812, young John's wife gave birth to their third son, William Henry Drake, at Coimbra, Portugal, while John was involved in a brief attempt to lay siege to the city of Burgos in Spain. This son, known always as Henry, travelled with his parents to postings in the West Indies. At the age of 15 he also joined the Commissariat, in Barbados. Three years later, in 1831, he obtained his first commissioned rank, and was sent to the newly established Swan River colony in Western Australia as a junior Commissariat officer. There he served for 17 years. At Swan River he met and married Louisa Purkis, with whom he produced five children, one of whom died young. In 1848 Henry was sent to Tasmania, and from there to

Saint John, New Brunswick. In 1854 he was called back to London and dispatched to Crimea, via Athens and Varna, with the rank of Assistant Commissary-General. While away from his family he wrote numerous letters and also kept a journal, which he continued to add to for over ten years. Transcripts of these entries survive.[23] In Crimea he distinguished himself, was promoted to Deputy Commissary-General, and was for a time in charge of the depot at Balaclava. At the end of the Crimean War he was decorated by all the allied powers.

Among those letters were reports of Henry Drake's encounters with "cousin" John Marshall, who was born in Jamaica, a son of the Rev. Edward Marshall, and married to Elizabeth Horn (see Figure 2.2). This relative's story is told in Chapter 13.

In 1856 Henry and his family returned to London for two years before being posted overseas again. During that time they lived on Regent's Park Terrace, two doors down from another William Marshall (a grandson of Dr William and Dorothy) and his wife Mary (née Benthall), a granddaughter of William and Grace and therefore his first cousin. Mary's brother Arthur Benthall and his wife, Alice, also lived close by. (Their stories will be told in more detail in Chapters 16 and 22). These families dined together regularly, and in 1857 Henry Drake's daughter Charlotte married Charles Henry Marshall, a son of William and Louisa Bentall. They were married by the Rev. Stephen Hawtrey (the mathematics teacher – see Chapter 2). Henry's journal provides valuable insights into the social relationships between the Benthalls and Marshalls that were living in London at that time, as well as a glimpse of the young Alfred Marshall.

The thumbnail photograph in Figure 3.2 was taken during that period in London. Henry is wearing all his medals, namely: Companion of the Order of the Bath (British), Chevalier of the Legion of Honour (France), Officer of the Order of St Maurice and St Lazarus (Sardinia), Order of Medjidie 4th Class (Turkey), and a campaign medal with clasps for the battles of Alma, Balaklava and Sevastopol.

Henry was posted to South Africa in 1859, where his wife died in 1862. He married again a year later to Elizabeth Lucy Wood, and his career took him next to Australia and New Zealand. In 1871 he became Sir William Henry Drake, KCB, and was appointed Director of Supplies and Transport at the War Office. He retired in 1877 and died in 1882.

Henry and his family reappear later, in Chapter 26.

## Chapter 4

# MERCHANT MIGRATION: WILLIAM BENTALL'S ANCESTRY

Our second patriarch, William Bentall, was descended from two families of some pedigree. This chapter and the next provide an account of them. There are two portraits of William Bentall in the Benthall Hall collection, one dating from 1782 and the other from about 1800. The later portrait is shown in Figure 1 at the beginning of the introduction, where the two patriarchs were first introduced. Full of character, it is much better executed than the one shown here (Figure 4.1), and so it is a shame that the identity of the artist is not known.

The 1782 portrait was painted by John Wright, who also painted portraits of several other family members to be discussed in due course.

Wright was primarily an engraver, miniaturist and art teacher, but he also painted a number of portraits of Totnes worthies. Here, Wright's subject was trying to look like a professional banker and patriarch.

William Bentall was born at Colchester, an ancient market town in the county of Essex, about 50 miles northeast of London. Before Roman times Colchester was an important Celtic centre of power known as Camulodunon. The Romans built a camp there and then a city with its own theatre and race track. The Normans later built a castle, and the town has been extensively developed since. William's father, John

Figure 4.1: William Bentall, ca. 1782

Bentall, was a prosperous wine merchant there, which in those days meant that he imported barrels of wine from suppliers in France, Portugal or elsewhere in Europe and bottled them himself, before selling the wine on to customers. John came from a small town named Halstead, about 12 miles outside Colchester, where his family had lived for several generations and had owned farmland, at least two of the local inns and a brewery. The family considered themselves to be part of the local "gentry," in part because they had the hereditary right to use a family coat of arms, owned farmland and could trace their ancestry to a village in Shropshire named Benthall, from which the family had originally taken its name (see Map 1).[24] The partial pedigree in Figure 4.2 delineates the origins of the family and William Bentall's connections to his ancestors in Shropshire.

The manor house at Benthall plays an important role in this family saga. The village of Benthall is located a couple of miles southeast of the parish of Much Wenlock, which was long dominated by Wenlock Priory, a monastic foundation that from early medieval times controlled most of the surrounding farmland. The village of Benthall is at the top of a steep escarpment known as Benthall Edge, where the River Severn leaves a broad flood plain and enters a narrow valley known as the Severn Gorge. The earliest well-documented "lord of the manor" – who controlled the village and farm, but was a tenant and owed feudal dues to the priory – was known as Anfrid de Benetal (or Benthall), and attended several local church and government assemblies between 1107 and 1120. Anfrid's descendant Philip was lord of the manor in around 1250; he had no sons, but his daughter Margery married a man named John Burnell. This John was a relative of Robert Burnell, Bishop of Bath and Wells, and tutor to the young Prince Edward, the future King Edward I. Soon after Edward became king, he appointed Robert as his Lord Chancellor. John Burnell was probably an illegitimate son of the Lord Chancellor, who is known to have kept a mistress named Juliana, and was rumoured to have fathered four sons and several daughters with her.[25] Robert Burnell became a major landowner in Shropshire. He built himself a grand country house (styled like a castle but with comfort rather than defence as its primary objective) in a village now known as Acton Burnell, about eight miles west of Much Wenlock. In 1283 he was visited there by King Edward, and hosted one of the earliest English Parliaments; the Lords met in his "castle" while the Commoners met in a barn next to it. When John Burnell married Margery, Robert arranged for him to become the lord of the manor of Benthall, and took the feudal rights away from the priory. He also appears to have arranged then for the grant of the coat of arms that has been used ever since by John's descendants. Robert's own coat of arms contained a crowned lion rampant, while John's also contained a similar lion, but of a different colour and with two tails.

The children of John and Margery dropped the 'Burnell' from their name, but their descendants continue to live at Benthall as feudal tenants of the Burnell family and eventually dropped the 'de' as well. Moving on 300 years and ten generations, the heir to the estate was named William Benthall, and he was living there in 1540. This William had three sons. The eldest, Richard, inherited the tenancy in 1562 and bought out the Burnell interest, thereby gaining full ownership of the property.[26] Richard and his children became wealthy by exploiting the limestone and coal resources on Benthall Edge, and in around 1580 construction of the manor house that is now known as Benthall Hall was funded mainly by shipping coal to downstream markets on the River Severn. In due course ownership of the business passed to Richard's first son, Lawrence, then to Lawrence's brother John, and then to John's son also named Lawrence. These three between them were responsible for decorating the house's interior with the plasterwork, staircase and panelling that still contribute to the charm of this National Trust property.

Grandson Lawrence's younger brother – yet another John, born in 1591 – was also a very successful merchant. He started his career

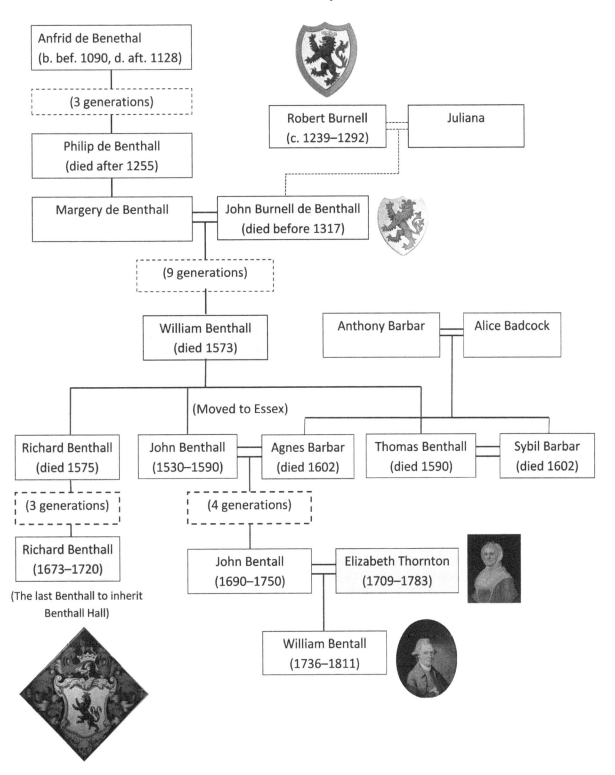

Figure 4.2: William Bentall's connections to the Benthall family in Shropshire

working for a silk merchant in London, but in 1618 he departed for India as an employee of the Honourable East India Company, arriving the following year. Soon afterwards he was sent to Gombroon, a port in Persia (now known as Bandar Abbas, in Iran), where the Company was trying to establish a post in order to participate in the silk trade. He was there for about 10 years. When he left, in 1628, he brought home with him 20 bales of silk, the proceeds from which allowed him to live comfortably for the rest of his life.

In 1645, during the English Civil War, the estate at Benthall Hall was garrisoned by Oliver Cromwell's supporters in order to control the coal supply. After the war was over, Lawrence had to pay a substantial fine for backing the Royalist side.[27] The house and estate passed through three more generations of Benthalls. The last of these, another Richard Benthall, had no children, but bequeathed the estate to his cousin, Elizabeth Browne. It passed from her to her eldest brother, John, and from him to their younger brother, Ralph. Fifteen years after Elizabeth's inheritance, Richard Benthall's sisters filed a lawsuit trying to overturn the original bequest and regain ownership. The case went to the House of Lords, and the Lord Chancellor found for the Browne family.[28] Ralph Browne had no children, so he left the estate to his wife, who then left it to her brother, Francis Blythe. It passed from him to his daughter and then his grandson, Francis Blythe

Figure 4.3: Benthall Hall, built around 1580

Harries, who sold it to Lord Forester, a local noble, in 1844.

Backing up now to the middle of the 16th century: William Benthall, the father of Richard, had two younger sons, Thomas and John, who married sisters Sybil and Agnes, daughters of Anthony Barbar, from Halstead, Essex. The two families established themselves in Halstead and dropped the "h" from their surname.[29] In both contemporary records and their personal wills, they are described as "*yeomen*": reputable middle-class owners of property that they managed.

John Bentall, the wine merchant in Colchester and father of our patriarch William, was the great-great-great-grandson of that John and Agnes Bentall.

The next chapter will provide an account of William Bentall's mother's family, and explain how it came about that William moved, at the age of 14, from Essex to Devon. Chapter 6 will provide an account of his subsequent life there.

## Chapter 5

# CLERICS, MERCHANTS AND BANKERS IN YORKSHIRE AND LONDON: THE FAMILY OF ELIZABETH BENTALL, NÉE THORNTON

**W**illiam Bentall's mother, John Bentall's wife, was christened Elizabeth Thornton. She was the daughter of Abigail Thornton (née Bulwer). There are quite fine portraits of Elizabeth and Abigail on show at Benthall Hall. Both paintings are accredited as "British (English) School" (see Figure 5.1).

Laura Benthall grew up with these pictures. In her *Annals* she wrote: "*the portrait of an old lady in a red dress by Gainsborough represents our great-grandmother. The young lady by Riley is her mother Mrs Thornton whose Christian name was Abigail.*" But those attributions are questionable.

Figure 5.1: Abigail Thornton (née Bulwer) and her daughter Elizabeth Thornton, Mrs John Bentall

The National Trust attributes Abigail's portrait to the 'circle of Michael Dahl' with a date around 1697, but that artist's career was based in London and did not take off until after 1696 so was unlikely to have had a 'circle' at that time that reached to Yorkshire. John Riley, referred to by Laura, died in 1691,[30] so if he was the artist, then this would need to have been painted before then. The painting has been damaged, and Abigail's right eye has been repainted, not very expertly, which accounts for her apparent squint.

Laura's claim that the second painting was by Gainsborough is also fanciful and unlikely, although Elizabeth's son-in-law's sister did marry into a family that knew Thomas Gainsborough well – a connection that will be described at the end of this chapter.

It is hard today to reconstruct the lives of people living that long ago, and most of what we now about them comes from church records of baptisms, marriages and deaths, and a few wills. Tracing back Abigail's ancestry, we know that her father was *"Thomas Bulwer of Whitgift, gentleman."* The village of Whitgift is in Yorkshire, on the banks of the River Ouse, about 18 miles west of Hull. Thomas was born around 1640, went to St Catharine's College, Cambridge, and graduated in 1660, having meanwhile been admitted in February 1659 to Gray's Inn, one of London's four professional associations for barristers. His will is in the archives of the Borthwick Institute, at the University of York. Several variations in the spelling of his surname appear in the surviving records, including *"Bulwere," "Bulwire"* and *"Bulwerd."*

Abigail was the youngest of three sisters. Her eldest sister, Martha, married the Rev. Peter Robinson, but died young, in 1699, and was buried at St Maurice, York. The next sister, Sibill, married the Rev. John Thomlinson at York Minster in January 1692. In 1693 they had a son, named William Henry Thomlinson, who in later life befriended William Bentall and exchanged letters with the younger man for several years, eventually appointing him as his executor.

It seems that in those days, people married often and died young. Abigail herself married twice, first to Robert Rudston, a draper, in 1692.[31] (Three years previously, Robert had married one Elinor Mason, when he was 24 and she was 22, but she died soon after.)[32] Robert died within a few years of marrying Abigail, and in June 1697 she married the Rev. William Thornton, rector of Birkin, a village about 16 miles south of the city of York and 18 miles west of Whitgift. If the painting dates from about that year, it would be pleasant to imagine that it was a wedding gift, possibly depicting Abigail in her wedding dress.

The Rev. William Thornton's father and grandfather had both occupied the same post before him. Meanwhile his brother, John Thornton, became the patriarch of a very wealthy family of merchants and bankers who were helpful to the Bentall family 100 years later. The pedigree (Figure 5.2) shows the relationship between Elizabeth and the Thornton family.

During the English Civil War, the Rev. Robert Thornton, the Rev. William's grandfather, was ousted as rector of Birkin and *"tyed to a Horse Tayle, and dragged in that manner prisoner to Cawood Castle. He survived the Usurpation and was repossessed of his Living."*[33] Grandfather Robert died in 1665 and was succeeded by his son, also named Robert, who himself died in February 1697, at which point William took over the parish.

Abigail and William Thornton had several children, of whom at least four lived to adulthood. Those were Robert (born 1698), who became a clergyman; John (born 1700); Elizabeth (born 1709), who became the woman in the red dress in the portrait above; and Margarett. Abigail died in 1716 and William died in 1718. By then Robert was at university, but there is no record of where John, Elizabeth or Margarett went to live after both parents died. Most likely they became wards of their uncle, John Thornton, William's older brother, who was a prosperous merchant based at Hull, a port on the River Humber.

By the end of the 17th century, this John Thornton had become one of Hull's leading exporters of Yorkshire's products, especially woollen cloth and lead, conducting much of his trade with the Baltic countries.[34] In 1709 he acquired a grand house on the High Street, where he brought up his four sons and one daughter, named Sarah, who married her father's apprentice, William Wilberforce. They became the grandparents of the famous politician of the same name, now regarded as being primarily responsible for Britain's decision to abolish slavery in its colonies.

John Thornton's will, dated 1726, includes bequests of £50 apiece to his nephews Robert and John Thornton and nieces Elizabeth and Margarett Thornton.[35] This is the primary evidence that confirms the existence of Abigail's three siblings. There is also a record of a baptism at Birkin, in 1703, of Charles Thornton, son of William, but he is not mentioned in John's will so presumably had died by then.

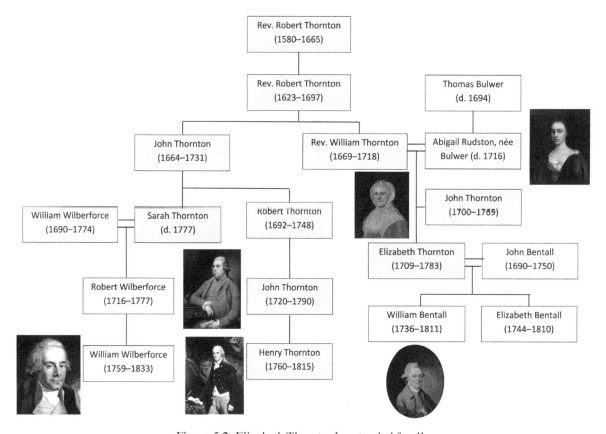

Figure 5.2: Elizabeth Thornton's extended family

This Hull merchant had several very famous descendants, and his family's story has been told many times, but is summarised again here since some of those descendants played such important roles in the lives of the Bentall family. In addition to the famous William Wilberforce, the most notable were his grandson, another John Thornton; his great-grandson Henry; and the novelist E.M. Forster, Henry's great grandson.

After John Thornton died in 1731, his eldest son, Robert, moved to London and continued to build his business interests there while retaining interests in Hull.[36] He became a director of the Bank of England in 1732, while continuing to operate a merchant house in the Russian Trade, now with an office in London as well as continuing connections with Hull. John Thornton's second son, Godfrey, also moved south and ran a separate merchant house. After Robert died, Godfrey Thornton took his brother's place as a director of the Bank of England.[37]

Robert's son, another John Thornton, also continued the family business, and became one of the richest men in England despite giving away half his income to charitable causes. This John Thornton is famous as a philanthropist and as one of the founders, with Henry Venn, of an evangelical Christian movement that became known as the Clapham Sect. He was a generous sponsor of Dartmouth College, New Hampshire, and likewise of John Newton, the onetime slaver who experienced a religious conversion and among other claims to fame authored the hymn "Amazing Grace." Most accounts of this John Thornton's life state that he was likewise a director of the Bank of England, although there is no actual record of this and it is almost certainly not true.[38]

After the first John Thornton died, his house in Hull passed to his Wilberforce son-in-law, who also continued in the Russia Trade and grew wealthy. The house is now known as the Wilberforce House and is a museum. William and Sarah's elder son, another William Wilberforce, married Hannah Thornton, daughter of Robert Thornton and therefore his first cousin. Another son, Robert, produced a grandson, also named William, and this is the William who became *"one of the great men of the age."*[39]

Grandson William went to Cambridge University and there became friends with William Pitt, son of the leading politician of the same name (and later 1$^{st}$ Earl of Chatham) who in various roles, including that of prime minister, had steered Britain through the Seven Years' War that engulfed Europe. William Wilberforce and William Pitt the Younger (himself prime minister from 1783–1801, and again from 1804–1806) were both elected to Parliament in 1780 and remained friends for life. Indeed, *"When Wilberforce bought a house in Wimbledon, Pitt moved in with him for extended periods."*[40]

The younger John Thornton had three sons, Samuel (1754–1838), another Robert (1759–1826), and Henry (1760–1815). All eventually became Members of Parliament. Henry started as an apprentice in the family business, but in 1784 he joined a banking partnership that became known as Down, Thornton & Free. Under his direction, the bank grew to be one of the largest in London, in part by fostering the growth of provincial banks throughout the country.

There are well-known portraits of the younger John Thornton, by Thomas Gainsborough, of Henry Thornton, by James Ward, and of William

Wilberforce, by Karl Anton Hickel. These are shown in Figure 5.3.

William Wilberforce MP became a devout evangelical Christian, and joined forces with his second cousin, Henry Thornton, so that when Henry bought a new house in Clapham, Wilberforce moved in with him for four years, and when Henry enlarged the house, their mutual friend William Pitt designed the library. Under Wilberforce's leadership, backed by Henry's organising capabilities and allies such as Hannah More, this group was successful in achieving a remarkable spiritual and moral revival of British society. The Clapham Sect also changed the way the British thought about and managed their colonial expansion. Thus, the growth of Empire evolved from being a purely political and mercantile endeavour to being one of spreading an evangelical Christian morality to "heathen" nations. This planted the seeds for many of the tensions that still bedevil international relations.

In his day, Henry Thornton was possibly better known for a book of prayers than for his economic writings, but he was a serious economist, responsible for an article on the effects of "paper credit" that was still highly regarded 100 years later by John Maynard Keynes and his peers. As a result, he has been described as *"the father of the modern central bank."*[41]

But we need to return to the story of Elizabeth and her brother, yet another John Thornton. Family tradition, as documented by Laura Benthall, is that this John became a *"Portugal merchant"* who, *"having resided for many years in that country, and thus become accustomed to a warm climate, was thus advised on his return to England to settle in Devonshire."* Elizabeth's life remains undocumented until 1734, when she married John Bentall, the wine merchant in Colchester, Essex, who was introduced in Chapter 4. She was 25, he was 43, and they were married in Colchester, but we don't know how long she had been living there. In those days a wine merchant imported wine in barrels, bottling it locally for sale, therefore it would be fanciful but not absurd to imagine that John Bentall had met John Thornton in Portugal while negotiating the purchase and shipment of barrels of port, and through him met Elizabeth.

John Thornton settled at Kingsbridge, South Devon, having married a woman named Letticia, (or Letitia) who was *"a great beauty, but the match was not a happy one."*[42]

Figure 5.3: John and Henry Thornton, William Wilberforce (L–R)

According to Laura, John and Elizabeth Bentall produced four children in Colchester. Of these, the first, named John, was born in 1735, died as an infant. The second was named William, born on 20 December 1736 and baptised on 11 January 1737, the third, also named John was born on 6 June 1738 and baptised on 6 July 1738, and the youngest, a daughter, also named Elizabeth, was born on 24 February 1744 and baptised on 22 March that year.[i]

Laura wrote of John Bentall:

*He was standing one day on the bridge at Colchester when a cry was raised of 'two boys fallen into the water'. Mr. Bentall called out 'Twenty guineas to whoever will save them'. A man jumped in and brought the boys to land, when our great-grandfather recognised his own sons, the younger of whom, John, was past recovery. William, the survivor, and one daughter, Elizabeth, were his only remaining children.*

There is a burial record for this younger John on 7 May 1742 that reads "*John Bental, a child drowned at Middle Mill*".

John Bentall died suddenly in 1750, while on a business trip to Portugal, and was buried there. John Thornton…

*…sent for his nephew William Bentall, whose mother, then a widow, continued to live at Colchester until the marriage of her daughter Elizabeth to Thomas Mendham, which took place in 1764. Mrs Bentall then came to join her son at Kingsbridge, and afterwards removed with him to Totnes, where she died in 1783 and was buried near the north door in Totnes church.*

The story of William's life after he moved to Devon will be resumed in Chapter 6, but a brief interlude is required in order to summarise the life and family of his sister, Elizabeth. As noted by Laura Benthall above, in 1764 she married Thomas Mendham, a lawyer in the Court of Chancery and secretary to the Master of the Rolls, the chief judge of that court. Elizabeth gave birth to seven children between 1770 and 1785, but only two, Sybilla and Louisa, survived childhood. In the words of Laura:

*On January 1st, 1810, Louisa being delicate in health, and ordered to a mild climate, her mother [Elizabeth] wrote to ask her brother to receive his nieces on a visit for the winter. Uncle John [John Bentall, third son of William Bentall] escorted them down, and every care was taken of the poor invalid, but consumption was too deeply rooted, and she died in a few weeks, and was buried with her grandmother in Totnes church. Her mother died the following day. Sybilla became much attached to her cousins [the children of William Bentall], and after the death of her parents, she came to live in Totnes in order to be near them.*

---

[i] A family prayer book owned by William's father has been used by five generations of his descendants to record family births, marriages and deaths. That states that William was born on 20 December 1736, "*at half an hour past eight at night,*" and that Elizabeth was born on 24 February 1844, "*at ½ an hour past 9 o'clock at night.*" Two pedigrees certified by the College of Arms give William's birth date a year later. But the baptism record for William has a date of 11 January 1737, and the register makes it clear that this followed immediately after December 1736. However the record of Elizabeth's baptism is dated 22 March 1843, but also shows that the next month was April 1744, indicating that the parish had reverted to the older custom of starting a new year after Lady Day, the 25th of March.

This cannot be strictly accurate. A memorial in Totnes church does say that Louisa died in January 1810, but her mother Elizabeth died in May, four months later. Between these two dates Thomas Mendham made a new will, at a time when his wife was still alive but Sybilla was his sole heiress-at-law and next of kin. He died in 1812, and this was presumably when Sybilla moved to Totnes for a while.

Three years later Sybilla Mendham married her first cousin the Rev. Claude Jamineau Carter, son of Thomas Mendham's sister Sarah. He was named after his great grandfather, Claude Jamineau (1664–1727), a Huguenot merchant based in London. This man has been described as a 'cloth merchant' but he and his brother David Jamineau made their fortunes by trading in Venetian beads and other trinkets used by slave traders to buy their slaves from African warlords. Claude Jamineau's daughter, Frances, married William Carter, "*of Bullingdon House, Bulmer, Essex*". They were the grand parents of Sybilla's husband. That village was where the portraitist Thomas Gainsborough grew up, and there is a fine painting of Frances and William by Gainsborough in the Tate collection, though not currently on display. Their daughter, the younger Claude's aunt, married a Mr Andrews and there

is a painting by Gainsborough of that couple at the National Gallery. The portraits of mother and daughter (and their husbands), all dressed in finest silks, (presumably imported by Jamineau) deserve to be seen side by side more often.

Laura wrote that that the Rev. Claude "*went to the University as a young man, but afterward joined the army and served in the Peninsular War.*" We know that Claude became a deacon in 1787 and then was re-admitted in 1804 to Corpus Christi College, Cambridge, after which he was ordained, so while it is possible that he was in the army, his service would have been much earlier than the Peninsular War (1807–1814). He was rector of Great Henny, Essex, from 1811 to 1833. Dramatically, on 26 March 1833 "*he was seized with an apoplexy in the pulpit just after announcing the text of his Sunday's sermon; and died about the same hour two days after.*"[43]

Sybilla died in 1835 without children. As a result, a suit was filed in the Court of Chancery in 1836 by the surviving nephew of Thomas Mendham and several charities, under the name of *Carter v. Bentall*. John Bentall (third son of our patriarch William) was the nominal defendant, being the executor of Sybilla's will as well as one of its beneficiaries, although there

Figure 5.4: Portraits of the Rev. Claude Carter's relatives by Thomas Gainsborough

were several other defendants to the suit. The case was heard by the Master of the Rolls, who found in favour of the Bentall side. Given that Thomas Mendham had been secretary to an earlier Master of the Rolls and himself a clerk of the Petty Bag (see digression below), and that John Bentall also was at the time of the hearing likewise a clerk of the Petty Bag, it may not be surprising that the judge found in favour of the people he knew and worked with.

## DIGRESSION: CLERKS OF THE PETTY BAG

While the position of Secretary to the Master of the Rolls was a meaningful one bearing significant responsibilities, the duties of clerks of the Petty Bag were apparently trivial. Nowadays the Master of the Rolls is the second most senior legal officer in England, but in the 18th century the job was specifically associated with the Court of Chancery, which dealt with civil disputes, including those over wills, trusts and other types of financial agreements. The court was also responsible for numerous legal chores, which were handled by a small army of obscurely titled clerks.

In *Bleak House*, written by Charles Dickens in 1851–1853, the Court of Chancery was the target of some of his most brilliant and mordant wit.[44] By then, some of the more obscure offices of the Court had been abolished: clerks and deputies of the Hanaper and the Cursitors went in 1835; the posts of Chaff Wax and his deputy were not abolished until 1852. However, the state of affairs while Thomas Mendham and later John Bentall served as clerks of the Petty Bag, whose responsibilities were described in about 500 words in a report by a Parliamentary commission that starts:[45]

> *The Clerks of the Petty Bag Office are three in number; their duties are, to make out all attachments of privilege, to draw all declarations and pleadings for and against officers of the Court of Chancery, and also on traverses of escheats and lunacies. To make out scire facias's, and all other proceedings on recognizances acknowledged and inrolled in the Court of Chancery, and on all bonds given on writs of ne exeat regno, supplicavits, lunacies, and idiotcies. To make out all re-extents and liberates on statutes staple. ... They are also to make out writs of congé d'elire for electing of archbishops and bishops, with the royal assents, patents of assistance, and writs of restitution of temporalities thereto belonging, ...*

Their duties were many and very clearly onerous, but the description ended: *"They are to give daily attendance at their office, for dispatching the business aforesaid. At the present time, the business of the office is transacted altogether by a deputy or under clerk."* It seems that in practice, the primary – possibly the only – role of the three clerks was to appoint this deputy, and make sure that he did his job.

# Chapter 6

## WILLIAM BENTALL: FROM MERCHANT TO PROVINCIAL BANKER

It was noted in Chapter 4 that in around 1751, our patriarch William Bentall moved to Devon to apprentice with his uncle John Thornton. He attended school at Kingsbridge and in due course went into business under John's supervision. William became friends with two medical students there, William Marshall and Christopher Searle. His mother, Elizabeth, continued to live in Essex with William's sister, also Elizabeth, until the latter married Thomas Mendham in 1764 (see Chapter 5). Once her daughter was provided for, William's mother moved to Devon to live with him. But while she was still living in Essex, William visited her relatively frequently, and while there he formed a warm friendship with his mother's first cousin, the Rev. William Henry Thomlinson, Rector of Rochford and son of Abigail's sister Sibill (see Chapter 2).

These two Williams, 45 years apart in age, wrote letters to each other regularly for many years.[46] Thomlinson appointed William as his sole executor and left him his library and furniture when he died in 1774, at the age of 82. From their correspondence we can obtain some sense of William's growing business interests as a merchant trading in grain and cider. In 1771 Thomlinson wrote to William suggesting that it might be time for him to find a wife, mentioning that if William had nobody in mind in Devon, then he knew of a young lady in Essex who might be suitable, "*a certain Judy.*" William replied:

*I do assure you that I have at present no engagement upon my hands to any lady in Devonshire or anywhere else and shall always pay great deference to your judgment in the choice of a Wife as well as everything else. Beauty is what I should not much prefer any lady, for having seen numberless matches where that was the principal motive very unhappy among them that of my late Uncle Thornton[47] often occurs to my memory. A great or little fortune would not make much difference as I hope I am now nearly able of my own industry to maintain a wife in the private and retired way I would choose to live. The principal thing that I should most regard would be the temper, as I think that most material towards making my future life happy. With a good-natured young lady who would choose to live private and retired and keep but little company I couldn't fail of living according to my wishes.*

William's early business career was principally as a grain merchant at Kingsbridge, with some additional trading in cider, wool and wine. But at around the time his mother moved to live with him, he bought large house in Totnes, situated between the river and "The Plains," a street next to the town marketplace and close to the town wharf. He also acquired leases on several cellars and warehouses next to this house, a row of smaller houses, and a nearby quay. This area of Totnes on the river bank had originally been a marsh, but over several centuries various steps had been taken to reclaim the land and make it usable, the construction of the weir upstream being chief among these. By 1719 the costs of maintaining the weir had bankrupted the town; as part of the effort to repay its debts, the Corporation leased out a number of town properties to local merchants for a period of 2,000 years, in return for lump-sum payments and some small annual rents. One of the richer men in town, John Brooking, leased some of the available plots next to the river, but soon after sold them to John Clarke, who built a fine mansion on one and used the others as warehouses (see Chapter 2). These were the properties that William Bentall acquired from John's son Richard.

William's friend Christopher Searle became a surgeon at Kingsbridge, where his sister Grace also lived and kept house for him. Christopher and Grace were the children of William Searle, who was heir to an ancient but not wealthy estate at Allerton, near Dartington, a few miles inland from Totnes, and who also owned farms in other neighbouring parishes. Grace had inherited some farmland from her grandmother, so was financially independent. Evidently William Bentall remained romantically cautious following his letter to Thomlinson above, but in 1777 he married Grace, when he was 39 and she was 32 or 33 years old.

There are two paintings of Grace Bentall, née Searle, at Benthall Hall (see Figure 6.1).

Figure 6.1: Grace Searle, Mrs William Bentall

The first one is not memorable, and is not on display – the depiction of her pet dog is probably a better likeness than that of her. The second painting is another by John Wright, dated 1782, and shows Grace with her second son, Thornton, who was born in February 1781.

Silhouettes of Christopher Searle and of a "*Captain John Searle*" are at Benthall Hall. The one on the left in Figure 6.2 shows Christopher, who was born in 1744 and lived at Kingsbridge, and the one on the right is John.

Laura Benthall wrote:

*Uncle Christopher was very handsome and agreeable, and Miss Wells* [a second cousin, once removed, of Dorothy Chadder], *a lady of great beauty, fortune and good family in the neighbourhood, but some years older than himself, fell in love with him. He did not appreciate the compliment, and tried hard to stand out against her fascinations, but her perseverance was irresistible, and having lost his guardian sister he at last yielded to his fate. It was not a happy marriage, and she did not live may years, but she left him all her property.*

At the age of 72 Christopher was thrown off his horse and broke his thigh. Thus crippled, he moved to Totnes to live with his nephews there.

There are two possible Captain John Searles, father and son. National Trust records indicate that the silhouette at Benthall Hall (Figure 6.2, right) shows the younger one. The older John (1742–1826) was Christopher's elder brother by two years; he inherited the financially troubled Allerton estate after another elder brother died from a fall while hunting on horseback.[48]

Figure 6.2: Christopher and John Searle

This John Searle was a naval captain and married a woman named Frances Yarde (1748–1823), sister of the rector of Allerton. He became a freeman of the borough of Totnes in 1783. The younger John (1783–1841), their son, *"went to Oxford and was for many years senior captain in the South Devon Militia."* He was *"an extravagant man"* and John senior was eventually forced to sell the Allerton estate, which had itself been steadily losing money. After the estate was sold, the father, the "Uncle John" of Laura Benthall's annals, lived at Totnes together with his wife, Frances.

As part of the marital negotiation, William Bentall entered into a marriage settlement with Grace Searle. William Searle, Grace's father, and Richard James Luscombe acted as trustees. Much of the document dealt with the disposition of his properties in Totnes, namely:

*A messuage or dwelling house, once the property of Richard Clarke, clothier … Three chambers over a cellar called the Middle Cellar and a staircase or stair plot thereto belonging … That row of houses lying on the south part of the said dwelling house and cellar … A quay known as Harvie's Quay.*

This complex of buildings would remain the basis for his business and those of his son William Searle Bentall and grandson, another William Bentall, for the next 95 years. As noted above, the houses and the cellar were governed by a 2,000-year lease from the borough of Totnes, whereas the quay had been the subject of a 99-year lease, of which about 40 were then unexpired. In around 1922 a local historian created a diagram of the area, now in the Totnes Municipal Archives (see Figure 6.3). It clearly indicates the location of Harvey/Harvie's Quay, the Middle Cellar, a house between them and

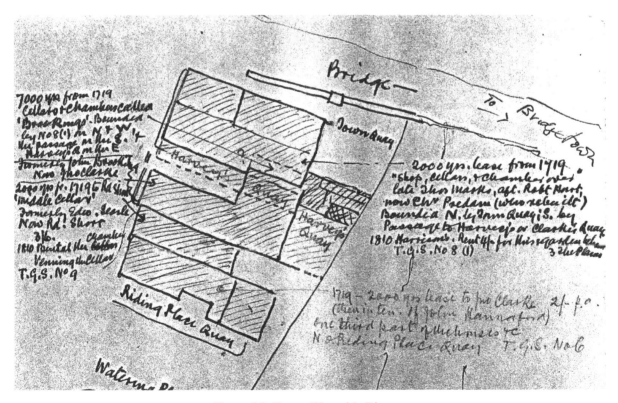

Figure 6.3: Totnes Waterside Diagram

another building – the "*row of houses*" to the south of the cellar.

Cherry and Pevsner described the Totnes riverside in 1989:

*Next to the bridge an intriguing group, enterprisingly converted for the local preservation trust: TOTNES WATERSIDE, by Harrison Sutton Partnership, 1986–7. Its core is a long, narrow two-storey range of chequered brick, with coved eaves and domestic windows of the early C18. It runs back from the river and perhaps was a merchant's house ... Parallel to it a rubble warehouse and, linking the two, a house 'lately erected' in 1824, its handsome five-bay frontage reinstated, and accessible from a new promenade above the river.*[49]

It is clear from the diagram that the alley known then as Harvey's Quay is now named

Figure 6.4: WB front door

Symon's Passage, and the fine doorway in the long façade of chequered brick was once the front door of the Bentall house. The photo (Figure 6.4) gives an impression of what the original house might have looked like.

It also seems certain that the house "*lately erected in 1824*" was a second house added by William Searle Bentall.

After William and Grace were married, she produced six children in just over eight years: four sons and two daughters (see Figure 6.5), whose lives will be accounted for in subsequent chapters.

As noted already in the introduction and illustrated there in Figure 2, two of the sons, William Searle and Thornton, married two daughters of Dr William Marshall. The elder daughter, Elizabeth, married Samuel Adams, who was Dr William Marshall's nephew. The younger daughter, Louisa, married another William Marshall, son of Dr William Marshall's brother the Rev. John Marshall – in other words, yet another nephew of Dr William Marshall (see Chapter 2). These intermarriages created a set of political and business alliances that extended well beyond the narrow provincial environment of Totnes.

William Bentall was a shrewd businessman, and at in due course he went into partnership with other local gentlemen and founded a private bank. According to Laura, "*A very friendly feeling existed between our grandfather and his cousin Henry Thornton, M.P. for Southwark, the great friend of Wilberforce, and author of the prayers that bear his name.*"[50] In 1792 William "*at the suggestion of his cousin, Henry Thornton, joined with Messrs. Wise and Farwell in establishing the bank* [known as "The Totnes Bank"], *himself becoming the manager.*"

In 1796 William was admitted as a freeman of the Borough of Totnes, and in 1799–1780 he served his first term as mayor, and was mayor again in 1808–09. These were important milestones for a serious merchant at Totnes.

When William Bentall was appointed for his first term as mayor, it was in the middle of a crisis: *"On the 21st February, 1799, at two p.m., the south-east pinnacle of the tower of Totnes Church was thrown down by lightning and the church nearly destroyed."*[51] The churchwardens

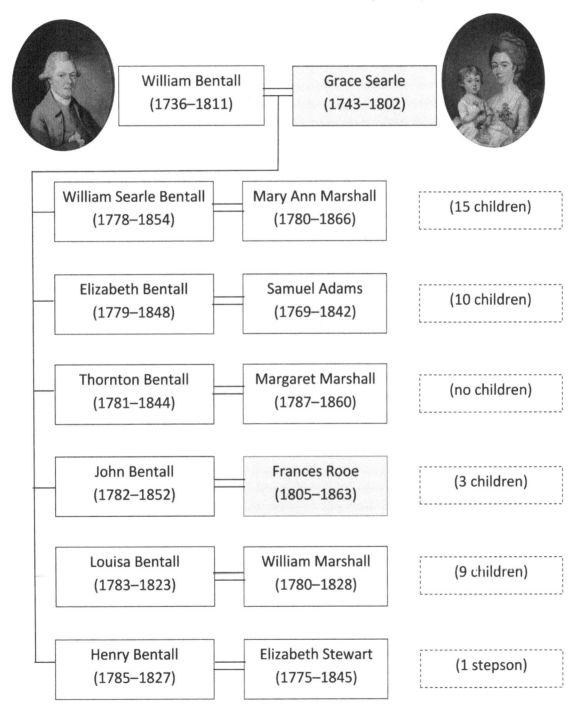

Figure 6.5: William and Grace Bentall's children

tried to impose a *"church rate"* on the parishioners to pay for the repair, but several objected on the grounds that it was customary for the mayor and burgesses to *"do such repairs at their own costs."* This became a lawsuit while William was mayor, and which the Corporation lost.

William's partnership, the Totnes Bank, flourished, but his family life did not. Grace died in 1802, aged 59, just before the birth of her first grandson. Nine years later, on 10 March 1811:

*...that grandson took a walk with his grandfather to Sharpham Lodge before breakfast; the old man walked as usual to church, looking in on his way on his daughter Elizabeth and her young baby Mary, promising a longer visit after the service. He took his accustomed seat in the Aldermen's pew beside his son Thornton* [his second son, Laura's uncle – see Figure 6.5]. *He stood up at the commencement of the singing, but suddenly fell dead in Uncle Thornton's arms.*

William and Grace were both buried at Dartington.[52]

## DIGRESSION: THE SEARLE FAMILY

In 1966 Paul Benthall deposited a large number of Searle family documents with the Devon County Records Office, some going back to the 13th century. An early John Searle, son of Nicholas Searle, held lands at Allerton in 1388–1389. Subsequent generations of the family called themselves by various names: Searle, Searell and Allerton. Over the years, various family members with access to those documents have tried without success to identify a clear line of descent, as evidenced by several elaborate pedigrees in the Benthall Hall archives, but for purpose of completeness, some account is due.

What can be gleaned with a degree of confidence from those efforts is that the father of John, Christopher and Grace Searle was William Searle of Allerton, born in 1715 and buried at Dartington in 1782, who in 1739 married Elizabeth, the daughter of John Fox of Totnes.

This William's father was John Searle of East Ogwell, who inherited the Allerton estate in 1714 from a relative, another William Searle of Allerton, who had died childless that year. The exact relationship between the two men is unknown. John Searle of East Ogwell married Grace, daughter of John Knowling, at Loddiswell. This Grace left lands at Loddiswell to her granddaughter Grace Searle, who married our patriarch William Bentall.

John Searle of East Ogwell was the son of Nicholas Searle of East Ogwell and Anne, daughter of Richard Leare of East Ogwell and Ipplepen. Nicholas Searle was himself the son of John Searle of Denbury and Mary, daughter of Christopher Gould of Buckfastleigh.

John Searle of Denbury (living in 1616) was the son of John Searle the Elder of Denbury and Anne, daughter of John Soper. How this ties back to the 14th-century landowners is still to be discovered, and how any of it ties back to other Searle relatives in the neighbourhood is likewise anyone's guess.

# PART II.
## CHILDREN OF THE PATRIARCHS

The six chapters in Part I provided an account of the origins and lives of our two patriarchs together with those of their wives and siblings, and it foreshadowed the intermarriages of their children. Part II concerns the lives of these children, six of them belonging to William Bentall and nine to Dr William Marshall. Some stayed close to home, but others travelled farther afield: to the West Indies, South Africa, India and China. Moving through time, the branches of the respective family trees multiply, and as noted in the introduction, subsequent parts of this book will narrow the focus of attention to a few specific branches that have both Bentall and Marshall connections, while brief summaries of the other branches are provided here.

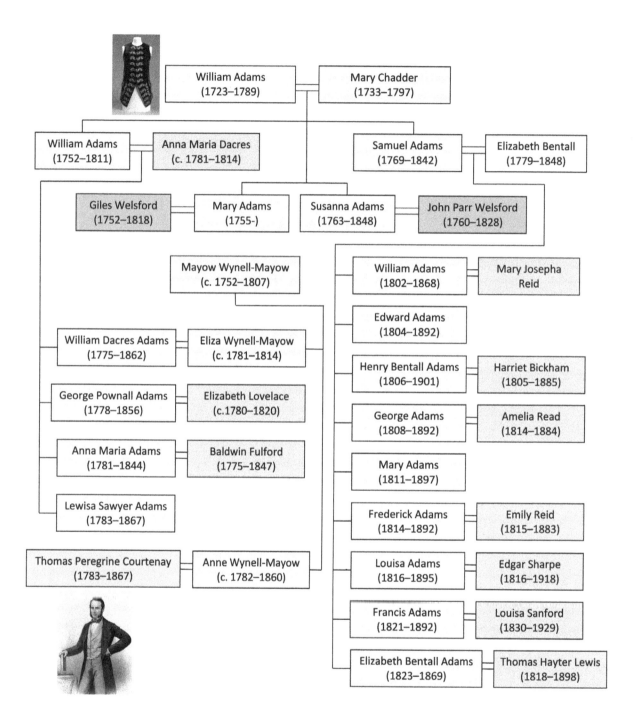

Figure 7.1: The Adams family

## *Chapter 7*

# MERCHANTS AND POLITICIANS:
# ELIZABETH BENTALL AND THE ADAMS FAMILY

The first of the children to account for is Elizabeth, eldest child of William and Grace Bentall, who married Samuel Adams, the youngest son of Dr William Adams and Mary Chadder. Since other members of the Adams family also played an important role in the lives of the Bentalls and Marshalls (although none were present at Dorothy's birthday party in 1822), a brief account of Samuel's parents and siblings is called for at this stage.

Dr William Adams was an important figure in the Totnes community, being a medical doctor and a resident freeman. The Royal Albert Memorial Museum in Exeter has a velvet waistcoat that was made for him when he was in his thirties.

Dr Adams married Mary Chadder and had five children: first a son, also of course named William; then three daughters named Mary, Sarah and Susanna (or Susan); and much later another son, Samuel, who eventually married Elizabeth Bentall. The chart (Figure 7.1) shows some of the key members of this clan.

In addition to the children of William and Samuel, the chart shows two of their sisters, Mary and Susanna, who married two brothers named Welsford. The chart also shows the relationship between William Dacres Adams and Thomas Peregrine Courtenay, who will become

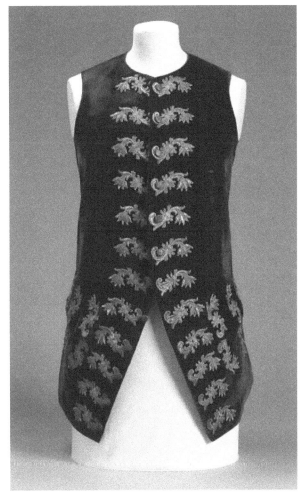

Figure 7.2: The Adams waistcoat

one of the most important people in this book, and whose life is covered in more detail in Chapter 10.

## William Adams MP and his family

The eldest son of Dr William and Mary Adams, another William, became Member of Parliament for Totnes after making a lot of money as a merchant. There is not much on record about his early commercial ventures. He is supposed to have told a friend that "*in 1766 he had been employed 'in a mercantile house in Liverpool'.*"[53] If this is true, he would have been only 14 at the time, but perhaps he was indeed that precocious – after all, he was appointed mayor of Totnes for the first time at the age of 28.

When this William returned to Devon in around 1770, he was initially in a partnership with his father, and lived for a while at Plymstock, near Plymouth, before moving back to Totnes. In 1783 that partnership was dissolved and taken over by a new partnership with his new brother-in-law, Giles Welsford,[54] who had married William's sister Mary Adams in 1782 and been admitted as a freeman of Totnes the same year. Giles became an important figure in the town in part because he and William Adams also became very successful merchants, winning numerous contracts to supply wheat and other supplies to the Royal Navy at Plymouth. He was later a target of food riots that broke out in 1800, when the price of wheat skyrocketed due to the provisioning needs of the fleet.[55] But he had many talents. In 1785 he was awarded a contract by the borough to repair and subsequently maintain the Totnes weir and the banks of the Mill Lake (see Chapter 1). In 1797 he built a fine house at 36 Fore Street which was thereafter known as "The Mansion." A century later it became the local grammar school, and it is currently an adult learning centre and library.

In 1774 William Adams, the future MP, married Anna Maria Dacres. She was the daughter of Richard Dacres, who had been the secretary of the English garrison in Gibraltar before retiring to Leatherhead. Her two brothers both became vice-admirals.[56] William and Anna Maria produced four children who lived to adulthood:

The first, William Dacres Adams, born in December 1775 at Plymstock, became private secretary to two prime ministers, and later was appointed a Commissioner of Woods, Forests and Land Revenues. The second, George Pownall Adams, born 1779 at Totnes, became a cavalry officer and ended up as Major-General Sir George Pownall Adams KCH. The third, Anna Maria Adams, born in 1781 at Totnes, married Baldwin Fulford, and one of her sons was a witness at Dorothy's party. The youngest, Lewisa[i] Sawyer Adams, was also born in 1783 at Totnes and was baptised there on 25 June 1783.

After the birth of Lewisa, her mother was chosen – one might say tapped – to be the wet nurse for Princess Amelia, who was born on 7 August 1783, the 15th and last child of King George III. There can be no doubt that this was arranged by the king's doctor, George Baker, father of Dr Thomas Baker, Dr William Marshall's brother-in-law. As a result, the Adams family was awarded a small pension. Princess Amelia was a spirited young woman, but contracted tuberculosis in 1798 at the age of 15, suffered from a severe case of measles 10 years later, and finally died in 1810 from erysipelas, an acute infection. Anna Maria went back to Hampton Court to help nurse Amelia through this last illness.[57]

William Adams was elected mayor of Totnes three times, in 1780–1781, 1788–1789 and 1797–1798. (He was also the recorder of Totnes from 1807 until his death in 1811.) In 1796 he decided to enter Parliament and found a seat at Plympton Erle, a small borough near Plymouth, where the local landowners controlled the corporation and

---

[i] On some documents it was spelled "Louisa."

Figure 7.3: William Dacres Adams, by Sir
Thomas Lawrence

sold the borough's Parliamentary seats to the highest bidders when it came to election time. But William still maintained his roots at Totnes, and in around 1800 he purchased a grand mansion, named Bowden House, just outside the town.

In 1801 one of the Totnes MPs resigned his seat, and William Adams was then returned in the by-election unopposed, thereby surrendering his seat at Plympton Erle.[58] By that time the electoral roll – i.e., the resident and non-resident freemen – comprised about 60 names, of which a substantial number were connected to William either by business or family (or both). Thereafter until his death in 1811, William made sure that new members of the Bentall and Marshall families, as well as of his own, were appointed freemen as soon as they reached an acceptable age. Modern histories of the period refer to the "Adams–Bentall–Marshall interest" when describing the tight control maintained by those families over the Totnes elections. More details of this period will be provided in Chapter 10.

William's two sons, William Dacres (W.D.) and George Pownall (G.P.) Adams, attended a small private boarding school in Moreton Hampstead, where they met another student named Baldwin Fulford, who later married their sister Anna Maria.[59] Both brothers were admitted as freemen of Totnes, W.D. in 1798 and G.P. in 1800 (bolstering support for Dad's election in 1801).

W.D. Adams joined the Home Office as a clerk in 1791, but in 1804 he became private secretary to William Pitt the Younger when the latter was elected prime minister for the second time, and was present at Pitt's deathbed in 1806. Later, from 1807–1809, he was also private secretary to the Duke of Portland while the latter was prime minister. In 1810 W.D. became one of the Commissioners of Woods, Forests and Land Revenues, responsible for managing all Crown properties. He was close friends with another ambitious politician, Thomas Peregrine Courtenay, and the two of them married two sisters, daughters of Mayow Wynell-Mayow. When William Adams decided in 1810 to retire from Parliament at the next election, he and W.D. jointly settled upon Courtenay as a suitable successor. William died some months before the election was due, and Courtenay was elected unopposed in the resulting by-election. With the continued support of the Adams–Benthall–Marshall interest, he remained an MP for Totnes until the passage of the Great Reform Act in 1832. During those years, Courtenay played an important and influential role in the Bentall and Marshall families. An account of his life is provided in Chapter 10, and further details of his influence will appear in Chapters 13, 14, 16, 17 and 43.

W.D. Adams became friendly with the highly regarded portraitist Sir Thomas Lawrence, who painted a very fine picture of him which cannot be reproduced here, but the engraving in Figure 7.3, made from that portrait, is in the British Museum collection.[60]

W.D. Adams had five children. His eldest son was William Pitt Adams (1804–1852), the next was Rev. Dacres Adams (1806–1871), followed by Mayow Wynell, Elizabeth and Herbert George Adams. A son of the Rev. Dacres Adams became the Rev. William Fulford Adams (1833–1912) and was a friend of the artistic polymath William Morris. The Rev. William's son, another William Dacres Adams (1864–1951), became an artist.

George Pownall (G.P.) Adams, the younger son of William Adams MP, became a cavalry officer, distinguished himself in battle both in Ireland in 1803 and then at Mysore, India, in 1809.[61] He was promoted to colonel in 1813 and then to major-general in 1819. In 1831, he was made a Knight Commander of the Royal Guelphic Order. He served as mayor of Totnes in 1828–1829 and remained involved in local politics after the Great Reform Act of 1832, but without success.

As noted above, W.D. and G.P. Adams' sister Anna Maria married Captain Baldwin Fulford, owner of a substantial estate about nine miles west of Exeter. Baldwin and Anna Maria had 14 children, one of whom, William Fulford, was present at Dorothy Marshall's family reunion, as her great-great-nephew (he of the grandiloquent signature in the bottom right corner of Figure 3.4). This William's early career was as an army officer in the Royal Artillery, but he ended it as a prison governor. At a Select Parliamentary Committee on Prison Discipline in 1863, he gave evidence *"with the assurance of one who had mastered the art of deterrence and achieved an appropriate reputation at Staffordshire county gaol."*[62] He was in favour of the penal treadwheel as the most effective form of hard labour and also agreed that *"prisoners might be whipped during the period of their imprisonment."* At a later gathering, the International Penitentiary Congress held in London in 1872, he was reported as saying that *"he was required to be present at every infliction of corporal punishment in his prison, and that he was invariably ill in consequence. Still, he believed it impossible to dispense with it in a prison where, as was the case with his, the prisoners were thoroughly degraded and vicious."*[63]

It is startling to discover that the young man who signed the register at Dorothy's birthday party ended up in that position. However, his eldest brother, named Baldwin like his father, was known locally as "Baldwin the Bad," since he *"was extravagant with his finances and by 1861 had accumulated over £60,000 of debts, which he fled the country to escape."*[64] Another brother, Francis, joined the church and became the Anglican Bishop of Montreal. Another brother, John, became a rear admiral in the Royal Navy.

One of Anna Maria's daughters, Eleanor, married her first cousin Herbert George Adams, the son of W.D. Adams, and they too had several children, not documented here.

## Samuel and Elizabeth Adams and their family

In 1800 Samuel, the younger brother of William Adams MP by 18 years, married Elizabeth Bentall, the eldest daughter of our original William Bentall. This couple lived at Totnes for several years after they married. (William Bentall visited her on the morning of his death – see Chapter 6.) Samuel was admitted as a freeman of the borough in 1792 and was appointed mayor in 1809–1810. He became a barrack-master, first at the Berry Head barracks outside Torquay (see Map 2), then later at the Hounslow barracks, where his family eventually moved. Samuel was born on New Year's Day, 1770, a birthday he shared with John Searle, brother of Grace, while under the new style calendar William Bentall was born on New Year's Eve.[ii] According to Laura, these three gentlemen always celebrated together, "*sitting up to drink healths as the clock struck.*"

There is a painting at Benthall Hall of Elizabeth as a child, together with her elder (by 13 months) brother William Searle (see Figure 7.4).

The artist was the same John Wright who painted the portraits of their parents. The back of the painting gives a date, 1782, which if correct means the subjects were aged four and three respectively at the time of sitting.

Samuel and Elizabeth Adams had ten children (one of whom died in infancy and is not shown in Figure 7.1). There was some adventure in their lives, and for a time some ongoing connections with the Benthalls and Marshalls, but those did not endure. Nonetheless, there are presumably a number of living Adams descendants who might be interested in reconnecting with their distant cousins. The following details of Samuel and Elizabeth Adams' children's careers and families have been assembled from various genealogical websites, including census records and newspaper archives.

The first child, named Mary, died in infancy. The second, William Adams was appointed as a Totnes freeman in 1827. He was given a job at the Office of Woods, Forests and Land Revenues, courtesy of his cousin W.D. Adams, and rose to the grade of principal clerk. He

Figure 7.4: William Searle and Elizabeth Bentall as children

married Mary Josepha Reid and died in 1868 at West Molesey. They had eight children, including Horace Adams, a captain in the Royal Navy, who retired to Totnes and was mayor there in 1904–1905, and Canon Arthur Adams, who died at age 74 while riding his motorcycle.

The third child, Edward Adams was educated at the Royal Military Academy, Woolwich. He joined the Royal Staff Corps in 1825, transferred to the 88th Regiment of Foot (Connaught Rangers) as lieutenant in 1829, and was promoted to captain in 1839, remaining in that post until at least 1847. By 1851 he was back in London, as superintendent of Bridewell Hospital. He appears in the 1861 census in the Chelsea Barracks, unmarried, as a colonel on half pay. In 1881 he was listed as a major-general, living in Kensington with his sister Mary.

The fourth child, Henry Bentall (H.B.) Adams was appointed as a Totnes freeman in 1828, married Harriet Bickham in 1835, and had a son, Dr Henry Adams, and two daughters, Emily and Ellen. He too was appointed, in May 1824, as a junior clerk in the Office of Woods, Forests and Land Revenues; became an assistant clerk in 1838; and acted as a "minute clerk" until 1852, when the department was reorganised and he retired on a modest pension. Henry died in Reigate, Surrey, in 1901. He witnessed the signatures of two of the Marshall boys when they accepted John Bentall as their legal guardian (see Chapter 13).

Next was George Adams, who was in the East India Company's Civil Service, and married Amelia (or Emilia) Read in 1833, in Bengal. They lived in Calcutta before retiring to Somerset, and very friendly there with Edward and Clementina Benthall. Their son, George Henry (G.H.) Adams, went to Australia and became a sheep farmer in Queensland. G.H. was in contact there with his cousin Charles Henry Marshall (see Chapter 26); he and Charles travelled back to England together in 1872. In January 1906 G.H. married his cousin Ellen Adams, daughter of H.B. Adams (see above), when he was 70 and she was 65. George and Amelia also had five other children. Some information about his marriage and his father-in-law is available online.[65]

Next came Mary Adams, who died unmarried at Reigate, Surrey, after looking after her brother Edward (see above) for many years.

After her came Frederick Adams, who was in the East India Company's military service. He married Emily Reid and died in 1892. They had six children, one of whom died as a child. Charlie Adams emigrated to Australia and was also in contact with his cousins, G.H. Adams and Charles Henry Marshall. He became the manager of a sugar plantation at Goondi,

Queensland, and died in 1913. Two other sons of Frederick and Emily became civil servants.

The eight child, Louisa Adams, married Edgar Sharpe (1817–1918), an accountant. They retired to Reigate and died there. They had a daughter, Clara, born in 1855 who lived with them until they died and died unmarried at age 79.

Number nine was Francis Adams, who married Louisa Sanford and became another clerk in the Office of Woods, Forests and Land Revenues. They had six sons and two daughters. He died in 1892 and she died in 1929, aged 99.

Lastly, Elizabeth Bentall Adams married an architect named Thomas Hayter Lewis, who became a professor at University College London (UCL) in 1864. She died in 1869. He married again and died in 1898.

Figure 7.5: Thomas Welch

## DIGRESSION: THOMAS WELCH

There is a record of another Totnes partnership that was wound up in December 1803, this one between James Harrison, Thomas Welch, William Adams and Giles Welsford.[66] Both James Harrison and Thomas Welch were admitted as freemen of Totnes in 1778, and Thomas Welch was mayor in 1814–1815.

Thomas Welch died suddenly in 1820 during a service at St Mary's Church, falling into the arms of William Searle Bentall while reciting the fourth verse of Psalm 144: *"Man is like a thing of nought: his time passeth away like a shadow."*[67] This was in the same pew where William Bentall had died in similar circumstances nine years earlier, falling into the arms of his son Thornton.

The reason for this digression is that there is a portrait of Thomas Welch at Benthall Hall (see Figure 7.5), also by John Wright and dated about 1782. It is not known how this became part of the Benthall portrait collection.

Figure 8.1: Elopement from Bristol[i]

_____

[i]  "Bumbrusher" was a slang term then for a schoolmaster. In fact, the couple were pursued by a schoolmistress, her brother and the landlord of a popular tavern, so this picture cannot be taken as historically accurate.

# Chapter 8

## NOTES ON A SCANDAL: ISABELLA AND WILLIAM MARSHALL

The eldest son of Dr William and Dorothy Marshall was another William Marshall (1774–1864). He, like his grandfather and uncles, went to Oxford and became an ordained clergyman. He held a clerical post at Putney, London, for a while, and later a fellowship at Balliol College, Oxford, where for a time he was a proctor – i.e., a university official responsible for student discipline and conducting examinations. In 1816 he married, at Totnes, a young woman named Isabella Caroline Clark Ogilvie Perry-Ogilvie (1793–1832), the eldest daughter of Richard Vining Perry and Clementina Clerk (or Clark).[ii] (For reasons to be explained, they later added the surname of Ogilvie.)

### The Bristol Elopement

Isabella's parents went through two marriage ceremonies: the first in March 1791 at Gretna Green, the first village across the Scottish border, where they could be married without parental consent; and then another, in October 1792, at an English church. The reason for this is that Richard eloped with Clementina, a wealthy heiress, when she was just 14 years old. A warrant was issued for his arrest on the capital charge (i.e., an offence punishable by death) of abduction and rape. The couple fled the country, but when Clementina became pregnant, they decided to return and Richard surrendered to face trial. Thus, most of the first year of their daughter Isabella's life was spent in jail while her father awaited trial. Eventually he was acquitted. The story was exactly what the London press needed to boost sales, and it became the talk of the town. The cartoon reproduced (Figure 8.1) is just one example, less scabrous than some, of the material that was published.[68]

---

ii The name is spelled variously in different places as Clerk, Clerke, Clark and Clarke.

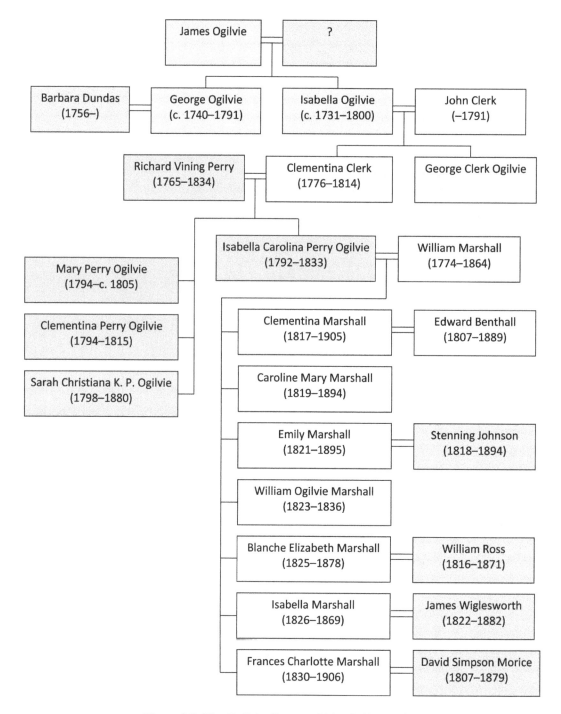

Figure 8.2: The Ogilvie, Perry and Marshall Families

The family tree in Figure 8.2 provides some genealogical background to this Marshall family, and in particular to the story that has become known in history as the "Bristol Elopement" or "Perry-Ogilvie Affair."

An account of the affair was written by one of the defence lawyers and published in 1794, shortly after the trial's conclusion.[69] In 1966 Paul Benthall also wrote an account which he circulated among his family, based on the earlier publication and on his study of an extensive collection of contemporary documents now at Benthall Hall, including letters written by Richard and Clementina themselves. Other accounts have been published recently by Anne Stott and Naomi Clifford, but without access to the Benthall Hall archive.[70]

The abbreviated account of this event presented here draws on all these sources. Paul Benthall's version is more detailed than Stott's, but it differs in some minor respects from her version and from the original account published by the defence lawyer shortly after the trial. Since Paul had access to original contemporary letters, his account may be more accurate in some respects, but equally he was at times more interested in a good story than in strict historical accuracy, so another careful study of the material may be in order. The quotes in the account here whose sources are not otherwise identified are from Paul's version.

One strand of this complicated story starts an ocean away, in Jamaica, where a Scotsman named George Ogilvie, born in Banff, Aberdeenshire, around 1740, had made his fortune as the owner of a sugar plantation named Langley Park. In the 1780s he returned to his native Scotland, bought another estate and country house, and in 1785 married a woman named Barbara Dundas, "*a daughter of the 24th laird of that ilk.*" George had a sister named Isobel (or Isabella) who married a man named John Clerk, "*a native of Banff, and variously described as a shoemaker and a merchant.*" The Clerks had two children, George and Clementina. George Ogilvie, with no children, initially settled his Jamaican estate on his nephew George, after providing an annuity for his wife Barbara.

There is a miniature of George Ogilvie and an oil painting of Barbara at Benthall Hall (see Figure 8.3).

Figure 8.3: George and Barbara Ogilvie

The miniature of George is a watercolour on ivory, painted around 1775 by John Bogle, and is on show for visitors. The oil painting of Barbara dates from about 1800 and is attributed to Sir William Beechey. It is not currently on show, although the hat makes it quite memorable.

The second strand of the story starts in 1758 in Bristol, where a schoolmaster and prominent Quaker named Jacob More founded a girls' boarding school, to be run by his two eldest daughters, and where one of his younger daughters, Hannah, was educated. Hannah More became a teacher and eventually the school manager herself. But she also blossomed as a playwright, became a member of the original Blue Stockings Society[iii] and was drawn into the Clapham Sect, where she worked with William Wilberforce and Henry Thornton and wrote in support of the abolition of slavery. As her literary career advanced, it became increasingly difficult for Hannah to fulfil her responsibilities at the family school in Bristol, and in 1789 she handed over its management to a group of five sisters: Selina, Mary, Virtue, Fanny and Susan Mills.

In 1786, at the age of 10, Clementina Clerk was taken by her aunt Barbara to Bristol and was enrolled in the school, at that stage still being run by Hannah but soon to be taken over by the Mills sisters. Four years later George Ogilvie, for reasons that are unknown, executed an amendment to his deed of settlement, designating Clementina as his sole heiress instead of her brother. George Ogilvie died the following year, in January 1791, and Clementina's father, John Clerk, died the very next month.

iii A society founded in the 1750s as a women's literary discussion group: https://en.wikipedia.org/wiki/Blue_Stockings_Society (retrieved April 2019)

According to Paul Benthall, "*Selina Mills broke the news to Clementina, who was much affected and had to be revived with wine and honey. She remained in low spirits and complained of headaches. Her moving letters to her bereaved mother and aunt still survive.*" But Clementina was now a wealthy young woman: it soon became known in Bristol that she had been left £12,000 in cash and an income of £6,000 a year, worth maybe 100 times that in spending power as of 2019.

There was in Bristol at that time a young man named Richard Vining Perry, a surgeon and apothecary, whose sister, Elizabeth, known as Betsy, kept house for him. Richard first encountered Clementina while walking on the downs outside Bristol, and although they did not speak, they subsequently "*corresponded by means of a servant, who passed on their notes.*"

Things progressed quickly. In March 1791 "*Richard offered to take Clementina to Scotland and to marry her there, and she agreed.*" He and a friend, a young attorney named Baynton, concocted a plan to this effect. First, they induced a servant girl at the school named Betty Baker to leave and take a job instead with Richard. Then they came up with a pretext to get Clementina allowed out of the school. On 19 March a footman in livery arrived with a chaise and a note requesting that she accompany him to meet a relative who had arrived from Scotland. But instead, Clementina was dropped off near Richard's house. "*There a post coach soon arrived – a coach with a driver, four horses, and two postilions, one mounted on each nearside horse. At about 11 p.m. the coach set off for the north with Richard, Clementina, Betsy Perry, Betty Baker, and ... Baynton.*"

Before reaching Worcester, there was an accident and the coach overturned. No-one was seriously injured, but Baynton left the party and returned to Bristol having sustained a black eye and other superficial head injuries. The rest of the party changed horses and continued north. It took them 37 hours, including stops and further changes of horses, to cover the 290 miles to Gretna Green – i.e., at an average speed of almost eight miles per hour. Just before arriving the coach overturned again, and this time both Richard and Clementina needed to have their heads bandaged. "*They reached Gretna on the 21st* [of March] *and the marriage was immediately performed according to the law of Scotland. The minister was a tall and powerful man, originally a tobacconist by trade, and said to be grossly ignorant. Locally he was known as 'the bishop of Gretna'.*" After a night's rest, they started back towards London.

Meanwhile back in Bristol, Mary and Virtue Mills, two of the school's mistresses, went looking for Clementina and on the evening of 20 March found Baynton, who admitted his part in the affair. That evening another post coach, containing Mary Mills and her brother Thomas, set out in pursuit of the fugitive couple. Mary and Thomas were about 60 miles from Gretna Green when the two coaches met, as Richard and Clementina travelled back after their Scottish marriage. According to Paul Benthall:

*On a rather narrow road in the midst of a lonely moor in Westmoreland*[71] *they* [Richard and Clementina] *encountered their pursuers and the two coaches drew up more or less side by side. Mary Mills put her head out of the window of her coach and violently exclaimed 'For Christ's sake, for God's sake, let me speak to Miss Clerk'. Richard, standing before the others in his coach, pointed a pistol at Mary and said 'There is no Miss Clerk here; it is*

*Mrs. Perry. Not one word. By God, go on'.*[72] *The last words were addressed to his drivers, who accordingly went on.* [The other] *coach with its four horses could not be turned on the narrow road, and had to proceed about three miles before it could turn and resume its pursuit.*

The pursuers soon gave up, while Richard and Clementina made their way to London and met with an elderly lawyer, a relative of Aunt Barbara, who would have nothing to do with the affair:

*No doubt he explained that under several ancient statutes the abduction of a woman by force was a hanging matter, and the crime was made worse if the victim was under 16 or if she possessed substantial property. So, Richard made hasty arrangements to leave for the Continent.*

Clementina wrote to her mother and to Selina Mills, assuring them that she was well and happy, "*but of course was not believed.*"[73] Hannah More became involved, as did William Wilberforce and Henry Thornton. A reward of £1,000 was offered for Clementina's return. The couple left London – she disguised as a boy – and made their way to Ostend in Belgium, still accompanied by Betsy Perry, Betty Baker and Richard's apprentice from Bristol, named Samuel.

Paul's version continues:

*In England the affair became a matter of national interest. Isabella was more concerned with her daughter's welfare than in getting Richard hanged – in fact she steadfastly and repeatedly refused to take any action against him – but to most others his arrest and trial became a matter of extreme importance.*[74]

*Richard's movements on the Continent at this time are obscure because he took pains to conceal his whereabouts. How he overcame the difficulties is not known, though a year later he and Clementina were issued with French passports (which still survive). It seems that they first went to Paris, but there they found the Revolution in full swing, so they left for Flanders. Eventually they arrived in Ghent, where they rented a house for a year, an act that gave them certain privileges as citizens of the town, which later helped them to escape arrest.*

The two passports are reproduced below (Figure 8.4).

Mary Mills caught up with the couple in Ghent, and tried to have them arrested without success. Under orders from higher authorities, the magistrates in Ghent conducted a search of some houses in the city, but *"only Samuel was arrested and he was soon released for lack of evidence..."*[75] In September 1792 Clementina wrote to say that she was expecting a baby; soon after, she and Richard decided to return to England. According to Stott, the return to England was precipitated by the French occupation of the Netherlands. Paul, on the other hand, believed that their motivation was chiefly financial, since Clementina had no access to her inheritance overseas.

*By October they were back in England and on the 15th they were married by banns in the parish church of St. Leonard's, Shoreditch. How they passed the winter is not known, but on 26th February 1793 a daughter was born*

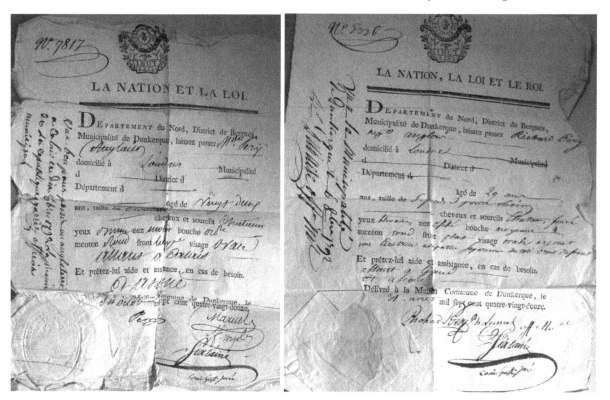

Figure 8.4: Clementina and Richard's French passports, 1790

*in a farmhouse belonging to a friend called John Gretton of Nunn Green, Peckham Rye, Surrey* [now part of the London borough of Southwark]. *According to one account the birth took place at night in a barn, but this seems wildly improbable especially in view of the season of the year. The baby was christened Isabella Caroline Clerk Ogilvie Perry.*

In May, Richard was arrested and imprisoned in a succession of London jails: first Newgate, then the King's Bench, and finally Borough Prison in Southwark, where he was joined by Clementina and Isabella. The prison keeper was impressed by her loyalty, and according to the contemporary account he "*accommodated them with his own house, a very good one, airy and well furnished, where they lived, he unfettered, and both unbarred, as well as it was possible for an open prison to afford, patiently waiting for the day that is past.*"[76]

The trial took place in Bristol in April 1794. On the first day, "*the Court was packed and there was a crowd of about a thousand in the streets outside.*" Barbara Dundas attended, as did Clementina, with Isabella in tow, and her brother George. (Clementina was visibly pregnant again, and would give birth to twins five months later.) "*Richard was charged under three ancient statutes. An essential part of the charge in each case was that force was used in the abduction. Richard's life therefore depended on whether he had in fact used force in abducting Clementina.*"

Selina Mills and her sister Mary gave evidence, as did the ex-tobacconist Scottish minister, who arrived and gave evidence while drunk. Most of the trial was taken up with arguments as to whether Clementina should be allowed to give evidence: the prosecuting counsel argued that a wife could not give evidence either for or against her lawful husband, while the defence argued that the public interest demanded her testimony. The judge sided with the defence, and Clementina swore under oath that she had known exactly what she was doing and had "*never once wished to leave Mr Perry.*"

The judge summed up, as quoted in the contemporary account of trial, "*Gentlemen of the jury, the Counsel for the prosecution have done their duty; and independently of Mrs. Perry's evidence, the evidence on the part of the prosecution, is so very slight that you cannot hesitate a moment in finding the prisoner Not Guilty.*" This same account ends with the words: "*On the acquittal, the Hall resounded with the acclamations of the people for about half an hour.*"

According to Paul:

*…the cheering was taken up by the crowds in the streets outside. The principal characters in the court shook hands or embraced, and even Aunt Barbara kissed Clementina, also of course did Selina. Little Isabella was kissed many times. When Richard and his wife eventually came out of court, exultation knew no bounds. The crowd removed the horses from a carriage that they found nearby and drew the happy couple in triumph through the principal streets of the city.*

Figure 8.5: Richard, Clementina and Isabella Perry Ogilvie

Once the trial was over, Richard and Clementina adopted the surname Ogilvie in addition to Perry. But before finishing the story of their lives, it is time to examine the portraits of them that are housed at Benthall Hall (see Figure 8.5).

The first two are silhouettes of Clementina and Richard, dates uncertain. The other three are miniatures, executed in watercolours on ivory. The miniature of Richard Perry is dated about 1805 and attributed to Andrew Plimer. The other two are said to be of Isabella. The portrait of her as a child in 1796, by John Bogle, is specified as such by an inscription on the back. The provenance of the last portrait is more enigmatic; nonetheless, the National Trust catalogue lists it as "*Isabella Caroline Clarke Perry Ogilvie, Mrs. William Marshall Ogilvie, attributed to John Cox Dillman Engleheart*".[77]

Paul's account of the case also mentions the silhouette of Clementina: "*A portrait of her when she was grown up shows a striking but rather angular face with a prominent roman nose, too large for beauty. Her hair, large specimens of which still exist, was light brown inclined to auburn, and her eyes were blue-grey.*"

After the trial, Richard and Clementina lived for a time in London, and he unsuccessfully stood for Parliament in a by-election for the Windsor constituency in 1797. Surprisingly,

the couple remained on friendly terms and in correspondence with Selina Mills and Hannah More. Clementina died in 1814 and was buried at Bath Abbey. Richard, now the owner of the Langley Park estate, moved to Jamaica, where he was recorded in 1816 as having 176 slaves and 186 animals. He died in 1834.

As noted above, Clementina was expecting twins at the time of the trial. Christened Mary and Clementina, they were born in Scotland in 1794. Paul mentions that in addition to Isabella and the twins, "*two more girls arrived, making five in all. The history of the younger daughters has not been recorded, but a portrait of one, called simply Mary Ogilvie, survives.*" Although no further trace of this Mary Ogilvie has been found, recent research has identified the other younger daughter as Sarah Christiana, born in 1798.

Isabella, the eldest sister, married the eldest son of William and Dorothy Marshall soon after her mother died, and moved with him to Totnes, together with her younger sisters, Clementina and Sarah Christiana. Clementina made a will in 1816 and died the following year. She left her share of the Jamaican estate to be split between Isabella and Sarah Christiana "*when she shall come of age.*" The witnesses were Sarah Marshall, Thornton Bentall and Samuel Hannaford, and the executor was the Rev.

William Marshall.[78] By implication, the other two sisters must have died previously.

Sarah Christiana had simply been given the family name Perry when she was baptised at Stanwell, Middlesex, but like the rest of her family she soon took the name Ogilvie in addition. She was one of the witnesses at Dorothy's birthday party, and in 1835 she was in correspondence with her niece, the daughter of Isabella, also named Clementina. In 1841 she was living or staying with her brother-in-law, Isabella's husband. However, by 1851 she had been consigned to a private lunatic asylum named Brislington House, on the outskirts of Bristol. In 1858 she was admitted to another private lunatic asylum near Bristol named Fishponds, and she then moved to a third, named Northwoods, where she died on 3 March 1880, aged 82. Sarah Christiana was buried at St Peter's Church, Frampton Cotterell.

Selina Mills was meanwhile sucked into the orbit of the Clapham Sect, through which she met and married Zachary Macaulay, governor of Sierra Leone and another antislavery activist. They had a son, Thomas Babington Macaulay, the famous politician and historian and first Lord Macaulay.

As noted above, Clementina Clerk's uncle George Ogilvie executed before his marriage a deed of settlement handing over to trustees his entire Jamaican estate to hold for his nephew George.[79] Upon marriage to Barbara Dundas, he executed an additional deed that charged the estate in Jamaica with payment of an annuity of £400 to her. Later he wrote a codicil to the original deed designating Clementina as the beneficiary, instead of her brother. The estate in Jamaica and these various deeds and their amendments created plenty of problems. One lawsuit, *Ogilvie v. Dundas and others*, which

went all the way to the House of Lords in 1826, was nominally between Clementina and her brother George, and it revolved around whether the cost of Barbara's annuity should be borne by George Ogilvie's Scottish estate or his Jamaican estate. Another, *Marshall and others v. Wedderburn and others*, was about whether George's son was entitled to any part of the Jamaican estate.[iv]

## William and Isabella Marshall

As noted above, shortly after her mother died Isabella married the Rev. William Marshall, the eldest son of Dr William and Dorothy Marshall. They settled at Totnes, where he became a curate of a nearby parish and chaplain to a seamen's chapel at Brixham. This William was admitted as a freeman of Totnes in 1811 and appointed mayor in 1817–1818. Their first four children were born there: three daughters, Clementina, Caroline Mary and Emily, who attended Dorothy's birthday party in 1822; and then a boy, William Ogilvie Marshall.

Isabella's husband, the Rev. William Marshall, was appointed vicar of Newport Pagnell in 1822 and held that position until February 1831. Their three younger daughters were baptised there: Blanche, Isabella and Frances Charlotte.

While occupying this post, the Rev. William became embroiled in some embarrassing publicity.[80] The story was told in a speech by John Wilks, secretary of the Protestant Society for the Protection of Religious Liberty, who would later become a Member of Parliament. In a speech that he gave in 1825, he said that on 29 July of that year "*two persons, of decent*

---

[iv] More lawsuits followed—they never seemed to stop.

*appearance, dressed soberly in black, with nothing unclerical in their exterior – nothing improper in their demeanour – waited on the Rev. William Marshall.*" They were representing the "*General Baptist Revivalist's Society*" and, not being aware that William was a "*clergyman of the parish*," were soliciting subscriptions to build a chapel at Newport Pagnell. Outraged, the vicar summoned a constable and a magistrate – who had to be recalled from a cricket match – in order to put them in "*a common gaol*," where they were interrogated. William declared that their intention was to overturn the Establishment, and as a result they were sent to the county jail at Aylesbury for three weeks of hard labour. However, the local MP "*heard of this piece of ecclesiastical tyranny ... rode twenty miles across to Aylesbury ... went to an attorney whom he employed*," and in due course obtained their release. The Rev. William was forced to compensate the injured men £50, in addition to paying their attorney's expenses and for a public apology to be printed in the county newspapers.

In 1831 the family moved to Chickerell, near the port of Weymouth in Dorset, where William was appointed rector. Paul wrote an account of their arrival:

> *Mother and daughter* [Clementina] *went ahead to occupy the rectory, leaving William to follow with their servants. The found the rectory was reputed to be haunted, and no local person could be found to spend the night there with them. Rather nervously they went to bed together in a double bed with a feather mattress, covered with an eiderdown quilt. During the night a storm blew up with thunder and lightning, and suddenly they were seized by a tremendous force which*

*pressed them both down in the soft bed till they could move neither hand nor foot. Their screams were unheard and no help came for hours; but with the morning someone from the village arrived and found that the plaster ceiling had collapsed.*

They survived the incident, but Isabella died not long after, in January 1833.

After slavery in the West Indies was abolished in 1833, William claimed, and was presumably paid out, £2,628 16s 8d[v] in compensation for the 144 slaves emancipated from the Jamaican estate that he and Isabella had inherited. He sold the property in 1834, by which time it was of little residual value. He lived on at Chickerell until his death in 1864.

As noted in the introduction, Clementina, the eldest daughter, married her first cousin Edward Benthall, who became a judge in the Indian Civil Service. Their story is told in Chapter 17, and those of their descendants in Parts IV and V. Here are brief summaries of the lives of the other children of the Rev. William and Isabella Marshall, based on census data and other sources.

**Caroline Mary Marshall**

Clementina's eldest sister was born in 1819 and never married. She was visiting her sister Emily (see below) when the 1881 census was taken, and in 1891 was living with two servants at 10 Langston House, Newport Pagnell. She died in 1894, and her executor was her nephew Octavius Arthur Benthall (the eighth child of Edward and Clementina Benthall – see Chapter 29).

---

[v] Equivalent to about £250,000 in today's money.

## Emily and Stenning Johnson

Emily was born in 1821. In 1845 she married the Rev. Stenning Johnson, who became rector of Rumboldswhyke, in Chichester, Sussex, where they lived for about 40 years, and where Caroline Mary was staying in 1881. In 1891 they had moved to Eastergate, a few miles away. They had ten children, and probably still have living descendants. Stenning died in 1894; his executor was "*E. Johnson*," probably his wife but possibly a daughter. Emily died in 1895.

## William Ogilvie Marshall

William, Clementina's only brother, was born at Totnes in 1823, but died in Chickerell in 1836.

## Blanche Elizabeth and William Ross

Blanche was baptised at Newport Pagnell in 1825. She travelled with Clementina and Edward Benthall to Jessore, Bengal, in 1841. Not long after they arrived, she married an army surgeon named William Ross and settled in the town of Hooghly, on the east bank of the Hooghly River north of Calcutta. William Ross was the son of a Scottish Presbyterian minister at Crawford, Lanarkshire. In Clementina's diary there is a touching entry that records Blanche's fourth consecutive miscarriage. William retired in 1859 and the couple moved to Brighton, where that year Blanche produced a son, named William Marshall Ross. William senior died there in 1871, and Blanche died in 1878. Her estate was administered by her late husband's brother, the Rev. Alexander Johnstone Ross,[81] in trust for their son, who was a troubled young man, as indicated by a number of newspaper articles. On 8 May 1883, the *St. James Gazette* contained this story:

*Master Nicholson, one of the Lunacy Commissioners, sat with a special jury yesterday at St. Clement's Inn Hall, to determine the state of mind of William Marshall Ross, of Cranbourne Hall Lunatic Asylum, Jersey. The petitioner was the Reverend A. J. Ross, vicar of Stepney, the paternal uncle of the respondent. The alleged lunatic was twenty-four years of age. His father died intestate on the 19th of July, 1871, leaving some property. The boy was sent to school in Brighton, and his conduct became so extraordinary that he was removed to Essex, and placed under the care of the Reverend Mr. Rayner. While there he threw his bedclothes out of the window, and afterwards ran away to Southend, getting into a train while it was in motion. He was found in London partly clothed, and when asked why he was running away he said that he came to London to set up as a costermonger. The petitioner was consulted by the boy's mother, and Dr. Langdon Down, of the London Hospital, was called in in 1876, and the boy was sent to an asylum in connection with that institution. While there he improved somewhat as to his mind, but became morally worse. He escaped several times, and was ultimately sent to Normansfield, where the London Hospital had another asylum. He again, however, made his escape. His mother died in January, 1878. In October, 1879, he was certified to be insane. A few months afterwards the Court of Chancery handed over the income from £4,000 to his uncle for the benefit of the nephew, who was then sent to the asylum at Jersey, where he now remains.*

*Evidence having been given by several doctors, all of whom expressed their opinion that the young man was insane, the court adjourned.*

Another article published around 20 May 1883 stated:

*William Marshall Ross, a young gentleman of considerable fortune and respectable connections, is under remand at Brighton on a charge of assaulting a telegraph boy employed by the railway. The prisoner has quite recently been liberated from a lunatic asylum. He is believed to be insane.*

A few days later he was sentenced to two months' hard labour.

Three years later, on 3 September 1886, an obituary was published in the *London Evening Standard* that read: "*ROSS. – August 31, at Albert Road, Peckham, of rapid consumption, William Marshall Ross, only son of the late Surgeon-Major Ross, of Brighton, aged 27.*"

### Isabella and James Wiglesworth

Isabella was born at Newport Pagnell in 1826, and in 1861 she married her father's curate at Chickerell, the Rev. James Langton Wiglesworth. They had four children, but these left few traces in any genealogical records. James Henry was born in 1862, but his subsequent career is unclear. Dorothea Isabella was born in 1863, but died at the age of six and was buried in Sussex. Lionel William was born in 1865 and travelled to Australia in 1900. Charles Alexander was born in 1867.

Isabella died at Chickerell in 1869. Census records for 1871 and 1881 show that James

moved with his three surviving children to a parish not far from Newton Pagnell, but after that, there are few signs of where he or his sons lived and died.

### Frances Charlotte and David Simpson Morice

Frances Charlotte, Clementina's youngest sister, was born in 1830, and was also baptised at Newport Pagnell. She married a solicitor named David Simpson Morice, who went to Westminster School. She bore him nine children, but also had a troubled life. The couple are listed together in the 1851 census (when Frances' sister Isabella was visiting) along with two of their children: Francis David (born 1849)[82] and Amy Clementina (born 1850).[83] A later newspaper article records a son named John who died in January 1858, aged just 11 weeks, in Brighton. Another boy, Alfred, was born later in 1858, but died the following year. The 1861 census lists two more children, Henry Edward (1853–1926) and Gertrude Frances (1855–1893, unmarried), as living with their father but without their mother, who was at that time a patient at the Royal Lunatic Asylum (now known as the Royal Cornhill Hospital) in Aberdeen, Scotland. A year later Frances was back in London, and another child, Lucy Elizabeth, was born in 1862 (who died unmarried in 1943). Two more children were subsequently born: William Ogilvie Marshall (1864–1947) and Cuthbert Charles Duguid (1867–1942).[84] But on 23 April 1868, Francis was finally admitted to the Ticehurst House Hospital (an asylum nowadays part of the Priory Group), where she stayed until her death in 1906.[85] Her husband died on 2 April 1881, in London. His will was proved

on 20 May; the executors were his eldest sur-
viving sons, the Rev. Francis David and Henry
Edward Morice,[86] along with his daughter Amy
Clementina Morice, spinster.

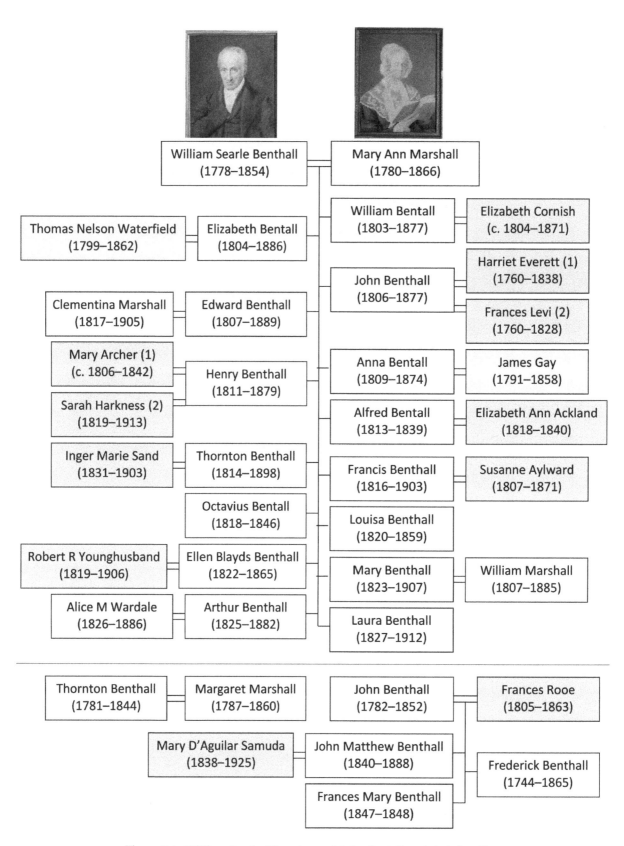

Figure 9.1: William Searle, Thornton and John Bentall and their families

## Chapter 9

# THE BANKER'S SONS: WILLIAM SEARLE, THORNTON, JOHN AND HENRY BENTALL

Figure 6.5 showed the children of William and Grace Bentall, including their four sons: in order of appearance, William Searle, Thornton, John and Henry. The youngest, Henry, played a minimal role in the lives of the rest of the family, but the other three were in business together and jointly were responsible for 25 children.

As noted earlier, the two eldest sons, William Searle and Thornton, married two sisters, Mary Ann and Margaret Eleanora Admonition Marshall respectively, who were the daughters of Dr William and Dorothy Marshall (née Chadder; see figures 2.2 and 6.5). After the death of their father, William Searle inherited his property and his businesses, and for several years he and Thornton lived together, along with their wives, in the big house on The Plains, as documented in Dorothy Marshall's 80th-birthday-party register. While Thornton and Margaret had no children, they helped raise William Searle and Mary Ann's 15, all of whom lived to adulthood.

John Bentall was a stockbroker and clerk of the Petty Bag in London, and he did not marry until he was in his fifties. But before then, he became the legal guardian of seven orphans, the children of William and Louisa Marshall (née Bentall), who were ultimately sent to Devon and became part of the extended families of their two elder uncles, William Searle and Thornton. (The story of William and Louisa Marshall is told in Chapter 13.) John participated to some extent in the raising of these 22 children (and later on his own three), and also with his brothers in business and politics.

This chapter provides an overview of the lives of these four brothers, and the next two will go into more detail of their business and political ventures. Figure 9.1 provides an overview of their children.

**William Searle and Mary Ann Bentall**

As has been told already, William Searle Bentall (1778–1854) was the son and heir of a prosperous merchant and banker, our patriarch William Bentall. William Searle[i] grew up in the large house in Totnes between The Plains and the river Dart, which his father had bought from Richard Clarke (see Chapter 2). It is likely that he was educated at Totnes Grammar School, which in those days had a single master and was based in one room in the Guildhall, but was considered to be of a high standard, and indeed required its students to dress in formal attire similar to an Eton jacket.[87] From the start, William Searle was groomed to take over his father William's

---

[i]    William Searle Bentall was known by both his baptismal names in order to differentiate him from his father.

Figure 9.2: Mary Ann Marshall and William Searle Benthall

businesses, including his partnership in the Totnes Bank. In 1801, at the age of 23, he married Mary Ann Marshall, shortly after her cousin Samuel Adams had married William Searle's own sister Elizabeth.

William Searle has already appeared in this book, accompanied by the same Elizabeth – i.e., in the portrait shown in Figure 7.4 by John Wright. The seven portraits in figures 9.2 and 9.3 depict him and his wife Mary Ann at various stages in their lives. The first, also by John Wright, shows Mary Ann as a child; it was painted a few years after the portrait of William Searle with his sister. The first silhouette is of William Searle (ca. 1830), the second is of Mary Ann (ca. 1850), and the last is of William Searle again (also ca. 1850).

The two watercolours shown in Figure 9.3 were painted by William Searle and Mary Ann's youngest daughter, Laura, around 1850. The photograph is of Mary Ann in old age, with Laura.

William Searle was active in Totnes business (and in politics until the passage of the Great Reform Act of 1832) and was mayor three times. The banking partnership he inherited from his father continued, and in 1817 the partners opened a second bank in Newton Abbot, about eight miles north of Totnes (see Map 2). However, the whole enterprise unravelled in around 1840, when two additional partners in the Newton Abbot bank ran out of money due to risky investments in Newfoundland cod-fishing. All the partners of both banks were

Figure 9.3: William Searle and Mary Ann Benthall (née Marshall), by Laura Benthall

Figure 9.4: Thornton Bentall's armorial tea set

forced into bankruptcy in 1841. These activities will be explained in more detail later.

After the bankruptcy proceedings were completed, William Searle and Mary Ann moved to London and lived for a time at 17 York Street, Portman Square. By then their surviving 14 children (one had drowned in 1839 – see Chapter 19) were living elsewhere. (The big house in Totnes was bought by William Searle's brother John Bentall; later it passed on to the next William Bentall, eldest son of William Searle and Mary Ann.) By 1851 the aging couple had moved back to Totnes. In 1852 their second son, John (see Chapter 17), was appointed vicar of Willen, a village in Buckinghamshire, and William and Mary Ann followed him there together with their two unmarried daughters, Louisa and Laura. William Searle died in 1854. Mary Ann continued to live at the vicarage in Willen until 1859 and then joined her third son, Edward, at Sherborne, Dorset, where she died in 1866.

## Thornton and Margaret Eleonora Admonition Bentall

Thornton Bentall (1781–1844) started in his brother William Searle's footsteps, but travelled farther afield. In 1799 he was sent to London, to work as a clerk in the office of Down & Co., which was at that time the name of his grandmother's cousin Henry Thornton's bank (see Chapter 5). Laura Benthall wrote that Henry Thornton *"was very kind to our uncles Thornton and John when they were in London as young men, frequently inviting them to his house."* (In the case of Thornton Bentall, this is corroborated by letters from William Bentall to Thornton when the latter first went to work for Down & Co.)

After two years learning the banking business in London, Thornton took time off and obtained a position as a purser in the East India Company's Maritime Service. He sailed on the East Indiaman *Ann* in September 1801, on a voyage to Madras and Calcutta,[ii] and then back by November 1802.[88] (Thornton chose a good time to travel: in September 1801 a preliminary agreement was signed that made the East India convoys much safer, only for war to resume in 1803.)

A possible by-product of this voyage survives in the form of pieces of a porcelain tea and coffee service – some of which are on display at Benthall Hall (see Figure 9.4) – made in China

---

[ii] Today Madras is known as Chennai and Calcutta as Kolkata. I have adopted the policy of using the names of cities and countries that were in use at the time, rather than converting them all to their 21st-century equivalents.

and decorated with the Bentall coat of arms, per Thornton Bentall's original commission.[89] There were in fact two editions of this tea set. Family oral history holds that the family gathered to inspect the delivery when the original shipment arrived from China, but the butler tripped while carrying the precious goods into the drawing room, shattering half the set. Replacements were then ordered from a porcelain manufacturer in Staffordshire, but the differences between the two can be discerned by an experienced eye. There are inherent problems with this story, if expert opinion on the likely dates is to be believed. The National Trust acknowledges Thornton Bentall as the original owner, but dates the Chinese set's manufacture to around 1795, several years before his voyage. In any event, family opinion is that the Chinese artists did a very poor job of representing the tail on the leopard.

In 1805, three years after returning, Thornton married Margaret Eleanora Admonition Marshall, the youngest daughter of Dr William and Dorothy Marshall. (There is no record of her parents' motive for giving her such an unwieldly set of names.) After they married, they travelled for several weeks by coach through England, as far north as Yorkshire and then back through Shropshire, Gloucestershire and so to Devon.

There is a small pocket diary that Margaret used during the first year of their marriage to keep track of daily living and travel expenses, but without much in the way of personal details. Nonetheless it does mention a visit she and Thornton made to Clapham, London, to have dinner with Henry Thornton MP in the company of one Lady Teignmouth. Lady Teignmouth's maiden name was Charlotte Cornish (1759–1835), and she was an aunt of William Floyer Cornish, who married Elizabeth Marshall,

the elder sister of Mary Ann and Margaret (see Chapter 12). Charlotte had married John Shore, who became Governor-General of India and was subsequently given the title of Baron Teignmouth. He became a convert to the ideas of William Wilberforce and Henry Thornton, and bought a house at Clapham in order to be part of that community.

Thornton and Margaret settled at Totnes, and Thornton joined the other local bank, known as the Totnes General Bank, founded by William Adams MP but at that time owned by a man named Walter Prideaux. In due course Thornton became Prideaux's partner. He also became a lieutenant in the Totnes Volunteer Infantry.[90] There are silhouettes of Thornton and Margaret at Benthall Hall, and also a small porcelain figurine of Thornton (see Figure 9.5). The two silhouettes date from 1831, the figurine from about 1835–1840.

Thornton and Margaret had no children of their own, but had an active role in raising those of his brother and her sister. As noted in Chapter 3, they all moved into the big house on The Plains in 1810 and hosted Dorothy's birthday party there in 1822.

In addition to his banking business, Thornton invested in other ventures that are described in more detail in Chapter 11, some in partnership with his brothers. He was twice mayor of Totnes.

By 1830 Thornton and Margaret had moved out of the big house, and that curious cohabitation of brothers and sisters was no more. Initially they lived in another house at Totnes, on Lower Main Street,[91] but in 1841 they were living at Bowden House, a grand mansion a few miles south of Totnes that had been bought by William Adams MP and was at the time owned by his son, Sir George Pownall Adams (see Chapter 7).

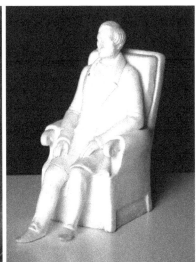

Figure 9.5: Thornton and Margaret Bentall (née Marshall)

Thornton died in 1844. His brother William Searle, by then living in London, paid £21 to the London Cemetery Company for a plot in the Highgate West Cemetery, where he erected a family vault (Vault 1173, square 17). Thornton was buried there, as were seven other relatives, the last in 1903. Margaret soon moved to live with William Searle's clergyman son John, first at Stanwell, near Hounslow, then at Willen, where she was joined by William Searle and Mary Ann. She died there in 1859.

## John Bentall

John Bentall (1782–1852) was not present at the reunion for Dorothy Marshall's 80th birthday, nor is there a picture of him at Benthall Hall or elsewhere. But he played such an important role in the lives of so many of the other family members that an account of his life is needed.

Paul Benthall wrote a memoir in 1940, based on oral and not very accurate recollections of his family stories, and said:

*My great-great-grandfather* [i.e., our patriarch William] *was succeeded by his son* [William Searle] *who lived in the same house, where he and his wife brought up sixteen children* [inaccurate – actually 15] *and adopted four more* [actually seven]. *In the same house lived the brother of the owner and his wife* [i.e., Thornton and Margaret], *and also another bachelor brother* [i.e., John]; *the latter however gave them all a good deal of anxiety because he was an atheist, and he was only allowed to stay in the house on condition that he never spoke to the children. However, one of his sisters read the Bible to him every night, and he eventually became converted after which he was the children's greatest friend.*

Although charming, there are is another problem with Paul's account, in addition to the arithmetical errors. At the time when John might have been a corrupting influence on the children, he was living and working in London, so can have been no more than a visitor to Totnes.

The first record of John's career is in the London Metropolitan Archives, signed on 24 May 1803, when he was 21 years old: "*It is ordered that the said John Bentall be admitted into the freedom of this City by redemption in the Company of Pattenmakers after paying unto Mr. Chamberlain for this City's use the sum of forty-six shillings and eight pence."* It was necessary to become a freeman of the City of London in order to conduct business there, and there were dozens of so-called livery companies (descendants of the medieval trade guilds), such as the Worshipful Company of Pattenmakers, from which a young man could choose to join in order to satisfy this requirement.

John benefitted from family connections, both to his uncle Thomas Mendham and to his grandmother's cousin Henry Thornton. It is possible that John also started his career at the same banking office in London as his brother Thornton, but it is more likely that he went to work in the office of his uncle Thomas, who was a clerk of the Petty Bag and secretary to the Master of the Rolls (see Chapter 5) – more likely, that is, because John was himself appointed, in 1812, a clerk of the Petty Bag and held that position for almost 30 years.

Before being appointed to that not very onerous office, John set himself up in London initially as a wine and tea merchant, but later as a stockbroker as well. From 1811 until around 1818 he was listed as a stockbroker at 2 Hercules Court, Threadneedle Street. He then moved to 37 Craven Street, where he lived and kept his office.[iii] In due course, two of his nephews, Thornton and Frank, would live there as well, and his brothers William Searle and Thornton stayed there when they visited London.

By 1838, legal reform was in the air. Between 1838 and 1842 John and another clerk of the Petty Bag were required to provide detailed accounts of their emoluments, and on 10 August 1842 their positions were abolished by Parliament passing *"An Act for abolishing certain Offices of the High Court of Chancery in England."* In compensation, John was granted an annual pension of £411 5s for life.[92]

John remained unmarried until 1838, whereupon (aged 53) he married Frances Rooe (aged 32) and bought a house near Torquay, retaining an office in London.[93] In August 1840 Frances gave birth to a son, John Matthew, then in 1844 another son, Frederick, followed in 1847 by a daughter, Frances Mary. Sadly, the daughter died not long after her first birthday. John died in 1852 and his wife died in 1863.

The two sons both became army officers. Frederick joined the British Army in 1863, became a lieutenant in the 3rd West India Regiment in 1864, was sent to Sierra Leone, and died there of fever in 1865, aged 21. His elder brother, John Matthew, saw active but inglorious duty as a captain in South Africa during the Zulu War of 1879, according to the following commentary:[94]

*Captain, J. M. Benthall, 1st Dragoon Guards.*

*Captain John Matthew Benthall was born at Upton, Torquay on 6 August 1840, the family home was "Furzewell House". In March 1857 he became an Articled Clerk to John Gridley, an Exeter solicitor, but he did not take to this profession and asked his guardian, the Rev. John Benthall of Newport Pagnell,* [sic] *to help him obtain a commission in the army. Eventually he passed the examination and, obtained by purchase, a commission as an Ensign in the Military Train as from 20 December 1859. After his marriage to Maria Samuda he exchanged into the Dragoon*

---

iii The house next door, no. 36, had been occupied many years earlier by Benjamin Franklin, and is today a museum.

*Guards. The regiment arrived in Natal on 10 April 1879 he served as Captain of "C" Troop, on 26 May he was put under arrest for sleeping in an ambulance after getting wet through, he was released with a "Devil of a Wigging". Retiring on half-pay 1 February 1882 he became Lt-Col. 31 December 1882 and died on 2 June 1888.*

Maria Samuda, whom John Matthew married in 1864, was the daughter of Joseph D'Aguilar Samuda.[95] The Samuda family was descended from a Portuguese family of Sephardic Jews, but had been "*seduced by social ambitions to forsake their ancestral faith.*"[96] Joseph and his brother were engineers, and were early shipbuilders of iron steamships for the Royal Navy. One of the founders of the Royal Institution of Naval Architects, Joseph was a pioneer in the promotion of "atmospheric railways" (driven by air pressure delivered to the train through a pipe laid beneath the track), including among others the ill-fated attempt to build such a railway from Exeter to Torquay via Totnes between 1845–1847. He was also a member of the Metropolitan Board of Works and a Member of Parliament.

John Matthew and Maria had one son, John Lawrence Benthall CBE (1868–1907). John Lawrence married Emily Maud Bradshaw, and descendants of theirs survive today. He became a director of Vickers, an engineering company working largely in defence, and for a time lived at Powderham Castle, ancestral home of the Courtenay family near Starcross, on the Exe Estuary in Devon, and close to where several of other Benthall and Marshall descendants also settled (see Map 3).

## Henry Bentall

Henry, the youngest son of William and Grace Bentall, married Elizabeth Stewart (née Hawes), in 1812. Eleven years his senior, Elizabeth was the widow of Alexander Stewart, who had been a surgeon on East India Company ships and had written a very influential article about best medical practices at sea. Thus, Henry acquired not only a wife but also a stepson, likewise named Alexander. The wedding was at St Olave's, in the London borough of Southwark, and the witnesses included William Hawes (Elizabeth's father), Sybilla Mendham (daughter of Thomas – see Chapter 5), Henry's brother John Bentall, and John and Jane Marshall (whose lives will be described in Chapter 12).

The new family moved to Bridgetown, Barbados, where Henry had obtained a position as Collector of Customs. Henry died on the British Virgin Island of Tortola in 1827, but the cause of his death is not recorded. Elizabeth stayed on in Bridgetown, and her son Alexander also became the Collector of Customs there. Elizabeth died in 1845. Alexander died in 1848, on board the steamer *Thames* while travelling from England back to Barbados, leaving a wife who erected a memorial tablet to her husband and mother-in-law in the local cathedral.

# Chapter 10

## POLITICAL INTERESTS IN TOTNES: 1770–1832

### Political Background

Chapter 1 provided a summary of the political history of Totnes up to around 1770, around the time that William Bentall moved there, during a period when the town leaders had begun to exert more influence on the choice of their Members of Parliament. At that time, the recorder of the borough was a gentleman by the name of Browse Trist, who owned a large mansion a few miles from the town named Bowden House (later bought from his heirs by William Adams MP, and occupied by Thornton Bentall in 1841–see above). He had been elected long previously, in 1747, to the position of recorder, which conferred substantial local power. Under his leadership a deal was struck with the local aristocracy, and *"at the general election that year the corporation, under Trist's influence, 'agreed to choose one ministerial man, the other a country gentleman'."*[97] A few years later Trist stood himself and was elected as the borough's "gentleman" MP. In 1761, when Dr William Chadder (Dorothy's father) was the mayor of Totnes, Trist won another contested election, and afterwards he wrote to the prime minister, Thomas Pelham-Holles, 1st Duke of Newcastle:

*After the most bitter and virulent reflections on my character and conduct, and the falsest insinuations to my friends by Mr. Southard, the chief cause of the opposition, there were 53 votes for myself, 51 for Mr. Lloyd, 22 for Mr. Spooner, and 26 for Captain Graves; which is about 2 to 1, notwithstanding £150 bribes were tendered to a number of freemen the night before the election: but to show the virtue of a Totnes freeman, not one single person would desert my interest by accepting the offer. Such honesty!*[98]

Trist retired from Parliament two years later, but stayed on as recorder until his death in 1777, the year that William and Grace Bentall were married, and around the time when William Adams, Dorothy's nephew, returned to Totnes and went into business with his brother-in-law Giles Welsford (see Chapter 7).

Meanwhile, the Corporation found itself in greater financial difficulty than usual, largely due to the costs of maintaining the weir and the church. In 1774 a difficult, and apparently not very permanent, decision was made: the custom of holding lavish dinners at the Corporation's expense was abolished, save for once a year on the day of the mayoral election.

In 1780, while the younger William Adams was mayor, one of the town's two MPs, a Mr Brown, donated £1,000 to the Corporation toward rectifying its finances. The money was used to pay off a few debts, to make repairs to and landscape the grammar school, and – ironically, given the difficult decision of six years before – to convert a building used previously as a corn and seed market into a "*mayoralty house*" suitable for holding "*Corporation Dinners and other Publick entertainments.*" This included the construction of a large ballroom, adjoining the Bentall properties on The Plains.[99]

In 1784 another MP, the Hon. Henry Phipps, donated £800 to the corporation which was used to pay off more debts. But the weir again proved costly: a contract for £359 was approved for its repair.

In 1786 the mayor, at that time Arthur Farwell, was given a raise. The following text, taken from the minutes of the meeting, provides a vivid example of the style of the time, and several of the names are familiar:

*Present Mr Mayor, Reynell Michell Esqr, Justice, Mr Christopher Predam, Mr Arthur Farwell, Mr George Farwell, Mr William Adams the younger, Roger Birdwood M.D., John Wise Esqr, and Francis Yarde Clk, Masters and Counsellors of the said Borough.*

*Whereas it hath been found by Experience that the sum of Fifty pounds and fifteen shillings heretofore allowed to the Mayor of this Borough for his yearly salary is very insufficient to answer the expenses of the several feasts and entertainments officially given by him, It is therefore hereby ordered and agreed, that the said salary or sum of Fifty pounds and fifteen shillings shall be augmented and increased to*

*the sum of Eighty pounds and that every future Mayor from this time having already served that office for the said Borough shall be entitled unto and have and receive out of the Incomes and Revenues of the Corporation the sum of Eighty pounds for his salary instead of the sum of Fifty pounds and fifteen shillings heretofore usually paid and allowed.*

*It is also ordered, that a Contract or agreement be forthwith entered into by the Mayor for the time being, or the person who shall be this day chosen Mayor, with Mr Giles Welsford for the repairing and keeping in repair as well the Wear called Totnes Wear and the walls, trips and gullett there and the walls of both, as also the walls banks and fences of the Mill Lake on both sides from the Rails or Gratings of the Mill to the Wall at the higher or North end of the said wear for and during all such term and number of years as Mr Jas Harrison now hath of and in the said Mills called Totnes Mills for and at the yearly sum of Twenty pounds.*

Two years later, William Adams was mayor again, and he served a third term in 1797–1798. This last term was after he had bought a Parliamentary seat at Plympton Erle (see Chapter 7).

It took some time before William Bentall became fully integrated into the Totnes community. He was not appointed a freeman until 1796, although he fairly quickly became mayor, for the 1799–1800 term. Soon after, in January 1800, his daughter Elizabeth married Samuel Adams, William's younger brother.

It was in July 1799 that the church was again struck by lightning, causing the southeast pinnacle to fall onto the roof below. The repairs, carried out by a builder named Mr Denny, cost £2,832, which the town could not pay in full, but instead paid interest on the debt at 5% while the aldermen tried to raise money. A few years later William Adams contributed £600, and the Duchess of Bolton £1,000. But in 1834, when a formal investigation was undertaken, Denny was still owed £661, and others, including William Searle Bentall and William Dacres Adams, were also owed money by the town.[100]

## William Adams MP

As noted in Chapter 7, the younger William Adams became MP for Totnes in 1801, being voted in unopposed at a by-election. The voters included: his brother-in-law Giles Welsford; his brother Samuel Adams; his two sons, William Dacres (W.D.) and George Pownall (G.P.) Adams; two of his wife's brothers, John and Richard Dacres; William Bentall and his son William Searle Bentall; Richard Marshall, son of Dr William Marshall; John Searle, a relative of William Bentall's wife, Grace; and several members of the Farwell and Wise families, William's banking partners. William Adams MP had by then purchased Bowden House from the Trist family, and so qualified as a "country gentleman." In 1807 he was also elected as recorder of Totnes.

Over the next 10 years, the Adams–Benthall–Marshall clan was in control.[i] William Searle Bentall served his first term as mayor in 1804–1805. Thornton Bentall was admitted as a freeman in 1804, shortly before he married Margaret. Henry Bentall was admitted as a freeman in 1808, his brother John Bentall in 1811. William Bentall,

our original patriarch, served again as mayor in 1808–1809. Samuel Adams took his turn in 1809–1810, Richard Marshall in 1811–1812, Thornton Bentall in 1812–1813, and William Searle Bentall had the job again in 1813–1814.

Richard Marshall's brother-in-law George Farwell was mayor in 1810–1811. The Farwell family had lived at Totnes for generations, and there are almost as many Farwell names on the list of Totnes mayors as Adams, Bentalls and Marshalls combined. Each generation had family members named George, Christopher and Arthur, and they all participated in the mayoral musical chairs. Among this generation, Richard Marshall was married to George Farwell's sister, Jane, while George's brother Christopher, at one time a colonel, was a partner in the Totnes Bank, being run by William Bentall. Although connected by marriage to the Marshalls, George Farwell was not quite part of the clan. He was an attorney, the Totnes town clerk, and an agent for the Duchess of Bolton, whose family owned a lot of land around Totnes and traditionally had been able to nominate one of the borough's MPs.

William Bentall died in March 1811, and as mentioned above, his eldest son, William Searle, inherited his partnership in the Totnes Bank. In August that year, William Adams decided not to stand again in the Parliamentary election scheduled for 1812, and, after consulting with his son W.D. Adams, recommended Thomas Peregrine Courtenay take his place. As noted in Chapter 7, Courtenay and W.D. Adams had married sisters. William Adams died rather suddenly the following month, but by then both George Farwell and the Adams–Benthall–Marshall clan had met Courtenay, and they went along with electing him uncontested. This was a small change in the protocol: Courtenay was neither local nor a landowner, but an ambitious politician.

---

[i]   Modern histories of Totnes politics refer to the "Adams–Bentall–Marshall interest," but it would be surprising if that terminology was in use at the time.

## Thomas Peregrine Courtenay

Courtenay was a political ally of W.D. Adams, as well as his brother-in-law. Indeed, he played such a crucial role in the fortunes of the Bentall and Marshall families between 1810 and 1832 that a brief account of his life is due. The *History of Parliament* series of books contains two articles describing Courtenay's political career, one for the period 1790–1820 and a second for 1820–1832. The quotations below are taken from the online versions of those.[101]

Thomas Peregrine Courtenay was born in 1782, the second son of the then Bishop of Exeter, who came from an ancient aristocratic family. Following in the footsteps of his elder brother, his father, grandfather and great-grandfather (and several other relatives), Thomas was admitted to Westminster School as a scholar in 1796, at the age of 14. It is possible that he first attended Exeter Grammar School, where he would have been taught by the Rev. John Marshall (see Chapter 2). In 1799 he was appointed as a clerk in the War Office, and there found a mentor in Charles Long, an under-secretary at the Treasury, who helped him move up the ladder in various government offices, becoming a deputy Paymaster General in 1807. The second article referred to above says this about his personality:

> *Courtenay, a younger son who saddled himself with a large family, was described in 1815 by his former patron, Charles Long, as 'one of those persons who will lose nothing for want of asking'. He was certainly a dedicated place-hunter, but he had a modest talent as a political pamphleteer and proved a capable administrator when put to the test.*

Figure 10.1: Thomas Peregrine Courtenay (1782–1841)

*Courtenay, described by Lord Ellenborough in 1829 as 'a man of undignified manners and appearance' but 'certainly a clever man', was an efficient if rather officious secretary to the Board of Control, where he provided an element of stability during his long tenure of the post. Liverpool had Canning's authority for asserting in 1820 that 'no office ever had an individual more completely conversant with every detail belonging to it'.*

In 1805 he married Anne Mayow, sister of Elizabeth Mayow, who had married W.D. Adams a year before. Given Courtenay's Devon roots, family connection and political competence, it is not surprising that William and W.D. Adams picked him to replace William as MP for Totnes.

Although Courtenay was elected unopposed in the 1811 by-election, for the general election the next year the Farwell faction put up candidates against Courtenay and his chosen colleague, Ayshford Wise, one of the partners in the Totnes Bank. With two members to be elected, each freeman cast two votes, and the two candidates with the most votes were elected. On this occasion, 36 votes were cast for Courtenay, 31 for Wise, and then 29 and 22 respectively for the candidates of the opposing faction. By then the list of voting freemen included: William Searle, Thornton, John and Henry Bentall; Richard, Edward and the Rev. William Marshall; Giles Welsford and his son; W.D. and G.P. Adams; Richard Dacres (brother-in-law of William Adams); and two more Farwells.

For the next 20 years, a period in which the political pressures for reform were dividing the country, Courtenay was able to keep his seat and exert a strong influence over who should be elected as the other MP, doing deals where necessary with the Farwell faction. (Additional details are provided below.) He also moved up the political ladder, and in 1812 was appointed secretary to the Board of Control (known officially as the Right Honourable Board of Commissioners for the Affairs of India), which managed the British government's growing involvement in its Indian colony, and which was run officially by a number of commissioners, supported by the secretary. In 1813 Courtenay was also made the "Colonial Agent" for the Cape of Good Hope.[ii] In 1828, with the Duke of Wellington as prime minister, he became a member of the Privy Council, was appointed vice-president of the Board of Trade and moved up to become one of the commissioners of the Board of Control.

Over that period, the relationship between Courtenay and the Bentalls in particular became quite intimate, as attested by a letter written by Courtenay over 8–9 June 1824 and mailed the following day. It was sent to Totnes from London and addressed to "*my dearest Thornton* [Bentall]." The first half of the letter, written on the 8th, is an account of a trip to Essex that Courtenay made in the company of John Bentall, to visit John's cousin Sybilla (née Mendham) and her husband the Rev. Claude Carter at the Great Henny parsonage (see Chapter 5). They also visited another family named Bentall who lived nearby, distant cousins of the Devon Bentalls. The tone of the letter is that of a brother, rather than just their elected MP. Courtenay refers to John's report of a visit to another distant cousin where there was a small family gathering: "*the young people were all Bentalls, their Arms and Crest are like ours and John found that he saw a great likeness in one of the young men to our William* [probably the eldest son of William Searle Bentall]." At the end of their trip, Courtney and John Bentall returned to John's house on Craven Street, where Courtenay spent the night and wrote this first half. (The contents of the second half, which provide even more remarkable evidence of his connections with the Bentalls and Marshalls, will be summarised in Chapter 13.)

The Bentalls were, in turn, able to help Courtenay with one of his other projects: finding evidence for his elder brother's presumptive claim to the title of Earl of Devon, which had been in abeyance since 1556. William Searle Bentall was helpful in handling the genealogical research.[102] As a result, in 1831 Courtenay was able to present a case to the House of Lords based on a family tree showing that the notorious 3rd Viscount Courtenay of

---

[ii]  A Colonial Agent was nominally the official who represented the interests of a particularly colony in London.

Powderham (known as "Kitty," then living in Paris after being caught *in flagrante* in a homosexual relationship) was in fact the legitimate heir to the earldom. His motive for this was that, since Kitty had no children, the next in line for that title would be Courtenay's elder brother, William, Kitty's second cousin. The petition was successful, the title was officially revived, and Kitty died in 1835. At this point William Courtenay succeeded to both titles, Viscount Courtenay and also Earl of Devon. In doing so, he became the owner of Powderham Castle, near Starcross, about six miles south of Exeter (see Map 3), as well as extensive estates in Ireland.[103]

**Catholic Emancipation**

As the decade moved on, the borough of Totnes thought it had recovered from its long decline. In 1823, when Richard Marshall was mayor, "*it was resolved to accept the proposal of the trustees of the Totnes Turnpike for repairing Totnes Bridge.*" This was not carried out, but the next year "*an Act of Parliament was obtained by the Turnpike trustees authorising the rebuilding of Totnes Bridge.*" [104] In 1826 the foundation stone of a new bridge was laid, and a celebratory procession ensued. The new bridge was opened in 1828, and still stands today. This must have increased the traffic around the house in The Plains. Also, in 1824, when Thornton Bentall was mayor, a proposal was presented to the Corporation to enlarge the church, and a plan to this effect was adopted, though eventually only partially implemented.

But while these capital projects were going on, changes were taking place in the fabric of English society that would eventually undermine the cosy, inbred political structure of

Totnes. The years 1820–1832 encompassed the "*Catholic Emancipation, the trial of Queen Caroline, the pursuit of 'Old Corruption' and the Great Reform Act, when the United Kingdom came as close to revolution as it has been in modern times, and began its long transition to democracy.*"[105]

The major events listed above were all debated at Totnes as fiercely as elsewhere. Nor was the borough afraid to project its opinions nationally. In 1820 King George III died and his eldest son duly became King George IV. The younger George had an estranged wife named Caroline who had left Britain in 1814 and allegedly become mistress to Joachim Murat, King of Naples and brother-in-law to Napoleon Bonaparte. When George III died, the British government offered her an annuity of £50,000 to stay out of the country, but she came back and caused great embarrassment to the new king and government.[106] They wanted a divorce, and could only obtain one with the approval of Parliament and on the grounds of adultery. Parliament duly drew up a "Bill of Pains and Penalties" to enact this, but popular opinion was divided, and some inhabitants of Totnes sent a petition to London in support of Queen Caroline. According to Fisher's account:

*The following month the news of the withdrawal of the bill of pains and penalties was marked by a "general illumination" in which only the corporation declined to participate. It appears that the mayor summoned "above 100 mob constables," but so few responded to his call that the aldermen were "compelled to turn mob constables themselves" and patrolled the streets all night. Nevertheless, "the windows of the mayor's house, with a few others, were shattered."*

Somewhat fortunately for the windows on Totnes High Street, Caroline died in May 1821, and the issue subsided. But the next big issue that divided the electorate and the public was that of Catholic emancipation, namely the dismantling of laws that restricted the ability of Catholics to hold public office and become Members of Parliament. By 1825, most if not all members of the House of Commons, including Courtenay, were in favour of "Catholic relief," but the House of Lords was against it. As the town worthies began to think about who to nominate as candidates in the election due in 1826, the question of support for or opposition to this cause became a burning one. This was also the year of a major financial crisis, and many banks in the West Country failed, although the two banks in Totnes managed respectively by William Searle and Thornton Bentall survived.

At that time, the Adams-Bentall-Marshall interest supplied six of the aldermen and at least 24 freemen. The main rival interest, managed by the attorney George Farwell, was that of the Vane family, which had inherited the local landholdings owned by the Duchess of Bolton. The new owner was her grandson William Vane, who assumed the surname Powlett, and whose elder brother was Henry Vane, Lord Barnard. (Their father was the Earl of Darlington.) George Farwell, as noted earlier, also happened to be the town clerk, the brother of Christopher Farwell (a partner in the Totnes Bank), and the brother of Jane Farwell, who had been married to Richard Marshall. He was mayor in 1810–1811 and again for two years in 1818–1820, while his brother Christopher was mayor in 1821–1822 and again in 1826–1827.

A so-called "independent party" – i.e., a group of freemen who were not tied either to the Farwells or to the Adams-Bentall-Marshall interest – approached Lord Barnard and suggested that he should stand for Parliament with their support. However, his response was to approach Courtenay instead and do a deal. As a result, "*afterwards the Adams-Bentall-Marshall interest and the Farwells agreed to provide 'mutual support' in order to secure Courtenay and Barnard's return.*" In response, the independents introduced a new candidate, named Baldwin, who was against Catholic relief and even convinced the Farwells to switch sides, to appoint 20 new freemen who would swing the vote in their favour, and to try to remove three aldermen on the grounds of non-residency. Nonetheless, the 1826 election returned Courtenay and Lord Barnard, despite the fact that they both favoured Catholic relief.

In February 1829, a meeting of about 600 people took place in Totnes, attended by General Adams, Thornton Bentall and George Farwell, among others, where a petition in opposition to the Roman Catholic Relief Act was unanimously approved. However, the Act duly passed later that year.

## The Great Reform Act of 1832

By 1830 the pressure for wider reform was growing, and a reform bill had been proposed that was designed to provide fundamental changes to the structure of Parliament. "*A radical newspaper declared in 1830 that Totnes was 'as corrupt a borough as the villainy of the borough system presents' and alleged that the corporators and their relatives were being 'provided for at the public expense'.*"[iii] By then the term "Old Corruption" had become a catchphrase in the popular imagination, and there was growing

---

[iii] This topic is discussed at greater length in Chapter 43.

political pressure to change the traditional ways in which public officers were rewarded.

Courtenay decided to drop his alliance with Lord Barnard (who now was able to call himself the Earl of Darlington, since his father had been honoured with an even more prestigious peerage), and arranged instead a deal with Baldwin, the candidate put forward in the previous election by the independents as opposed to Catholic Relief, but who was, like Courtenay, opposed to the reform movement. The reasons for Courtenay at this point preferring Baldwin to Barnard (who also opposed reform) are not clear, but probably related to his need to conciliate the voters who had opposed him earlier. The clan again prevailed: Courtenay and Baldwin were elected for Totnes, although the Devon County seat was won by a reformist candidate. A few weeks later, a "reform dinner" was organised in Totnes to celebrate the election of the latter. According to Fisher, "*The mayor, William* [Searle] *Bentall, 'endeavoured to check the exuberance of joy' by arresting two boys for letting off firecrackers, and the inhabitants responded by breaking his windows.*"[107]

Yet another Parliamentary election was held in May 1831,[108] in which the freemen again defied popular, pro-reform opinion in the town. This time the candidates were again Courtenay, Barnard/Darlington and Baldwin. The votes were 56 for Courtenay, 43 for Baldwin, and 39 for Darlington. "*After Courtenay and Baldwin were declared elected, they were 'saluted with continual yells, hisses and execrations', and that evening their effigies were paraded through the streets and then quartered and burned.*"

This new Parliament passed the Great Reform Act in 1832. The constituency of Totnes was enlarged sufficiently for it to retain the right to elect two MPs; however, the eligible voting base was expanded to include any householder paying more than £10 annually in rent, while non-resident freemen were disenfranchised. Upon the next election, held in 1833 under the new rules, Courtenay realised that he had no chance of winning again and retired from public life. The new MPs were two local solicitors, Jasper Parrott and James Cornish, the latter of whose father was also a solicitor at Totnes, and whose uncle, William Floyer Cornish, was married to Elizabeth Marshall (see Chapter 12).

After the passage of the Great Reform Act a Parliamentary commission was set up to "*inquire into the municipal corporations of England and Wales.*" In 1834 the commission published a scathing indictment of the fiscal irresponsibility of the Borough of Totnes, naming names. That document will be discussed in more detail in Chapter 43. In 1839, when another election was coming due, a local newspaper dredged up all the earlier allegations of corruption. To assess the validity of the accusations, it is necessary to know much more about the people involved, so further discussion of this topic is also included in Chapter 43.

Courtenay was a loyal supporter of the Tory party of his time, but not against all forms of change. When he retired in November 1832:

*...he issued a lengthy farewell address to his constituents, in which he entered into a detailed historical defence of Toryism and a condemnation of the* [Lord] *Grey ministry's record. He declared his support for a fixed duty on corn, retrenchment wherever possible, abolition of the East India Company's monopoly of the China trade, church reform, the present poor law system, protection for factory children and slave emancipation with compensation to the planters.*[109]

Courtenay subsequently published this speech as a pamphlet, which can be accessed today as an e-book, courtesy of Google.[110] Excerpts from it are also quoted in Chapter 43.

It would be interesting to study Courtenay in greater depth. When he died, *"An obituarist described him as 'a man of business, very assiduous and efficient'."*[111] Throughout his career, he was insecure about his own personal income and ability to support his family. He died in 1841, drowning off the beach at Torquay. After he died, his elder brother, the Earl of Devon, was concerned that his eight sons were struggling to maintain themselves, and wrote to the prime minister, Robert Peel, to ask for help in finding them jobs. *"A clerkship at the India board was eventually found for the youngest son, and Devon reported that they were 'now all placed in some way of earning their livelihood'."*[112]

## Chapter 11

# BUSINESSES AND BANKRUPTCY

The intertwining of family, business and politics described in the previous chapter must have made for interesting dinner conversations, and clearly it was a successful strategy, in spite of the fact that notionally William Searle and Thornton Bentall were banking competitors in Totnes, as partners respectively in the Totnes Bank and the Totnes General Bank.

When the patriarch died, William Searle Bentall inherited his father's properties and business interests, including the banking partnership. In 1817 the partnership that owned the Totnes Bank created a new bank under a separate partnership agreement at Newton Abbott, about six miles north of Totnes, known as the Newton Bank.

In a directory published in 1822,[113] Thornton is listed as part of a banking partnership known as Prideaux & Bentall,[114] but also known locally as the Totnes General Bank (whose office building, intriguingly, seems to have been part of the riverside complex owned by William Searle). But Thornton was also involved in other, diverse business activities, often with William Searle or his younger brother John.

In another 1822 directory Thornton Bentall is listed as a wine merchant in London at 3 Capel Court, Bartholomew Lane, which was just around the corner from the Bank of England and the Stock Exchange, and close to the banking office of Pole, Thornton, Down and Scott at 1 Bartholomew Lane, where Thornton had apprenticed as a teenager. John Bentall was listed at the same address as a stockbroker. In an 1823 directory Thornton no longer appears, while John is listed at that address as a *"stock and tea-broker."*

William Searle and Thornton collaborated as investors in real estate. As noted in Chapter 1, the town of Buckfastleigh, about five miles upstream from Totnes on the River Dart, had been the centre of a thriving wool industry for hundreds of years. In medieval times, the local abbey[115] owned *"extensive sheep runs on Dartmoor, seventeen manors in central and south Devon, town houses in Exeter, fisheries on the Dart and the Avon, and a country house for the abbot at Kingsbridge."*[116] Like most abbeys and monasteries, it fell into ruin after the Reformation, and in 1800 the site was purchased by a local businessman named Samuel Berry, who built a large woollen mill and salvaged the ancient stones to erect a neo-Gothic mansion, dubbed Buckfast Abbey, on the same site. However, Berry went bankrupt in 1813, and the Bentall brothers bought the house and the farmland around it.[117] In 1828 two other members of the Berry family also went bankrupt, and William Searle Bentall became a part owner of two more fields in the neighbourhood.[118]

It is not clear whether the family ever made a serious attempt to live at Buckfast Abbey. One of William Searle's children, Edward (see Chapter 17), attended the grammar school at Buckfastleigh, but he lived with the headmaster, and his letters home to his mother indicate that the Abbey was being redecorated by Thornton but occupied by Samuel and Elizabeth Adams (see Chapter 7). In around 1828 they moved out – probably to move to Hounslow, where Samuel was the barrack-master – and the mansion at Buckfast Abbey was leased out to a Royal Navy captain named Thomas White, later a rear admiral. He wrote books[119] and helped restore the church at Buckfastleigh, where he and his wife were eventually buried. There are a number of versions of an engraving of the house by an artist named McClatchie; the version shown in Figure 11.1 was issued as an early postcard, and carries the title *Buckfast Abbey, Devon. 1828. The Property of Mrs. Benthall*. A similar version also appears on the market from time to time, entitled *The Property of Mrs. Benthall to Captain White RN. View of his residence is respectfully inscribed*.[120]

In the next generation, Frank Benthall, one of the sons of William Searle, arranged to be designated "Lord of the Manor of Buckfast" and liked to write about the "Benthalls of Buckfast," although he certainly never lived there. This topic is dealt with in more detail in Chapter 21.

Back in Totnes, in 1823 William Searle and Thornton Bentall took a lease on the Totnes Town Mill, in partnership with Thomas and Joseph Hakewill, who were fullers (i.e., woollen clothmakers). The four also signed a lease on the fishing rights to the river, in return for which they agreed to keep the weir in good repair.[121]

William Searle, Thornton and John Bentall engaged in a variety of other businesses, either individually or in collaboration. One such short-lived venture stands out, with consequences

Figure 11.1: Buckfast Abbey

that remain relevant even today. In 1824 or possibly 1825, some Devon entrepreneurs, including Thornton and two of William Searle's banking partners, decided to enter the insurance business. The South Devon Insurance Company was established by a Private Act of Parliament,[122] and started to sell fire, life and marine insurance policies.

According to an advertisement in the *Liverpool Mercury* in April 1825, the managing directors included two of William Searle's partners in the Totnes and Newton banks, Ayshford Wise and Nicholas Baker. Thornton Bentall was a director (although the advertisement misspelled his surname "*Benlatt*"), and so was the Rev. George Baker, vicar of South Brent, and a number of other worthies.

This insurance company lasted only two years before it was wound up, but it had some collateral impact. The main trace of its short existence is a legal case known as *Shore v. Bentall*, which has been much cited as a legal precedent in all manner of highly technical legal texts relating to marine insurance law, both in the United Kingdom[123] and the United States.[124]

An article in the *North Devon Journal* on 7 August 1828, provides an account of the litigation. The plaintiff, Mr Shore, was a miller, proprietor of another Totnes mill, and owner (or part owner) of a cargo vessel named *Record*, which was insured with the South Devon Marine Insurance Company. On 18 February 1827 the ship arrived at Dartmouth from Weymouth with a cargo of corn, but had trouble finding a pilot so delayed its passage up the river until the next day. It then headed up the River Dart, but ran into problems with a high wind and dropped anchor. The anchor dragged, and the ship ran aground and turned on its side. The insurance company, in the person of Thornton Bentall,

refused to pay, on the grounds that the master of the vessel had not used due diligence in his handling of the ship. The case was won by the plaintiff, however, and is now the precedent under which many marine insurance claims are still decided, that an insurance company is generally liable for losses due to misconduct or negligence of a ship's captain or crew.

An 1830 directory of Totnes[125] provides further insight into the Bentall business activities at that time, as well as information about where various family members lived. The directory lists first the "*nobility, gentry and clergy*." This section includes William Searle and Thornton Bentall, along with "*Mrs. [William] Adams*," "*Major-General Geo. Pownall Adams*," "*Richard Marshall, esq*," the "*Rev. Wm. Floyer Cornish B.A.*," several Farwells, etc. According to that directory, William Searle and Mary Ann Bentall were living on The Plains, while Thornton was living on Lower Main Street, as were Christopher Farwell and the Rev. Arthur Farwell. Dr Richard Marshall was listed as living on Upper Main Street (but was not listed as a practising surgeon: well before 1830 he had moved to Chatham to take up a position as assistant barrack-master, while also apparently keeping a house at Totnes).

The directory additionally lists professionals and traders by category. The two banks are listed, referred to by the names of the partnerships, not their trading names. There is a section labelled "*Miscellaneous*" which includes this listing: "*Bentall William and Thornton and Co. woollen manufacturers, Plains*."

Other examples of the activities of William Searle and Thornton Bentall come from the *Exeter Register of Shipping*, which lists a number of vessels in which one of the two brothers (along with their banking partners) had a part share. The *Prince Regent* was owned by Andrew Howard and the four partners in the Totnes Bank. The *Fume*, the *Brothers* and the *Lord Duncan* were part-owned by Thornton in his capacity as a partner in the Totnes General Bank.

## Banking Ups and Downs

As noted earlier, in 1825 there was first a stock market crash and then a banking crisis, which started in the West Country but soon spread to the capital. In December that year, two major London banks failed, including Pole Thornton & Co. (a successor of Down & Co.), the bank where Henry Thornton MP had been one of the senior partners and where Thornton Bentall had apprenticed, but was then being managed by Henry Thornton's son, Henry Sykes Thornton.[126] However, the two Totnes banks and the Newton Bank survived, although another bank in which Walter Prideaux, Thornton's partner in the Totnes General Bank, had another partnership did fail.[127] William Searle Bentall later stated that the partners in the Totnes and Newton banks refrained from sharing the profits of their banks between 1825 and 1833, in order to restore their finances.

But the crash of 1825 brought about big changes in banking rules and regulations, with joint-stock banks gradually replacing the old partnerships. In about 1835, the business of the Totnes General Bank was acquired by the Devon & Cornwall Banking Company and became a branch of this larger enterprise, with Thornton remaining as branch manager.

## Bankruptcy and its Aftermath

In 1841, after several years of difficulty, the Newton Bank failed and brought down its partnership, and with it also the Totnes Bank. On 17 February 1842 a meeting of the Commissioners of Bankrupts was held in Exeter. William Searle Bentall attended in person to explain the failure, and the local newspaper provided a detailed account of his speech. He laid the blame squarely on two of his partners, Wise and Baker, who had taken loans from the Newton Bank on their personal promissory notes, invested the money in the Newfoundland cod trade, lost it all, and thus brought down both banks and their other two partners. An account of the hearing was published in the local newspaper, which provides insights into the character of William Searle Bentall:

*On Tuesday the 17th inst., was the second meeting of the Commissioners under the Fiat of Bankruptcy against Messrs. Wise and Co., of Totnes. The number of Creditors was so great that the Commissioners adjourned from Webb's Hotel to the Town Hall, where Mr. Bentall, the acting partner, made a point of attending, and voluntarily gave the following statement of the affairs of the Bank. He commenced by saying, – It is my earnest desire to fulfil the painful duties that devolve upon me to the best of my ability, and to state as clearly as lies in my power the circumstances connected with our unhappy failure; but our accounts not being completed, I cannot at present undertake to give a correct statement of our affairs, but I wish to convey to you such particulars as appear to me to be most important to be communicated at this time. The business of the Totnes Bank has generally been steady, and produced a regular profit, so that although we have met with many losses, and in the year 1825, when we were obliged to make great sacrifices by the sale of Stock, and also suffered severely from the failure of our London Bankers, yet by the Partners refraining from dividing their profits from March 1825 to Sept. 1833, the affairs of the Bank were restored to a healthy state. In the year 1834 Mr. Baker proposed to resign his Share in the Totnes Bank, on condition of having half the profit of the Newton bank, and it was agreed that the new concern of each Bank should take off all the accounts, except such debts as were of a doubtful nature. It was agreed that these debts should be consolidated in one account, to be settled at a future time. This consolidated account at Totnes consisted partly of debts secured by Policies of Insurance, which, instead of affording an annual income increased the amount of debt, for not only was the interest left in arrear, but in some instances were obliged to pay the premium on the Policies of Insurance lest they should become void. The present amount of the Totnes portion of these unsettled accounts augmented by the accumulation of interest and premiums paid, is £13,181 9s. 3d., but I cannot venture to calculate on the securities being worth as much, and have only reckoned them in £4,000, although I trust that they are much under-rated in that sum. In Mr. Bentall's statement of the liabilities and assets of the Bank, we noticed that the securities and good debts exceeded one half of the amount of the liabilities, exclusively of a large amount of doubtful debts, a claim on the Newton bank for £22,000 for cash advanced, and a demand on the old firm for the deficiencies in the consolidated account above alluded to, making*

*altogether several thousands more than the entire liabilities. In this financial statement the private properties of the Partners was not taken into consideration.*

*Mr. Bentall then proceeded to say, that having been informed that the Newton Bank intended to endeavour to evade the debt which it owes to the Totnes Bank for cash advanced, on the ground of a loss by the Newfoundland Trade, he could assure the Creditors that the Totnes Bank was in no way concerned with that Trade, and that neither he nor Col. Farwell had any individual interest in it, and that the Newton bank had only taken a small portion of it in discharge of a debt due from the original Trader. The principal Share in this Business belonged to Messrs. Wise and Baker, independently of the Bank, and these gentlemen had given their individual Notes of hand for the Capital which they borrowed from the Bank. On the 5th Sept., 1839, Mr. Bentall learnt from Mr. Baker, that including the losses by the Newfoundland Trade, and his own and Mr. Wise's Notes of Hand, the Newton Bank was minus more than £40,000. Astonished at this statement, Mr. Bentall called upon his Partners to examine whether they had the means of satisfying the claims of the public, and the private property of which the Partners declared themselves to be possessed was found to be much more than sufficient to pay all demands, and therefore it was thought right to continue the business of the Bank. In the year 1840, Mr. Wise having failed in raising a sum of money on his property, Mr. Bentall a second time expressed his fear of the solvency of the Bank, and urged the impropriety of exchanging its Creditors, but was assured by both Mr. Wise and Mr. Baker that they should soon place its affairs in a better state; and he again wrote in July last, to recommend a suspension of payments before the stock dividends were received, but his opinion was overrules by his Partners, who were confident of overcoming their difficulties.*

*Mr. Bentall, then in a very feeling manner, expressed his gratitude for the very friendly and kind feeling manifested towards him by the creditors of the bank, and assured them that the calamity which had caused so much distress to the public, had been the source of inexpressible misery to himself, but although he could not now expect that the creditors would receive the full amount of their debts, yet he trusted that the loss would not be so great as many persons had anticipated.*

*We never witnessed under such circumstances, a more gratifying reception than Mr. Bentall met with from the whole assembly, and we think his appearing so promptly before the creditors of the bank to afford every information in his power, does him much credit.*

In 1843 all of William Searle's assets were put up for auction, including his share of the Buckfast estate, his buildings in Totnes and his life insurance policy. Two auctions were advertised. The first was held in September 1842 at the Seven Stars Hotel, in the centre of Totnes, where five lots were auctioned off.[128] Lots 1 and 2 comprised Buckfast Abbey (owned by William Searle together with Thornton) and some surrounding property, and were described as follows:

[Lot 1: A half part of] *…the mansion house, consisting of a dining room 20 ¼ feet by 16 feet, height 13 feet, drawing room 24 ½ feet by 17 feet, height 13 feet, small breakfast room, two kitchens, seven bed rooms, two of which have good dressing rooms, cellars, coach house, stables, two orchards, and a productive walled garden. The house is built on part of the site of the ancient Abbey of Buckfast, the picturesque ruins of which stand on the property, and the sitting rooms command delightful views of the surrounding scenery, including the river Dart, which flows at the extremity of the grounds, a lawn in front extending to the river Dart, and intersected by a mill leat, which affords great facilities for irrigation; also two fields called Little Butt Meadow and Sheppen Park, labourers' cottages and gardens, and a barn, the whole containing about 17 acres.*" [The property is occupied by] *Captain Thomas White R.N. and Edward White, Esq. as yearly tenants.* [This was Buckfast Abbey, and as noted earlier, the other half was owned by Thornton Bentall.]

[Lot 2:] *The entire fee simple of and in the watered meadow, called Great Butt Meadow, partially intersecting the last lot, and containing about 5 acres, 2 roods of valuable pasture land, watered by the mill leat that flows through it. The field is now in the occupation of Edward White, Esq. as yearly tenant. The proprietors of Lot 1 and their tenants will have a right to the use of a pathway across this meadow, to and from the lawn and Little Butt Meadow comprised in Lot 1.*

The next two lots were properties in Totnes. The first was a "*substantial dwelling-house*" in Fore Street, Totnes, "*now in the occupation of Mrs. Jacobs, Silversmith, consisting of a handsome shop, a dining room, drawing room, four* best bed rooms, two good servants' bed rooms, a water-closet, two kitchens, a wash house, and two productive walled gardens..." This was on lease until 1856, "*at the low rent of £30 per annum, in consideration of the very extensive improvements which have been made by the tenant.*" The other lot was:

> ...*a dwelling-house and premises in Victoria-street, Totnes, now in the occupation of Mr. William Foale, Carrier, as yearly tenant, and only about fifteen years since erected. The property comprises two coach houses and two cider cellars, a parlour, two bedrooms, a kitchen and offices, all on one floor, besides excellent garrets over, stables with hay lofts over them, a stable yard with pump and other requisites.*

The fifth and final lot consisted of two life insurance policies, for £100 and £50 respectively, payable on the death of William Searle Bentall, "*subject to continued payment of the annual premiums of £2 2s, during his life.*"

The second auction, in December 1843, was for the sale of five separate lots situated on The Plains, in the centre of Totnes. Most of these were the properties that William Bentall had bought prior to moving there 70 years previously. *The London Gazette* described Lot 1 as "*A dwelling house lately occupied by William Searle Bentall; also the flower garden and green-house between it and the river; a dwelling-house adjoining that, and lately occupied by Miss Marshall; also the court and shrubbery in front of these houses.*"[129] "Miss Marshall" was almost certainly Sarah Marshall, sister of Mary Ann and Margaret. (For more details of her life, see Chapter 12.) The second dwelling-house was probably the one described by Cherry and Pevsner as "*a house 'lately erected'*"

in 1824, *its handsome five-bay frontage reinstated, and accessible from a new promenade above the river.*"[130]

Lot 2 was "*A large building on the south side of lot 1, consisting of a coal cellar and wine cellar, in the occupation of William Bentall and Henry Adams, together with a large wareroom over, with extensive lofts over; also a good sitting-room, about sixteen feet square, with bedrooms, a water closet, and other offices for a family residence.*" The wareroom also extended over another cellar, belonging to a Mr Richard Venning and not part of the lot; however, above that cellar were additional "*closets*" lately used and held by Miss Marshall, separate from the wareroom, and those were included.

Lot 3 was "*A counting-house, cellar and large warehouse over, with a wharf adjoining the Riding-place-quay, and now in the occupation of Henry Adams, Coal Merchant, as tenant.*"

Lot 4 was "*A dwelling-house occupied by the Devon and Cornwall Banking Company; also a large coal cellar and wine cellar, situated behind the said dwelling-house, extending to the Town quay, with large rooms over the same.*" This lot also included a "*verandah or green-house*" at the west end of the shrubbery in Lot 1.

Lot 5 was "*A dwelling-house occupied by Mr. William Bentall; also a large wine cellar behind it, with the Auction Mart over the cellar, the whole extending from the Plains to the Town quay.*" This William Bentall was the eldest son of William Searle Bentall, and his story is covered in Chapter 15.

Comparing the above descriptions with those contained in the original William Bentall's marriage settlement with his bride Grace Searle (see Chapter 6), it seems that by 1843 the family had increased its real estate holdings substantially. The original settlement included the original house bought from the Clarke family, a 'middle cellar, with three chambers above it, and a 'row of houses' south of that. By 1843, a large extension had been added to the original house, plus a second house next door, and those buildings constituted Lot 1. The "*Middle Cellar*" described in the marriage settlement had been divided, and part was occupied by Mr Venning, but the rest made up Lot 2. possibly including part of the "*row of houses*" next to Riding Place Quay. Lot 3 comprised the rest of that "*row of houses.*" Lots 4 and 5 were not mentioned in the marriage settlement, but it also seems that the family had acquired the underlying lease of the bank building on the north side of Harvey's Quay, with its associated cellars (Lot 4), and of the buildings to the north of that (Lot 5). It is likely that these included the mayoralty house and ballroom constructed in 1780 (see Chapter 10). In May 1806 the ballroom had been redeveloped to become the "*Totnes New Theatre.*" By 1843 the theatre was no longer in business and the space was merely described as an "*auction mart*," while the cellar below contained the stock for the younger William Bentall's wine business.

It is not entirely clear what transpired at those auctions, since no record has been found, but it clear that the family rallied round to retain ownership of Buckfast Abbey and the riverside properties, including the old house and at least some, if not all, of the cellars and warehouses.[131] For example, as noted earlier, a younger son of William Searle's, Frank, a solicitor who acted on behalf of his father during the settlement of the bankruptcy, eventually became the sole owner of Buckfast Abbey, having presumably acquired his father's share at the auction and then bought out the other half from his uncle Thornton. Some further explanation of the subsequent ownership of these properties will be given in Chapters 15 and 21.

# Chapter 12

## THE OTHER MARSHALL CHILDREN

Chapters 8 and 9 provided accounts of the lives of three of Dr William and Dorothy Marshall's nine children. That leaves three more daughters and three more sons, some of whom have already appeared in previous chapters. Their lives are summarised here.

**Three Sisters: Elizabeth, Sarah and Anne**

The eldest daughter, Elizabeth, married the Rev. William Floyer Cornish in 1804. William's parents were Dr James Cornish, another medical doctor at Totnes,[132] and Sarah Cornish (née Searle).[133] William later became the rector of Hook, Dorset, in 1827. The couple had no children, and both died at Totnes. This oil painting of Elizabeth (Figure 12.1), by an unknown artist, is at Benthall Hall, and was probably painted around 1850. The whereabouts of the painting of William are unknown, but a photograph of it survives.

Figure 12.1: Elizabeth Marshall and the Rev. William Floyer Cornish

The Cornish, Marshall and Bentall families were interconnected in various ways, usually – but not always – cordially. (Some of those connections have already been outlined in the chapters above.) When Elizabeth Marshall was widowed, old and frail, one of the servants at the old house on The Plains, named Ann Dart, was sent to look after her. She will reappear later in this narrative.

Sarah Marshall was born in 1783. She was married in 1843 by her brother the Rev. William Marshall, then at Chickerell (see Chapter 8), to Benjamin Hamilton, when she was 60 and he was 59. The couple lived at Croydon. She died there in 1849, shortly after a *"frightful fall."*[134] He died in 1858, and they were both buried in the Benthall vault at Highgate Cemetery.

Anne Gowan Marshall was born at Totnes in 1784[135] and died there, unmarried, in 1835. Sadly, there is no other information about her to be found.

**Richard Marshall**

Dr William and Dorothy's second son, Richard (1776–1859), started his career as a medical doctor. It is not clear whether he apprenticed locally with his father or another local doctor in Totnes, or in the army. He married twice. As noted in Chapter 10, his first wife was Jane Farwell, whose family had been prominent burgesses at Totnes for several generations. She died in 1815 after giving birth to five children: one son, yet another William Marshall, and four daughters.

Richard then married Sally Ford, and with her had one more daughter. Sally and all of Richard's children were at Dorothy's 80th birthday party, as well as Sally's sister, Peggy Ford, and their children's governess, Miss Borrow. Richard was admitted as a freeman of Totnes in 1797, and was appointed mayor in 1817–1818 and again in 1822–1823. He was also appointed, as early as 1805 according to one record, as an assistant barrack-master in Chatham, Kent. It is not clear how he divided his time, but certainly by 1835 he was living at Chatham, and in 1839 he moved to Maidstone and became master of the cavalry barracks there.

Richard's only son, William Marshall, was born in 1808. He became a clerk at the War Office, and spent his entire working career there. This William married his first cousin Mary Bentall, who was still to be born at the time of Dorothy's party. (They were introduced briefly in Chapter 3 as friends of Henry Drake and their story is told in Chapter 22.) The eldest daughter, Jane Farwell Marshall, was born in 1809 and never married. She lived with her father until he died, and died herself in London in 1865. Another daughter, Ellen, was born in 1811 and died in 1828.

The other two daughters, Louisa (1812–1880) and Marianne (1814–1855), both married, to Richard Darke Edgcumbe and Edward Thompson respectively, and they both have living descendants. Richard Darke Edgcumbe (1811–1862) was an officer in the Honourable East India Company's Maritime Service,[136] and then a surgeon working at the Western Asylum in Marylebone, London, but he was also the heir to an estate in Devon that traced its ownership in the family back to before the Norman Conquest. Once retired from his naval career, he lived with Louisa in Pimlico, London. Meanwhile, Marianne (also spelled Mary Ann) and Edward Thompson (1790–1884) lived at Salters' Hall, in the City of London, and then at Wilmington House, near Dartford, Kent, and both were buried at St Michael's Church, Wilmington. Edward was a solicitor and a clerk for the Worshipful Company of Salters.

That information and the story of Richard's last child was told by one of Marianne's daughters who wrote reminiscences of her family that included this paragraph about Richard:

*After some years he married a Miss Ford, the youngest of two maiden ladies who lived together on a comfortable income. I may say he married both ladies for they were inseparable and never did anything and scarcely dare think anything without appealing to each other. Sally and Peggy were their names. My grandfather had proposed to a Miss Adams of Sharpham, who was a cousin of his and of good family but in some way it did not come to anything, he would probably have found in her a partner more congenial to his fine mind and tastes. By this marriage there was one little girl, Margaret, who became the pet of her brothers and sisters, one and all being devoted to her. She was very clever, especially in drawing and cutting out all those groups of flowers and figures in black and white paper in my scrapbook were cut out by her. She died at the age of 13 of consumption.*[137]

## John and Jane Marshall

Whereas Dr William and Dorothy Marshall's eldest son went into the Church, and the second became a doctor like his father, the third one, John (1770–1850), went to sea. At the age of about 15, around the time when the new French Republic executed King Louis XVI and then declared war on Great Britain, he obtained a posting on a ship belonging to the Honourable East India Company's Maritime Service, initially as a "captain's servant." The Maritime Service ran convoys of ships from London to India and sometimes also to China; a return voyage took between 14 and 20 months. John first sailed on the maiden voyage of the East Indiaman *Brunswick*, which left London in January 1793 and returned in August 1794, after visiting Bombay and Canton, China.[138] His next voyage, as 5th mate, was on the *Kent*, leaving in May 1795 and returning in February 1797. That voyage was made under 'letters of marque', which gave the captain the right to attack and capture enemy vessels. He sailed as 3rd officer on the *Houghton* from April 1797 to July 1798, and as 2nd officer on the *Hugh Inglis* from May 1800 to December 1801. The record is incomplete from then until 1807, whereupon he captained the *Diana* on two consecutive voyages, from July 1807 to June 1809 and February 1810 to October 1811.

On the first outbound voyage of the *Diana* there were about 30 passengers, mainly military officers and HEIC employees, but also five unmarried women, including one named Jane Campbell.[139] The ship arrived at Calcutta on 17 March 1808, and John Marshall and Jane Campbell were married there the following week. The *Diana* sailed again on 21 August and joined a convoy of eight other East Indiamen and HMS Albion, a 74 gun 'ship of the line'. Another passenger on board was William Christopher (W.C.) Ord, a private merchant who had boarded previously at Madras and whom John had befriended.[140]

The convoy left Madras on 5 October but on 21 and 22 November they encountered "*the great hurricane of November 1808*" (also later referred to as "*Albion's hurricane*"). The Diana had four feet of water on the gun-deck and had to "*cut away the foremast*" to survive.[141] Most of the ships "*limped in to Cape Town in various states of distress.*"[142] Three of the merchant ships never arrived. In December, while still at sea and recovering from that ordeal, Jane gave birth to a boy, who was referred to as E.O. Marshall, but who died at Cape Town in January. When they were back in London, they were able to attend the marriage of Henry Bentall to Elizabeth Stewart (see Chapter 9).

After the next less fraught 1810–1811 voyage, John Marshall retired from the Maritime Service. The family lived off his modest pension for a few years, but in 1815 John was appointed president of the Lombard and Discount Bank, in the Cape Colony,[143] a post he held until 1842. This posting was obtained through the influence of T.P. Courtenay, who was then the Colonial Agent for the Cape of Good Hope (see Chapter 10). John and Jane went on to have two more sons and two daughters, who were brought up at Cape Town. The sons were named Francis Ord and William Ord Marshall, in tribute to John's friend W.C. Ord, and the girls were Emma and Anna Jane.

In 1821 John and Jane returned to visit England, on leave with their children and servants, and so were able to attend the reunion for Dorothy's birthday at Totnes in 1822. The two eldest children, Francis Ord and Emma Marshall, were able to write their names on the attendance sheet, but the younger two, William Ord and Anna Jane, were too young to leave more than their "marks."

John had a lively mind. While at the Cape, he became interested in mechanics and meteorology, as well as banking strategy.[144] In 1821 he wrote a pamphlet entitled *Description of a machine denominated the lifting dock, the model of which was exhibited in Table Bay, on Monday, the 3d of December, 1821*. In 1825 he also wrote a letter to a local newspaper on the theory of storms, based on his experience in 1808. This appears to have been highly regarded at the time and anticipated the later work of William Redfield (of New York) and William Reid, governor of Bermuda. As noted above, Reid's paper discussed Albion's hurricane and quotes from the log of the Diana. An article published in 1839 contains the following paragraph:[145]

*THE LAW OF STORMS.*

*By letters from the Cape it appears that the Secretary of State for the Colonies having forwarded to the Governor Lieut.-Col. Reid's work on Storms, with a request that public attention might be called to the subject, the Governor directed that a short printed compendium of the Theory [see Athen. No. 565,] together with Hints for Observers, prepared by Mr. Maclear, the Astronomer Royal of the Colony, should be delivered to all commanders of vessels sailing from Table Bay. To these papers have been added, at the suggestion of the Astronomer Royal, a very interesting letter from Mr. Marshall (formerly commander of one of the Hon. East India Company's ships), published nearly fourteen years since in the Cape journals, wherein he offers an explanation of the nature and character of tropical storms, and points out how to escape from their greatest danger, so closely resembling the theory of Mr. Redfield that the coincidence is quite remarkable. Col. Reid observes, that the hurricane referred to in Mr. Marshall's letter is among the anomalies, inasmuch as it had but little if any progressive motion. "This," says Mr. Maclear," is sufficient to account for the circumstance of his [Mr. Marshall] having made no allusion to the progressive motion of hurricanes; it being thus admitted by Col. Reid that the hurricane, described by Mr. Marshall, had but little, if any, progressive motion, although in Mr. Marshall's opinion, that it had a rotary motion, may be safely inferred from his figurative analogy between the centre of a hurricane and the vortex of a whirlpool." – but without reference to this particular question, Mr. Marshall's letter is both valuable and interesting.*

John finally retired to Sussex in about 1840, and died there in 1850. Three of the four children led conventional but not uninteresting lives. The two girls were both married at Cape Town. Emma married Samuel Blackaller Venning. Their eldest child was born there, but the couple then moved back to London and had four more children, born in Chelsea and Clapham, including William Marshall Venning (1841–1906). Samuel was depressive and committed suicide in 1848. Anna married Henry Francis Demergue, who was employed by the Madras Civil Service, but he died at sea in 1840. They also had children.

The younger brother, William Ord Marshall, became a précis writer and librarian at the War Office. He was described by a contemporary as "*a most urbane gentleman.*"[146] In 1882, having retired from the War Office, he married Elizabeth Middleton Beloe. (A year later, William Marshall Venning married Maud Henrietta Beloe, Elizabeth's younger sister.) After William Ord Marshall died, in 1900, Elizabeth helped found an organisation named the League of the Empire, whose mission was "*to help spread a greater sense of imperial loyalty and unity by correspondence between children throughout the Empire.*"[147] Her house became the League's headquarters, and in 1918 she was awarded a CBE.

The life of the elder brother, Francis Ord Marshall (born 1812), was more colourful and unconventional. In 1831 he married Eliza Jane Glasse, who came from a fairly conventional family but whose parents were estranged. The marriage was performed by his cousin the Rev. John Benthall (second son of William Searle and Mary Ann Bentall – see Chapter 17).

Francis then took a job as a clerk in the House of Lords, but in 1836 he moved to Samarang, on the Indonesian island of Java, to work as an engineer on a sugar plantation, leaving Eliza in London. He settled down there with a Chinese woman named Teh Ing Njo, who bore his first child in 1839 and then four more. One of their Dutch descendants, Ralph Ravestijn, has a genealogical website on which his family's history is detailed (in Dutch)[148] and has written extensively elsewhere about this specific family.[149]

Eliza also gave birth to a boy in Chelsea in 1839; he was baptised Francis Glasse Marshall in 1842, at about the same time as William Marshall Venning, also born in Chelsea.

In 1854 Francis senior was back in England and became an enthusiastic member of the Royal Thames Yacht Club, where his brother William was also a member. He owned several racing yachts, of which the most successful were Vestal and Thought, which competed in several prestigious regattas, documented with lithographs in the Illustrated London News (see Figure 12.2, overleaf).

While in London he started yet another relationship, with a woman named Ursula Hutchins, who already had an illegitimate son, born in 1850 and baptised at Boulogne-sur-Mer. (That boy's natural father was William John Duff Roper, who died in 1858. Roper was a writer, the author of *Chronicles of Charter-House*, a history of that institution as a monastery, a hospital and a school.) After her initial liaison with Francis, Ursula married a man named Symes,

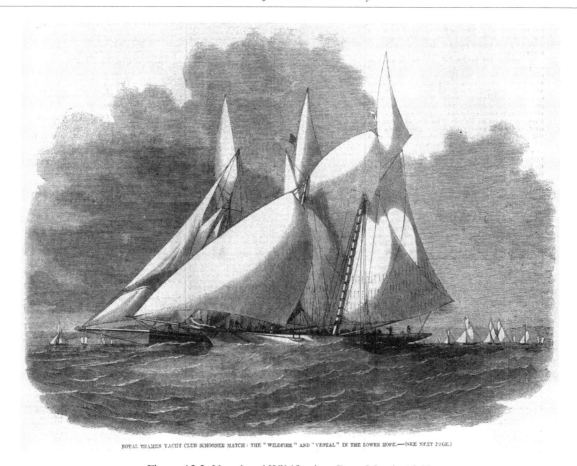

BOYAL THAMES YACHT CLUB SCHOONER MATCH : THE "WILDFIRE" AND "VESTAL" IN THE LOWER HOPE.——(SEE NEXT PAGE.)

Figure 12.2: Vestal and Wildfire in a Race Match, 1857

Figure 12.3: Ellen and Thomas Marshall

but left him after he assaulted her, and Francis took up with her again in 1857 or 1858. At this point, or possibly earlier, Francis appears to have adopted Ursula's son, who took the name William Norman Duff Roper Marshall. Eliza and Francis eventually divorced in 1861, and the messy story of his entanglements is recorded in the divorce papers.

Meanwhile, Francis's children in Java, whose mother was Teh Ing Njo, grew up and flourished. Francis returned to Java and died there in 1870. The photographs (Figure 12.3) are of two of those children, Ellen (with her husband and family) and Thomas Marshall.

## Edward Marshall

Edward, the youngest of the four sons of Dr William and Dorothy Marshall, was the most distinguished. He started his career in April 1798 as a clerk in the "Accomptant's Department" at the War Office, with a salary of £80 a year.[150] In 1806 he became private secretary to Sir Arthur Wellesley (later to become the Duke of Wellington), who at that time was serving as Chief Secretary for Ireland after returning from a military career in India. When Wellesley was given command of the expeditionary force that landed in Portugal in 1807 and launched the Peninsular War, Edward returned to London and went back to the War Office as a senior clerk. In that position he worked for 19 years under Lord Palmerston, who was Secretary at War from 1809 to 1828. Not long after,[151] he was promoted to the position of Chief Examiner of Army Accounts, head of one of the two departments that made up the War Office. He worked there in that position until he retired in 1849, serving under 13 subsequent Secretaries at War.

Edward retained an interest in the politics of Totnes. He was admitted as a freeman in 1810 and in 1825 he became embroiled in the political fight going on there (see Chapter 10). He wrote a letter to one of the candidates – Henry Vane, Lord Barnard – complaining "*about the 'hostile proceedings' of 'Farwell and his party', who had 'aggrandized themselves' within the corporation 'at our expense'.*"[152] In the end, the Courtenay and Barnard supporters agreed to support each other and were duly returned at the election in 1826. "*Marshall warned Barnard that the 'misconduct of your agent* [i.e. Farwell] *would have put your return at hazard' had they not held him in such high regard.*"[153]

Edward also retained an interest in helping his family. In 1828 he wrote to Courtenay: "… *as it was you who obtained for my brother* [John Marshall – see above] *the presidency of the Cape Bank, I am extremely sorry to inform you that your well-intentioned endeavour to promote his welfare has eventually been a disservice, because the salary was inadequate.*"[154] As noted earlier, two of Edward's nephews, William (son of Richard Marshall) and William Ord (son of John Marshall), were given positions and had long careers at the War Office.

In addition to his own career at the War Office, Edward became an early shareholder and director of the Van Diemen's Land Company. Van Diemen's Land was the name then given to the Australian island of Tasmania. The company, founded in 1825 by "*a group of London merchants who planned a wool-growing venture to supply the needs of the British textile industry,*"[155] was granted 250,000 acres of land in Tasmania on which to raise sheep. The other shareholders included Richard Marshall and Peggy Ford, Richard's sister-in-law. John Bentall was their stockbroker, and their dividends were signed for by young Thornton Bentall, son of William Searle Bentall, who worked for his uncle John until he became a member of the stock exchange himself (see Chapter 20).

A book by Matthew Boyd published in 1871 provides some interesting insights into Edward's character and temperament and some of its anecdotes deserve to be repeated here:[156]

> *Lord Palmerston and Mr. Marshall did not always ride their horses together. The former, one day, directed Mr. Marshall to prepare for transmission abroad an important document, which instruction the latter had most carefully carried out, sending the paper by a clerk or messenger to his lordship, then in his own room. In its perusal, Lord Palmerston came to the word 'waggon,' which his amanuensis had spelt with one 'g.' Not taking the same view of orthography, his lordship said to the messenger, 'Take that back to Mr. Marshall' (of course unsigned by his lordship). In a few minutes the messenger returned with two dictionaries, one or both of which authorised the word being spelt either with one 'g' or two. 'Carry back these books to Mr. Marshall, and assure him I do not require to be told how to spell waggon;' and he dashed the books on the floor.*

On another occasion, Palmerston walked into Edward's office one morning and gave him an urgent task to complete. As he left, he quietly locked the door and put the key in his pocket, which Edward only discovered when he tried to go out for lunch. He was able to ring a bell to summon help and to have the lock picked. In Boyd's retelling of the story, when Palmerston returned later that day, Edward said to his boss: *"My lord, I am now no longer a*

*schoolboy; I am as old, if not older, than your lordship, and I must beg your lordship in future not to lock my door."*

Despite these clashes, Palmerston defended Marshall when necessary. In February 1822 the "Army Estimates" were being debated in the House of Commons, and Edward was singled out by an MP named Hume as someone who

> *"had 700l. a year, and received besides 150l. for preparing estimates to be laid before the House. Now the time required for this could not be more than two or three days; and he really thought the sum considerably too much. He should be happy to do it himself for less, and should think himself very well paid."*[157]

Palmerston's reply was loyal:

> *"The labour of making out the estimates, so far from being the work of two or three days, occupied several months, and if any fault could be imputed to his majesty's government, it was, that the persons employed in this labour were inadequately paid."*

One more of Boyd's anecdotes deserves repeating:

> *There was a standing joke against the Chief Examiner of Army Accounts, which, I am told, lasted during the war, and indeed more or less to the day of his death. 'Ah, Marshall, you know it was you who selected Sir Arthur Wellesley to command the army of the Peninsula.' Marshall was an extremely sensible man, and I never saw him ruffled in the least with all this banter, to which he always submitted in great good humour. I was anxious to know the precise origin of a joke I*

94

*had heard so often, and he told me the whole story, with much more of a highly interesting nature in reference to the 'Iron Duke,' during the period through which he was associated with him in Ireland. He said: – 'I was in the habit of keeping up a close correspondence from Dublin with an esteemed colleague of mine in one of the Government offices at Whitehall, and much of that correspondence related to the illustrious statesman and general under whom I was then serving ; for he was, even at that time, "illustrious" as the hero of Assaye. I described Sir Arthur to my friend as the most remarkable public man with whom I had ever been thrown into communication, for there was nothing, however abstruse, in public affairs which he could not at once master.' 'I presume,' continued my friend, 'when a general was wanted to meet the great Napoleon in Spain I must have expatiated on the qualifications of my own chief as better suited than any other, in my humble opinion. It appeared, of which I was entirely unaware, that my letters, with which I had taken some pains for the information of one whom I very much esteemed, but never contemplating they were to be seen beyond himself and his own immediate circle, were regularly perused by Lord Castlereagh, Sir Arthur Wellesley's earliest patron and staunchest supporter in the Cabinet; and he,*

*I conclude, was not displeased to hear even the opinion of a young Treasury official who had presumed to write so much ad libitum regarding his chief the Secretary of State for Ireland; for occasionally, on the receipt of the news of some victory in Spain, if I accidentally met Lord Castlereagh, he would stop and say: "Ah, Marshall, you formed a correct estimate of Lord Wellington in Ireland," adding, as he pointed his finger to his head, "I knew it was here."' 'That, my dear friend,' addressing me, 'is the full extent of my share in the appointment of Sir Arthur Wellesley to command that army whose achievements culminated on the plains of Waterloo.'*

As one of the senior functionaries at the War Office, Edward was able to find jobs for two his nephews, William and William Ord (see above).[158] Later in Edward's career, in 1839, Thomas Babington Macaulay was appointed Secretary at War. Macaulay would eventually become Lord Macaulay and a famous historian. He was the son of Selina Mills, the schoolmistress responsible for Clementina Clerk, and a witness at that famous trial (see Chapter 8). Edward must have known of the connection between Macaulay's mother and his sister-in-law, Isabella, but one might wonder whether he ever mentioned it.

Figure 12.4: Mary and Alexander Marshall

Edward was still single at the time of his mother's 1822 reunion, but the next year he married Mary Faulder, the daughter of a well-known bookseller with a shop on Bond Street, London. They had two sons, Edward and Alexander (whose silhouette is shown in Figure 12.4), and two daughters, Mary (also pictured below) and Anna, who died in infancy.

Edward junior married Caroline Augusta Shearburn and also ended up with a job at the War Office, while Alexander married Frances Lavinia Bartlett, and both have descendants alive today. Sadly, Mary died at Teignmouth in 1839, aged about 13.

## Chapter 13

# CAPE TOWN, MAURITIUS AND LEITH: WILLIAM AND LOUISA MARSHALL

We come now to the story of Louisa Bentall, who married the William Marshall who was the youngest son of the Rev. John Marshall (see Chapter 2). William and Louisa were the grandparents of Professor Alfred Marshall, and their lives have been misrepresented by some of the professor's biographers. William was born at Exeter and was baptised by his own father in 1780. It is likely that he was a student at Exeter Grammar School up to the point when a career needed to be chosen. His older brothers had all taken holy orders, but William decided instead to become a mariner, and at the age of 15 he became a captain's servant in the Honourable East India Company's Maritime Service,[159] following in the steps of his cousin John, who was three years ahead of him.

Like his cousin John, William's first ship was the *Brunswick*, a 1,200-ton East Indiaman whose nominal owner was Thomas Newte Esq., and whose captain was Thomas Palmer Acland. John Marshall had sailed on the maiden voyage of that ship, and William signed on for its second one. The *Brunswick* sailed from London in May 1795, travelling to Bombay and China. For that voyage, Acland had acquired a 'letter of marque' and the ship sailed as part of a convoy bringing troops to invade the Cape Colony (then owned by the Dutch). At the end of 1796 William was

promoted to midshipman, and he arrived back with the ship in July 1797. Six months later, the same ship but with a new captain, James Ludovic Grant, also with a letter of marque, set out again on the same route, returning in August 1799, by which time Marshall had moved up to the rank of 6th mate. He served on four more such voyages: the next three on the *Canton*, all under letter of marque, by the end of which he was promoted to chief mate – i.e., second in command after the captain – and the final one aboard the *Surat Castle*, as chief mate under Captain Alexander Robertson. That voyage was completed in May 1809.[160]

On 19 January 1810 William resigned from the service, and on 16 February he married Louisa Bentall in the parish church of Totnes. The witnesses signed their names as *"Wm Bentall, Elizth Adams, Wm Adams, W. S. Bentall, and Wm Bentall Jr."*[161]

Portraits of William and Louisa, used to (and may still) exist and photographs of them survive (see Figure 13.1).

Soon after the marriage, William and Louisa embarked for Cape Town, where he had been appointed Assistant Paymaster General for the army garrison there. There is no doubt that this appointment was made by T.P. Courtenay, and was arranged even before the marriage, with the help of William Adams MP, who was a witness to that marriage. It is likely that Courtenay, whose father was the Bishop of Exeter, knew this William Marshall; indeed, they probably attended school at Exeter together, although Courtenay was two years younger. Twenty years later, Courtenay was deeply involved in both the Cape Colony and the India Board of Control, and was being groomed as the next MP for Totnes.

William and Louisa arrived at Cape Town on 1 October 1810. It was four years after the Dutch had surrendered the territory to the British for the second time, and their arrival coincided with the British naval expedition to capture the island of Mauritius from the French (an endeavour that was complete by 3 December 1810). The British had been ambivalent about whether the expense of occupying Cape Town was worth the effort, since it was not self-sustaining economically but of strategic value nonetheless: whoever controlled that port could control all trade between Europe and the East Indies. In 1810 *"the Cape Garrison contained almost 6,500 soldiers, giving it a larger capacity than either Gibraltar or Malta."*[162]

In due course William bought a house and "erf"[163] with a large stable and several detached buildings, one of which became his official office as paymaster. The house address was 5 Buitenkant, while the nearby office was on Roeland Street. Today, those are two of the major streets in the centre of Cape Town.

Louisa bore four children at Cape Town, two of whom survived infancy. Mary was born in 1811 but died before the end of the year. William was born on 16 August 1812. John was born on 1 June 1814. Charles was born in July 1815, but died within a week.

Figure 13.1: William and Louisa Marshall

After five years at Cape Town, William was appointed Assistant Deputy Paymaster General for Mauritius. He sold his Cape Town house in March 1816 and moved to Port Louis, the capital of this new colony. At that time Mauritius had an acting governor, but no official "Council of Government." The colony was officially bilingual, with British rule over still a mainly French-speaking population. Soon after arriving, William changed jobs again, becoming one of two joint police commissaries – the other being a man named Journel, from a French family that had lived there for over 30 years.

In December 1817 the provisional government, seeking funds, put up for auction the *"farm of the batelage"* – essentially the job of harbour master, but including the exclusive right to control the shipping and landing of goods at the main harbour of Port Louis for a period of two years. William bid for and won the position, to be paid for in two instalments, but within a few months discovered that he had seriously overpaid: he could not make enough money from it to cover his living expenses, and was rapidly using up his savings. In April 1818 he wrote to the acting governor, explaining that he could not pay the next instalment and pleading for relief.[164] Partly, he said, this was because some of his boats and implements had been destroyed by a hurricane the previous month, but also because whereas he had been led to believe that the port would be kept open to foreign ships until March 1820, it had suddenly been shut to them just weeks ago – that is, two years sooner than he expected.

The story behind the closure is complicated, but of interest, since it is one of the places where the biographers of Professor Alfred Marshall seriously misrepresent his grandfather's record.

At that time the Navigation Act of 1651 barred any trade with British colonies except using British vessels. When applied to the new colony, this had caused a huge drop in the exports on which the island economy depended. In March 1817 the governor, Sir Robert Farquhar, obtained permission to waive the law for a year, and as a result the volume of trade – and with it, the harbour fees – grew substantially. Farquhar returned to England that November and a new acting governor, Major General Gage John Hall, was appointed, and it was he who arranged for the auction. In doing so, he privately instructed the auctioneer, Colonel Draper, to force the price up to $24,000 (Mauritian dollars[i]) if he could. After the bidding went above $17,500, William was unknowingly bidding against the auctioneer (as Draper himself later confirmed), and allowed himself to be coaxed up to $23,000 per year.

The contract started in January 1818. Ominously, soon after, according to the memorial later written by William to the acting governor, several ships in the harbour were seized for bringing in *"prohibited goods the landing of which under certain restrictions had heretofore been permitted."*[165] Then, on 28 February and 1 March, Mauritius was hit by a monster hurricane, unequalled again in its devastation until 1892. Of the 41 vessels in harbour, only one rode out the storm; the other 40, including a British frigate, HMS *Magicienne*, were driven ashore or wrecked. The town and countryside were also severely damaged. At the end of March, the port was again closed to foreign ships, prompting William's letter to Hall in April. His request for relief from his contract turned on three arguments: (a) that until now, the *"farm of*

---

[i] Five Mauritian dollars were equivalent to one pound sterling.

*the batelage*" had "*never* [been] *sold for more than $11,225 per annum*"; (b) that he had been led to believe that the port would remain open to foreign ships at least until March 1820; and (c) that the hurricane had destroyed his boats, sheds and implements, at a cost of $28,000 to replace.

Hall objected to the letter, but agreed to forward it to London so long as William revised it to refer only to the hurricane and not his other complaints. William did so, but the letter was never forwarded. In December 1818 Hall was recalled, to be replaced briefly by Colonel John Dalrymple, and then in February 1819 by Major-General Ralph Darling. William wrote a revised petition, dated 31 December 1818, enclosing copies of the first and second drafts of his original petition. In March 1819 Darling forwarded this third revision, plus the earlier two and an affidavit from the auctioneer confirming that the auction was in fact rigged.

William was also caught up in another of Hall's other priorities, albeit a more salutary one: the suppression of the slave trade. In 1807 the British government had passed an act prohibiting the transportation of slaves, and the Royal Navy had established the West Africa Squadron to enforce the ban. But slaves already on the island of Mauritius, who accounted for well over half the population, remained legally enslaved: they were registered by their owners and could still be bought or sold. Furthermore, it seems that there was a lively but illegal trade in newly imported captives who were sold surreptitiously to plantation owners. Hall wanted to stop that illegal trade, and he instructed William to go after suspected cases. This caused a pushback from the French estate owners, and in March 1818 William was named in a complaint after he (at the direction of Hall) sent his police to remove a number of slaves from the estate of their nominal owner, on the basis that they were recent illegal acquisitions.

William was still signing documents as one of the joint police commissaries in May 1818, but in June he was replaced by a man named Warren. It is not clear how he then supported his wife and rapidly growing family. Five more children were born in Mauritius: Edward in 1816 (probably December), Louisa Maria on 5 March 1818, Charles Henry in December the same year, Henry in 1821, and Thornton on 6 March 1822. Figure 13.2 provides additional details of these children and their families.

In 1821 the two eldest sons, William and John, were sent back to England to live with their uncles and aunts at Totnes. Mary Ann Bentall sent a letter in September 1821 to Miss Helen Davidson,[ii] who had been governess to the Bentall children in Totnes but had since moved on to another career, in which Mary Ann wrote about the arrival of the two boys and the fact that the elder, then aged nine, was attending Totnes Grammar School as a boarder. The boys' signatures appear under the list of witnesses at Dorothy Marshall's birthday party in 1822.

Sometime later, William senior travelled back to England and then moved to Leith, the port of Edinburgh, in time to have his address listed in the *Edinburgh and Leith Postal Directory* published in May 1823, in which he described himself as a merchant.[166] Louisa remained at Port Louis with her five other children, but died on 24 March 1823. The cause of her death is not known, but the 1817–1824 cholera pandemic reached Mauritius in 1823,[167] so that may have been the reason.

It took a year to organise the return of the other children to Britain. In Chapter 10 there

---

[ii] For more details on this letter, see Chapter 14.

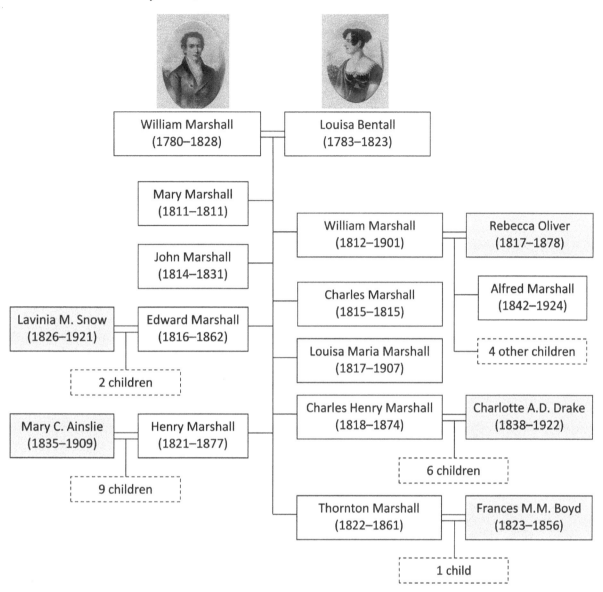

Figure 13.2: William and Louisa Marshall's children

was an account of the first half of a letter that T.P. Courtenay started to write to Thornton Bentall on 8 June 1824, while paying a visit to Essex in the company of John Bentall. That letter was in two parts; the following day, after staying overnight at John's house on Craven Street, Courtenay resumed writing:

*We arrived in Craven Street too late for me to send this by the post which I am very sorry for as I fear you will be disappointed at getting no letter for two days … On my arrival*

*here after a most tiresome dusty journey. I was greeted with the intelligence that all William Marshall's children would probably be in London in a few days as Mrs. Jennings* [her role in this is unknown] *has received a letter from their father to that effect. John is most discomforted as Mrs. Garfield* [probably John's housekeeper] *cannot possibly accommodate them. I shall write to Hounslow* [to Elizabeth and Samuel Adams] *on the subject today and if I find that your sister does not wish to have them there I have made up my mind to take the whole of a Coach which carries six inside and set off myself with all the family as soon as they arrive but I cannot help having some hope that the Captain of the ship will have sense enough to send them immediately to Totnes.*[168]

The five younger children travelled to England, accompanied by a black servant, on a ship named the *Hero of Malown*, which arrived at Falmouth on 5 June 1824 and then sailed on to London.[169] Maybe they went initially to Devon, but documentary evidence indicates that fairly soon young William and his brother Charles – and, therefore, presumably all the others as well – went to their father in Scotland, since William wrote later about the "taws," a peculiarly Scottish instrument of corporal punishment,[170] and Charles on his honeymoon took his new wife, Charlotte, to see the house he had lived in as a child, and his father's grave.[171]

When William senior first moved to Leith, he gave his address as "*2 John's Place, Links.*" The house with that address today is almost certainly the same one, and is situated at the end of a terrace with a view of Leith Links, nowadays a park but once one of the earliest golf courses. He listed his residence there in the directories for 1823–1824, 1824–1825 and 1825–1826, but not in 1826–1827. In the 1827–1828 directory he relisted as "*Wm. Marshall (of the Devon Insurance Co.)*" with a home address at 30 Constitution Street.[172] Meanwhile, the South Devon Marine Insurance Company had its own listing at 37 Charlotte Street. As noted in Chapter 11, this company had been set up in 1825 by a group of Totnes bankers including Ayshford Wise, Nicholas Baker and Thornton Bentall. It closed down soon after the directory was published, but it seems that William was

briefly representing the company in Leith while it was still in business.

William died in January 1828, and was buried in the churchyard of the South Leith Church. A gravestone was eventually erected with an inscription "*William Marshall-Died 17th jan 1828 aged 47 formerly Paymaster RN.*"[173] The area was redeveloped and the cemetery is no longer there. It is not clear when the inscription was carved, or who paid for it.

William died without a will. His brother-in-law John prepared the necessary paperwork for probate, and declared the value of the estate to be just under £2,000. A formal assignment of guardianship was drawn up and signed by six of the seven children in March 1828. The youngest son, Thornton, being only six years old, was considered too young to participate. Louisa's signature was witnessed at Exeter by her uncle Richard Collins and his son John. The signatures of John, Edward and Henry were witnessed at Hounslow by Samuel Adams and his housekeeper. The signatures of William and Charles Henry were witnessed by William Dacres Adams and Henry Bentall Adams at the Office of Woods, Forests and Land Revenues on Whitehall Place, London.[174]

In due course the children – or certainly most of them – were moved back to Totnes and became part of the extended households of William Searle and Thornton Bentall. Then they moved on, and by the next generation had lost touch with most of their Bentall relatives, although they kept in touch with each other. The biographers of Alfred Marshall took a great interest in them. Figure 13.2 provides a summary of the orphans' families, and their stories are told in Part III.

## DIGRESSION: "COUSIN" JOHN MARSHALL

When I decided to track down the people present at Dorothy's 80th birthday party, the signatures of "*W. Marshall*" and "*J. Marshall*" posed a problem. I assumed that Louisa's husband, William Marshall, had returned to England by then and made the trip to Totnes before heading up to Leith. That explained – for the time being – the first signature but not the second.

I started making a search for relatives named John Marshall that might have been alive in 1822. William had a younger brother named John, but he had died in around 1810. William and Louisa's third child was named John, but Alfred Marshall's biographers had stated that he had survived for less than a year.[175]

However, I had read that there was a "*cousin John Marshall*" who had passed through Calcutta in around 1843 and was mentioned in the diary kept by Clementina Benthall, née Marshall (see Chapter 17). With no sign of any other, I concluded that the most likely candidate for this elusive "*J. Marshall*" was in fact the son of the Rev. Edward Marshall, of Mount Moses, Jamaica, and who might also be the same John who met his cousin Clementina in Calcutta. I posted an inquiry on the *Genealogists' Forum* website, and the administrators there quickly located all the information about his birth, marriage, children and eventual death in 1855, in the Crimean War, where he met Henry Drake, the grandson of Sarah Chadder (see Chapter 3). It was due to that set of posts that I made the acquaintance of Megan Stevens, who was trying to track down the same man while editing Henry Drake's journal.

Nonetheless, when the formal assignment of guardianship was unearthed in the Kew National Archives, it became clear that the John Marshall who was the son of William and Louisa had not in fact died in infancy at Cape Town; and soon after that, the letter referred to above from Mary Ann Bentall to her ex-governess Helen Davidson established that he had been sent back to Totnes in 1821. (More details of that letter are provided in Chapter 14.) This made it clear that the two witnesses were in fact the two eldest sons of William and Louisa, William and John.

But the visitor in Calcutta in 1843 and the man in Crimea in 1855 were one and the same person, and story of this "cousin" John Marshall is worth telling anyway. He was the son of William's elder brother, the Rev. Edward Marshall, and his wife Elizabeth (née Horn), who lived in Jamaica. John was born there in 1809 and was a great-nephew of Dorothy's. He married Elizabeth Salmon[176] and became an army surgeon, initially in the 65th Foot Regiment and then in the 84th Foot. Their first daughter, Clara, was born in Coventry in 1844. He was posted to Madras, where a second daughter, Mary Emma, was born in 1846. In 1848 a son, John William, was also born in Madras, as was another daughter, Caroline, in 1850. By this time John was with the 15th Hussars, and another daughter, Emily, was born in Bangalore in 1851. Their last child, Dora, was born in Brecon, Wales, in 1854, and by then John was listed as a surgeon in the 31st Regiment. In August 1854 he was promoted to the rank "Staff Surgeon of the First Class" and sent to Crimea to support the British Army there.

Sadly, a death notice appeared in *The Morning Chronicle* on 9 March 1855: "*At the hospital, Kulalee, on the Bosphorus, to which place he had been invalided from the Crimea, Staff-Surgeon (first class) JOHN MARSHALL, senior medical officer in charge of the second division of the British army before Sebastopol.*" He had died on 10 February, of "*fever.*" His widow received a pension and lived until 1901. She and two of her daughters were buried at Bath.[177]

Henry Drake (see Chapter 3) was also at Balaclava as part of the Commissariat, and in a letter written in November 1854 he reported Dr John Marshall's arrival, since when he met the doctor, he learned that "*W.M.*" had referred John to him. ("*W.M.*" being the young William Marshall who was a clerk at the War Office and married Mary Benthall – see Chapter 22). In a few subsequent letters Drake noted that he had seen Dr Marshall again, but a letter in January reported that he was sick and another in February that he had been sent back to Scutari.

# PART III.
# THE BENTALL-MARSHALL GRANDCHILDREN

Part II provided accounts of the lives of the children of William Bentall and Dr William Marshall, as well as brief summaries of their subsequent descendants who did not have both Bentall and Marshall genes. Part III continues with the stories of those descendants who *did* have both Bentall and Marshall ancestry – i.e., the 15 children of William Searle and Mary Ann Bentall (née Marshall) and the seven orphans, the children of William and Louisa Marshall (née Bentall). The names of these children and their spouses were summarised in Figures 9.1 and 13.2.

## Chapter 14

## THE EDUCATION OF MERCHANT CHILDREN

Before going into detailed accounts of the lives of these people, I would like to make some general observations about how they were educated. As far as we know, their parents and their parents' peers were typically educated either with a private tutor or at a local grammar school. Most of those sent up to Oxford or Cambridge were destined for an ecclesiastical career, to obtain a degree and then proceed through the process of ordination. Some also went to those universities in preparation for becoming lawyers. William Bentall, the patriarch, had attended the local grammar school at Kingsbridge when he moved to Devon. His children did not move away from Totnes until their teens. The same was probably true of the children of Dr William Marshall.

But by the end of the 18th century, the fashion in education had evolved: it was now seen by the merchant classes as well as the aristocracy that in order to be well educated and ultimately successful, their children, especially the boys but also some girls, needed to attend school as boarders. Indeed, by 1821 even the lone Corporation-appointed master at the Totnes Grammar School – who was paid a small salary and required to teach two students free of charge, but was also permitted to charge for others to attend – was accommodating boarders

in his own house. A similar arrangement was in place at Buckfastleigh.

At the established ecclesiastical schools, such as Eton, Winchester and Westminster, the education received for free by the "scholars"[178] was subsidised by fee-paying students, known as "town boys" or "oppidans," living nearby as boarders under the care of a landlady. The sons of the nobility and landed gentry might start their education at the local grammar school, but then increasingly they would move on to be a boarder at such a school, after which the more intelligent ones would go up to Oxford or Cambridge, even if not intending to become a clergyman or a lawyer.[179] The merchant class began to adopt the same approach. As noted in Chapter 2, Dr William Marshall's elder brother had married into the Hawtrey family, and as a result, his nephew Edward had attended Eton College as a scholar. Of the nine sons of William Searle and Mary Ann Bentall (see Figure 9.1), five attended Westminster (three as scholars, the other two as town boys); one attended the grammar school at Buckfastleigh as a boarder, and then went to the East India College at the age of 17 to prepare for a career in the Indian Civil Service; while two joined the Royal Navy and trained to be naval officers. (The education of one other brother, Henry, is something of a mystery, to be discussed in due course more fully – see Chapter 18).

The Bentalls were probably introduced to this idea by Courtenay, whose family had been attending Westminster School for generations (see Chapter 10). Courtenay, while working in government offices around Westminster, habitually kept an eye on the young scholars at Westminster school. In 1818 he hired one of the brightest of these, named Thomas Nelson (T.N.) Waterfield, before he could graduate from Cambridge, to work first as a clerk at the Board of Control, and then as his private secretary. Courtenay also hired Waterfield's father at about the same time. Eight years later, T.N. Waterfield married Elizabeth Bentall. Well before then, when Courtenay first got to know the Bentall and Adams families, he encouraged them to think about Westminster School. The eldest son of William Searle and Mary Ann Bentall, William, was admitted as a King's Scholar in 1817, William Pitt Adams in 1818, and John Bentall and Dacres Adams both in 1820. Later, both Thornton and Frank Bentall attended Westminster School as town boys, and the youngest boy, Arthur, was a Queen's Scholar (Victoria having acceded to the throne by then). For the Bentalls, this must have represented a substantial cultural shift from a provincial to a national perspective, which possibly first took root when Thornton and John Bentall, William Searle Bentall's younger brothers, launched their careers in London.

A number of other Bentall cousins were also at Westminster, some close, others more distant. Thornton Marshall, the youngest of the orphans (see Chapter 28 and Figure 9.1), attended in 1835. Several members of the Thornton clan, fourth cousins of the Bentalls, also attended the school. All the sons of T.N. and Elizabeth Waterfield were there, as were nine of their grandsons and at least five great-grandsons.[180]

A letter written by Mary Ann Bentall in September 1821 to an ex-governess named Helen Davidson and mentioned already in Chapter 13, provides some insight into how these younger Bentalls' and Marshalls' education was managed. In part it reads:

*I should have answered your letter before this, but I have hardly found any time lately for writing, having had all my children at home for some weeks and much other company. We are now dispersing a little. John returned to school last week and William will go to Cambridge in about a fortnight. I believe I have not written to you since the arrival of our two little Nephews from the Mauritius [see Chapter 13]. They are very pleasant children. We have sent the elder to Mr. Cleave's school[181] as Boarder and the younger who is about Thornton's age stays with us. I enclose a letter I have found written by Thornton a long time since which will show you that he sometimes thinks about you, he has lately left off his frocks and looks much better in boy's clothes.[182] Anna attends Mrs. Backet's school as I found the boys occupied Miss Coombe's[183] time so much that she was not well attended to. She likes school very much and I think improves there. Your little favourite Louisa is now at a very interesting age, and is in some danger of being spoilt among so many great boys who are all very fond of indulging her. She is a sweet-tempered little girl in general. Francis does not yet articulate well but he speaks better and is much improved in other respects. Octavius is a fine lively child and is a great pet with the family. Henry and Alfred go on very well with Mr. Eaton and are good tractable children at home.[184]*

The letter does not mention Elizabeth, and the three youngest daughters were not yet born in 1821, so we don't know a lot about their education, but the record shows that they were a talented group too. Of the six daughters, four married and became baby factories, bearing six to eight children each, though several of those died young. Two remained unmarried, of which one, Louisa, has left a very faint imprint on posterity, but the youngest, Laura, whose *Annals* of her Bentall and Marshall relatives have been much quoted in earlier chapters, was a gifted artist and a friend and mentor to two more generations of her nephews and nieces. The portraits she painted of her parents, as well as a photograph or Laura with her mother, were shown in Figure 9.3.

Mary Ann's letter provides a sense also of how the Marshall boys, soon to be orphaned, were educated. The two eldest, William and John, were sent back to England from Mauritius, aged nine and seven, and William was promptly sent to live with the local schoolmaster. But, as described in Chapter 12, the next eight years were difficult for them and their younger siblings. No details of their later education have been found.

This was a period during which the British Empire was expanding fast, driven as much as anything by the economic opportunities it offered. Most of these children went on to participate enthusiastically in that endeavour, putting to good use the merchant tradition that they had grown up in. Their stories are told in Chapters 15 to 28.

## *Chapter 15*

# RESPONSIBILITIES OF A FIRSTBORN: WILLIAM AND ELIZABETH BENTALL

The next William Bentall (1803–1877) was the eldest of the 15 children of William Searle and Mary Ann Bentall. He started his life with every advantage in the context of the provincial borough of Totnes, since his father was a successful banker at the centre of a political coalition that had influence in the national government. He was awarded a scholarship to Westminster School in 1816, and went up from there, on another scholarship, to Trinity College Cambridge, in 1821. But like many others of his time, he did not graduate, and moved back to Totnes after a year or two. For a while, it seems he worked in his uncle Thornton's bank, known as the Totnes General Bank (see Chapter 11). Reminiscences and letters attributed to his younger brother Edward indicate that he was "*the sporting member of the family*."[185] In 1831 he married Elizabeth Cornish (ca. 1805–1871). Their portraits are on show at Benthall Hall (see Figure 15.1).

Figure 15.1: William and Elizabeth Benthall, née Cornish

This Elizabeth's story is not typical of its time. She was the daughter of Hubert Cornish, a Bengal judge, who was the younger brother of both James Cornish, the Totnes solicitor whose son was elected an MP in 1832 (see Chapter 11), and the Reverend William Floyer Cornish, who married Elizabeth Marshall (see Chapter 12). When Hubert retired, he brought back with him from India his mistress and their two illegitimate daughters, and settled them near Totnes at a residence known as Black Hall. According to one descendant of the Cornish family, "[Elizabeth's] *father disapproved of her marriage, but although he did not receive her and her husband at Black Hall afterwards he did provide for them financially.*"[186] The most likely reason for such disapproval was political: Hubert's nephew James Cornish was an attorney in Totnes, and a leading supporter there of the Great Reform Act of 1832 (see Chapter 10). He was elected as an MP for Totnes after the Act passed, thereby replacing the candidate representing the Adams-Bentall-Marshall interest.

After Thornton and his banking partners sold the Totnes General Bank to the Devon & Cornwall Banking Company, and then William's father, William Searle Bentall, became bankrupt through the collapse of his own banking partnership, it was left to young William to pick up the pieces, and he appears in due course to have become the owner of all the five lots that had been advertised for auction (see Chapter 11). Once the bankruptcy had run its course, William moved into the main house on The Plains, by the river in Totnes, and eventually became owner of the house and the commercial wine cellar just north of it, out of which he ran his business as a wine merchant. He entered into a partnership with a Mr Lloyd and they ran a cider making and bottling business on the south side, in one of the buildings facing Riding Place Quay. This business traded under the name of Bentall Lloyd & Company, Ltd, and continued for many years after William's death.

The 'auction mart' above the wine cellar in due course became the "New Masonic Lodge," and the dwelling house between them became a lodging house, occupied by a "*lodging house keeper*" and several lodgers.

In the 1841 census Elizabeth was at Totnes, living in the Mill House, while William was visiting his brother John at Westminster, and his profession was listed as "*merchant.*" In a directory published in 1848 he was not listed under the heading "*Gentry, Clergy etc.*," but was entered several times under other categories, as: a coal (and culm)[i] merchant; an insurance agent for both the British Commercial Life Insurance company and Phoenix Assurance, a fire insurance company; a timber merchant; and a wine and spirit merchant.[187] In the 1851 census he was listed as the head of the household on The Plains, and he described his profession as "*Wine, Spirit, Timber, Coal and Wholesale Cider Merchant.*"

William briefly had another role as an agent for the Australian Agricultural Company. He was contacted by this organisation in 1841 and asked to recruit 50 "*suitable shepherds*" to emigrate and help support the development of sheep farming in New South Wales. Nineteen shepherds sailed aboard the *London* in November 1841, and another 22 in March 1842 on the *Ganges*, both ships arriving eventually at Port Stephens, north of Newcastle.[188] This connection probably came through his uncle Edward Marshall, who was involved in the development

---

[i] Culm was a type of coal found in Devon and was cheaper than anthracite.

of sheep farms in Tasmania, then known as Van Diemen's Land (see Chapter 12).

William also appears to have been friends with Charles Babbage, famed inventor of the "Difference" and "Analytical" engines, precursors to modern computers. An article published in 1885 gave an account of the connection between Babbage and Totnes, quoting a letter from the Rev. James Powning, then headmaster of Totnes Grammar School, who wrote:

*We have no School record of Mr. Babbage, unless it be the 'insculpture' of his name on one of the desks. Shortly after I came to Totnes – now more than thirty years ago – I remember Mr. Babbage, accompanied by his friend, Mr. W. Bentall, of this town, coming to revisit the old school where he had received his early training, and pointing out where he usually sat.*[189]

That visit must have taken place in the 1850s, so there is no doubt about which William Bentall this was. What is not clear is how the pair became friends, since William was 12 years younger than Charles, and they did not overlap at Cambridge. Presumably their parents had business and some social connections. Charles Babbage's grandfather, Benjamin Babbage, had been a Totnes goldsmith, and was mayor in 1754–1755, while his father, also Benjamin (1753–1827), started in the family business but became a banker and moved to London. The Babbage family had property in Teignmouth, from where Charles was sent to school first at Exeter, then at Totnes.

On 19 January 1860, disaster struck. An "*alarming fire*"[190] broke out at one o'clock in the morning at the New Masonic lodge (i.e., the former theatre and auction mart). Before

it could be extinguished, the Lodge, the bank building next door, the lodging house, and a great part of the wine cellar were gutted. An omnibus driver of the Seven Stars Hotel, named Hodge, was trying to help put out the fire, but fell into the river and drowned. A newspaper report reads:

*The Freemasons alone, by the destruction of their new decorations, fittings, plate and jewels will lose upwards of £500 and we regret to say that Mr. Bentall is a far heavier sufferer having lost his entire stock of wine in bottle from 800 to 1,000 dozen of the finest old wines which cannot be replaced. His wines in cask however were mostly saved but his loss is estimated at £1,500 to £2,000.*[191]

William was only partially insured, even though he was an agent for Phoenix Assurance.

Other information about William and Elizabeth Bentall is quite fragmentary. There is an anecdote from 1837[192] that mentions a friendship between this William and his three-year-old neighbour, William John Wills, who would go on to co-lead the ill-fated "Burke and Wills" expedition in 1861 from Melbourne, on Australia's southeast coast, to the Gulf of Carpentaria, on its north coast. They both died tragically on their return journey, after their camels died and they ran out of food. A year later, William Bentall became mayor of Totnes, and was instrumental in arranging for a memorial to be erected in honour of William John Wills in the middle of The Plains, just outside his house.

In 1871 William testified at an inquiry held at Totnes by the Special Commissioners for English Fisheries into the "*legality of fishing weirs, milldams and fixed engines in the river*

*Dart.*"[193] In his testimony he referred to the weir and his uncles' responsibility for keeping it in repair, as lessees of the Totnes Mill.

In 1873 a railway line was laid from the main Totnes railway station to the Totnes quay. The line – "*for goods traffic only, and horse-operated*"[194] – ran right in front of William's house and other buildings on The Plains, down to the quay a few hundred yards south of them.

Although William and Elizabeth had no children, they lived together for 40 years in the house where he was born. William outlived Elizabeth by six years, died in 1877 and bequeathed all his property to his youngest sister, Laura.

# Chapter 16

# WESTMINSTER CONNECTIONS: THE WARDALES, WATERFIELDS, GAYS AND BENTHALLS

This chapter provides an account of the lives of three children of William Searle and Mary Ann Bentall: their two eldest daughters, Elizabeth and Anna, and their youngest son, Arthur. It has been mentioned several times in these pages that cousin marriages were encouraged in the 19th century, and that intermarriages within related families were common. Several examples of this phenomenon have been presented already, but the families of these three children of William Searle Bentall went to town on the idea, as shown in Figure 16.1.

As shown in this very incomplete but still fairly bewildering pedigree, Elizabeth Bentall married Thomas Nelson Waterfield, while her next sister, Anna, married James Gay. Anna and James had four children. The eldest of these, another James, married his second cousin Rose Gay, thereby inheriting a comfortable estate in Norfolk. Two of the others exchanged vows with their first cousins (i.e., the children of Elizabeth and T.N. Waterfield): Louisa Gay married William Waterfield, and Edward Gay married Ellen Waterfield.

Anna and James Gay's other daughter, Susannah, married the Rev. John Wardale. In due course Arthur Benthall, the youngest brother of Elizabeth and Anna, married Alice Margaret Wardale, John's younger sister. There

was another branch of the Wardale family, and Francis, the son of John and Susannah Wardale, married Edith Maude Wardale, whose father was his third cousin. Edward Waterfield, the son of William and Louisa Waterfield, married Edith's sister Winifred.

Two other names are shown on this diagram, since they will turn up in minor roles in subsequent pages: Edith Elizabeth Wardale (daughter of John and Susannah, so both niece and great niece to Arthur Benthall) and Philip Gay Waterfield.

**Elizabeth and Thomas Nelson Waterfield**

Thomas Nelson Waterfield was educated at Westminster and Cambridge. He was admitted as a scholar at Westminster in 1814 (two years ahead of William Bentall), became captain of the school and was awarded a scholarship to Trinity College, Cambridge, a year ahead of the normal time. But he did not stay long enough to graduate. His obituary in the 1862 *Annual Register195* provides an explanation, albeit a partly inaccurate one:

*Circumstances ... marked out a different course for him. Mr. (afterwards the Right Honourable) Thomas Peregrine Courtenay,*

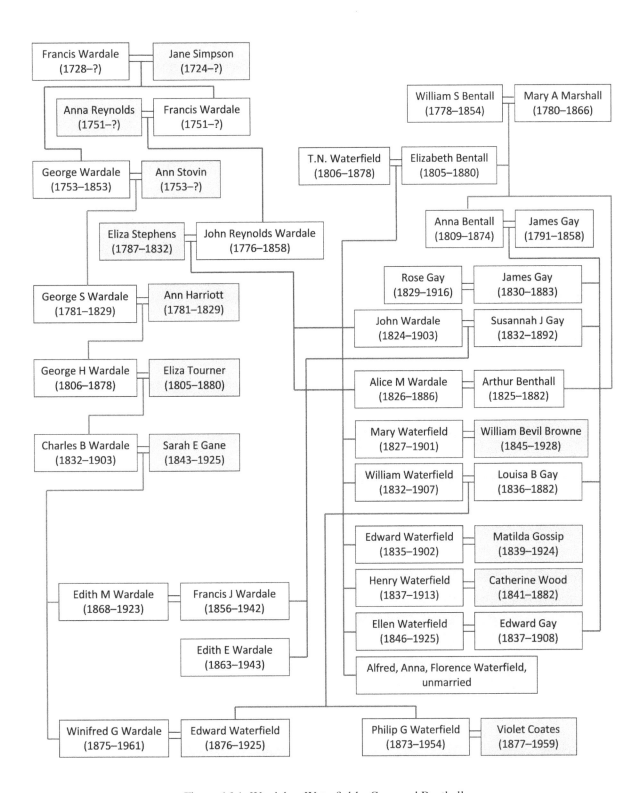

Figure 16.1: Wardales, Waterfields, Gays and Benthalls

*then Secretary to the Commissioners for the Affairs of India, having received important support from Mr. Waterfield's family, who had influence in the borough of Totnes, obtained for Mr. Waterfield an appointment at the Board of Control, and nominated him his private secretary. He continued in the same capacity with Mr. Courtenay's successors until 1839, when his elevation to the highest grade in the office removed him to more responsible duties. During the wars in Afghanistan, Scind, Gwalior, the Punjab, and Burma, the most important papers were in his custody, and the most important duties devolved upon him. He might be called the confidential adviser to the several Presidents of the Board.*

The problem with this account is that Courtenay picked Waterfield to be his private secretary (and also found a job for his father) in 1818, several years before the Waterfield and Bentall families became connected by marriage.[196] Courtenay's letter to Thornton Bentall in 1824 mentions that "*Old Mr. Waterfield and his son came to call on me last night*," but it was not until 1826 that T.N. and Elizabeth were married. It is most unlikely therefore that Courtenay hired T.N. in order to repay a favour to the Bentalls. Rather, he kept an eye out for promising graduates from Westminster School because he wanted competent staff.

However, the rest of the obituary is accurate. His great-grandson, John Percival Waterfield, wrote a memoir that describes T.N. Waterfield as:

*...at his peak, probably the most influential London civil servant in the development of British interests in India*".[197] *... He never went to India himself (he turned down an invitation to go as Lord Ellenborough's Private Secretary for reasons of career security, and his frail health also probably came into play) but he was in a strong position of influence to send his two younger brothers, his sons and other relatives into the Indian Army or civil administration. There were at least two Waterfield Major Generals and several Colonels, all of our part of the family, in the 19th century Indian Army, as well as a large number of civilian administrators and less senior army officers. We have photographic portraits of Thomas Nelson and his wife Elizabeth, née Benthall, framed and on the stairs here at Somerton. They must have been among the earliest portrait photographs. They look full of character, grave, but with a humorous smile in his case, and a gaze of kindly sympathy in hers.*

Copies of these portraits – although the identity of their subjects is not altogether certain – may be glimpsed in Figure 22.4.

T.N. and Elizabeth Waterfield lived in the middle of Westminster School, on Dean's Yard Terrace. (Other family members were frequent visitors, and a reunion was held there in 1851 to celebrate the 50th wedding anniversary of William Searle and Mary Ann Benthall.)[198] They had 11 children, first a daughter named Mary, then three boys who all died as infants, then four more boys who survived – William, Edward, Henry and Alfred – and finally three girls in succession, Anna, Ellen and Florence. The eight that lived to adulthood are shown in Figure 16.1. They and their descendants include many distinguished people.

The eldest daughter, Mary Waterfield, was a guest at one of Henry Drake's dinner parties in 1858 (see Chapter 3). She remained unmarried until at age 44 in 1871 she married the Rev. William Bevil Browne, who was then aged 26. She had a son, Arthur Bevil Browne, the following year. The disparity in age is surprising, but both Mary's husband and son were interesting people. William Bevil Browne attended Trinity College, Cambridge, and in 1870 was admitted to deacon's orders (the first step in the process of ordination as an Anglican priest) in Malta by the Lord Bishop of Gibraltar.[199] He became a curate at Salcombe, on the south coast of Devon, where he compiled plant lists that earned him a place in a *Dictionary of British and Irish Botanists and Horticulturalists*, then a vicar in Northamptonshire, before retiring back to Devon, this time at Shaldon.

The son, Arthur Bevil Browne, went to Winchester College, then up to Christ's College, Cambridge, where he earned his bachelor's degree as "7th Wrangler."[200] He then decided to take holy orders, and in 1905 became acting priest-in-charge of an Indian Mission in Durban, South Africa.[201] In 1936 he wrote a book entitled *The way and the faith: A study in early church history*. He died in 1937, having spent the last nine years of his life as a teacher at a girls' boarding school in Wiltshire.

The eldest son of T.N. and Elizabeth Waterfield, William (1832–1907), was awarded a scholarship to Westminster in 1846. He decided not to go up to Oxford, attending instead the Imperial Service College in Windsor, and duly entered the Indian Civil Service in 1852.[202] He worked his way up the ranks and became Accountant-General for the North-Western Provinces and Oudh, and finally Comptroller-General for the Government of India from 1877–1880. He also wrote a book, *Indian ballads, and other poems*, which was published in 1868 by Smith, Elder & Co.

William Waterfield married twice. His first wife was his first cousin, Louisa Bentall Gay (1836–1882). They were married at Westminster Abbey, where apparently *the choir sang from Beethoven*. Four of their children lived to adulthood; one, named Katherine, was at the time of the 1871 census a child visiting Totnes with her great-uncle William Bentall (see Chapter 15), her grandmother Anna Gay (see Figure 16.1 and further details below), and her great-aunt Laura Benthall (see Chapter 22).

After Louisa died, William married again, this time to Matilda Rose Herschel, granddaughter and daughter, respectively, of the astronomers William Herschel and Sir John Herschel. There are photographs of her at the National Portrait Gallery, but these are not accessible online. William met Matilda through her brother Sir William Herschel, 2nd Baronet, whom he knew from the East India College. This younger William Herschel invented fingerprinting, or at least, was the first to promote it as a reliable way of identifying people, recording William Waterfield's fingerprints as proof that they did not change over time.

When William retired from India, he leased a small estate near Dawlish, in Devon, named Eastdon House, where he lived with Matilda Rose and several of their children. The local church was in the village of Cofton, and in about 1890 he arranged for his cousin, the Rev. Charles Francis Benthall (see Chapter 33), to be appointed vicar there. Matilda Rose was the church organist.

One of William and Matilda Rose's children was Sir (Alexander) Percival Waterfield, who was a major force in reforming the system of recruitment for the British Civil Service.[203]

His son, John Percival Waterfield, who wrote the memoir referred to above, was in the British Foreign Service, Ambassador to Mali, and connected to NATO.

The second son of T.N. and Elizabeth was Edward Waterfield, who also joined the Indian Civil Service. He married Matilda Georgiana Gossip in India and they had several children together. One was the Rev. Reginald Waterfield (1867–1967), principal of Cheltenham College (a boarding school founded in 1841) and later dean of Hereford Cathedral. Another was Alfred Waterfield (1873–1948), who was born in India but spent most of his life managing plantations in what was then British Guyana.

T.N. and Elizabeth's next son, Henry (1837–1913), ended up as Sir Henry Waterfield GCIE KCSI CB. He was the financial secretary to the India Office for 23 years.[204] He married twice and had numerous children.

The next, Alfred, also joined the Indian Civil Service, but died unmarried.

Two of the other three daughters, Anna (1842–1903) and Florence (1847–1902), died unmarried. But, as noted at the outset of this chapter, Ellen Waterfield (1844–1925) married her first cousin Edward Gay (1837–1908), younger brother of Louisa Bentall Gay. They had three children, including a daughter Margaret, who married Christopher Charles Campbell Lilly. Margaret and Christopher's son, Geoffrey Laurence Lilly, was an enthusiastic genealogist, and copies of some of the pedigrees he compiled found their way back to at least one of the Benthall researchers and are now in the family archive at Benthall Hall.

Some of the Waterfield children and their descendants have made a lasting impact on British history, and they have many descendants who are alive and well. There were cordial relations between the Benthall and Waterfield families until at least 1992, when John Percival Waterfield, memoirist and Elizabeth's great-grandson, travelled to Shropshire to attend the funeral of Paul Benthall, my father and Elizabeth's great-nephew.

## Anna and James Gay

Anna (1809–1874) married James Gay in 1827 at Totnes. James was a grandson of John Gay, of Aldborough Hall, Norfolk, and a son of another James Gay, of Champion Hill (now in the London district of Southwark) and Gimingham, Norfolk, from the latter's marriage to Susanna Jennings. James junior was appointed a freeman of Totnes when he married Anna, but his career was as a solicitor in London. The couple had four children, all of whom have been introduced already as three of them married cousins:

James Gay (1830–1884) married his second cousin, Rose Gay, and inherited a second mansion in Norfolk, named Thurning Hall. Susannah Jennings Gay (1832–1892) married the Rev. John Wardale (1824–1903) , rector of Orcheston St Mary, Wiltshire. Their daughter Elizabeth Edith Wardale was one of the first women to be educated at Oxford University. She was awarded a PhD from the University of Zurich, and then returned to Oxford, where as a lecturer and tutor she became an authority on the Old English language and literature.[205] C.S. Lewis was one of her students, and wrote in a letter to his father in 1922:

*By the way I was wrong about Miss Waddell: it turns out to be Miss Wardale – an amazing old lady who is very keen on phonetics and pronunciation. I spend most of my hours with her trying to reproduce the various clucking, growling and grunted noises which are apparently an essential to the pure accent of Alfred – or Aelfred as we must now call him ....*[206]

Louisa Bentall Gay (1836–1882) married her first cousin William Waterfield, son of T.N. and Elizabeth Waterfield, on 2 June 1864 at Westminster Abbey. Edward Gay (1837–1908) married his first cousin Ellen Waterfield, William's sister.

In 1841 Anna and James were living in Croydon. In the 1851 census they were listed as living in Hornsey, north London, as were their daughter Susannah, niece Mary Waterfield and brother(-in-law) Arthur Benthall.

James died in 1858. The records are not clear: it may be that he died at Totnes, but was buried at Highgate Cemetery.

In both the 1861 and 1871 censuses Anna Gay was listed as visiting her brother William at Totnes, suggesting that she in fact lived there after her husband died. She died in 1874 and was buried at Orcheston St Mary, this being the parish where her daughter Susannah lived. The chancel of that church was rebuilt in 1883 and contains memorial windows to both James and Anna.

## Arthur and Alice Benthall

Arthur was the youngest son of William Searle and Mary Ann Benthall. He attended Westminster from the age of about eight, and was admitted as a scholar at the age of 13, in 1838. In 1843 he became a mathematics student at Clare College, Cambridge, and was admitted to Lincoln's Inn, one of London's four Inns of Court, the same year. For three years he commuted from Cambridge to London to fulfil the residential and academic requirements of both institutions. In 1848 he was both awarded his bachelor's degree from Cambridge (with a mediocre result)[207] and called to the Bar. However, he never practised as a barrister. In 1850 he took a position as a clerk at the General Post Office. In 1855 he married Alice Margaret Wardale, sister-in-law of his niece Susannah Wardale (née Gay). There is no record of children.

Henry Drake's journal (see Chapter 3) mentions several dinners with Arthur and Alice in 1856 and 1857, and they probably attended the wedding of Charles Henry Marshall to Charlotte Drake (see Chapter 26). They were living at 22 Gloucester Crescent, close to Regent's Park and a block from where the Drakes lived on Regent's Park Terrace,[208] but by the 1861 census they had moved to Kent. At the time of the 1871 census they were living at Kingston, Surrey, and three of the children of Edward and Clementina Benthall – Clement, Madeleine and Bertha – were staying with them.

Arthur had a distinguished career at the General Post Office. From the starting position of Clerk, he rose to Under Secretary around 1873, Inspector-General of Mails in 1877, and Third Secretary in 1881. In 1891 an account of the 50th-anniversary celebrations of the Uniform Penny Post said that *"he supervised the relations of the department with the railways with an astuteness and cordiality that left nothing to be desired."*[209] This was a crucial function, for in those days the railways were what made it possible to provide several mail deliveries a day in urban areas. Arthur was much involved in the logistics of establishing a parcel post, which happened in 1883, shortly after his death. While at the General Post Office, he became acquainted with the novelist Anthony Trollope, as well as another novelist named Edmund

Yates, a regular contributor to the periodicals published by Charles Dickens.

Anthony Trollope, 10 years older than Arthur, worked at the General Post Office from 1859 to 1867. *The Letters of Anthony Trollope*, edited by N. John Hall,[210] contains one that reads in part: "*My dear Benthall I'll write to Mr Howes. His cantankerousness can't hurt me. I shall be very happy to shake hands with you tomorrow. Yours always, Anty Trollope.*" It would be interesting to discover how well they knew each other, and why Arthur asked him to intervene with Mr Howes.

In 1869 Edmund Yates was the head of the Missing Letter Department at the Post Office. He was also a novelist, whose works were serialised in a magazine published by Charles Dickens called *All the Year Round*. His novel *Wrecked in Port* was serialised over 1868–1869; characters in it included a schoolmaster named the Rev. George Benthall, his wife Gertrude (or Gerty) and a local curate named Mr Trollope.[211]

In 1882 the 28th *Report of the Postmaster General on the Post Office* included this announcement: "*It is with sincere regret that I have to record the death of … Mr. Arthur Benthall, who held the office of Third Secretary… In Mr. Benthall the public service has lost an officer of proved ability and great experience.*"

The 1891 account quoted above also had this to say about him: "*The late Mr. Benthall was a valued and most trustworthy servant of the State. He had taken a good degree at Cambridge and soon rose in official life. … He was greatly respected in the railway world.*"[212]

Alice died not long afterward, in 1886, at Newton Abbot. There are no known portraits of either husband or wife, and their lives seem to have been rather colourless, at least in comparison to those of his brothers. One would like to know if Arthur, so apparently studious a boy and diligent a public servant, ever had much fun.

# Chapter 17

## SERIOUS YOUNGER BROTHERS: THE REV. JOHN AND JUDGE EDWARD BENTHALL

John Bentall was the third child and second son of William Searle and Mary Ann Bentall. Edward was the next child after John. Their families also liked to intermarry, and the partial pedigree in Figure 17.1 (overleaf) shows these connections.

Edward Benthall married his first cousin Clementina Marshall, and they produced nine children. Their eldest daughter, Edith, married her first cousin William Henry Benthall, John's son. That couple produced three sons, but no grandchildren ensued. Of the other eight children of Edward and Clementina, only three gave them grandchildren, and only the youngest of those grandchildren, Charles Francis Benthall (see Chapter 33), has living descendants today.

### The Reverend John Benthall

The first 30 years of this John's life were full of promise, but he then had to endure ten years of disappointments before settling back into a more comfortable, and eventually happy, middle and old age. Like his elder brother William, he attended Westminster School as a scholar and later went up to Trinity College, Cambridge. Unlike William, he did graduate, in 1828, after which he moved back to Westminster to work as an "usher" – i.e., a junior teacher – while going through the process of becoming an ordained minister. In May 1835 he married Harriett Everett, and they produced two boys: John Everett Benthall was born in May 1836, William Henry Benthall in July 1837. But not long after, in August 1838, Harriett died and was buried in the north cloister of Westminster Abbey. Eight years later John, the elder son, also died and was buried there. There is a small memorial to them both in the north cloister.[213]

The three pictures (Figure 17.2) are at Benthall Hall. The watercolour on the left is of John Benthall (senior) as a teenager. The two miniatures were painted in about 1840 by Margaret Gilles: one of Harriet, executed after her death, and one of the two boys. The latter's hair styles and costumes are bizarre by modern standards, but the letter written by Mary Ann Bentall and quoted in Chapter 14 makes it clear that small boys were then dressed in frocks up to the age of about seven, and that mothers often liked to keep a son's hair as long as they would a daughter's.

In spite of the loss of his wife, John's home in Little Dean's Yard, Westminster, remained a base in London for visiting family as well as a boarding house for students at the school.[214] The 1841 census for that household lists John; his sons, John and William Henry; his brothers

William, Frank and Arthur; his uncle and aunt William Floyer and Elizabeth Cornish; and five servants.

In 1846, shortly before John junior died, a new headmaster was appointed at Westminster School, which had been starved of funding by the Abbey and had suffered a severe decline in pupil numbers.[215] The new head realised that discipline had broken down and that as a teacher, John Bentall was *"unable to control his*

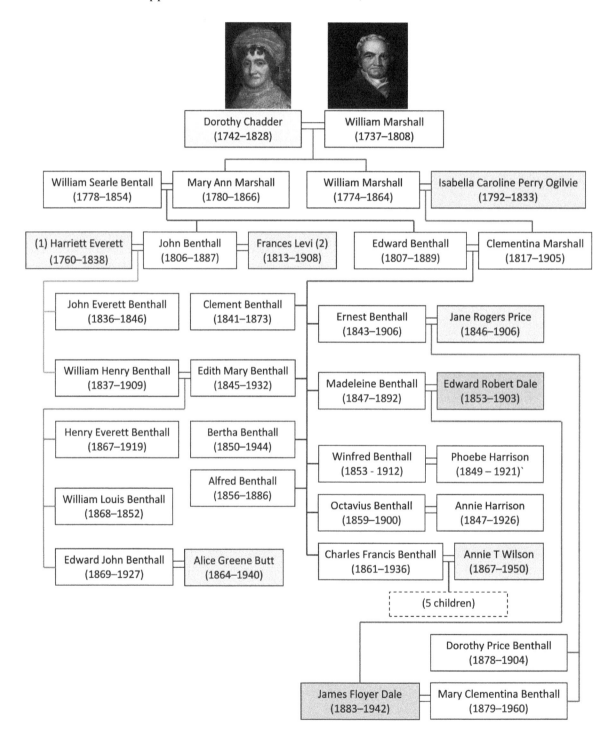

Figure 17.1: John and Edward Benthall, and their children

Figure 17.2: John Benthall, his first wife, Harriett, and their children

*pupils.*"[216] So, John was fired. He obtained a position as chaplain to the Hounslow Barracks, where his uncle Samuel Adams had been barrack-master until his death in 1842 (see Chapter 7). It is not clear how John obtained this position, since Samuel was several years dead and his widow, Elizabeth, had by then moved to Mitcham, in southwest London.

John remained a point of support for his extended family: in the 1851 census, at his new house in Stanwell (nowadays just south of Heathrow Airport), he listed himself, his aunt Margaret (widow of Thornton Benthall and known as "Aunt Thornton") [217], his sisters Louisa and Laura, and three of his brother Edward's children – Clement, Ernest and Edith Mary – who had been sent back from India not only to be educated, but also to avoid the diseases then rampant in Bengal. The stories of Edward and those children will be told later, but are also documented in a book about the challenges faced by families in India at the time.[218]

In 1852 John was appointed vicar of Willen, a village in Buckinghamshire that is now part of Milton Keynes. There was a fine Georgian church, a large vicarage house suitable for John's extended family, and the appointment was reserved for alumni of Westminster School. John's predecessor was the Rev. George Phillimore, whose mother was named Almeria Thornton, whose grandfather was Godfrey Thornton, a first cousin of John's great-grandmother Elizabeth (née Thornton). John moved into the vicarage with his entourage: his aunt Thornton, his sisters Louisa and Laura, his nephews Clement and Ernest, his niece Edith Mary, and his surviving son, young William Henry, although the latter had been sent to Marlborough School so only returned during the holidays. It was not long before John's parents, William Searle and Mary Ann Benthall, also moved in.

Gradually, various of these family members either died or dispersed. William Searle Benthall died in 1854. Louisa died in 1859, followed by Margaret in 1860. Mary Ann moved out after the death of Louisa, and ended up at Sherborne with her next son, Edward (see below). Once Mary Ann moved out, so did Laura, and by then John had found a new wife, named Frances (or Fanny) Levi. Her father lived in the village of Moulsoe, about three miles from Willen. They married in 1861. Although born in 1813, Fanny had never previously married.

John wrote three books: *Lectures on the Liturgy*; *Sons of the Hebrew Poets in English Verse*; and *Gleanings of the Harvest Field, or Thought in Verse on portions of the Church Services*. One of John's students at Westminster school who wrote a book about his time there, listed these publications and added: *"It is to be hoped that Mr. Benthall will allow a wider circulation to the latter volume, which is, at present, printed for private circulation only, as*

Figure 17.3: Fanny Levi

*from the sweetness and simplicity of the language and the piety of the thoughts expressed it would be welcomed in many families."*[219]

John died at Willen in 1887, while Fanny lived on to the age of 95, dying in 1908. As noted above, John's surviving son William Henry Bentall married his first cousin, Edith Mary Benthall – yet another cousin intermarriage. Their stories (and those of their children) are told in Chapter 30.

## Edward and Clementina Benthall

Edward Benthall (1807–1889) was the fourth child and third son of William Searle and Mary Ann Benthall. Clementina Marshall (1817–1905), his wife, was the eldest daughter of the Rev. William Marshall and Isabella Caroline Clarke Perry Ogilvie (see Chapter 8). Thus, Edward and Clementina were first cousins, as Figure 17.1 shows. His signature and her "mark" can be seen on the attendance sheet from Dorothy's 80th birthday party in 1822. There are pictures of them both at Benthall Hall, and they play a crucial role in this story, since it was their descendants who eventually bought that house and later arranged for it to be acquired by the National Trust.

The two silhouettes in Figure 17.4 are marked in one corner as *"taken at the Hubard Gallery"* in 1840 or 1841. The Hubard Gallery was a travelling enterprise, founded originally to exploit the artistic talents of a young prodigy named William James Hubard, but later the name became a brand used to promote the works of other artists, both in the United States and Britain.

James Benthall has written an unpublished account of Edward's early years based on extensive family correspondence.[220] This summary is

Figure 17.4: Edward and Clementina Benthall (ca. 1840)

based on and quotes from his research. "*Edward went to school at Buckfastleigh Grammar School. In his early boyhood he learned to handle a boat, to shoot and to fish with his elder brother William.*" In 1825 Edward was admitted to the East India College, Hertfordshire, with letters of recommendation from both his uncle John Bentall and Charles Bathurst MP, the latter "*at the request of Mr. Courtenay.*"[221] He was there for less than two years, but in that time studied Classics, Mathematics, Political Economy and Law, as well as the Sanskrit, Persian and Hindustani languages. He was then sent to India, arriving at Calcutta in May 1827. Once there he rose slowly through the bureaucratic ranks. Postings to various towns north of Calcutta, initially as

an assistant to the local magistrate and/or tax collector, led eventually to his appointment, in 1836 at the age of 30, as the magistrate and tax collector for Dinajpur, a town about 225 miles north of Calcutta and now in the north western corner of Bangladesh.[222] In January of 1839 he became due for extended leave, and left Calcutta for his first visit back to England since his original departure 12 years previously.

Meanwhile, Clementina was growing up too. The account of her family in Chapter 8 left her in 1831 together with her mother, Isabella, trapped under a collapsed ceiling. Isabella died soon after, leaving Clementina in a household with her father, a brother and six younger sisters. In the summer of 1835, when she was approaching her 18th birthday, Clementina and her cousin Louisa Marshall – one of the seven orphaned children of William and Louisa (see Chapter 13), and a few months older than Clementina – spent nine months in London seeing the sights, meeting their relatives under the avuncular eyes of William Searle and his brother John Bentall, and being entertained by William Searle's sons Henry, Thornton and Frank, who by then were all living in London (see Chapters 18, 20 and 21).

Clementina kept a journal, now in the Benthall Hall archives, that shows her to be a talented writer and a competent pianist, and which provides an interesting picture of how tourists spent their time then, not to mention the intricacies of the Bentall and Marshall family dynamics. In between bouts of unspecified illness, while in London she walked miles every day visiting her extended network of relatives. She lived for part of the time with Elizabeth and T.N. Waterfield at Westminster, and also spent a month with Edward Marshall's family at Ramsgate, and another with Richard Marshall's family at Chatham. Among the relatives she spent time with in or near London were: William Marshall, the eldest of Louisa's brothers; Thornton Marshall, Louisa's youngest brother; James and Anna Gay (see Chapter 16); her cousins Marianne Thompson and Louisa Edgcumbe (daughters of Richard Marshall – see Chapter 12); John and Harriett Bentall (see above); William and Mary Adams (this William being the eldest son of Elizabeth and Samuel Adams – see Chapter 7); and "*Mr & Mrs Drake*" (probably John and Maria – see Chapter 3). There is also an elusive reference to a "*Mrs Henry Bentall*" (just possibly the widow of the younger brother of William Searle and John Bentall – see Chapter 9 – but she was living in Barbados).

When Edward returned to England his first priority was to find a wife. And where better to look for one, than among his friends and relatives? Thus, in March 1840, he married Clementina Marshall at Totnes. In the census taken in April 1841, the couple were staying with their uncle Thornton Bentall and his wife, Margaret, just outside Totnes at Bowden House, which was still owned by the Adams family but leased to Thornton (see Chapter 9). In July of that year they embarked together from Portsmouth on the East Indiaman *Southampton*, accompanied by Blanche Marshall, Clementina's younger sister, and also with a nurse, since Clementina was eight months pregnant when they left England. Upon leaving Totnes she had started to keep another diary, which she maintained for the next 12 years. That diary is now held by the Centre of South Asian Studies, Cambridge, together with over 200 letters written by or to Edward and Clementina. Members of her family, probably her grandchildren, created first a hand-written copy and then a partial typed copy of the original handwritten diary. These are more easily readable, although neither is a perfect or complete transcription.[223]

The diary provides a detailed account of their departure from Portsmouth, Clementina's seasickness and confinement, and the birth of their son, Clement Edward, on 28 August, "*about four degrees north of the equator*." They arrived at Calcutta in November, and Edward was offered a position as a judge in Jessore, a town about 75 miles north of Calcutta and now part of Bangladesh.

Clementina gave birth to two more children at Jessore – Ernest in 1843, and Edith in 1845 – but they were prone to illness, and Edward and Clementina eventually decided to send all three of their children home to England in 1847, to live with his brother John and sisters Louisa and Laura at Stanwell (see above).

Clementina continued to be a close observer of everything around her, and wrote extensively about the fauna and flora that she encountered. She was also quite a good painter: nine of her watercolours are in the collection at Benthall Hall, although not all of them on show. Figure 17.5 shows her painting of the judge's house at Jessore.

Edward and Clementina moved in 1847 to Alipore, a residential neighbourhood about five miles southwest of Calcutta, where he became a sessions judge (i.e., dealing with criminal cases) for the districts around that growing metropolis. Their fourth and fifth children were born there,

Madeleine in 1847 and Bertha in 1850. But Edward's health was poor. His medical report in 1852 stated that he had:

*…never been in good health for the last five years, suffering from dysentery, dyspepsia, painful neuralgia and rheumatic affections. Last year he suffered severe neuralgia in his loins. His body is emaciated except for a distended abdomen. Mercurial tonics and regulated regimen have been tried without beneficial effect. Needs complete change before the end of the cold season. Should go to the cape or to New south Wales for at least 2 years.*[224]

Figure 17.5: The house at Jessore

Accordingly, Edward and Clementina took an extended vacation at Wynberg, close to Cape Town. Their next child, Winfred, was born in September 1853 on board ship while in transit, like his eldest brother.[225] At some point during this period Edward also found time to make a collection of South African seashells, many of which are still used as decorative embellishments at Benthall Hall.

In 1855, owing to his continuing poor health, Edward decided to resign from the East India Company's service. By then, travel to and from India was more tightly organised: this time the family (Edward, Clementina, Madeleine, Bertha and Winfred) took a paddle wheeler from India to Suez, then a train overland to Port Said, and finally another ship from there back to England. They travelled back with 13 cases of arrowroot, which were probably then sent on to the Crimea as treatment for cholera and dysentery, diseases that were ravaging soldiers there.

Although still in his late 40s, Edward retired on a full pension, which enabled him to lead a comfortable life. He and Clementina settled in Sherborne, Dorset, due to the town's reputation for excellent boys' and girls' schools. Edward became a magistrate, and a governor of Sherborne School. Clementina produced three more boys: Alfred in 1856, Octavius in 1859, and Charles Francis in 1861. Edward's mother came to live with them in her old age, and died there.

Edward died in 1889, but Clementina lived on until 1905. The stories of their children are the subject of Part IV.

Figure 17.6: Edward and Clementina Benthall in retirement

# *Chapter 18*

## HENRY BENTHALL: COAL, WINE AND GRANITE MERCHANT – AND SERIAL BANKRUPT

Henry Benthall (1811–1879), the next child of William Searle and Mary Ann, lived a colourful life in London. He was introduced briefly in the preamble to this book. No information is known about Henry's education, save for the fact that he did not follow his elder brothers to Westminster or the East India College. He seems to have been more interested in emulating his uncles Thornton and John Bentall, finding employment in London at the age of 16 or 17 with a bank on Pall Mall. In 1835 he was a frequent escort to Clementina and Louisa Marshall while they sojourned in London; a favourite activity was rowing the girls along the Thames on his boat.

Henry married a widow named Mary Archer in 1840. She had been born Mary Walker in 1809, the daughter of a watchmaker, and her first husband was William Newham, whom she appears to have married at the age of 15 or 16, and with whom she had a son named James William Newham (born in 1825). This husband died, leaving her with enough money to provide an education for her son. She married again, to a man named James Archer, but he died shortly after, so she married Henry.

In later life, Henry's stepson (i.e., Mary's son by her first husband) wrote a memoir, published as *The Diary of a Prison Governor*,[226]

in which he described the next ten years of his stepfather's career, and from which much of this biographical information is taken. It is from James William Newham that we know that Henry Benthall "*was tall, short sighted, and deaf*"; began his career as a "*clerk in Duckett and Morland's Bank, Pall Mall*"; became a coal merchant; and then unwisely launched a wine business as well, on credit. The latter was initially very successful, but Henry and his family lived extravagantly at 18 Cecil Street, Strand, then a modestly reputable street running from the Strand to the river Thames. Needing extra funds, he entered into a dubious business arrangement:

*…two sharks, brothers named Hill, … persuaded Mr. Benthall to become a 'general merchant'. He fell into their trap and was soon completely ruined by them. They ordered all sorts of merchandize in his name …which they sold for their benefit, at less than the cost price, giving Mr. Benthall worthless bills for the amount. He did not see that he was being victimized but thought, as he did in all his subsequent ventures, that he was on the high road to fortune.*

In 1840 he was arrested for debt and sent for some months to the Queen's Bench Prison, in Southwark. In stepson James's words:

*... bankruptcy in those days moved very slowly, it was next akin to chancery ... Mr. Benthall's debts amounted to about £15,000 and some months elapsed before he was released from prison. During his detention my mother lived with him in his rooms and I occasionally slept there; such proceedings were winked at for a consideration in those days. ... the wine trade was lost but the coal trade was kept together by me and in my name.*

Eventually Henry was released, and he moved back home to 18 Cecil Street. In 1841 the house was burgled.[227] He reported the incident and a few days later was able to identify some of the stolen goods, including a case containing Chinese counters, made from mother-of-pearl, each marked with a Chinese decoration and engraved also with the Bentall crest.[228]

Henry continued in his coal business, with James acting as his *"clerk and collector."* Mary succumbed to cancer of the uterus in 1842, but James continued to lodge with Henry. In 1843 Henry married again, to Sarah Ellen Harkness. James and Sarah did not get along: he was rude to her, and she threw him out. Consequently, James found another job, as a clerk for a solicitor named Fry, and for several years had no contact with the Benthalls. In 1851, however, Henry walked into Fry's office to inform James that *"a clerk was wanted at Maidstone Gaol"* and that he had recommended him.[229] James got the job, rose to become the assistant governor there, and finally became governor of a larger prison in Canterbury.

No mention of Henry's first wife or stepson was made in any Benthall family archives, but Sarah Ellen was liked. In 1846 Laura Benthall, then aged 19, visited the couple in Croydon and drew Sarah's portrait, shown in Figure 18.1. The miniature of Henry, a watercolour on ivory, dates from about 1840, but the artist is unknown. Both pictures are now at Benthall Hall.

In 1849 Sarah gave birth to a son named Albert. The 1851 census lists the family as living in Battersea, London, but in around 1852 all three moved to 14 Chatham Place, at the end of a cul-de-sac at the north end of Blackfriars Bridge. They lived there until 1866, and Henry used that address as a base for his various subsequent business ventures.

In June 1852 Henry filed a prospectus to launch a new company known as the "Australian and General Emigration Company."[230] In 1854 he helped launch a new insurance company, "London and Continental," listing himself as its actuary.[231] In 1854 a provisional committee was set up to explore the development of a new railway line in the Australian colony of Victoria, between the towns of Geelong and Ballarat. Somehow, by 1856 Henry Benthall had become a member of that committee, while his brother Frank Benthall (see Chapter 21) was listed as its "Parliamentary Agent."[232] They were unable to raise the necessary capital and the project was taken over by the colonial government, but the line was eventually built based on the committee's initial engineering plans. In 1857 a new joint-stock company, "The Alliance Steam Navigation Company Limited," published advertisements to raise capital. Its office was at 14 Chatham Place, and Henry was one of two listed "auditors." (A newspaper report announced the *"collapse"* of the company in

Figure 18.1: Sarah Ellen and Henry Benthall

January 1882,[233] long after Henry had ceased to be involved).

In 1861 or perhaps earlier, the "Port Nant Granite Company" was founded to quarry granite in a remote part of Wales, and Henry was listed as the "Company Secretary" in a *Directory of Joint Stock Companies* published in 1867.[234] Meanwhile, Henry seems to have maintained his business as a coal merchant in the borough of Southwark, conveniently located across the Thames on the other side of Blackfriars Bridge.

The five-story block on Chatham Place was at first entirely residential, but by 1850 much of the space had been leased by lawyers and insurance offices, which is presumably how Henry became involved in the insurance business, among his other ventures. Number 14 was

at the end of the row, and some of the flats had views of the river and the bridge. The building can be seen in Figure 18.2, at the far left of the engraving.

The details are fuzzy, but it appears that for a while that two adjacent addresses along the row, nos. 13 and 14, were owned by the "Governors of Bridewell Hospital" and overseen by a Mr Duncan, who appointed Henry as his agent, responsible for collecting rent from the other tenants. Each building had a stairwell that gave access to two individual flats on each floor. The best flat at no. 14, on the stairwell shared by Henry's flat, had a bay window overlooking the river, and was rented by the Pre-Raphaelite painter Dante Gabriel Rossetti together with his brother William, since the bay window provided a good light for painting.

Rossetti's wife and muse, Lizzie Siddal, also lived there. At some point Mr Duncan offered the group the second floor of the adjoining flat as well, opening up a passageway to connect the two properties.

Thus, Henry collected rent from Rossetti, arranged for necessary repairs, and even recommended a dressmaker for Lizzie when she needed one. A collection of Rossetti's letters was compiled by his brother William and published in 1895. William comments that *"My brother's landlord in Chatham Place was a legal gentleman, Mr. Benthall."*[235] A postal directory from that time lists the occupants of 14 Chatham Place as: *"W.M. Rossetti, art."*; *"D.G. Rossetti, art."*; *"Henry Benthall, M.A."*; and a *'Thos. Keates'*. There is no evidence that Henry had ever obtained a university degree, let alone any legal or actuarial qualification, but he must have been a convincing talker.

In February 1862 Lizzie died in her flat from an overdose of laudanum mixed with brandy. Her neighbour Mr Keates was a consulting chemist by profession, so it may have been he who provided the drug. Henry was among the jurors at the inquest, as were Clara Siddal (Lizzie's sister) and the controversial poet Algernon Charles Swinburne, among others.[236] The next tenant was another painter, G.P. Boyce, a friend of Rossetti's, whose watercolour of the view from the bay window, *Blackfriars Bridge: Moonlight Sketch*, is in the Tate collection.[237]

At about that time formal plans were published for construction of the Victoria Embankment, and it became clear that these buildings would eventually be demolished to make way for the

Figure 18.2: Blackfriars Bridge (including 14 Chatham Place)

new streets and railway lines. While it would be several years until works began, the insurance companies started to move out, and Henry saw an opportunity to make some money. By 1865 he was the owner of both 13 and 14 Chatham Place, and so, when the Metropolitan Board of Works, which was overseeing the project, finally requisitioned the buildings, Henry became due £4,444 in compensation.

However, by then Henry was once more in deep financial trouble. In December 1866 he negotiated with a number of creditors, and reached a settlement to "*pay them two shillings in the pound by two equal instalments of one shilling each at three and six calendar months,*" while his creditors agreed "*not to sue, arrest, attach or take in execution the debtor.*"[238] It is not clear who those creditors might have been, but in 1867 Henry moved back to the Strand, with an address at 28 Norfolk Street, and continued to work as a contractor. (The following year, Henry's brothers Frank and Edward filed claims with the Metropolitan Board of Works to secure their rights as Henry's mortgagees with regard to 13 and 14 Chatham Place.) In 1869 he put in a bid as to manage the paving of much of the new Embankment road, presumably planning to use granite from the Port Nant Granite Company in Wales, but did not win the contract.

There are two photographs of no. 14 Chatham Place in the London Metropolitan archives, taken just before it was demolished to make room for the construction of the Thames Embankment and a new Blackfriars Bridge, which at the time of writing can be seen on a web site about Lizzie Siddall.[239]

Henry bounced back from his second bankruptcy and became involved in another granite company, this one quarrying the rock on the island of Lundy, about ten miles off the north coast of Devon. In 1862 the owner of Lundy had recognised granite as a possible source of income and sent a sample to that year's International Exhibition in London. The following year, two brothers named McKenna negotiated a lease and launched a company to open and work quarries on the island:

> *£25,000 was said to have been raised before a second share issue attempted to raise this to £100,000. It was wrongly implied there was a contract to supply granite to the Thames Embankment. Huge sums were spent on laying out quarries, tramways, a shipping place, cottages for an estimated 200 workers, as well as improvements to the farm which was part of the lease. By July 1865 three quarries were in production and a ship was acquired to carry granite across [to the mainland].*[240]

But the granite turned out to be of poor quality, and financial controls were lacking:

> *By 1869 the company was in liquidation. A contractor, Henry Benthall, bought the assets but William McKenna still held the lease and made it impossible for him to work the quarries. Eventually the liquidator took over when McKenna relinquished the lease, but Benthall was soon bankrupt.*

And so, poor Henry wound up in bankruptcy court for a third time, in 1872. After that, he and Sarah moved to the village of Hampton, near Hampton Court. He died in 1879, but Sarah lived on for another 34 years, until 1913.

Their son, Albert, became a physician, initially practising medicine in London in a partnership named Benthall and Lovegrove which was dissolved in 1876. In 1879 he married Rosa

Cooke in Kingston, Surrey. He became interested in the legal, ethical and political issues related to workers' compensation, wrote a series of articles published in *The Lancet* between 1900 and 1907, and became a "medical referee" under the Workmen's Compensation Act 1906. But Albert, like his father, was also a serial bankrupt: first in 1883, again in 1902, a third time in 1906, and yet again in 1921.

During the 1911 census Albert and Rosa were living in Hampstead with Albert's mother, Sarah, then aged 92, and their four children: Gilbert, Margery, Francis Bernard and Arthur Lawrence. Gilbert Benthall (1880–1961) served as an artillery officer in the First World War and subsequently became a civil servant, print collector and amateur art historian. His books were never published, but his working papers are archived at the Paul Mellon Centre for Studies in British Art.[241] When Benthall Hall was put on the market in 1934, Gilbert wrote letters to various family members to rally support for its purchase (see Chapter 34). Arthur and Francis Bernard both married and had descendants. Margery never married, but visited her cousins at Benthall Hall a few years before her death.

# Chapter 19

## DEATHS BY DROWNING: ALFRED AND OCTAVIUS BENTALL

Two of William Searle and Mary Ann Bentall's sons, Alfred and Octavius, decided to join the Royal Navy. Both eventually drowned, at opposite ends of the world. After leaving the Navy, Alfred became the commander of a merchant ship. By fathering a child out of wedlock, he made himself an embarrassment to his family, who were increasingly engaged in the moral revival pioneered by the Clapham Sect. When he died near Venice, aged 26, records of his existence were largely expunged from the family narrative. His younger brother, Octavius, remained a naval officer in training, and had recently been promoted to the rank of lieutenant when he died on the North Island of New Zealand, aged 28. A memorial to his early demise was carved in stone.[242] Both travelled more widely and accomplished more than we expect today from people in their twenties. Below are their contrasting stories.

### Alfred Bentall

Compared with the amount of information available about his other brothers, the fifth son, Alfred (1813–1839) is almost entirely absent from family records, and no portrait of him survives. From public records, however, it has been possible to document his short and rather sad life.

Alfred chose a nautical career, and became a "volunteer, 1st class" on HMS *Aurora* in May 1826, aged just 13. This was a "fourth-rate" frigate, carrying 40 guns, that had been captured from the French in 1814. Alfred remained on the *Aurora* until August 1829. During that period, the ship spent most of its time in the West Indies. Alfred was then transferred to HMS *Galatea*, having been promoted to midshipman in 1828. This was a fifth-rate ship, with slightly fewer (36) guns. When Alfred joined the *Galatea* the captain was Charles Napier, who had installed some innovative technology:

*…an experimental system of his own design of paddles that the crew would work via winches on the main deck. The paddles proved useful for manoeuvring at speeds of up to 3 knots in windless conditions. On 12 September 1831 Galatea towed the line-of-battle ship Caledonia by means of paddles alone.*[243]

In 1832 Alfred transferred to HMS *Excellent*, a gunnery training ship moored permanently at Portsmouth. As a midshipman there, he passed the seamanship exam in 1832 and the navigation exam in 1833.[244] He continued to be on the

135

*Excellent's* muster until March 1834, when he transferred to HMS *Canopus*, an ageing third-rate (84-gun) ship that had been captured from the French at the Battle of the Nile in 1798. Alfred was ranked "mate" and sailed on her to the Mediterranean. However, in June of that year he was discharged, for reasons unknown, both from that ship and the service *"per order of Rear Admiral Sir Thomas Briggs."*[245]

How Alfred spent the following 12 months is likewise unknown, but in May 1835 he did a deal with his uncle John Bentall, who purchased *"sixteen sixty-fourth shares"* (i.e., a quarter-share) of a 269-ton merchant brig named *Permei*, majority-owned by one Edward Robson Arthur. Alfred, at the tender age of 22, was duly appointed "master" of this vessel, which advertised itself as trading *"Eastward of the Cape of Good Hope."* Alfred took out a life insurance policy for the sum of £500 which was left in the hands of his uncle John as collateral for the purchase.

In July 1835 the ship was advertised in the *Asiatic Register* as due to leave London on a voyage to Singapore and Manila, but a last-minute change of plans saw Alfred sail it instead to Constantinople (now Istanbul). An article in the *Morning Post* of 25 July 1835 described some of the cargo onboard:

*SYMBOLIC PRESENTS TO THE SULTAN. – By the English vessel Permei, which has just sailed from London for Constantinople, his Majesty's Government has sent, as a present to the Sultan, three powerful entire dray horses, and two beautiful blood horses, accompanied by two of Tattersall's[246] men to attend them during the voyage. It is presumed that this is a delicate but, at the same time, pointed way, symbolically conveyed, according to Eastern customs, and which cannot give offence to any party, of warning the Sultan of his critical situation. It need scarcely be added that the three overpowering dray horses represent Russia, the two beautiful blood horses Turkey, at present closely allied; and the two persons watching over them England and France, whose constant occupation is not only to prevent too close acts of intimacy, but also to endeavour to preserve the blood horses from being kicked to pieces by the gigantic dray horses.*

The *"critical situation"* that inspired this strange gift defies any simple summary. The Crimean War was still 20 years away, but the British were already much concerned about the growing power of Russia in the Black Sea. The Ottoman Empire had included much of the coast along the Black Sea, the Balkans, and Egypt; but after a short war with Russia, under the 1829 Treaty of Adrianople, it ceded Georgia to Russia and opened the Dardanelles (the narrow passage between the Mediterranean and the Black Sea) to commercial vessels.

Meanwhile, the Ottomans were facing a dangerous rebellion in Egypt. With help from Britain and France unforthcoming, they turned to their erstwhile enemies, the Russians, who were happy to send troops for a price. a secret article inserted into a subsequent treaty, signed in 1833, whereby the Ottomans agreed to close the Dardanelles to foreign warships if the Russians asked them to do so. The British discovered the agreement, and were rightly troubled by the possibility of a growing alliance between Russia and the Ottoman Empire. Lord Palmerston, then Secretary of War, was *"stung into action,"*[247] albeit at a diplomatic level for the time being.

Hence the gift of horses. But the choice of the *Permei* to ferry them is intriguing. Edward Marshall was then an under-secretary at the War Office, and his nephew Alfred happened to have a recently acquired vessel ready to sail. Mere coincidence?

In any event, the voyage was completed successfully, and the following year, in September 1836, Alfred left again for Mauritius and Ceylon. The *Permei* started on its return voyage on 23 April 1837, passed the Cape on 28 June, and arrived back in London in mid-September.[248]

On his return, Alfred found himself to be the father of a three-month-old daughter. Ellen Bentall was born on 20 June 1837 and baptised at St John the Evangelist Church, Wapping, on 22 October 1837. The baptismal record gives her father's name as Alfred Bentall (occupation: "*Mariner*") and her mother's name as Elizabeth Ann Ackland. They were not married.

The following month, Alfred made a Will, with the help of his brother Frank. It refers to the loan from his uncle John that had been used to buy a share of the *Permei*, and to the insurance policy taken out as collateral. After bequests to his executors (his brothers Henry and Frank), Alfred left the rest of his estate "*for the support, maintenance and education of my reputed or illegitimate daughter named Ellen by Elizabeth Ann Ackland, now of Chapel Street in Devonport in the county of Devon.*"

He had been scheduled to leave London for Algoa Bay, Singapore and Canton with the *Permei* on 15 October, but this was delayed until 15 November. He arrived back at Glasgow a little over a year later, in February 1839, and then made his way with the ship back to London.

A marriage record shows that Alfred and Elizabeth Ann were married at St Botolph's Aldgate on 1 October 1839, and lists the bride's father as Joseph, a "*carpenter.*"[249]

But soon afterward, Alfred set off again aboard the *Permei*, headed for Trieste. On 7 December 1839 the ship ran aground in a thick fog near Venice. Three weeks later, according to a newspaper article, Alfred "*lost his life, together with his faithful carpenter and second mate, R.P. Saggs, in their strenuous endeavours to complete the salvage of the cargo. He was a skilful and intrepid mariner and a truly kind-hearted relative and friend.*"[250] (The newspaper report referred to a place named "Talle," but today there is no such place, so it is likely that this was a misspelling of "Porto Tolle," a small town about 40 miles south of Venice in the Po Delta.). Alfred's Will was proved in February 1840.

Three months later, in May, Elizabeth Ann gave birth to another child, a son. She made a will, signed on 1 June of that year, which starts: "*I, Elizabeth Ann Bentall, of Hoddesdon in the county of Hertford, widow, bequeath to my sister Jane Caddy of Devonport the sum of five pounds.*" Everything else was to be left "*in trust for my daughter Ellen Bentall and for my son at present unnamed.*" The executors were Alfred's brothers, Thornton and Frank, both then living in London.

The baby was baptised Alfred Bentall on 17 July 1840, again at St John's in Wapping, and mother and son returned to her sister's house at Davenport, near Plymouth in Devon. The baby died 10 days later and was buried at Plymouth on 29 July. Shortly afterwards Elizabeth Ann also died there. Her will was proved on 20 October. These events created a niggling legal issue. Under English law, the posthumous birth of Alfred's legitimate son meant that his original Will was no longer valid and therefore he could be declared intestate. In May 1842,

Frank filed for annulment of the original probate and was given a "Grant of Administration" to manage Alfred's estate on behalf of the surviving daughter.

It has been possible to identify Elizabeth's sister Jane Caddy and her family in 1839,[251] but there is no trace of that family in the 1841 or any later census, nor is there any further trace of Ellen. [252] It is fair to assume that the orphaned girl became part of Jane's family. The most plausible explanation of the lack of any record of the Caddy family in any subsequent UK census records is that they emigrated to one of the colonies. When Frank filed for the new Grant, he probably knew whether she was alive or dead, but his application says nothing about her. Ellen may have been raised as Ellen Caddy, but without any clue as to where they went, this is a story yet to be told.

## Octavius Benthall

Like his elder brother Alfred, Octavius Benthall (1818–1846) joined the Royal Navy, but unlike Alfred he remained there for the rest of his career. He is recorded as being a mate on HMS *Trinculo* in 1835, transferring as a mate on HMS *Albion* in 1837 and then being promoted to midshipman later that year. His entry in *A Naval Biographical Dictionary* reads:

> *Octavius Benthall died 21 April, 1846. He was drowned while attempting to cross the bar of Hokianga Bay, New Zealand, in the pinnace[i] of H.M.S. OSPREY. This officer passed his examination 8 Sept. 1837; and served for some time as Mate, on the*

*Mediterranean, Home, and East India stations, in the MAGICIENNE 24, Capts. Fred. Thos. Michell and Rich. Laird Warren, ALBION 90, Capt. Nicholas Lockyer, and OSPREY 12, Capt. Fred. Patten. He obtained his commission 1 Sept. 1845; then became Additional Lieutenant of the AGINCOURT 72, bearing the flag of Sir Thos. John Cochrane; and ultimately perished, as above.*

There are two silhouettes of him in the Benthall Hall collection, as shown in Figure 19.1: the one on the right is dated 1831, when he was 13, and the one on the left dates from about 1840, when he was 22. The 1840 version looks as though it might be from the same artist as those of Edward and Clementina (see Chapter 17), but this is speculation.

The wreck of the *Osprey* was a sad affair. The ship had been launched at Portsmouth in 1844, the very latest design of brig, only to be wrecked in New Zealand two years later, on 11 March 1846. It took some time for the news to reach Britain, but an extensive account was printed in *The Times* on 15 September 1846:

> *The following account of the loss of this beautiful vessel is taken from the New Zealander of March 28:– "It is with the deepest regret we have to announce the loss of this beautiful brig-of-war, mounting twelve guns, on the western coast, about 18 miles to the northward of Hokianga, on Wednesday, the 11th inst., about 3 o'clock in the afternoon. On Tuesday, the 10th inst., the Osprey made the western coast, and was enabled to take an observation, which proved that she was in the latitude of Hokianga; but the weather coming on thick and hazy, she kept off the land until the evening, when it cleared away. She then*

---

[i]  A pinnace was a small boat carried on board a larger one, used to ferry goods and passengers from ship to shore.

Figure 19.1: Octavius Benthall

*stood in, fired two guns to announce to the pilot at Hokianga that she was off the harbour, and again stood to sea for the night. On the following morning, on nearing the coast, a high southern headland, similar to Hokianga, was seen, with what was presumed to be the pilot's house; but which, subsequently, proved to be a white spot on the cliff. Soon afterwards, perceiving a red flag run up, it was confidently anticipated that it was the entrance of the Hokianga, and the brig stood on, over the surf, bringing the northern and southern heads in one. After crossing the breakers, which were judged to be the three of Hokianga, the vessel touched ground; but it was thought that she was just merely on the bar, over which she would soon forge; but almost immediately she struck again with increased violence, and succession of shocks brought the alarming conviction that she was ashore, and that it was not the entrance to*

*Hokianga but that of Haere-kino, or False Hokianga. The guns were instantly hove overboard, and the masts cut away, which falling, with the sails set towards the shore, dragged the vessel still higher on the beach. On the tide receding, the vessel being about half-way between high and low water mark, the officers and crew were enabled to land about 2 o'clock on Thursday morning, with their small arms and some dry ammunition, which had been fortunately saved on deck, the greater part having been thrown overboard. The vessel stands upright on her keel, in the sand, and is but slightly injured, the heel of the keel only being knocked away. The stores are being landed, and the crew are assisted by 150 natives, who are well disposed, and behave very friendly and peaceably. Two of them had been caught pilfering, and had been taken into custody. After the stores are all taken out of the Osprey, there is no hope*

139

*of her floating without a number of empty casks to raise her, or of hauling her off. The shore on that part of the western coast is extremely shallow for a long distance outwards, with a heavy surf and breakers continually rolling in, even when the wind is off the land: so that no vessel of proper size and power could approach with safety sufficiently near to render the Osprey efficient assistance in hauling off. This untoward circumstance has arisen, it appears, from mistaking the headlands; and likewise from being misled by the hoisting of the red flag, similar to the practice at the true Hokianga, to apprize vessels that there is sufficient water for them on the bar. From information we have received we learn that this little harbour of Haere-kino is precisely a miniature of Hokianga, and the principal native chief has adopted the plan of the pilot at the latter place, to announce high water to the smaller vessels that may approach his settlement. We consider that some measures should be taken to prevent the future recurrence of similar disasters to large vessels. The harbour of Hokianga itself, although a bar harbour, can be approached and entered with proper precautions; therefore the accident should not, in any degree, tend to the detraction of it. If some wooden beacon, or some other landmark, was erected at Haere-kino, and public notice given, the access to Hokianga would be more easily ascertained, and the strand of Haere-kino more certainly avoided. The Aurora schooner, of Hokianga, is employed to convey the stores of the Osprey to that port, and the Adelaide brig has sailed from here to take them on board for their ultimate destination. Her Majesty's ship Racehorse likewise sailed on Thursday morning, for the Bay of*

*Islands, to be in communication with the officers and crew of the Osprey."*

Nobody was hurt during the initial grounding, but a later report in *The Times*, on 30 October, added this: *"On the 21st of April last, Lieutenant Octavius Benthall, R.N., drowned in endeavouring to cross the bar of Hokianga Bay, New Zealand, in the pinnace of Her Majesty's ship Osprey."*

A long and very turgid account of the entire saga was published in 1858.[253] The book does provide an interesting account of the customs and culture of the native Maori tribe led by chief Pukeroa, and of the difficulties the passengers and crew faced in finding their way back, by land, to *"civilisation."* But the *"moral and scriptural illustrations"* advertised on its title page include long digressions on biblical themes – for example, the travails of the Apostle Paul when caught in a storm in the Mediterranean. And there are a number of very bad poems, of which this is an extract.

*And so with thee, poor BENTALL; from England's shore you came,*
*Thy heart beat high with joyous hope, for honour and for fame;*
*That earthly honour yours – but short the time you bore it here,*
*For ocean was thy couch of death, the sands thy funeral bier.*

However, the book does eventually provide an account of this second accident. It appears that a schooner arrived at the site of the *Osprey*, and had left for Hokianga with the Osprey's pinnace in tow. Before they reached the harbour, the pinnace was cast off and sent ahead, with Lieutenant Benthall in command together with the schooner's owner and three other crew members, hoping to make it into the harbour before dark. The details are not clear, but the boat was spotted by a local man being rowed towards land, but it then capsized in the surf, causing everyone on board to drown.

# Chapter 20

## INVENTING INTERNATIONAL TOURISM: THOMAS BENNETT, BORN THORNTON BENTALL

The sixth son of William Searle and Mary Ann Bentall was born in 1814 and named Thornton in honour of his grandmother and uncle (see Chapters 5 and 9–11). He worked in London for several years in finance, but at the age of 31 he left England in a hurry, leaving behind a mountain of debt and a collection of *"stuffed birds,"*[254] to start a new life first in Denmark and then in Norway under the assumed name of Thomas Bennett.

Like his brothers, Thornton was well educated, probably initially at the Totnes Grammar School. In 1829, aged 15, he moved from Totnes to London, where he indentured himself to his uncle John and attended Westminster school as a town boy (see Chapter 14). He did not attend university, but set himself up instead as a stockbroker and money scrivener[i] under his uncle's guidance. He lived with John at 37 Craven Street, Westminster, until 1839.

In the summer of 1838, he spent time in Devon. A letter written by Clementina Marshall that September notes that Thornton drove some of his cousins from Totnes to Shaldon, where she was holidaying. By 1840 Thornton had become his father's primary contact in London for borrowing money as William Searle attempted to

stave off his impending bankruptcy (see Chapter 11). A letter survives, dated 27 April 1840, in which Thornton enclosed half of a banknote for £1,000, and said that he would send the other half under separate cover. In June that year Thornton travelled to Devon for financial consultations with his father. He took the train to Southampton (a service that had just opened in May), followed by a steamer to Torquay, where he asked William Searle to have a horse available so that he could get to Totnes.

In the 1841 census Thornton described himself as a stockbroker, and as living or staying at Chevening, Kent, with Arthur Cornish,[255] Samuel Lorne, and a Mr and Mrs Box. However, the electoral register listed his office address: 1 Copthall Chambers, London.

By 1845 he had moved to Croydon, just south of London, and had invested large sums of money – some borrowed, some invested on behalf of others – in railway shares.[256] Later that year he fled the country, leaving nothing in his apartment except his stuffed birds, and moved first to France, where he changed his name to Thomas Bennett before moving on to other parts of Europe. (Back in England, "Thornton Bentall" was declared bankrupt with debts of £50,000 or more, equivalent to several million pounds in today's money, but no

---

[i]   The job of a money scrivener was to help people obtain loans, from either other individuals or banks.

142

serious attempt was made to find him.) In April 1848 he was in Copenhagen, teaching English to private students. At that time, he started to keep a journal, and later recollected in a letter to his family:

*I must first remind you that in 1848 a war broke out between Denmark and Prussia, the first war in Europe since the Battle of Waterloo. At that time, I was in Copenhagen and gave lessons in English to a wholesale merchant named Staehr. He was very kind to me and introduced me to all his family, amongst whom was a younger brother, 18 or 20 years old, who like many other men had volunteered to join the army as common soldiers. The evening before his departure from the city I accompanied him to take farewell with his family and seeing a tear in his eye on parting, it struck me that it might be a little consolation to them if he had a friend to go a little way with him; so I said: "I have nothing to do for a day or two, therefore I will accompany you on the first day's march if you like." He and his family appeared delighted at my offer, and his brother a couple of years younger than himself said, "Well I can also get away and will accompany you."*

*So it was agreed that we should both accompany the soldier and come back together. Both of the brothers spoke English. We started on the following morning*

*On the march the surgeon of the regiment, who spoke English, came to me and asked me to accompany them to the war, saying I might be very useful to him in attending to the wounded. I said that I was not doing much in*

*Copenhagen and that if I could make myself useful I had no objection.*

Thomas thus for six weeks became a volunteer medical orderly, earning himself an effusive letter of recommendation in June, after the initial fairly short-lived conflict was over.[257] He then moved to Christiania, in those days a Swedish town, but renamed in 1924 as Oslo, the capital of Norway. He obtained a job as secretary to the British Consul, became an English teacher at a local school,[258] and started making travel arrangements for visitors who contacted the consulate. A year later, in 1849, he set up a store, which he called Bennett's Bazaar, where he offered a variety of imported products for sale, as well as the services of a travel agency.

Thomas Bennett was proving quite the travel entrepreneur. By 1851 he had opened several scheduled carriage services between Oslo and other nearby towns, using imported carriages built in Britain to his specifications. This business was short-lived, but others flourished, and he quickly established himself as an authority on tourism. In 1853 George Bradshaw, the initiator of the railway guides that bore his name, paid a visit to Oslo to meet Bennett, but died there of cholera. Over the next 20 years:

*...it fell to Bennett to traverse the length and breadth of the region, from Copenhagen to the Arctic Circle, establishing new carriage routes, stabling for horses, guides and inns. Hitherto, currency exchange and payment for services in remote areas had been a problem, but Bennett triumphantly overcame this hurdle through an innovative system of coupons and vouchers–an early forerunner of traveller's cheques and credit cards.[259]*

In 1861 Jules Verne made a trip to Oslo to discuss with Bennett ideas for new books, and it may have been during those discussions that Verne began to consider the logistics of travelling around the world in 80 days. In one of his later books, *The Lottery Ticket*, "Mr. Bennett" himself makes an appearance. Thomas also entered into correspondence with Charles Darwin on the subject of hair-colour variations among Norwegian horses. Thomas died in 1898, but the Bennett travel agency continued in business for almost another 100 years, with offices throughout Scandinavia and in New York.

There are many mysteries about Thomas Bennett's early years in Oslo and the extent to which he remained in contact with his English brothers and sisters. A biography of Thomas Bennett written in 1925 and family records claim that he returned to England in 1853, and that his mother, Mary Ann, provided funds to start the tourism business. Given her circumstances at the time, this does not seem likely, since his father, William Searle, had lost all his savings in the bankruptcy proceedings ten years previously.

Perhaps, then, some other member of the family gave him financial support. Bennett certainly travelled to England in 1860, and while there adopted an English boy named Frederic, then aged about six. He applied for a British passport for himself in June of that year, and then in August applied for one for Frederic, after which he brought Frederic back with him to Oslo. The family tradition is that this foster son was the "*son of his older brother, Franz,*

Figure 20.1: Thomas Bennett, a.k.a. Thornton Bentall or Benthall

*who was widowed and could not look after the child.*"[260] But Thomas/Thornton's brother Frank Benthall, whose story is told in the next chapter, did not marry until 1861. Only one of Thomas's other brothers, the Rev. John Benthall, was widowed, but he did not have a son of that age. Whether or how Frederic was related to Thomas has not yet been determined, but it is certainly possible that Frederic was the illegitimate son of either Thomas himself or one of his brothers – and of those, Frank was the least unlikely to have been the father. But attempts to trace a possible mother have been unsuccessful.

Once back in Oslo, Thomas hired two young women, sisters, as his housekeepers. In 1864 he married one of them, Inger Marie Sand, and they produced three children together: Charles, Alfred and Francis. Their descendants live in Norway and Sweden today, and have visited Benthall Hall on several occasions.[261]

There are no portraits of Thomas in the English family archives, but his Nordic descendants have numerous family pictures, including the recently colourised photographs shown in Figure 20.1. The first shows Thomas, Inger Marie, their three young children, and Frederic standing at the back. The second shows Thomas in old age.

## Chapter 21

# PUTTING THE 'H' BACK IN BENTHALL: FRANCIS BENTHALL, SOLICITOR, BARRISTER AND ANTIQUARIAN

Francis (1816–1903), known as Frank, the seventh son, attended Totnes Grammar School, and then moved on to be a town boy at Westminster. He became articled to a solicitor named John Cole, and was admitted to the Queen's Bench in 1839. He then joined a partnership named Freeman, Bothamley and Bentall.[262] Like his uncle John (see Chapter 9), he paid the necessary dues to be given the "Freedom of the City of London" and so be allowed to conduct business there.

In 1835, as Clementina's teenage journal indicates (and a letter Frank wrote almost 70 years later confirms), he was also living, together with his brother Thornton (i.e., Thomas Bennett), with Uncle John at 37 Craven Street. According to Clementina, Frank played the guitar and had already started to collect antiquarian books. After John Bentall retired and went to live in Devon, Frank moved in briefly as a boarder with his brother the Rev. John Bentall at Little Dean's Yard, in the centre of Westminster School. But by 1846 and until at least 1850, he was listing his address as 14 York Street, Portman Square,[263] but in the 1851 census he was listed as a visitor with his sister

Elizabeth Waterfield at Dean's Yard Terrace (also close to Westminster School).

In 1842, when William Searle Bentall went bankrupt, Frank acted as his father's lawyer during the drawn-out process of selling off the family assets. As noted earlier, he also filed the paperwork required to sort out the estates of his brother Alfred and Alfred's wife, Elizabeth.

From his early years he devoted much of his spare time to antiquarian studies. He became a Fellow of the Society of Antiquaries of London in 1841, collected a large library of antiquarian books, bought property in the parish of Benthall, Shropshire, and was generally obsessive about the genealogy of the Benthall family.

In 1843, he went through the formal procedure of obtaining a Royal Licence in order to put the "h" back into the family name. He even filed a petition in court to change the name under which he had been admitted to the Queen's Bench, thereby creating a precedent for future legal decisions. Meanwhile he apparently convinced the College of Arms to designate him "Lord of the Manor of Buckfast," since by then (or at least some time soon after) he had bought out his father's and uncle's interest in the Buckfast Abbey property (see Chapter 11).

On 9 July 1845 Frank was required to testify at his brother Thornton's bankruptcy hearing, where he was as evasive as he could be. The court record from that day reads:

*Mr. Bentall, a brother of the bankrupt, was then examined ... :He did not know positively where his brother was, but believed he was in some part of France. He had seen a letter from him since he had left this country, but not one addressed to him ([the] witness). It was dated from a place called Morcluse, between Boulogne and Calais. He had directed communications to his brother addressed to him there, under the name of Richards, 'Poste Restante'. The last was on Monday or Saturday. The witness here said that he was so much confused by the troubles and anxiety he had undergone on this matter, that he could only state his belief and not positively. He believed that the bankrupt took £100 with him. He saw him shortly before he left on the 16th or 17th of June last. [Thornton] told him he was going. He was not a married man. All the communications from the bankrupt had been directed to another of his brothers. He (the witness) was a loser to a considerable amount more than £1000, and he was also responsible for £4000 or £5000 more. Nearly the whole of his family was involved. He (witness) held some doubtful securities in the shape of returned bills, but none other.*

Frank's testimony pleaded ignorance as to his brother's accounts and how Thornton had handled the large sums of money entrusted to him.

On 31 December 1849 Frank removed himself from the partnership with Freeman and Bothamley. He became an independent solicitor, a commissioner for oaths in Chancery and a "Parliamentary agent."[264]

In June 1855 he arranged for the sale of many of his antiquarian books by auction at Sotheby's.[i] In 1859, he married a widow, Susanna Bates (née Aylward), the Rev. John Benthall officiating, at St George's, Hanover Square. (Her first husband, a surgeon, had died the previous year.) In 1861 he decided to switch careers and become a barrister, and was admitted to the Bar in 1864. He practised as a conveyancer, a specialist kind of barrister then engaged in drafting legal documents concerned with land and trusts within the jurisdiction of the Court of Chancery, but who did not appear as an advocate in court.

According to family records, Frank was a bigoted anti-Catholic. After acquiring the Buckfast Abbey estate, eventually he sold most of it to a man named Gale, on the explicit understanding that Gale would not sell it to the Benedictine monks who wanted to re-establish a monastery there. Mr Gale reneged on that commitment, to Frank's fury. A few smaller properties around Buckfastleigh remained in the family, passing through several descendants until they were sold in about 1980.

Susanna died in 1871 and was buried in the family vault in Highgate Cemetery, whereupon Frank moved to Silsoe, Bedfordshire. He also bought three adjoining cottages on Barton Road, as well as some gardens nearby, in order to store the collections of pictures and his remaining books. He made alterations to the interior of the cottages, the better to display the artwork, and arranged for a Mrs Payne to open the premises to visitors, furnish them with catalogues and

---

[i] A suspicious mind might note the date as being close to the presumed date of the birth of Thomas Bennett's foster-son, Frederic (see Chapter 20).

answer their questions. He named the renovated building "Boteler Lodge" after a local worthy who had died in 1647 but was descended from a Shropshire baron of the 12th century.

Figure 21.1: Francis (Frank) Benthall[265]

A book was published in 1848 (and reprinted in 1858) named *The Baronial Halls and Picturesque Edifices of England*,[266] with numerous illustrations and a text by Samuel Carter Hall, who is now remembered, if at all, as the model for Pecksniff, one of Charles Dickens' more infamous characters. One article in that book discusses the history of Benthall Hall and the family that built it, and mentions that it was no longer owned by a family member. But there is a footnote there that says: *"There is a small estate in the parish belonging to their descendants, the Benthalls of Buckfast, in Devonshire."* This information can only have come from Frank, since the "Benthalls of

Buckfast" was his invention, and he had indeed bought a small piece of land in the parish. Since he spent a lot of time researching the records of the borough of Much Wenlock, he may have thought that having a small pied-à-terre there would be useful. In any event, it would appear that at least that article in Hall's book was in fact supplied by Frank.

Later Frank gave all of his research on the Much Wenlock and Benthall parish histories to a friend named Vaughan, who published them, including extensive family trees, in the *Transactions of the Shropshire Archaeological Society*.[267] The 80-page article, entitled "Extracts from the Registers of the Parish of Much Wenlock, with Notes" includes this preamble:

> *The following extracts were carefully made from the original records by one of the senior Fellows of the Society of Antiquaries... By his kindness they were committed to the writer to be put in a more digested form, and so offered to the Archaeological Society of a County which he loves well, and with which his family have been so long connected."*

It is intriguing that Frank preferred to allow others to publish his research rather than put his own name on the work.

Frank Benthall died in 1903, and was buried in the family vault at Highgate Cemetery, as had been his wife when she died in 1871. He left behind an interesting will, written about a year before he died. Comprising 11 pages of double-spaced typescript, its first seven pages list a full 55 individually identified relatives (most of whom are named in this book). It also contains a remarkable clause designed to forestall any lawsuits among the beneficiaries: *"I direct that in the event of proceedings being taken for the administration of my estate by the Court of Chancery the person or persons on whose behalf those proceedings shall be taken shall immediately forfeit all interest in my … estate …*"; with the residual estate to be placed in trust "*for the restoration and preservation of sepulchral memorials of the dead*" (six of which were specifically identified).

# Chapter 22

## SISTERLY CONTRASTS: LOUISA, ELLEN BLAYDS, MARY AND LAURA BENTHALL

The catalogue of the 15 children of William Searle and Mary Ann will be complete once the lives of the four younger daughters have been described. They illustrate the choices available, depending on temperaments and ambitions. Two, Ellen Blayds and Mary, like their elder sisters, married and produced large numbers of children, most but not all of whom survived to adulthood. The other two, Louisa and Laura, were spinsters, both occupying themselves first as housekeepers for their widowed brother, John, then for their "Aunt Thornton" (i.e., Margaret Benthall) and their mother Mary Ann in widowhood, and also for several nephews and nieces. Laura, the youngest, was also a good artist, and once independent of those responsibilities she became the author of a memoir that has been much quoted in this book, the owner of a boarding house, a traveller, and apparently an enthusiastic photographer. Here are their stories.

### Louisa Benthall

Louisa (1820–1859) lived with Aunt Thornton almost all her life, first at Totnes, then at her brother John's house at Stanwell, and then at his Willen vicarage (see Chapter 17). She was to some extent a housekeeper for John,

and a surrogate parent to the three eldest children of Edward and Clementina (see Chapter 17). There are a few letters surviving from Louisa's correspondence with her sister-in-law Clementina, but otherwise very little else to say about her, aside from the fact that she did have an influence on the career of at least one of her nephews, Clement Benthall (see Chapter 29).

The images in Figure 22.1 of Louisa and the next sister, Ellen Blayds, are digitally enhanced from a photograph of a photograph of sketches made by their youngest sister, Laura.

### Ellen Blayds Benthall, Mrs Robert Romer Younghusband

Ellen Blayds Benthall[268] (1822–1865) was living with her brother William and his wife, Elizabeth, in the Mill House at Totnes during the 1841 census. She married Robert Romer Younghusband in 1849. Robert was the son of Major-General Charles Younghusband. Robert and two of his brothers became models of a modern Major-General, while his two other brothers were killed in action in India.[269]

Charles Younghusband is named in Clementina Marshall's teenage diary in 1835 as someone who came to dinner and stayed the night with the Waterfields at Westminster,

Figure 22.1: Louisa and Ellen Blayds Benthall

but that was 14 years before Robert married Ellen Blayds, in November 1849, at Stanwell, Middlesex, where her brother John and his flock were living. At the time of their marriage Robert was a lieutenant in the Indian Army, and Ellen Blayds duly moved out there with him. She gave birth to nine children.[270] The first four were born in India, and of those, three survived past infancy: a daughter, Frances Mary; and two sons, Arthur Delaval and George William. The next, another son, Romer Edward, was born in 1858 in England, at Freshford, a village just outside Bath. The next after that, another son, Henry Buchanan, was born near Bombay in December 1859, but died at sea in 1861. Later that year, Alfred was born at Freshford, followed in 1862 by a daughter, Ellen, who died soon after birth. By 1865 the family were back in India. Ellen Blayds gave birth once more to a daughter that year, at Nasirabad, Rajputana, but she and the baby, named Ellen Edith, were both dead within a week.[271] Robert subsequently remarried, to Anna Shaw, with whom he had two more children, and retired to Clifton, Bristol. Three of his sons with Ellen Blayds also lived in India after being educated back in Britain. Among the beneficiaries from Frank's will were Francis Mary, two children of George William, and the widow of Alfred Younghusband.

## Mary Benthall, Mrs. William Marshall

Mary Benthall (1823–1907) married her first cousin William Marshall, the son of Dr Richard Marshall (see Chapter 12). This William, like his cousin William Ord Marshall, was a clerk at the War Office, courtesy of their uncle Edward Marshall.[272] During the 1841 census Mary, aged about 18, was visiting Edward Marshall (her uncle as well) at his home in St Pancras, London, while William was visiting or possibly lodging with his sister Louisa Edgcumbe. Mary and William married in 1843, and it must be supposed that Uncle Edward was supportive. They had eight children in total, but three died in infancy: Richard, Laura and Ernest William, who are named on the family vault at Highgate Cemetery (see Chapter 9).

In 1851 Mary and William were living on Larkhill Lane, Clapham, with daughter Mary, aged five, and sons Arthur, 2 years old, and Herbert, aged 2 months. Not long after, they moved to Regent's Park Terrace, St Pancras, where they became neighbours of William Henry Drake, their second cousin, and his wife, Louisa. As noted in the digressions at the end of Chapters 3 and 13, Drake was sent to Crimea before William and Mary moved to Regent's Park Terrace, but they still maintained contact with their cousin Dr John Marshall, and advised him to contact Drake when he arrived at Balaclava. After the Crimean War was over, the Drakes and Marshalls met for dinner in each other's houses, together with other Marshall and Benthall cousins, including Arthur and Alice Benthall who also lived close by (see Chapter 16).[273] Charles Henry Marshall (one of the seven orphans – see Chapter 26) came to visit these cousins in 1856, met there Charlotte, a daughter of the Drakes, and married her on 23

September 1857, which was also the wedding anniversary both of Charlotte's parents and of William and Mary Marshall.

During the 1861 census William and Mary were living at Regent's Park Terrace with their children Mary (aged 15), Arthur (aged 12), Herbert (aged ten), Ellen Jane (aged eight) and Frederick (aged three). In 1871 William had retired, and the five children were still living at the same address. By 1881 William and Mary had moved to Elmwood House, Croydon, together with Mary, Herbert and Ellen, those three children being unmarried. Herbert, a clerk in the India Office, died unmarried in 1889. In 1891 Mary, by now widowed, was living at Hastings, still with her daughters Mary and Ellen. Arthur was a civil engineer, and died unmarried in 1901. During the census that year, Mary was living at "*Woodgift,*" in Horsham, Surrey, still with Ellen but without the younger Mary. Mary senior died in 1907, and in her will left £1,115 14s 10d to her two youngest children – the Rev. Frederick Marshall and Ellen Jane Marshall, spinster – suggesting that daughter Mary predeceased her, although no record of her death has been located. William and Mary Marshall were both buried at Willen.

Their son Frederick became vicar of Ockley, Surrey, a few miles north of Horsham. He married Margaret Helen Young and the couple had five children. Their son Eustace, (born in 1893) produced in 1926 a son named Robin, whose family included two children born in the 1950s.

### Laura Benthall

Laura (1827–1912) was the youngest child of William Searle and Mary Ann Benthall. She died unmarried. Like Louisa, she lived as a companion to Aunt Thornton, following her from Totnes to Stanwell and then to Willen, where her mother also lived as a widow. But after Louisa and Aunt Thornton died and Mary Ann moved to Sherborne, Laura became independent and moved to London. When Mary Ann Benthall died in 1866, Laura was named as an executor of her mother's will, and her address then was given as "*30 Harley Street, Cavendish Square, Middlesex*" (Middlesex having since been subsumed by Greater London). During the 1871 census she was visiting her brother William at the old house on The Plains, Totnes, together with their sister Anna Gay and a niece, Katherine Waterfield, a daughter of William Waterfield, who was living with his wife Louisa (Anna's daughter) in India.

By 1877 Laura had moved to the village of Orcheston St Mary, where her widowed sister Anna was then living with her daughter Susannah and son-in-law, the Rev. John Wardale, rector of that parish (see Chapter 16). Her eldest brother, William Bentall, died that year and bequeathed her his entire estate. Laura then sold the old house and also three cottages on Church Lane, Totnes, which William had bought in 1869 from the Rev. Stenning Johnson and David Simpson Morice (sons-in-law of the Rev. William and Isabella Marshall – see Chapter 8).[274]

During the 1881 census Laura was staying with her nephew and niece William Henry and Edith Benthall and their three children at 33 Pevensey Road South, St Leonards-on-Sea, East Sussex (see Chapter 30). By 1884 she had moved back to Devon, settling at Dawlish where she bought and lived in a large house named "Rockstone."[275] In the 1891 census, and again in 1901, a person also listed there was Ann J. Dart, her occupation being "*Lodging Housekeeper.*" Ann had been a Benthall family employee all her life. In the 1851 census she was listed as a housemaid, aged 18, at the old house in Totnes.

In 1861 she was looking after Elizabeth Cornish, whose husband had died in 1858 and who herself died a year later in 1862. In 1871 she was back at the old house on The Plains, again as a housemaid, and in 1881 she was still there, but listed as a lodging housekeeper.[276] It must have been Laura's idea to install Ann at Rockstone to run it as a guest house for relatives (and presumably some paying guests too).

By 1911 Laura, then aged 83, had moved out of Rockstone and was living in a five-room apartment at 25 The Strand, in the centre of Dawlish. On the day of the census that year she had two visitors: one was Ann Dart, by then 78; and the other (who also signed the census form on Laura's behalf) was a great niece, Edith Elizabeth Wardale, a *"Tutor and Lecturer at St. Hugh's College, Oxford,"* then aged 48 (see Chapter 16).

Laura was an accomplished artist; several of the portraits at Benthall Hall were drawn or painted by her. She obtained her first passport in 1872 and appears to have travelled widely. Many years later she arranged an exhibition of photographs in Dawlish, including pictures of several European cities and art works. The reports of the event are not clear, but she may have been an early adopter of the Kodak camera, invented by George Eastman in 1888, and these were photographs she had taken herself. The Bennett family in Norway (see Chapter 20) has copies of portraits she painted of her parents, as well as two watercolours of Swiss landscapes that are attributed to her. The implication is that she visited her brother Thornton (a.k.a Thomas Bennett) there at some point and took those pictures as gifts; or, if she did not visit Norway herself, she may have sent the pictures over with her nephew Harry Benthall when he visited in around 1904.

While living at Willen, Laura produced a number of paintings of the vicarage, school and church which are now at the Centre for Buckinghamshire Studies, located in the County Council offices at Aylesbury. The one shown in Figure 22.2, a painting of the vicarage, has a hand-written note on the back saying, *"Mother holding flowers while Aunt gathers."*

Laura also wrote an extensive history of her grandparents and their families which has been an important source for the material in this book. She wrote the document originally in 1871, but continued to add to it until she died.

One photograph of Laura has already been shown, in Figure 9.3. Figure 22.3 features two more, the first of uncertain date, and the second taken at her flat in Dawlish in around 1910.

Figure 22.2: The Willen vicarage

Figure 22.3: Laura Benthall

Figure 22.4 shows a photograph taken in Laura's Dawlish flat in about the same year. That photo is now in the family archives at Benthall Hall. Most the portraits then on Laura's wall are now in the Benthall Hall collections and have been used as illustrations in this book. The portraits of Louisa and Ellen Blayds in Figure 22.1, which are not at Benthall Hall, were copied from this image. The two photographs at the top right are not positively identified, but may be of Thomas Nelson and Elizabeth Waterfield, as described by their great-grandson John Percival Waterfield in his memoir (see Chapter 16). Some of the silhouettes are not identified.

Figure 22.4: Laura Benthall's portrait collection

## Chapter 23

# A VICTORIAN TYRANT? WILLIAM MARSHALL, FATHER OF ALFRED MARSHALL

The remainder of Part III provides details of the lives of the orphaned children of William and Louisa Marshall (née Bentall) who were the subjects of Chapter 13. As with William Bentall, (the eldest child of William Searle and Mary Ann Bentall), the eldest of the Marshall orphans, another William Marshall, found a niche close to home and remained in it for most of his life. As the father of the illustrious Professor Alfred Marshall, this William Marshall's life and opinions have been scrutinised closely by Alfred's biographers. John Maynard Keynes, a possibly even more illustrious economist, wrote the first, an extended obituary, and was quite gentle, if slightly catty, describing him as

*a tough old character, of great resolution and perception, cast in the mould of the strictest Evangelicals, bony neck, projecting chin, author of an Evangelical epic in a sort of Anglo-Saxon language of his own invention which found some favour in its appropriate circles, surviving despotically-minded into his ninety-second year.*[277]

However, Ronald Coase, another illustrious economist and Nobel laureate, took issue with Keynes' characterisation:

*This is wrong. He was a man of great resolution and no perception... [He] was completely convinced of the correctness of his own narrow views, had little regard for the feelings or wishes of others, and thought it right to control the actions of those in his power by 'an extremely severe discipline.'*[278]

Coase's perspective, adopted later by Alfred's biographer P.D. Groenewegen, has become accepted as an accurate account of William's personality and his approach to parenting. The paper by Stevens cited earlier refutes much of Coase's evidence and largely restores the Keynesian version.

William was born at Cape Town in 1812, moved to Mauritius at the age of four, and then in 1821 to Totnes, where his uncle William Searle Bentall placed him at the age of nine in the Totnes Grammar School as a boarder. In 1823, when his father returned from Mauritius, William joined him in Scotland, where it is likely that he attended the Leith grammar school. After William's father died in 1828, his assent to the appointment of us uncle John Bentall as his legal guardian was witnessed by his cousins, William Dacres Adams and Henry Bentall Adams (see Chapter 13).[279] In 1829, about 18 months after his father's death,

William started as a clerk at his uncle John's office in London, but soon was found a position at the Bank of England, where he stayed for the rest of his working life. The published accounts suggest that this position was obtained thanks to John's influence. A young neighbour of John Bentall named Edward Oliver had joined the Bank of England in 1829, shortly before William, and the two worked closely together for most of their lives – indeed, Edward may have been a reason for William's career choice.

In 1835, when Clementina Marshall (who later married Edward Benthall – see Chapter 17) and Louisa Marshall, William's younger sister, spent several months in London as teenagers, William was in regular attendance as an escort and companion, and his uncle John Bentall gave a lavish dinner to celebrate his 23rd birthday.

In May 1840 William married Rebecca Oliver, sister of his colleague Edward Oliver. Edward and Rebecca were from Maidstone, Kent, and it seems that their clan dominated the butchery and leather industries in the area. Their father had been a butcher there, and their brothers – George and James – owned three butcher's shops in the middle of the town. A presumed relative, Joseph Oliver, was the owner of a large tannery in the village of Hollingbourne, a few miles from Maidstone, and other Olivers in the area were butchers and curriers.[280]

Alfred Marshall's biographers made much of the fact that on the marriage certificate, William Marshall stated his occupation as "gentleman," and that as such, marrying a butcher's daughter put him beyond the pale as far as his Bentall relatives were concerned. But there is scant support to justify that interpretation of the subsequent relationships between the respective families.

William and Rebecca's marriage produced five children. The eldest, Charles William, born at Camberwell in 1841, went to India in 1858, and eventually became a manager of what remained of the East India Company's silk-production venture in Bengal. The second son, the famous Alfred, was born at Bermondsey in 1842; he was sent to Merchant Taylors' School, on Suffolk Lane in central London, and then went up to Cambridge, where he read mathematics and ultimately became a professor of economics, responsible for key developments in economic theory between 1870 and 1920. Alfred was deeply interested in the concepts of supply and demand, the elasticity of demand, and the rigorous application of mathematics to their study.[281]

Two sisters came next: Agnes, born at Sydenham (formerly part of Kent, but nowadays a London suburb) in 1846; and Mabel, born at Clapham in 1851. The youngest brother was Walter, born at Clapham in 1853.[282] Walter went to St John's College, Cambridge, in 1870, where Alfred was then teaching, but was consumptive. Sometime later he travelled to the home of Jonathan and Susannah Ayliff at Grahamstown, South Africa, where it was thought the dry air might help him, but he died there in 1874.[283]

William worked as a clerk at the Bank of England for about 47 years. According to Groenewegen, Alfred Marshall's biographer, he spent two years in the Cash Book Office, and then a full 35 in the Clearer's Office and the Bills Office. In 1867 he was appointed a "supernumerary cashier" and spent four years in that section and then six more in the Cashier's section.[284] After retiring in 1877, he entertained himself by writing and publishing four long, rather bad poems and two books: *The Past, Present, and Future of England's Language*, and then *The Dangers and Defences of English Protestantism*.[285]

Sometime after 1871 the family moved to Great Malvern, Worcestershire, where Rebecca died in 1878. In 1881 the sisters Agnes and Mabel were living there with William, in a boarding house. In 1886 Mabel married the Rev. Ernest Guillebaud, rector of Yatesbury, Wiltshire. William moved in with them, and stayed until he died in 1901.

Many stories were told about William by his descendants, most of them disparaging. Coase quotes an account of his death give to him by a nephew of Alfred's, Claude Guillebaud:

*He told me that he and the other children were in the nursery when someone came in and solemnly announced, 'Grandfather is dead'. The children at first merely repeated what they had been told, and then they realised what had happened. In a spontaneous outburst of joy, they whooped and holloed and went around the nursery in Indian file, crying out all the while, 'Grandfather is dead'.*[286]

Coase furthermore tells us that William, in his youth, "*was made boss over the other children* [i.e., his siblings] *and kept them in order with a slipper*," and that his brother Charles "*disliked his brother's control at Totnes, and ran away and became a cabin boy*."[287] Groenewegen goes as far as to say that William's "*later published writings ... show an obsessive fascination with the instruments for inflicting corporal punishment on children*."[288] He quotes extensively from these writings and to that extent, the point is fair. However, attitudes then to corporal punishment were different. Every school – especially the more prestigious ones – saw it as an essential part of school life: "*Eton, Rugby, Winchester, Shrewsbury, Westminster, Merchant Tailors' and many other halls of learning were famous for their flagellations*."[289] The practice had become moderated to some extent by 1850, but William

was a product of his time and not necessarily far beyond the mainstream of the culture he grew up in. Indeed, Alfred's own summary was that his father was wonderfully unselfish and kindly intentioned, but unaware of the effect his extremely severe discipline had on his children.[290]

There do not appear to be any portraits of William, but the photograph of Alfred (Figure 23.1) is taken from that article written by Keynes.

Figure 23.1: Professor Alfred Marshall

# Chapter 24

# EDWARD MARSHALL:
## AN OFFICER IN A PEACETIME ROYAL NAVY

The second surviving son of William and Louisa Marshall (née Bentall), John, died aged 17 in Totnes. The third, Edward, enlisted in the Royal Navy in January 1829 – i.e., within a year of his father's death – at the age of just 12.[291] Coase rather whimsically compared Edward's career with that of Horatio Hornblower, the fictional hero of a series of novels by C.S. Forester set during the Napoleonic Wars, but this was anachronistic. The role of the Royal Navy had changed by the time Edward became an officer. In the almost 30 years that he served, steam gradually supplemented and then took over from sail. Edward's career rarely involved armed combat, and the task of the Royal Navy was to keep the peace rather than make war.

Edward graduated from the Royal Naval College at Portsmouth on 19 December 1836 and entered service as a mate, first on HMS *Sappho* and then on HMS *Caledonia*. He became a lieutenant in 1843 and was posted to HMS *Winchester*, which was stationed at Cape Town. There he was instrumental in impounding the Portuguese brig *Sociedade* on suspicion of being a slaver, as part of a two-man team sent to conduct a survey of the ship. They found on board 736 planks, designed to construct a slave deck, and 28 casks of water:

*…sufficient for the consumption of the officers, crew, and passengers (and the animals), which were on board the 'Sociedade' for the voyage from Rio de Janeiro* [Brazil] *to Benguela* [now in Angola] *and back again to Rio." Their report concluded: "We are of the opinion that 3,200 gallons of water would be sufficient for the officers and crew … and 400 slaves."*[292]

In 1845 Edward moved to HMS *Conway* and in 1847 to HMS *Nimrod*, under the command of Captain James Richard Dacres.[293] In 1851 he was still a lieutenant, in a squadron of ships based in Sierra Leone whose purpose was to enforce the British ban on slave trading. An early account of this obscure episode in British naval history starts thus: *"Coçioco, a usurping king of Lagos, then one of the chief centres of the slave trade, became troublesome and intractable."*[294] It was decided that a flotilla of armed boats, drawn from the Sierra Leone squadron, should accompany the local British Consul (based on Fernando Po, an island of Equatorial Guinea nowadays known as Bioko) under a flag of truce to negotiate with Coçioco. HMS *Bloodhound*, an iron-hulled paddle steamer with several guns and two masts as well, accompanied by several smaller "paddle-box" boats, crossed the bar at the entrance to the Ogun River, whereupon the *Bloodhound* went aground "*but the boats kept on in line, until they were fired at from both guns and musketry on shore.*" Fighting continued for the rest of the day. That night they refloated the Bloodhound and returned to the squadron. "*In this affair, which, though costly and ineffective, was most bravely conducted, the two Mates of the Niger were killed, and ten people were badly wounded, numerous others being hit by spent balls, etc.*"

A month later, a new and more powerful flotilla returned and tried again. But once more the Bloodhound ran aground, as did another steamer, the *Teazer*.

Another battle took place. "*Fifteen officers and men of the squadron were killed or mortally wounded, and no fewer than 63 people were wounded.*" The *Teazer* was refloated, but the *Bloodhound* remained stuck. The next morning the British ships regrouped and was able to bring both ships back to safety. Edward was notably involved in that foray: "*A general attack on the town was soon afterwards begun, the rocket boats, under Lieutenant Edward Marshall, making splendid practice, firing numerous houses, and at length blowing up a magazine* [i.e., an ammunition storage facility]." His name subsequently received a special mention in dispatches.

In 1853 Edward was appointed commander of HMS *Virago*, a first-class six-gun paddle sloop at that time stationed at Valparaiso, Chile, as part of the Pacific Squadron. In April 1854 a paddle-box boat sent out from that ship was able to rescue a group of 12 starving American soldiers representing the survivors of the ill-fated "Darien Exploring Expedition" that had become stranded on the upper course of the Chuquanaqua, a river now known as the Chucunaque, the longest river in Panama.[295] Not long after that rather inconsequential event, the *Virago* was dispatched to Kamchatka, the peninsula on the far eastern edge of Russia, where she became part of the squadron that participated in the siege of the Russian naval base at Petropavlovsk while Britain was fighting the Crimean War.[296]

In December 1855 Edward was appointed commander of HMS *Devastation*, stationed at Portsmouth, and in 1857 he was promoted to the rank of captain, but without a command, which probably means that he went on the retirement list with a pension. In 1860 he married Lavinia Maitland Snow at Exeter. In 1861 they had a son, Edward Lionel Marshall, and at the time of that year's census they were living at Cockington, a village between Totnes and Torquay. Their next child, a daughter, Evelyn Maitland Marshall, was baptised in 1862, by which time the family had moved to Lamerton, a village on the other side of Dartmoor. Edward died there later that year, apparently aged 45.[297]

In 1865 Lavinia married again, to a widower named Edward Baring-Gould, Lord of the Manor of Lewtrenchard, and produced two more children (Alfred and Leila). Edward Baring-Gould's eldest son by his first marriage was the Rev. Sabine Baring-Gould, a prolific writer and antiquarian, but probably most famous as the author of the hymn "Onward Christian Soldiers," which he composed in 1864.

Coase, as an example of Edward Marshall's elder brother William's obnoxious character in his old age, said that he attempted to censor the hymns being sung in his son-in-law's church at Yatesbury, and that he took particular exception to this one, since one of its lines "*smacked of popery.*" That information came from a

Guillebaud grandson. But William must have known that this hymn had been written by his former sister-in-law's stepson. Was that why he objected? Was this part of his mordant sense of humour?

Lavinia lived to the age of 92 and died in 1921. Edward Marshall and Lavinia's son, Dr Edward Lionel Marshall, moved to Virginia, USA, where his descendants still live.

## Chapter 25

# LOUISA MARIA MARSHALL: EVERYONE'S FAVOURITE AUNT

Everyone loved and respected Louisa Maria Marshall (1818–1907), the fourth of the "orphans." The information that came to John Maynard Keynes, via Alfred Marshall's wife, Mary, was that:

*She refused several offers of marriage because she wished to remain a centre of the large family & to keep them all together. … Alfred was so much overworked by his father that, he used to say, his life was saved by his Aunt Louisa, with whom he spent long summer holidays near Dawlish. She gave him a boat and a gun and a pony, and by the end of the summer he would return home, brown and well.*

Similarly, Ronald Coase wrote:

*Of Aunt Louisa, Mary Marshall tells us that Alfred Marshall was devotedly fond … She made the care of her brothers and their families her first duty in life. Alfred Marshall owed a special debt to her (and so do we) since it was his belief that the summer holidays he spent with her saved his life after being overworked by his father during the rest of the year.*

Louisa arrived back in England from Mauritius in 1824 with her four younger brothers. So far there is no information about how much time Louisa Maria spent in Devon and then in Scotland after returning, and tracing her subsequent life through the public record is not particularly informative. After her father died, she was first sent to Exeter, where her assent to the appointment of John Bentall as her legal guardian was signed there by her uncle Richard Collins (who had married Mary Marshall, her father's eldest sister – see Chapter 2). She probably moved to Totnes soon after. In 1835 she went to London with Clementina Marshall and spent time with all her cousins living there (see Chapter 17). In the summer of 1838, she was staying with the Bentall family at Totnes.[298] In the 1841 census she was listed as visiting or living in Exeter with her aunt Anna Buller (i.e., her father William's youngest sister).

Sometime after that Louisa went to live with another aunt, Eliza Furse, and her husband Philip, at their house, then called Kenton Cottage, in the village of Kenton, a mile or so inland from Starcross and a few miles north of Dawlish (see Map 4). (Eliza was the other of William's sisters who, like Anna, was reputed to have been a model for the characters in Jane Austen's *Pride and Prejudice* – see Chapter 2).

Louisa was certainly living at Kenton Cottage in November 1846, when she witnessed a codicil to her uncle Philip's will. She was also there for the 1851 census. By that time Philip Furse had died, but Louisa and Eliza continued to share the residence along with a housekeeper, a butler, lady's maid, kitchen maid and gardener.[299]

The young Alfred Marshall and his siblings spent their summers there with his 'Aunt Louisa' during the 1850s. Evidence for this, in addition to the information provided to Keynes by Alfred's wife, is provided by the journal of William Henry Drake (see Chapter 3), which mentions a trip taken by him to Devon in August 1857 with his wife and two daughters, the older also named Louisa Maria, and the younger named Charlotte, who was engaged to be married to Louisa Marshall's younger brother Charles (see Chapter 26). The Drakes stayed at Kenton Cottage, where they met up with Eliza Furse, Louisa Marshall and three of William Marshall's children: Alfred. Agnes and Mabel. From there they also visited Exeter and Totnes, where they dined with William and Elizabeth Bentall (see Chapter 15), still living at the big house on The Plains that William's grandfather had bought 80 years before.

Eliza died in 1858. Louisa Marshall was the executor of her estate, but Kenton Cottage was still part of Eliza's husband Philip's estate and passed to his daughter by an earlier marriage. Louisa moved on. In the 1861 census she was listed as staying with her brother Charles and his family in Marylebone, London. During the 1871 census she was visiting her brother William in Clapham. In 1874 her brother Charles Henry died (see the next chapter) and she became the executor of his estate. This dragged on for years. In the 1881 census she was listed as staying with her sister-in-law, Charlotte, Charles

Henry's widow, in Lewisham, Kent (but nowadays a borough of southeast London). In 1884 a notice was published in an Australian government gazette announcing the appointment of a local lawyer to make a final settlement of Charles Henry's assets there. The notice gave Louisa's address as "*Rockstone, Dawlish*" – i.e., the house in which her cousin Laura Benthall had recently purchased and where she lived for many years (see Chapter 22).

Louisa has not yet been identified in the census records for 1891, but in 1901 she was living at Bexhill, a seaside town in East Sussex. She died there in 1907. Her executors were her nephews, Charles and Alfred, the sons of her brother William, and her estate was valued at over £34,000, equivalent to about £3,400,000 today. How she accumulated that capital is unknown, but presumably it was through inheritance – from Eliza, and other aunts and uncles – combined with sound investment advice from her family.

As far back as 1855, Louisa and her aunt Eliza were subscribers to a society supporting missionaries in Africa, and there are indications that she was still doing that from Dawlish in 1900.[300] Louisa also maintained connections with the Hawtrey family (see Chapter 2), as evidenced by an acknowledgment in the Hawtrey family history, published in 1903.[301] And she maintained an active correspondence with her brothers wherever they happened to be.

# Chapter 26

## CHARLES HENRY MARSHALL: AN AUSTRALIAN PASTORALIST

Alfred's biographers also gave extended accounts of the life of the next orphaned brother, Charles Henry (1818–1874) since he played a critical role in helping his nephew Alfred to attend Cambridge. They quote Alfred's wife, Mary Marshall, as describing him thus: "*A favourite uncle was Charles Henry, who disliked his brother William's control at Totnes, and ran away and became a cabin-boy.*"[302]

The exact date when Charles Henry first went to sea is not known, but this "running away" story is not plausible. His brother William moved to London in 1829, when Charles Henry was just nine years old, which was too young an age – even in those precocious days – for someone to launch a naval career. If anything, that anecdote might more plausibly have been told about Edward, who did indeed join the Royal Navy while William was still at Totnes (see Chapter 24).

Charles Henry went to sea rather later, probably around 1833, but on a merchant ship rather than a naval vessel. According to the register of a ship named the *Princess Charlotte*, Charles was appointed third mate in 1839 for a voyage to the West Indies and back. That same register states that his previous appointment had been aboard the *Thomas Laurie*, built in Quebec in around 1815 and purchased by a Lieutenant

Langdon RN in around 1829. Langdon commanded this vessel on two or three round trips to Tasmania (then known as Van Diemen's Land), where he acquired 2,000 acres of land. Even after Langdon stopped sailing, the *Thomas Laurie* continued to make that voyage at least until 1838.

In 1841, back from the West Indies, Charles Henry was listed in the census as a "*mariner*" staying at Bowden House with his uncle Thornton Bentall. In 1842 he travelled again to Tasmania and took a job as a bookkeeper for the Van Diemen's Land Company, of which his relative Edward Marshall (of the War Office) was a director and Dr. Richard Marshall and Richard's sister-in-law Peggy Ford were shareholders (see Chapter 12).[303] This company's "Tenantry Report" from March 1843 lists "*Chas. Marshall, single,*" noting that he "*has capital & holds the situation of Book-keeper, [and is] a relation of Mr. Edward Marshall of the War Office.*" Charles Henry became the superintendent of the Woolnorth sheep station in the northwest corner of Tasmania, but resigned in January 1849 and moved first to Moreton Bay (then in New South Wales, but nowadays part of southern Queensland), and then by December 1849 to Ellangowan station, an estate on the Darling Downs (likewise a former New South

Wales region since subsumed by Queensland). By 1851 he had entered into partnership with Robert Tertius Campbell, who owned the nearby Glengallan estate comprising 60,000 acres and holding 15,000 sheep, 400 cattle and 30 horses.[304] Charles Henry was appointed as a magistrate in 1849–1850, and he bought out Campbell's interest in Glengallan in 1852. In 1855 he took on a new partner, a Scotsman named John Deuchar, a successful breeder of sheep, cattle and horses, and expanded his stock-breeding efforts on Glengallan over the next 10 years.

Charles Henry returned to England in 1856, and the following year he married Charlotte Augusta Dring Drake, second daughter of his second cousin Henry Drake. As noted in Chapter 3, Henry Drake had returned from Crimea in 1856 and taken up residence with his wife and two daughters at 21 Regent's Park Terrace. William and Mary Marshall (he from the War Office and she née Bentall – see Chapter 22) lived next door, at no. 19, so it is likely that Charles Henry's introduction to the Drake family came through them. The marriage took place in September 1857, officiated by the Rev. Stephen Thomas Hawtrey, a relative of Charles Henry's grandmother (and the man responsible for introducing the study of mathematics at Eton – see Chapter 2). After the ceremony, a party of 37 met for a wedding lunch. No guest list survives, but it almost certainly included William and Rebecca Marshall (see Chapter 23) and their children, William and Mary Marshall and theirs, and Charlotte's sisters as well.

Charles Henry and Charlotte then went on a honeymoon tour that took in Chester, the Lake District, Edinburgh[305] and York. They returned to Australia briefly, and their first child, Charlotte

Louisa, was born there in 1859.[306] They soon returned to London, and their second daughter, Amy, was born at Marylebone in 1860.

The 1861 census records that Charles Henry and Charlotte were then living at St John's Wood, London, with their two daughters, and that Louisa Maria Marshall was visiting (see Chapter 25). His occupation was specified as "*Wool Merchant*," so he was probably managing the sale of the wool produced on the Glengallan estate. He was also very much in touch with his brother William, and in 1861 provided the loan that enabled young Alfred, William's son, to go up to Cambridge to study mathematics.[307]

Figure 26.1: Charles Henry Marshall

Three more sons arrived during the next seven years: Thornton (1862–1894), Hawtrey Charles (1864–1927), and Bertram (1868–1901), known as 'Bertie'. In 1865 John Deuchar bought out Charles Henry's share of the Glengallan partnership, with a mortgage agreement that required him to pay in instalments over a ten-year period. Either just before or just after, Charles Henry bought a property named Balmore House, at Caversham, Oxfordshire, which had been built in about 1850 on 25 acres of land, but offered for sale by the owner after he sued his wife for divorce.[308]

Back in Australia, Deuchar went on a spree, building a fine new house on the Glengallan property. A gala opening party was held in September 1868. But when the expensive construction bill was compounded by a drought, Deuchar found himself unable to make the mortgage payments. Charles Henry was forced to foreclose on him in 1870, sell the mansion that he had bought at Caversham, and travel back to Australia with Charlotte to sort out the mess. They took with them their three-year-old son Bertie, but left their two daughters at a *"school for young ladies"* and their two older sons, Thornton and Hawtrey, with William and Rebecca Marshall (and possibly also Louisa) at Clapham, where they were home-schooled.

Charles Henry, Charlotte and Bertie stayed at Glengallan for three years, but he then arranged a new partnership, with W.B. Slade, enabling them to return to London early in 1874. Sadly, he died that October at Lewisham.[309] Charlotte, who was expecting another child, arranged for Bertie to join his brother Hawtrey in Clapham, under Rebecca's tutelage, while she gave birth in 1875 to their last son, baptised with his father's name: Charles Henry. In 1883 Charlotte married again, to William Knighton, eventually dissolved the Glengallan partnership with Slade in 1904, and died in 1922. The hill behind Glengallan is today known as Mount Marshall.

There is a small whiff of scandal related to Charles Henry. His family's oral tradition includes a belief that while living in Tasmania, he acquired a wife and fathered a child whom he kept secret from Charlotte until after his death. There is indeed a reference to the existence of this family in the Van Diemen's Land Company's "Tenantry Report" dated 31 August 1849. In the 1840s there was a substantial population of female convicts in Hobart, transported there from Britain and given jobs as domestic servants as long as they behaved. Many of the single young men must have been tempted.

## Chapter 27

# HENRY MARSHALL, AND THE SEARCH FOR A GENTRIFIED UTOPIA IN TENNESSEE

Henry Marshall (1821–1877), known as Harry, also travelled to Tasmania at the same time or soon after his elder brother Charles Henry. The same "Tenantry Report" of 1843 lists *"Henry Marshall, single"* with the note: *"Brother of Mr. Charles Marshall, has capital."* However, Henry soon moved on to India, setting himself up as a timber merchant in Calcutta. In 1849 he spent Christmas Day with Edward and Clementina Benthall at their home in Alipore, a suburb of Calcutta (see Chapter 17).

In 1854, aged 33, Henry married Mary Charlotte Ainslie, aged 18, who coincidentally had also been born on the island of Mauritius. Her father had also been a merchant in Bengal. Henry and Mary Charlotte had nine children. The first three, Alice Constance, Henry Edgar (known as Edgar) and Louisa, were born in Calcutta. The family was still there when Henry's nephew Charles William Marshall (Alfred's older brother) arrived, but left shortly afterwards, and the next child, Ethel, was born in Devon in 1859. They then moved to Gloucestershire, where William Ainslie (known as Ainslie) was born in 1861. During the 1861 census they and their five children were living at Miserden, near Stroud in Gloucestershire, together with a niece and a nephew, Julia and Charles White, from Calcutta. In the 1871 census they were listed as living in Bedfordshire with four additional children – Charlotte, Edward Athelstan, Herbert and Ada Beatrice – plus their niece Susan Frances Marshall, daughter of Thornton (see Chapter 28).

Groenewegen states that Harry *"operated a timber firm (Steel, Marshall & Company) from 1874, an enterprise financially assisted by his brother, Charles Henry."*[310] Harry died in 1877 and his will named his nephew Alfred Marshall as executor. Harry's son Edgar continued the timber business for a short while, but there is a notice in the *London Gazette* dated 29 June 1879 announcing the dissolution of that partnership.

The eldest daughter, Alice, married a solicitor named Frank Watts in 1895. They lived at Kew, and both died there (she in 1925, he in 1926). In 1880 the two elder sons, Edgar and Ainslie, travelled to the Unites States, to *"that new colony founded by Tom Hughes."*[311] Hughes, the author of *Tom Brown's Schooldays*, was a British politician who in 1880 founded a settlement at Rugby, Tennessee, *"designed as an experiment in utopian living for the younger sons of the English gentry."* This move must have gone well at the start, since their mother, Mary Charlotte, three sisters (Louisa Mary,

Ethel and Charlotte Helen) and their brother Edward Athelstan went out a year later to join them. Mary Charlotte moved back to England in due course, and died in Sheffield in 1909.

Edgar married Edna Ralston, an Englishwoman, in Kentucky in 1895, but died two years later. Edna then returned to England, dying in Gloucestershire in 1942. Ainslie married in the United States in 1902, but moved to Nairobi, became a dairy farmer there and died there in 1937. Louisa Mary married in Philadelphia, but moved back to England with her husband; they are both buried at Richmond Cemetery. Ethel, who never married, also moved back to England and died in Devon in 1937. Charlotte Helen moved back, married, and died in Gloucestershire in 1942. Edward married in Baltimore, Maryland, and died there in 1928. The youngest brother, Herbert, followed his family somewhat later to the United States, became a doctor, married, lived in Albemarle County, Virginia, and died there in 1939, survived by his wife who died in 1975. The youngest sister, Ada Beatrice, married James McNab, but he died soon after. She moved to Nairobi to join her brother Ainslie, and died there in 1934.

## Chapter 28

# THORNTON MARSHALL: AN ARMY SURGEON IN AUSTRALIA AND NEW ZEALAND

The most complete account of the life of Thornton (1822–1861), the youngest orphaned son, comes from two articles published in 1968 by the Whakatane and District Historical Society in their publication entitled "*Historical Review*".[312] During the two years he served as an army surgeon in New Zealand, from 1856 to 1858, he kept a diary which, together with information provided by his grand-daughter and great-grandson, formed the basis for these articles. Relatively little is known about his early life, but the details that come from that diary are poignant, and provide insights into his relations with his brothers and sisters, with whom he maintained a regular correspondence.

In Clementina Marshall's London journal (see Chapter 17) she refers to him as "*little Thornton*." He was admitted to Westminster School in 1835,[313] and was a frequent visitor to John Bentall's house on Craven Street. The documented record shows that he became a medical student at Guy's Hospital, with the help of a recommendation from Dr. Hawtrey, head master of Eton College, and studied medicine under John Clarke, a surgeon there.[314] In 1845 he was appointed as an assistant surgeon in the British Army and sent to Australia. In 1851 his regiment, the 11th Regiment of Foot, was in New South Wales, and in Sydney that year

he married a 28-year-old Irish woman, Frances Mary Merrick Boyd, known as Fanny, daughter of Major Alexander Boyd, of the 65th Regiment of Foot. Thornton and Fanny's daughter, Susan (Susie) Frances, was born in April 1852, and baptised in Adelaide, South Australia.

In 1855 Thornton was promoted to surgeon and transferred from the 11th Regiment of Foot to the 65th, his father-in-law's regiment, and moved to Wellington, New Zealand. Fanny was suffering from consumption and died there soon after they arrived. The first few entries in his diary provide a prayerful account of the last month of her life.

Over the next two years Thornton wrote about his patients, his arguments about religion with his neighbours, his regrettable tendency to lose his temper while doing so, and his concerns for the welfare of his darling daughter Susie. He wrote to, and received numerous letters from, his sister Louisa and brothers Charles Henry, William and Henry. His brother Edward is mentioned briefly in the diary, but does not seem to have been much of a letter-writer, and his whereabouts at any point in time must have been uncertain.

Figure 28.1: Thornton and Fanny Marshall

In January 1857 Thornton wrote:

*My late fatigue and anxiety has produced rather an injurious effect on my forehead. It is more painful and inflamed than usual. Indeed it is not improving at all, and on calmly considering it, I fear I cannot expect that it will get well.*

The editor of the *"Historical Review"* added the following:

*It was this injury, because it steadily became worse, that ultimately caused* [Thornton] *to return to England. It stemmed from an unsuccessful operation to remove a lump formed by the impact of a cricket ball when playing for his hospital team.*

It took some time to arrange, but in August 1858 Thornton embarked for England with Susie, his *"faithful servant Martin"* and 17 invalids. They landed at Gravesend, Kent, in December. Thornton consulted with two doctors. The first told him that an operation was out of the question, and the second

*told me he would heal the wound but that a cure was out of the question. He applied some lotion of Chloride of Lime, which for the past month has kept me in the most fearful pain & agony.*

After enduring this very painful treatment for some time, Thornton died in London in 1861. He was buried in the Benthall family vault at Highgate Cemetery.

Daughter Susie stayed for a while with her Boyd grandparents, then with her uncle Henry Marshall, until she married Legh Richmond Powell in 1876. She died at Newton Abbott, Devon, in 1938. Her daughter *"Miss B.M. Legh Powell"* and her grandson *"Mr G.V. Wingfield Digby"* provided a transcript of the diary to the Whakatane and District Historical Society, together with other (not always accurate) information about Thornton's life.[315]

# Part IV.
# The Next Generation
# of Benthalls

## Chapter 29

# CHILDREN OF THE RAJ

igure 17.1 introduced the children and some of the grandchildren of Edward and Clementina Benthall. It was their descendants who fell in love with Benthall Hall, the old ancestral home in Shropshire, purchased it, and then ultimately arranged for it to be acquired by the National Trust. Edward and Clementina produced nine children, but only four of those had children of their own.

Edith Mary Benthall (1845–1932) married her first cousin, William Henry Benthall (1837–1909), and had three sons.

Ernest Benthall (1843–1928) married Jane Rogers Price, worked at the India Office, retired and moved to Wales, and had two daughters, Dorothy Price Benthall and Mary Clementina Benthall (known for most of her life as Molly).

Madeleine Anna Benthall (1847–1892) married Edward Robert Dale, and had a son, James Floyer Dale (known as Floyer) and a daughter, known as May. The first cousins Floyer Dale and Molly Benthall eventually married, then bought Benthall Hall when it came on the market in 1934.

The youngest son, the Rev. Charles Francis Benthall (1861–1936), married Annie Theodosia Wilson (1867–1950), who insisted on being called Anne, even by their five children. Their sons, Edward Charles Benthall (known as Tom – see Chapter 35) and Arthur

Paul (known as Paul – see Chapter 37), arranged and helped to fund the transfer of Benthall Hall to the National Trust.

Of the four families above, only Charles and Anne's produced grandchildren, which is the reason why so many of the family records and portraits ended up with them, and eventually became part of the Benthall Hall collection.

Edward and Clementina's five other children – Clement, Bertha, Winfred, Alfred and Octavius – had no offspring, but the family has portraits of some of them, and in 1940 Paul Benthall described his recollections of his aunts and uncles in a memoir. The lives of these five are summarised below, and those of the other four families in Chapters 30–33, drawing partly on Paul's memoir.

**Clement Edward Benthall (1841–1873)**

As noted in Chapter 17, Clement was born at sea, about four degrees north of the equator, and was baptised after his parents reached India. He and his next two siblings (see Figure 30.1 for a portrait of all three) were sent home when quite young, to live with their uncle the Rev. John Benthall and aunts Louisa and Laura (and their great aunt Thornton). Clement's life has been summarised at least twice, by James Benthall in a privately circulated book,[316] and also by Vyvyen Brendon in a book entitled *Children of the Raj*.[317] These accounts are based on the copious letters from Clementina and Edward to their children and family, and replies from Louisa Benthall and others back to them.[318] According to Brendon, Clement

> *...was an anxious child with an earnest desire to please his parents but a tendency to lapses in conduct. In May 1850 he had to be rescued from drowning in a gravel pit to which he had been forbidden to go. ... not long after their* [his parents] *return to England he upset them afresh by announcing that he wanted to join the Army rather than enter the Church as they desired. He got his way with the help of his Aunt Louisa, who explained to his parents*

*that 'poor dear Clement feels very much the importance of the step he has to decide on'.*

Thus, Clement successfully applied for a cavalry cadetship in the East India Company Army (shortly before the European regiments of that army were merged into the British Army). After attending the cadet training course, he returned to India in 1858, and gained the rank of lieutenant in 1859, six weeks before his 18th birthday. Listed as an "Unposted Cavalry Officer," he was reluctant to engage in the pastimes popular with other officers, such as dancing, smoking, playing cards and drinking beer. He was given a variety of temporary assignments and was somewhat accident prone, suffering a painful injury to his foot in 1860, and a

Figure 29.1: Clement Edward Benthall

broken arm in 1864. Somehow, for reasons lost to history, he won an Indian General Service Medal for his participation in the Bhutan War of 1864–65. (This was not one of the more glorious British expeditions.) He was promoted to the rank of captain in 1867, but he was rarely healthy. He visited England in 1861 for a training course in musketry, and again in 1871, and was listed in that year's census as staying at the home of his uncle Arthur Benthall. He then returned to India, and died of gastritis in Allahabad in 1873.

There are numerous photographs of him in the family's possession, including those shown in Figure 29.1.

## Bertha Benthall (1850–1944)

Bertha was born in the Calcutta suburb of Alipore, but lived almost her entire life at Sherborne, Dorset. She never married. In 1940 Paul Benthall wrote of her:

*When a small baby she was delicate and had to be fed on asses milk and in order to get enough a whole herd of donkeys had to be bought. Her unkind brothers and sisters attributed her rather inferior intelligence to the asses, but even at the age of 8 she could write an excellent letter and she has always*

Figure 29.2: Bertha Benthall

*been interesting to talk to especially when she talks about her ancient relations. She was a pretty little thing and a few years ago was heard to complain that she was losing her looks.*

The two photographs shown in Figure 29.2 are among the family archives.

## Winfred Benthall (1853–1912)

Winfred was born in 1853, on board ship, like his eldest brother. while Edward and Clementina were traveling to the Cape Colony on medical leave. He travelled back with them to England in 1855. In due course he attended Sherborne School and Pembroke College, Cambridge, and became a doctor. He had a successful medical practice near Derby and was a consulting physician at the Derbyshire Royal Infirmary. He married a widow named Phoebe Mary Christiana Shaw (née Harrison) in 1892, but they had no children. Paul Benthall wrote:

> *"In about 1908 he* [Winfred] *retired and in order to be near us he settled down at Staplake, Starcross, within a mile of our home at Cofton. He saved my life at least once when I was very ill. He was fond of shooting and a great companion of Charles* [Charles Francis Benthall, Winfred youngest brother and Paul's father – see Chapter 33]."

Winfred died in 1912, followed by his wife in 1921.

## Alfred Elliott Benthall (1856–1886)

Alfred, the seventh child and fourth son, was born at Sherborne, Dorset. Like his brother Winfred, he attended Sherborne School and became a doctor, a fellow of the Royal College of Physicians of Edinburgh. However, he died at Sherborne in 1886, aged just 29.

## Octavius Arthur Benthall (1859–1900)

Octavius (known to all as Octo) was the eighth child and fifth son. In the previous generation they waited for the eighth son to use that name, but this time around the sisters were allowed to be counted. Octo enrolled at Hertford College, Oxford, in 1877, obtained bachelor's and master's degrees, and then was ordained. He served as the vicar of a couple of Dorset parishes close to Sherborne – first Oborne, then Haydon. In 1888 he married Annie Harrison, the sister of Phoebe, whom Winfred would marry four years later. Octo and Annie also had no children. He died in 1900, she in 1926. Paul Benthall never knew him, but wrote: "*A clever and amusing man … he could have gone far but he had no ambition and died fairly young.*"

## *Chapter 30*

# WILLIAM HENRY AND EDITH BENTHALL: ANOTHER COUSIN MARRIAGE, AND ITS DOWNSIDE

Edith Benthall (1845–1932) was the third child of Edward and Clementina. She was sent back to England with her two older brothers shortly before her third birthday, and the three of them stayed for the next seven years with their uncle the Rev. John Benthall (see Chapter 17) and great-aunt Thornton, plus aunts Louisa and Laura and cousin William Henry, when he was not away at boarding school.

William Henry Benthall (1837–1909), son of that same Rev. John Benthall, left Westminster School after his father was fired in 1846 and was then sent to school at Marlborough College, a boarding school founded in 1843 "with the prime purpose of educating the sons of clergy."[319] From there he went up to Clare College, Cambridge, where:

> *…he at once got the first classical scholarship. During his first long vacation a clerkship in the India Office was thrown open to competition, and Henry obtained it, but as he was allowed to keep his term at Cambridge, he entirely supported himself by his Clerkship, Scholarship and two small Exhibitions which he gained. He ceased to read hard, and played in the University [cricket] eleven, and was also*

> *known as a racket player. Notwithstanding, he obtained a third class in the Mathematics Tripos.[i] He afterwards became private secretary to Lord Ripon, Mr. Stanfield, Lord Salisbury, Sir Stafford Northcote, the Duke of Argyle, in succession.[320]*

Outside of work, he played county cricket for Middlesex for many years.[321]

In 1866 Edith married William Henry – another first-cousin marriage. There are three pictures of her at Benthall Hall (see Figure 30.1, overleaf). The first is an unfinished watercolour by Laura of the three siblings sent home from India – Clement, Ernest and Edith – dating probably from about 1850. It is hard to say which boy is which, but Edith is in the centre. The second is a portrait miniature, a watercolour on ivory, painted in 1905 by Maud Worsfold. The third is a photograph dating from about 1910, shortly after her husband died, when she was still in formal widow's weeds. She lived to the age of 87, dying in 1932.

---

[i] Traditionally "Tripos" was the name given to the exams at Cambridge University that qualified a student for a bachelor's degree.

177

Figure 30.1: Edith Benthall, wife of William Henry Benthall

William Henry and Edith Benthall had three sons, and retired to Pevensey Road, St Leonards-on-Sea, Sussex. (They also had a daughter, Edith, who died at less than two weeks old.) The eldest son, Henry Everett Benthall (born in 1867 and known as Harry), attended Tonbridge School before going up to St John's College, Cambridge. He became a chartered accountant, spent some time in India as chief auditor for the Bengal Central Railway, then returned to England, became a company secretary, and died unmarried in 1919.

The first of the portraits in Figure 30.2 is a watercolour of Harry, painted in around 1877 by his aunt Laura Benthall. The next is a silhouette of William Henry and Edith's next son, the Rev. William Louis Benthall, dating probably from about 1890.

Born in 1868, William Louis became known in the family as "poor cousin Will." He likewise attended Tonbridge School and then St John's College, Cambridge. He was ordained in 1892, and served as a curate in various parishes. The database of Cambridge alumni states that he *"disappears from Crockford* [in] *1911"* and *"went into retirement for reasons of health."* For

reasons of mental ill-health, that is – he lived on until 1952, but for 40 years in a lunatic asylum near Exeter. His mental instability had become apparent in 1903, when he was first admitted to Bethlem Royal Hospital. The admission register for that period is available on the internet, and it gives some indication of his parlous state of mind. One of the admitting doctors wrote:

*The patient suffers from delusions and stated that he had been persecuted by Freemasons in Germany on account of his affection for a lady who he does not know but whom he supposes 'is of high position' and intimately associated with the Freemasons.*[322]

The *"supposed cause of insanity"* was *"Overwork."* It is not clear whether the German lady was a persistent part of William Louis's delusionary life, but it is clear that he became increasingly obsessed with his supposed genealogy, and a number of his books are at Benthall Hall with handwritten annotations that indicate that he believed himself to be either the rightful King of England or the rightful Emperor of Abyssinia, or both. He was briefly admitted to

Figure 30.2: Henry Everett (Harry) and William Louis Benthall

Bethlem again in 1907; remarkably, later that year he was appointed chaplain at the Anglican church in Düsseldorf. He left that position in 1910, and was institutionalised permanently in 1911, at a mental hospital near Exeter. His relatives believed that the root cause of his insanity was not overwork, but that he was the product of two first-cousin marriages, the first between his grandparents, Edward Benthall and Clementina Marshall, and the second between their daughter Edith and nephew William Henry Thus, he had only 10 great-great-grandparents, rather than the normal complement of 16.

The third son, Edward John (born in 1869 and known as Ted), attended Tonbridge School but did not go up to university. He married Sophia Alice Greene Butt at St Leonards-on-Sea, Sussex, in 1901, and lived there for a while. In the 1911 census they were living at Bracknell, Berkshire. He died childless at Countess Wear, just outside Exeter, in 1927, not far from the asylum where his brother was living. Records of his wife are elusive, but after his death she lived at West Malling, Kent, and died at Exmouth, Devon, in 1940.

# Chapter 31

# A WELSH CONNECTION:
# ERNEST BENTHALL AND HIS WIFE, JANE PRICE

Ernest was the second child of Edward and Clementina Benthall. He was born in 1843 at Jessore, now part of Bangladesh. After several years living with his uncle John, he was sent to Sherborne School, leaving in 1861. He was described by his nephew Paul Benthall as *"a dull but kindly man with a large beard who held an unimportant post in the India Office."* He joined the India Office (the reorganised version of the India Board of Control and the East India Company – see digression below) in 1865, as a junior clerk in its Military Store department, was promoted in 1877 to the position of senior clerk, and retired in 1889.

## DIGRESSION: THE INDIA OFFICE AND ITS MILITARY STORE

From 1784 to 1858 the affairs of the East India Company were monitored by the British government through the so-called Board of Control, whose secretary for a period (1812–1828) was Thomas Peregrine Courtenay and where Thomas Nelson Waterfield also worked for many years (see Chapter 16). In 1858 the East India Company was abolished, as a consequence of the previous year's Indian Rebellion, and its affairs were taken over by a new government department known as the India Office, into which the Board of Control was merged.

*At the peak of its commercial activities in the early nineteenth century, the East India Company [had] employed more than three thousand labourers in its London warehouses, the largest single body of civilian manual workers in the metropolis at that time.*[323]

After 1858 most of these warehouses were closed, with the exception of the Military Store, which moved to new premises in Lambeth, southeast London, and continued in operation there until 1947. This department was responsible for purchasing all kinds of materials required by the army and civil government of India, from helmets to railway locomotives.

Figure 31.1: Jane (and her sister Dora, right) and Ernest Benthall

In 1876 Ernest married Jane Rogers Price, who came from a respected Welsh family living in the parish of Ystradgynlais, in the Upper Swansea Valley, about 12 miles northeast of Swansea itself. Jane's father, William Price,[324] was a successful surgeon who built a house there named Glantwrch. Her mother, Mary Jenkins, was the daughter of Elias Jenkins, who from around 1804 until 1850 was the part-owner and manager of the White Rock Copper Works, a copper smelting business in the Lower Swansea Valley. Jane was the elder of two daughters. She and her younger sister, Dora, are the subjects of a watercolour portrait at Benthall Hall labelled as being of "*Jane and her sister Dorothy*" by J.J. Johnson, from about 1860 and framed in Liverpool (see Figure 31.1).

A portrait of Ernest as a child, with his elder brother Clement and his sister Edith, is reproduced in Figure 30.1. A portrait of Ernest as an adult, drawn in pastel on brown paper by Percy E.T. Thomas in 1911, is shown in Figure 31.1. Like the portrait of Jane and Dora, it is at Benthall Hall but not on display.

Photographic portraits believed to be of Jane's parents, William and Mary Price, are also in the family archives at Benthall Hall (see Figure 31.2).

There are also a number of silhouettes of the Jenkins family, Jane's maternal ancestors. These are briefly described in Appendix A, together with more details about the Jenkins family, since they are not particularly relevant to narrative of this book, but did end up at Benthall Hall.

Ernest and Jane Benthall had two daughters. The elder, Dorothy, was born in 1878 in London. The younger, born the following year also in London, was named Mary Clementina but known as Molly for most of her life.[i]

---

[i] Until, that is, her cousin Paul married Mollie Pringle, at which point the family reverted to calling her Clementina, to avoid confusion.

The family lived in Kensington for many years, but when Ernest retired from the Military Store they moved to Jane's hometown of Ystradgynlais, where she had inherited the family home, Glantwrch, and some other property. Ernest served as Commissioner of Taxes there from 1897 to 1917, and also as a justice of the peace (JP) at both Ystradgynlais and Pontardawe, a Valley town about halfway to Swansea. Those being somewhat undemanding jobs, the family appears to have travelled: there is no record of them in the 1891 census, but in 1901 they were recorded as being at Bournemouth. Jane died in Wales in 1906, unfortunately preceded by her daughter Dorothy in 1904. Ernest and Molly continued to live in Wales until 1917. The details are somewhat uncertain, but newspaper articles published during that time indicate that they moved from Glantwrch to Ystalyfera House, in an industrial village three miles down the Swansea Valley on the River Tawe.[325] While Ernest collected taxes and acted as a JP, Molly kept herself busy with good works and some modest academic pursuits, including possibly writing a biography of her ancestor, Elias Jenkins.[326]

Molly's name is remembered in that area for a more curious reason. There was a small pottery a few miles south of Ystalyfera named Ynysmeudwy, which flourished between 1845 and 1875, and whose output has recently become sought after by collectors. Molly came to possess a number of stoneware mugs with lead glazing that she believed had been made there in 1862. In November 1917 she gave the mugs away to children in the neighbourhood, with inscriptions on their bases such as: "*To Rachel Winter from M.C. Benthall Nov. 1917. Made in 1862 at*

Figure 31.2: William and Mary Price

Figure 31.3: Benthall Mugs

*Ynysmeudwy Pottery Swansea Valley*" (see Figure 31.3). These are now known in the Valley as "Benthall Mugs."[327] There are no clues as to who these children were in relation to Molly, how the mugs came into Molly's possession, or how she knew that they had been made at Ynysmeudwy, since they are unlike any of its other products.

One reason for Molly's largesse may have been that Ernest decided that year to resign as Commissioner of Taxes and move to Devon – perhaps it wasn't worth the effort to take a box of old mugs with them. Ernest bought Countess Wear House, in a suburb of Exeter, and which is now a Grade II listed building. The move may have been prompted by the need to have some family close to the asylum where cousin Will was housed and this is where his nephew Ted (son of William Henry and Edith Benthall – see previous chapter) died in 1927, and where Ernest himself died in 1928. His obituary in the *South Wales Voice* of 28 Saturday 1928 includes this comment:

*Mr. Benthall took a great interest in his magisterial work, both at Ystradgynlais and Pontardawe and soon after his arrival in the locality he began to study the Welsh language. In a short time he became sufficiently proficient to administer the oath in the vernacular. He was an income tax commissioner for Breconshire*

*and always took a keen interest in local affairs up to the time of his removal in 1917.*

Molly inherited Countess Wear House and continued to live there after her father died. She also inherited a number of houses in Swansea, in and around a street named Benthall Place, a housing development on property that had probably once belonged to her parents.

She continued to take an interest in supporting young women, and in 1931 donated £1,500 to the Sisters of St Elizabeth of Hungary, an Anglican order of nuns, who used it to set up a hostel for high-school girls in Bunbury, Western Australia. This was named the "Mary Clementina Hostel for Girls" in Molly's honour.

The first photograph in Figure 31.4 (see overleaf) is of Molly (left) and Dorothy as children, and the other two are of Molly later in life.

In 1933 she married her first cousin Floyer Dale, son of Madeleine Benthall and Edward Robert Dale. The story of their subsequent lives will be told in Chapter 34, once the lives of her aunt Madeleine and uncle Charles have been covered.

Figure 31.4: Mary Clementina (Molly) Benthall

# Chapter 32

## MARRYING INTO MADNESS: MADELEINE BENTHALL AND EDWARD ROBERT DALE

Paul Benthall wrote the following paragraph about his aunt Madeleine Anna Benthall (see also Figure 17.1):

*A beautiful girl whose life was a tragedy. She married a Dorset squire of good family but no education called [Edward Robert] Dale. His mother was an epileptic and I think committed suicide. Madeleine had a miserable life and her husband eventually went off his head and committed suicide also and in a particularly horrid way. Meanwhile two children had been born, a boy called Floyer and a girl called May, who was beautiful and had a most sweet and charming expression but who died in an asylum a homicidal maniac.*

There is much truth to this story, though not everything can be corroborated. Madeleine was born at Alipore, Calcutta, in 1847, after Clement, Ernest and Enid had been sent back to England (as explained in Chapters 29–31). She stayed with her parents and came back to England with them in 1855. Her husband, Edward Robert Dale, was the son of James Charles Dale (1791–1872),[328] a distinguished entomologist who was High Sheriff of Dorset in 1843 and who had married Marianne Lucy Wylde in 1848, when he was 57 and she was 26.

Edward Robert was their second son, born in 1853. The older son was also an entomologist and Edward also had some interest in insects, but was more passionate about electrical machinery. He was awarded a patent in 1878 for the invention of "*Improvements in instruments or appliances for measuring curves*"[329] and demonstrated his "Patent Curve Meters" at the Tottenham, Edmonton and Enfield Industrial Exhibition in October of that year.[330]

Madeleine[331] married Edward in August 1881, several months after the death of his mother. Their daughter, Mary Clementina Farr Dale, known as May, was born in 1882, and their son, James Floyer Dale, in 1883, both at Godmanstone, near Dorchester.

During the 1891 census Madeleine and daughter May were living on Long Street, Sherborne, with a butler, nurse and housemaid, while Edward was staying at the Three Choughs, a pub in Yeovil about five miles away. Madeleine died the following year. In 1901 May was living with her grandmother Clementina and her aunt Bertha at Sherborne (see Chapter 29), while her father Edward was listed as a boarder at a house in Salisbury, where he amused himself by conducting experiments with electricity. An article in *The Taunton Courier* of 19 August 1903 describes his suicide and the ensuing inquest in gruesome and graphic terms. The details are not easy to read, even today, but that article is reproduced in Appendix B for readers who are interested.

In 1911 May was living at 2 Pevensey Mansions, St Leonards-on-Sea, with two visitors named Mary and Ann Shaw. That house was a few hundred feet down the street from her aunt Edith Benthall (see Chapter 30), who lived at 33 Pevensey Road until she died in 1832. May died in 1933, and her probate record reads: "*DALE Mary Clementina Farr of 2 Pevensey Mansions St. Leonards-on-Sea spinster died 19 August 1933 at Hellingly Mental Hospital Sussex Probate Lewes 6 October to Westminster Bank Limited. Effects £13309 13s. 10d.*" The sole heir to her estate was her brother. The suggestion that she was a "*homicidal maniac*" was probably passed down to Paul via May's aunt

Bertha, who was known as a fund of stories about her family.

James Floyer Dale (1883–1942; known as Floyer), whom Molly eventually married, did not have an easy childhood. He was not with either parent in the 1891 census, although the census that year does show a "*James Dale*" of the right age as a "*patient*" in Holborn, London, probably at St Bartholomew's Hospital. In 1893 he was enrolled in the Derby School,[332] an ancient grammar school that was then expanding to become a "*nationally known public school.*"[333] In the 1901 census "James F. Benthall," aged 17 and born at Godmanstone, was registered as a "pupil" living at Derby, so was still attending that school.

In 1903 he was elected as a "Student" of the Institute of Electrical Engineers,[334] and enrolled at the University of Manchester, as evidenced

Figure 32.1: Madeleine Benthall and Edward Robert Dale

by an entry in the Manchester University Roll of Service, commemorating members of the university who participated in the First World War.[335] However, he did not graduate, and in the 1911 census a "James George Dale," aged 27, single and born at Godmanstone, was listed as living at Barnes, southwest of London, with the occupation of "hiring motor cars," which at that time was not the simple business that we take for granted today. According to the Roll of Service, during the War he enlisted as a volunteer in a branch of the Royal Engineers that manned searchlights at ports along the British coast. Paul Benthall described him as *"one of the best and kindest of men but not blessed with many brains or much education and a trifle eccentric at times."*

Floyer and his cousin Molly (see previous chapter), four years older than him, were close friends and he long thought they should marry, but both were aware of the insanity in his family and the dangers of first-cousin marriages. They did tie the knot eventually, but only when she was decisively past child-bearing age. The wedding took place at Countess Wear on 17 October 1933, 11 days after his sister May's probate was granted, when Molly was 54 and Floyer was 50.

The rest of their lives together will be described in Chapter 34, after first covering the career and family of the youngest of Edward and Clementina Benthall's children in the next chapter.

Figure 32.2: Mary Clementina Benthall and James Floyer Dale

# Chapter 33

## AN UNLIKELY COUPLE: THE REV. CHARLES FRANCIS AND ANNE BENTHALL

Charles Francis Benthall (1861–1936), or "The Rev." as he was known to his family, including his children, was the youngest son of Edward and Clementina Benthall.

He was educated at Sherborne School and went up to Pembroke College, Cambridge, where he took a degree in Classics, Mathematics and Hebrew. He became a master at a school in Godalming, Surrey, and then attended Salisbury Theological College. In 1890, soon after being ordained, he was appointed vicar of Cofton, near Dawlish in Devon (see Map 4), on the recommendation of his cousin William Waterfield, who had retired from India and was living in one of the larger houses in the area (see Chapter 16). Charles Francis stayed in that position for 27 years.[336]

Paul Benthall wrote this about him:

*My father* [i.e., Charles Francis] *was one of the last survivors of that 18th century phenomenon the sporting parson. He delighted in all the humbler forms of what are now called 'blood sports' and are condemned by a large section of our town-bred population. But though he enjoyed the outwitting and killing of wild animals, his real interest in these pursuits lay in the study of the animals concerned, and in all the other natural phenomena that he came across in the course of his sport. His knowledge of animals and plants was unscientific, but remarkably wide and in some respects profound. Although apparently lacking in a musical ear (certainly he had very little interest in music), he could identify with ease almost any bird call that could be heard in the south of England, and could usually pronounce without hesitation on the sex of the bird, and even its motives for making the noise in question. It was a rare event for him to see a bird that he could not immediately identify on sight, even at distances when most people would distinguish little or nothing. For some fifteen years before I was born he had been studying butterflies and moths, and had made a large and fairly comprehensive collection. Some specimens supplied by him are illustrated in Barrett's "British Lepidoptera". The garden at Cofton Vicarage, though small and rather disorganised, became full of an astonishing variety of unusual plants which attracted many visitors. As a parson he was lacking in spirituality, and was handicapped by a complete inability to sing or intone. His sermons usually contained scraps of erudite knowledge which gave them interest and he was gifted with a fund of practical common sense and generous sympathy which made him many friends. As a correspondent he was laconic and he kept in touch with his family mostly by postcards. One of these addressed to his wife in London read – 'Old Mrs. Partridge died yesterday. So did my best ferret. Otherwise all well. – C.F.B.'.*

There is a very fine portrait of Charles Francis at Benthall Hall, painted by Alethea Garstin in around 1925, and the family has old photographs of him as a boy (see Figure 33.1).

His wife, baptised Annie Theodosia Wilson but who answered only to "Anne" or "A.T. Benthall" (1867–1950), was described by her son Paul as "*a gifted and complex person, not liked by everyone, but with a great many devoted and admiring friends ... but I can say with certainty that few mothers can have*

*been more loved by their children.*" Her father, James Leonard Wilson, owned a bookbinding cloth manufacturing business, and his father had moved to London from Yorkshire in 1815. Anne's mother was Adelaide Ann Fripp, whose family included several prominent watercolourists and an eminent surgeon.

After the age of 40, Anne started to develop her interest in art, as described by Paul:

*Her first enterprise was etching, with which she had some success, and from there she went on to water colours, tempera, pottery, and woodcuts. Her younger sister Helen became a professional painter in oils but in this medium my mother made little progress. These artistic pursuits were continued until in old age her sight began to fail. Her water colours of*

Figure 33.1: The Rev. Charles Francis Benthall

189

*Devonshire and French scenery reached their best between 1912 and 1918.*

Paul also wrote:

*Two well-known men became her friends. The first was Sir Frank Brangwyn, the painter, whom with a party of other students and disciples she used to accompany on painting expeditions in France. The second was Eden Phillpotts, the novelist and poet, who lived at Torquay and often came to see us. He was a keen gardener and had much in common with my father. My mother illustrated several of his books with water colour sketches.*

The first portrait shown (Figure 33.2), by an unknown artist, was painted when Anne was about 15; the next two are undated photographs, and the fourth portrait was painted by Dame Ethel Walker RA (1861–1951) in around 1940. The first and last are on display at Benthall Hall.

She also wrote a children's book entitled *When I Was*, published in 1913 by Gay & Hancock, with an introduction by Eden Phillpotts and which she also illustrated.

Anne and Charles Francis had five children, as shown in Figure 33.4. One of the curiosities of this family was that they were all known by nicknames.

"Tom" and "Paul" will be accounted for later in great detail. The eldest child (with an encumbered set of baptismal names) was known sometimes as Enid or more commonly as "Crow." She was an early example of a female undergraduate at Oxford, where she attended Lady Margaret Hall and read History. She was expected to be a star and win a first-class degree, but had a meltdown at the last minute and ended with a "fourth." Paul Benthall ascribed this to "*overwork.*" She worked in a munition factory and on farms during the First World War, and then became a social worker. She died relatively young, in 1931.

"Mick" married Arthur Armstrong, who was at school with Tom and became a barrister, and then a county court judge travelling around the west of England. Mick and Arthur had three children and have a number of descendants in Britain, New Zealand and elsewhere. The watercolour in Figure 33.4, on display at Benthall Hall, is of Paul and Mick, painted by their mother Anne in about 1915.

"Doit" was fortunate in her parents' choice of godfather, James Broad Bissell, who died in 1913, leaving a wife but no children. When James died, Doit inherited from him Bishopsteignton House, a fine building on the banks of the River Teign, plus other investments.

Figure 33.2: Anne Benthall

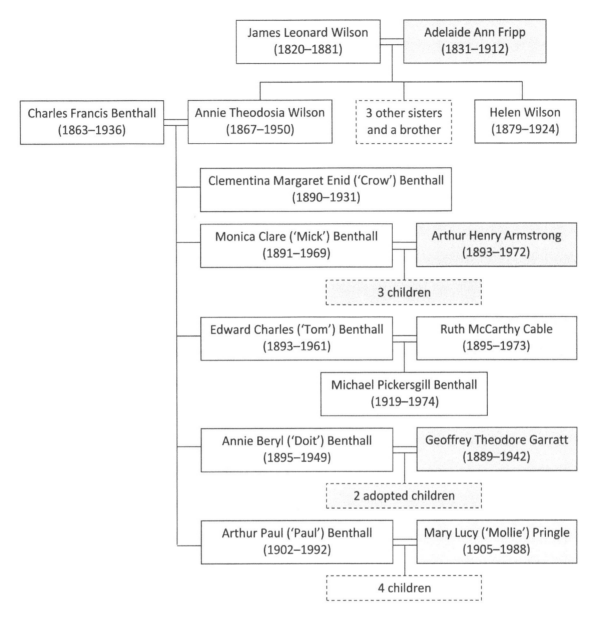

Figure 33.3: The family of Charles and Anne Benthall

Doit married Geoffrey Theodore Garratt, who had been educated at Rugby School and Hertford College, Oxford, and joined the Indian Civil Service in 1912. By 1916, when Doit first met him while visiting India, he had become an officer in the Indian Cavalry. They met up again in Tangier in 1920, and married soon after at Benthall Hall. They returned briefly to India, but soon left again and Geoffrey became a farmer, journalist and an active member of the Labour Party. At the start of the Second World War, aged 51, already a justice of the peace and having been awarded an MBE, he re-joined the army and was appointed a major in the Royal Pioneer Corps.[337] In 1942 he was running a training course on the disposal of land mines at the Pembroke Dock barracks when one or more of them exploded, killing him and 18 others. That disaster was hushed up and the details were not made public until 70 years later. Doit died in 1949. They had adopted two sons, and one of those has living descendants.

Figure 33.4: Paul and Mick Benthall

In 1918 Charles Francis decided to retire from his living at Cofton and, having inherited several legacies from his childless siblings, took a lease on Benthall Hall, which at that time had been empty for some years, probably since before the start of the First World War.[338]

During the three years that Charles Francis, Anne and their son Paul lived there, the house proved to be a magnet for family and friends. As mentioned above, Doit and Geoffrey were married at Benthall Hall in 1920, and some of Charles and Anne's grandchildren were baptised there. But after Paul finished his studies (see Chapter 37) and started to work, first in London and then in India, Charles and Anne decided to leave Benthall Hall and divide their time between Tangier and Devon instead, while attempting to sublease Benthall Hall until their own lease expired.

There was in those days a thriving expatriate British community in Tangier, including a number of artists. One of those was Anne's sister Helen, who had fallen in love with the city and bought a small house there in about 1912, followed by a much larger one in about 1921. When Helen died in 1924, Charles and Anne inherited the house and frequented it as their Moroccan base for several years after. It was during one of those visits that his portrait (see Figure 33.1) was painted.

Charles died in 1936. Soon after, Anne moved to Lindridge, a mansion owned by her son Tom and his wife Ruth (see Chapter 35), where she died in 1950.

## DIGRESSION: JAMES BROAD BISSELL (1846–1913)

James Broad Bissell's father was an "ironmaster" who had owned a foundry at Walsall, Staffordshire, and as a young man James was also involved in running the ironworks. After his father died, James sold the business, and for the rest of his life lived off the proceeds. He married twice, but had no children. His first wife was Julia Elizabeth Bagnall, whom he married in 1872. In around 1883 they moved to Diptford, in Devon, and in 1885 James stood for Parliament unsuccessfully as the Conservative candidate for Bristol (East). Soon afterwards they moved to Starcross (see Map 3) where Julia died in 1887. James became acquainted with other educated families in the area, including Charles Francis and Anne Benthall at Cofton, the Waterfields living at Eastdon, plus some descendants of Thomas Peregrine Courtenay and Hubert Cornish. Thus, when Doit was born in 1895, James agreed to be her godfather. He married again in 1897, to Edith Wolfe, daughter of the prebendary of Exeter, and they then moved to Bishopsteignton (see Map 3), where he served as a justice of the peace and vice-president of the Devonshire Association for the Advancement of Science, Literature and Art.

When he died his estate was valued at £95,506, or £76,219 after taxes (equivalent to about 60 times those figures in 2019). The executors were Anne Benthall and Philip Gay Waterfield (see Figure 16.1). He left a settlement of £10,000 to provide an income for his wife while she was alive, and after some bequests amounting to about £11,000, everything else, including the house, was to be held in trust for Doit, including the reversion of the settlement when his wife died. Curiously the beneficiaries of the other bequests included two granddaughters of T.P. Courtenay and a great-great-niece of the Rev. William Floyer Cornish, who had married Elizabeth Marshall (see Figure 12.1). After Doit died, Bishopsteignton House was sold by her sons and is now an assisted living residence.

# PART V.
## RETURN TO BENTHALL HALL

## Chapter 34

# MARY CLEMENTINA AND JAMES FLOYER DALE, CONTINUED.

In 1934 Mary Clementina (Molly) and James Floyer (Floyer) Dale, who we left as newly wedded in Chapter 32, purchased Benthall Hall and the 200-acre farm that surrounded it.

In Chapter 33 it was noted that Charles and Anne Benthall had leased Benthall Hall from the Forester family in 1918, but moved out again after three years and then sublet it for the last few years of the lease. But after the lease expired the Foresters were unable to find a new tenant, and the house remained empty. On 14 June 1934 Gilbert Benthall, son of Albert and grandson of Henry Benthall (see Chapter 18), saw an article in *The Times* newspaper announcing that Benthall Hall would be put up for auction on 14 July, made inquiries and was told that the asking price was £6,000, and that if the property was not sold it would be demolished and that the panelling would be shipped to the United States. Gilbert wrote to all the family members he could think of, and also to both the National Trust and the Society for the Protection of Ancient Buildings, asking if anyone could save it. The National Trust wrote back with regrets that it did not have funds available, and most of the others also sent regrets, but on 9 July Gilbert received a postcard from Mary Clementina Dale confirming that she and her husband had purchased the property: "*You*

*will be glad to know that the old hall has been bought by descendants of the W.B. who built it in 1535 who hope to live in it.*"[339]

The next year Floyer adopted his wife's surname, Benthall, to match their new residence. On 10 December 1935 *The London Gazette*, an official journal of the British government, contained the following announcement:

*I JAMES FLOYER BENTHALL, of Benthall Hall, Broseley, in the county of Salop, formerly of Countess Wear, near Exeter, in the county of Devon, Esquire, heretofore called and known as James Floyer Dale, hereby give notice that on the 24th day of October, 1935, I renounced and abandoned the use of my said surname of Dale, and assumed in lieu thereof the surname of Benthall; and further that such change of name is evidenced by a deed dated the 24th day of October, 1935, duly executed by me, and attested, and enrolled in the Enrolment Department of the Central Office of the Royal Courts of Justice on the 6th day of December, 1935. – Dated the 4th day of December, 1935. JAMES FLOYER BENTHALL. late James Floyer Dale.*

Two years later Floyer fell down a well in the backyard of Benthall Hall, probably as an attempt at suicide in the sad tradition of his family. This is the account written by Paul Benthall in 1940:

> *In the winter of 1937–38 Floyer got ill and one day Molly having left him alone for a few minutes in a chair in the West room, came back to find him gone but his gold watch and other valuables placed on a table beside the chair. As he was too weak to walk far and the weather was bitterly cold she started a search for her husband and before long he was found at the bottom of a well in a shrubbery behind the west side of the house. The well had always been a source of interest because there was always running water at the bottom of it and the current can easily be seen by peering down from the top. The shaft is about forty feet deep and to get Floyer out was a difficult and dangerous business, but Thomas [the gardener] and the butler managed it somehow though Floyer was helpless and had a broken arm. For months Floyer was very ill both physically and mentally, and when he got stronger physically he had to go to a mental hospital where he remains to this day.*

In 1941, as German bombers terrorised Britain and especially Greater London, Molly decided to lease Benthall Hall to Langley Place, a boys' school near Slough that wanted to move out of harm's way. Floyer was put into a hospital at Topsham, near Exmouth in Devonshire, and Molly took a job driving a canteen around the anti-aircraft gun sites on the hills of Exmoor, in North Devon. Floyer died in hospital in December 1942. While there, Molly also had her share of problems. According to Paul, who visited her in North Devon in 1944:

> *One night she was putting the van into a garage when the brake slipped off and the van ran over her, breaking her leg. She remained pinned underneath the van till morning and took a long time to recover from the consequences.*

Molly moved back to Shropshire in 1945 and continued to live at Benthall Hall. Around that time the family started calling her Clementina instead of Molly, to distinguish her from another Mollie Benthall, the wife of her cousin Paul Benthall, and who stayed (with her children) at Benthall Hall for several months in 1945 and 1946 while Paul was working in India, before settling in Devon in 1947 (see Chapter 37).

In 1952 Paul initiated a long conversation with the National Trust about it possibly acquiring the property. In 1957 the secretary of the National Trust finally visited Benthall Hall, and in a subsequent letter he wrote:

> *Yesterday morning I went for the first time to Benthall Hall and Mrs. Benthall [i.e., Clementina] took me round. The house was full of cripples having a holiday and Mrs. Benthall with her love of the place and the church seemed to me to be the nearest approach to a saint that I have ever met.*[340]

The following year the acquisition was completed, with an endowment of £45,000 provided by Paul, Clementina and Paul's elder brother Tom. Clementina continued to live there as the National Trust's tenant until February 1960, when her health began to fail. She died at a nursing home in Shrewsbury that September.

Before completing the story of the house and its revitalisation as a National Trust property, a fuller account of the lives of Tom, Paul and their wives is called for.

# Chapter 35

## MERCHANTS IN INDIA, PART 1: TOM ("SIR EDWARD") AND RUTH BENTHALL

The Rev. Charles and Anne Benthall, whose lives were described in Chapter 33, did not see eye to eye on all domestic matters. When their first son was born, Anne wanted to name him Tom, but Charles preferred Edward. Anne thought that she had won, but when the baby came to be baptised by his father, the Rev. Charles firmly announced his baptismal names to be "Edward Charles." Anne continued to call him Tom, whereas Charles, at least in writing, would always address his letters to "ECB." He was Tom to all his friends and close business colleagues, but when honoured with a knighthood he took the title Sir Edward Benthall.

Tom was a big man, six feet tall by the age of 13, and a formidable athlete in his youth. He was awarded a King's Scholarship to Eton College, and later went up to King's College, Cambridge, where in his first term he became a rugby "blue" (the university's highest sporting rank). When war was declared in 1914, he became an officer in a territorial battalion of the Devonshire Regiment, and was sent first to India and then on a relief expedition to besieged Kut in Mesopotamia (modern Iraq), where he was wounded and partly buried by a shell. He was invalided back to England and spent the rest of the war in the Intelligence Department of the War Office.

Tom married Ruth Cable in 1918. She was the daughter of Sir Ernest Cable (see Figure 36.1), who was born and grew up in Calcutta where his father had a job in the Customs House. When his father died in 1877,[341] Ernest was just 17, but he had to go to work to support his mother. His third job, which he started at the age of 21, was with a "managing agency" named Bird & Company, and in 1886 he became a partner in the business. Bird & Company had been founded in 1864 in Allahabad by brothers Paul and Sam Bird, and then relocated to Calcutta in 1870. Ernest guided the business through several crises, and by 1896 it employed 30,000 people in a wide range of industries, including transportation, coal mining and jute spinning. In 1903 he was elected president of the Bengal Chamber of Commerce, and in 1906 he was awarded a knighthood.

Bird & Company's lawyer in Calcutta was Herbert Sparkes, whose family was from Devon. Ernest met Herbert's sister, Lilian Sparkes, and they married in Devon in 1888, in due course producing four children. One died in infancy; the surviving three were Dawn, George and Ruth. George was born in 1891 and was expected to join – and inherit – the family business, but when the First World War started, he enlisted in the army and was killed fighting in Belgium in 1915. Herbert Sparkes retired to

Cofton, and Ernest Cable took a lease on a large mansion house named Lindridge, in the parish of Bishopsteignton about five miles away. In the words of Paul Benthall,

*"The Cable family generally lived near their relatives the Sparkes, and through the Sparkes family we came to know the Cable family and Tom met Ruth Cable. During the war Ruth went to India chaperoned by Anne and Doit to see Tom, and there they became engaged."*

That trip took place shortly after the death of Ruth's brother George.

Tom and Ruth married when the war was over, and their son Michael was born in 1919. In 1921 the family moved to India, and Tom joined Bird & Company. At that time also, Sir Ernest Cable was elevated to the peerage, as Baron Cable of Ideford. It was then quite easy to acquire such an honour, since not long previously the prime minister, David Lloyd George, had found a way to raise money for his party by selling titles. The going rate for a peerage was somewhere above £50,000, the equivalent of around £3,000,000 in 2020. The title also allowed Sir Ernest's children to flaunt their apparent superiority. As the daughter of a peer, Ruth's formal name became "The Honourable Mrs. Edward Benthall."

Ernest purchased the freehold of Lindridge and the surrounding estate in 1924, but died in 1927. A deal was made with his executors and the many minority shareholders in the Bird & Company conglomerate for Tom to take full ownership of the business, and for the others to be gradually bought out with its profits. This was not finally accomplished for another 20 years. Lindridge became the family home while Michael was at school in England (see Chapter 39 for an account of Michael's life).

Tom soon became a public figure in Calcutta. In 1931 he became the President of the Associated Chambers of Commerce in India, and then was selected to participate in the second Round Table Conference (held in London in September to December of that year to discuss constitutional reforms for India) officially representing the commercial interests of the Europeans then living in India. This involved long and difficult negotiations with Mahatma Gandhi and others in an attempt to have wording included in the draft agreement that would protect the European community from legal or administrative discrimination or from expropriation without compensation. During those three months he got to know Gandhi very well, and after Gandhi's death he wrote a memoir entitled "Reflections of Mahatma Gandhi".[342] Among other anecdotes, he wrote:

*These meetings recall certain unforgettable pictures to my mind. I see him sitting in a Queen Anne bergère armchair in the flat which my mother-in-law had lent us in Berkeley Square, an incongruous figure in the background of antiques and brocades. I see us after a very long sitting in the apartments of G.D. Birla at Grosvenor House Hotel, which ended at 2 a.m., and as he came to see me to the lift we weighed each other on a machine in the corridor. I turned the scales at 18 stone 4 lbs and he at 7 stone 5 lbs in two dhotis. How we laughed!*

As a result of his participation at that conference Tom was awarded a knighthood. Thereafter his formal name became "Sir Edward Benthall" and Ruth's "The Honourable Lady Benthall." Such were the niceties of the British honours system.

There are individual portraits of Tom and Ruth at Benthall Hall, both by painted by Glyn

Philpot but with ten years between them (see Figure 35.1). The portrait of Tom dates from 1925, while that of Ruth dates from 1935.

In 1939, at the start of the Second World War, Tom and Ruth moved to London where he had a job at the Ministry of Economic Warfare, which oversaw the conduct of spying, sabotage and intelligence in continental Europe. Lindridge became a refugee centre, housing children displaced by the war. When the German bombing started in 1940, Tom and Ruth left their basement flat in the centre of London and rented a "villa cottage" in Walton-on-Thames (a few miles southwest of London) and commuted into London every day. (During this time, when food was rationed and shortages frequent, Lindridge remained a source of protein, in the form of eggs and rabbits). In November that year, a stray bomb fell in a field close to Lindridge and blew out all the windows in the house. When Ruth heard about the details,

she wrote to a friend that *"the hens didn't ruffle their feathers … but laid scrambled eggs the next day"*.

Early in 1942, Tom was sent back to India to became Minister for War Transport in the Viceroy's Executive Council, the body responsible for governing the country. In 1945 he was awarded a second and more prestigious knighthood: Knight Commander of the Order of the Star of India.

After the war Tom was appointed as a governor of the British Broadcasting Corporation (BBC). He also continued to be involved in public life, and in 1953 led a government-sponsored trade mission to the Middle East, visiting Baghdad, Beirut, Damascus, Jeddah and Kuwait to promote British exports.[343] Later in that decade he began to suffer from heart problems and died in 1961. But before his death, he joined with his brother Paul, and cousin Mary Clementina to help fund the endowment

Figure 35.1: Ruth and Tom Benthall

required to complete the acquisition of Benthall Hall by the National Trust.

Not long after Tom's death, Ruth broke her hip, became bed-ridden, and moved to a flat in London. Michael arranged for the sale of the Lindridge estate, and the family portraits that had accumulated there were moved to Benthall Hall. Ruth died in 1973.

## DIGRESSION: MAURICE FOGT

Tom and Ruth were close friends in Calcutta with a French merchant named Maurice Fogt who, with his brother Georges, ran a business there.

Maurice-Pierre-François Fogt was born in Paris on 16 December 1890. His older brother named Georges was born in 1887. His father was named Henri, and his mother Celine.[344] It is likely that he became a medical student, but the earliest official record of his life dates from 1915, when he became an ambulance driver in the French army's "*59e Bataillon de chasseurs a pied*". By 1917 he had risen to the rank of "*Médecin aide-major de 1e classe*". Once the war was over, he resumed his studies and in 1919 he obtained his medical degree, with his thesis entitled "*L'Hematosalpinx par malformation congenitale*". He did not go into medical practice, although he remained for many years on the formal list of Army Reserve doctors. Instead he moved to Calcutta, where his brother Georges was already living and had married an English woman named Vera Louis Bryan in 1917. In 1921 it was reported in the official French papers that Maurice was awarded the Croix de Guerre and appointed a *Chevalier de la Légion d'Honneur*. A week later, another French newspaper announced that "*in Calcutta, Maurice Fogt, Chevalier de la Légion d'Honneur*", had married Doris Isabelle de le Pena, from London. Although born in England, she moved with her parents, Stanley and Minnie, to Montgomery Pennsylvania. How she then met Maurice is a mystery.

In 1940, Tom was working in London and he and Ruth had rented a small house in Walton-on-Thames, which was safer than their London basement when bombs were falling every night. Maurice lived with them there, since he had been *'bombed out of all his flats'*.[345] He went on to make broadcasts in French, and obtained some formal appointment within Charles de Gaulle's "government in exile". After the war, he moved to Le Tignet, a village in the south of France. During the 1950s Ruth complained a lot about her sciatica, and spent most of her time being treated by her personal doctor, Maurice, at his villa there. After Tom died, the family expected that she would move there permanently, but sadly he was diagnosed with cancer and died not long after.

Georges and Vera also had moved to London when war broke out and lived in Chelsea. They had a son, Maurice Peter Fogt, who became a Lieutenant in the Royal Ulster Rifles. He took part in the "Battle of the Bulge", also known as the "Ardennes Offensive" and died in the Netherlands in January 1945.

Maurice and Doris had a daughter named Mimi, who is the subject of a later digression–see Chapter 39.

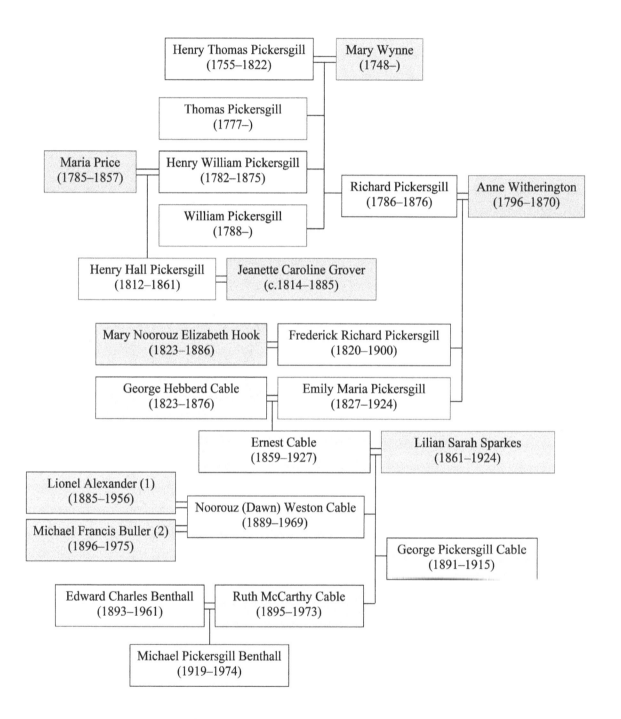

Figure 36.1: Pickersgill and Cable Family Tree

# Chapter 36

# THE PICKERSGILL PORTRAITS

Ruth Benthall's paternal grandmother was Emily Maria Pickersgill, whose father was a landscape painter named Richard Pickersgill, who himself came from a family of artists now much more famous than him, including his brother Henry William, his son Frederick Richard, and his nephew Henry Hall Pickersgill. The relationships between these painters and their connections to Ruth's grandmother are illustrated in Figure 36.1.

Two paintings by Richard's brother Henry William and two by his son Frederick Richard are on display at Benthall Hall. Figure 36.2 shows the two by Henry William Pickersgill.

There has been considerable confusion about these paintings. For many years they were both described as being portraits of Richard's daughter Emily Maria – i.e., Ruth's grandmother – and that may be the case with the one on the right. But the other is certainly not of her, based on recent research by Lucasta Miller, who

Figure 36.2: Henry William Pickersgill Paintings

has confirmed that it was exhibited at the Royal Academy in 1828 (one year after Emily Maria's birth) as *The Minstrel of Chamouni*, and that the sitter was in fact a young woman named Letitia Elizabeth Landon.[346] An engraving of this painting was then used as the frontispiece of the 1830 volume of *The Amulet*, a collection of essays and poems published annually by Samuel Carter Hall[347] and edited by his wife, Anna Maria. That volume also contained a poem written by Mrs. Pickersgill, likewise entitled "*The Minstrel of Chamouni*." But there was an underlying irony in this that was only apparent to the cognoscenti of the time: Letitia Elizabeth Landon (1802–1838) was a literary prodigy and a well-known poetess by the age of 20, publishing her poems above the initials "L.E.L." in *The Literary Gazette*, a weekly journal edited by William Jerdan. Her poetry was influenced by the "pastoral-erotic style"[348] as exhibited in the writings of Keats, Shelley and Byron. For example, Keats had written in "The Eve of St. Agnes" (a poem first circulated privately in manuscript and then published in 1820 in a less erotic version):

> *Awakening up, he took her hollow lute, –*
> *Tumultuous, – and, in chords that tenderest be,*
> *He play'd an ancient ditty, long since mute,*
> *In Provence call'd, "La belle dame sans mercy":*
> *Close to her ear touching the melody; –*
> *Wherewith disturb'd, she utter'd a soft moan:*
> *He ceased – she panted quick – and suddenly*
> *Her blue affrayed eyes wide open shone:*
> *Upon his knees he sank, pale as smooth-sculptured stone.*

In 1824 Letitia published her first book-length poem, *The Improvisatrice*. The first edition sold out within a day, and six more editions were printed by the end of 1825. It included this oblique reference to Keats' stanza.

> *My hand kept wandering to my lute,*
> *In music, but unconsciously*
> *My pulses throbbed, my heart beat high,*
> *A flush of dizzy ecstasy*
> *Crimsoned my cheek.*

In preparation for the publication of her book, Jerdan commissioned Henry William Pickersgill to paint a picture of a minstrel with a flushed cheek likewise entitled *L'Improvisatrice*, and it was exhibited in 1823. It depicted a young woman in Mediterranean dress playing a lute. The name of the sitter was not published, but may have been Letitia.

In 1825 Pickersgill painted and exhibited a formal portrait of Letitia, wearing a fancy Spanish hat and an abundance of décolletage, but his 1828 painting of the *Minstrel of Chamouni*, shown above, reverted to a more modest costume dress and did not identify the name of the sitter, although it would have been easily recognisable to anyone who knew her. In Miller's words, "*This more hygienic minstrel has attached prim pink ribbons to her lute, which she delicately plucks with a plectrum, as if afraid of touching the strings directly.*"[349]

By then Letitia was trying to make a change in her public image, since it was widely known within the London literary cognoscenti that she had given birth to two children out of wedlock, both fathered by Jerdan: the first, Ella, in 1823 and the second, Alfred, in 1826. She was not the demure, "*pure and simple peasant girl*" described in Mrs. Pickersgill's poem.[350] Most reviews were scathing. Whoever commissioned the painting – probably Jerdan – did not pay for it, so the painting stayed in the family.

Henry William and Richard Pickersgill were both born in London and baptised at a Nonconformist chapel in the district of Holborn. Richard married Ann Witherington, the daughter of a landscape painter, and their two children were Emily Maria and her elder brother, Frederick Richard Pickersgill, who also became a well-known painter. The two paintings by Frederick Richard at Benthall Hall are a portrait of a *Lady in a Persian Dress* – probably the artist's wife, Mary Noorouz Elizabeth, sister of yet another landscape painter, J.C. Hook – and a depiction of *Samson Betrayed* (see Figure 36.3).

Various attributions, as of 2018, have stated that the *Lady in a Persian Dress* was Ruth Benthall's great-grandmother. But if the sitter was indeed Frederick Richard's wife, then that would have made her Ruth's great-aunt.

A family anecdote is that Tom Benthall had *Samson Betrayed* hung next to his own portrait so that he could wave a hand in that general direction and invite visitors to look at the "*portrait of me as a young man.*"

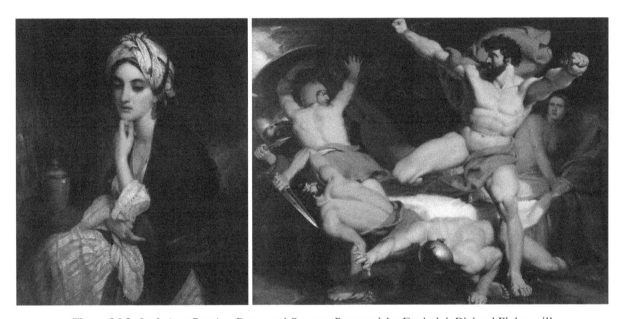

Figure 36.3: *Lady in a Persian Dress* and *Samson Betrayed*, by Frederick Richard Pickersgill

# Chapter 37

## MERCHANTS IN INDIA, PART 2: PAUL AND MOLLIE BENTHALL

Paul Benthall, the youngest son of Charles and Anne Benthall, followed his brother Tom to India, was also honoured with a knighthood, and became Sir Paul Benthall KBE. Figure 37.1 shows a portrait of him as a young boy painted by his aunt, Helen Wilson, alongside a much later portrait of him with his wife, Mollie, from 1984. Both of these are at Benthall Hall, together with the portrait of Paul with his sister Mick (see Figure 33.4).

Paul wrote extensively about his childhood and his life up until about 1953, and the quotations here are excerpted from his own notes. Six years younger than his sister Doit, he grew up in the vicarage at Cofton, near Dawlish in South Devon, where there were few other children. Some of the other families spoke "*the King's English*," but most of the local country people conversed in "*Demshurr*," a dialect that was "*almost unintelligible to strangers*" but in which Paul became fluent.

As a child Paul was beset with numerous health issues, and contracted pneumonia soon after being sent off to boarding school at the age of nine:

*There were no antibiotics in those days and pneumonia was always dangerous as well as*

Figure 37.1: Paul and Mollie Benthall

*very painful. I survived the crisis but pleurisy developed and the fluid in my pleural cavity turned septic. A large accumulation of puss pushed my heart out of place and forced the bones in my shoulder upwards into a strange deformity.*

His mother then reached out to Sir Alfred Fripp, her second cousin (and onetime surgeon to King Edward VII), who removed part of a rib in order to drain his lung. Soon after that he developed a fistula, which required another operation. The cause was thought to be tubercular, and since the only "cure" in those days for tuberculosis was fresh air, he returned home and lived in a shed in the garden, *"seldom entering the house except for meals, and never to sleep."* Then one morning, at the age of 12, he woke up to find that his right cheek was paralysed. Although diagnosed at the time as Bell's palsy, 60 years later a doctor told Paul that this was unlikely, and that the paralysis was probably caused by shingles of the mouth.[351] As a result, what schooling he obtained was at home.

Slightly before this latest affliction, in the winter of 1912 when Paul was approaching his eleventh birthday, his mother Anne had taken him and Doit on a visit to Tangier, Morocco, where his Aunt Helen had recently bought *"a modest bungalow with a small garden and a view over the Straits of Gibraltar."* They stayed for four months, and his mother hired a tutor to teach him Classical Arabic.

The next year it was decided that he should go to Eton. This was enabled by Doit having *"inherited a small fortune from her godfather"* (see Chapter 33), and for a year his elder sister Crow coached him in the garden shed, *"warmed by an oil heater,"* on the subjects required for him to take the entrance exam, which he passed in 1915.

In spite of his earlier lung problems, Paul took up rowing at Eton, but he continued to suffer from ill-health, including a case of rheumatic fever.

In 1918 Paul's parents moved to Benthall Hall (see Chapter 33), and thereafter he spent his school vacations in Shropshire. He developed a great love of the house and the surrounding countryside. In 1920 he went up to Christ Church, Oxford. In his first year he continued to demonstrate his rowing ability by becoming stroke of the college's first eight and successfully defending its position at the Head of the River Race. But he was subsequently diagnosed with a leaking heart valve, caused by the rheumatic fever, and advised to avoid all forms of energetic exercise, thereby ending his rowing career.

Even before going up to Oxford, Paul had decided that he wanted to go to India to work – spending the full three years at university was never his plan. His brother Tom, by then working in India, offered him a job there with Bird & Company.

But before going to India, Paul needed *"some preliminary training."* He attended a business training college, joined an accounting firm as an unpaid intern, and then in 1923 moved to Glasgow, where he worked for a colliery, doing office paperwork in the mornings and going *"down the pit"* in the afternoons as an assistant to the manager or surveyor. His work there was cut short by an attack of appendicitis that almost killed him:

*The ride in the ambulance over the bumpy Glasgow cobbles was a trip I shall never forget. The operation took place immediately on my arrival in the hospital without any preparation, and the anaesthetic was pure chloroform, an obsolete practice elsewhere but still favoured in such cases by some doctors in Scotland. The appendix burst as it was removed and peritonitis was only avoided by a small margin.*

One of Bird & Company's major businesses was the spinning and weaving of jute, a coarse but strong vegetable fibre grown primarily in East and West Bengal (the former nowadays part of Bangladesh, the latter of India) and used to make carpet backing, burlap, and other coarse cloth. Paul spent time in early 1924 studying the jute business, including more time in Scotland being shown around the jute mills of Dundee. Later that year he sailed for Calcutta to take up the position of "Mercantile Assistant" with Bird & Company. He spent two years at a jute mill near Calcutta and was then posted to a series of assignments throughout the region, before being brought back to the head office in Calcutta.

Paul went on his first home leave in 1928, and his second in 1932, on each occasion for six months and staying with his parents, who by then were living as retirees at Teignmouth, on the Devon coast. Halfway through the second of these furloughs, his parents received a letter from Warren Sparkes, a first cousin of Ruth Benthall (see Chapter 35) "*who on the way back from the east with his family had met a girl called Mollie Pringle who was coming to stay at Teignmouth.*" Paul and his mother went to call, and, as he wrote later: "*to condense an enthralling time into words, we got engaged in August about a week before I had to go back to India. When I sailed we had met a total of 19 times in all.*"

That December, Mollie travelled out to India with her sister. Paul took a train from Calcutta to Bombay to meet them, and he and Mollie were married there on New Year's Eve, 1932. A number of small paintings of Mollie Benthall's ancestors and relatives are in the National Trust collection, and her family background, together with images of those portraits, is covered in the next chapter.

Paul continued to work at Bird & Company in Calcutta until 1953. He became a partner in 1934, and was deeply involved in the management of the company's jute mills. When his brother Tom became more involved in public affairs in Britain as well as in India throughout the Second World War, Paul became one of the two senior partners managing the business. In that role he was able to make a decisive contribution to the war effort by manufacturing a huge number of cheap "parajutes" to resupply the allied troops besieged by the Japanese 31st Division at Kohima, in Northeast India. This is an abbreviated account of the story he told in his memoirs:

*During the cold weather of 1942/1943 General Slim struggling with the problem of supplying his armies,[352] conceived the idea that supply-dropping parachutes, which were scarce and expensive when made of silk or artificial fibres, could be made cheaply and in large quantities out of jute. A young officer came to our office to discuss the matter and a series of experiments was carried out. In a few weeks a practicable parachute had been devised but there was a difficulty in making large quantities of suitable cloth because the necessary reeds for the looms were not available and to have obtained more would have taken months. (A reed is a device for correctly spacing and ordering the warp yarns.) The point was referred to me as a serious obstacle to proceeding with the plan, but I was able to suggest a solution. Parachutes are usually made with a large vent at the apex which was supposed to act as a safety valve by allowing air to escape when the parachute opened with a jerk, thus preventing its bursting. I proposed to have no hole in the top, but to make the cloth with the next size in reeds to the correct size, which (incorrect) size happened to be available in large numbers. This would have the effect of making many very small holes in the cloth, dispersed at regular intervals, and a multitude of small holes might do as well as one big hole. The idea was tried out and found to work, and the jute parachute or "parajute" was ready for manufacture in quantity. However, all preparations having been made for mass production, no order was received and we almost forgot the matter.*

*Several months later a brigadier arrived in my office straight from the front with an urgent request from the C.–in- C. [Commander-in-Chief]. A British division was surrounded in the Arakan and there was a great need for parajutes. Could we make 200,000 in two months? I had to tell him that this was quite impossible, but we had made arrangements for their manufacture in many jute mills and we could start manufacturing in all of them the following morning. He explained that he could give me no formal order, and the C.–in- C. could not be quite sure that we would ever be paid, but he felt fairly confident that we would get our money. I took the brigadier round to see the chairman of the jute mills association, who agreed with me that it was in the best interests of the shareholders of the jute mills to supply the parajutes on these terms, and we undertook to do our best. To*

*await a formal order would have wasted at least a month. Our managers worked all night to get the production started in the morning. I forget how many parajutes were eventually made but the number came to somewhere near 200,000, and the cost was about £1 each against £10 or £20 for a conventional parachute. Eventually after a long argument with the government we got paid. As he records in his book "Defeat into Victory", Lord Slim got a severe reprimand for not buying through the proper channels. He replied that he "never wanted to find a more proper channel than those Calcutta jute men."*

*It may be claimed that the parajutes had a decisive effect on the war. The allies had almost complete command of the air and with the aid of thousands of parajutes they were able to supply our forces wherever needed; but the Japanese had to drag everything through mountains and jungles. They achieved little by surrounding a British force because it could be supplied from the air, but the surrounding troops soon ran out of everything and had either to die or retreat. Many died.*

Although relatively overlooked in modern history books, the battle of Kohima has been described as the turning point of the Japanese offensive into India in 1944 – the "*Stalingrad of the East*" – and was once voted by the British Army Naval Museum as "*Britain's Greatest Battle.*"[353]

After the war, in 1947, India gained independence. Paul became the senior resident partner in Bird & Company, and Vice-President of the Bengal Chamber of Commerce. In that capacity he twice met with Mahatma Gandhi, who was

211

publicly promoting a campaign to improve the Calcutta slums as a way to defuse the growing violence, and was demanding that the business community take charge of the project. In 1948 he was appointed president of the Bengal Chamber of Commerce, and spent much of the year meeting with senior officials and ministers in the Indian government. He took that position again in 1950, when the incumbent president was murdered by a mob. He was awarded a knighthood that year, and took the title of Sir Paul Benthall KBE. In 1953 he decided to retire from India and moved himself and his family back to England, where he took up residence in Surrey. He continued to run the London subsidiary of Bird & Company, and also took on several other part-time positions in the City of London, as a board member of the Chartered Bank (now Standard Chartered) and of the Royal Insurance Company (now RSA), and as chairman of the board of a trading company named Amalgamated Metal Corporation (now part of the AMC Group).

By 1957 Paul had negotiated an agreement with the National Trust and convinced Mary Clementina Benthall – then living at Benthall Hall, and who had told Paul that he would inherit the house when she died – that she should not bequeath the house to him, but rather donate it to the National Trust. He persuaded Tom to participate, and between them they found the money that the National Trust had decided it needed in order to take on the property. As part of the arrangement, family members were to be offered the ability to lease the house from the National Trust and make it their home, while keeping parts of it open to the public.

Clementina died in 1960, and in 1962 Paul and Mollie sold their house in Surrey and moved to Benthall Hall, thereby fulfilling an ambition that he had nurtured for 40 years. They worked with the National Trust management to prepare the house to be occupied as a family residence but also open to visitors in the summer. For ten years he divided his time between Benthall Hall and London, but retired from his business commitments in the City in 1972. They lived at Benthall Hall until she died in 1988 and he died in 1992.

Apart from his business career, Paul had a wide variety of interests. He was an avid sailor, and for much of his life he owned some kind of sailboat, the last of which was a dinghy that he kept in the Isles of Scilly. He was also an enthusiastic botanist. During the war he wrote a book entitled *The Trees of Calcutta and Its Neighbourhood*, which was published in 1946 and is now viewable in digitised form on the internet. As a result of that effort, he became a fellow of the Linnean Society of London, and later he was appointed chair of a Parliamentary committee on "Transactions in Seeds," whose unanimous recommendations led to the Plant Variety and Seeds Act of 1964. Meanwhile, he became a fellow of the British Chess Problem Society, which published a few of the problems he composed. Between 1962 and 1972 he spent much time in London engaged in genealogical research, in the days before the internet made it so much simpler. His writings on this subject have been invaluable while doing research for this book.

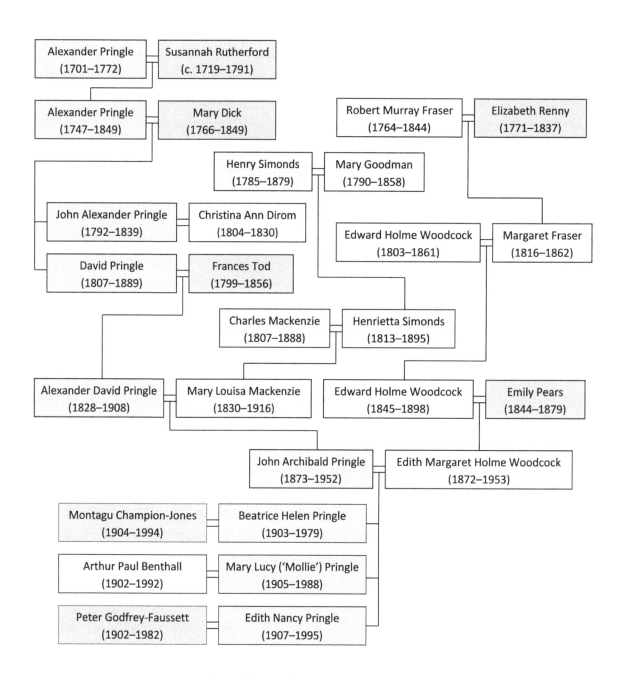

Figure 38.1: Mollie Benthall's forebears

# Chapter 38

## MOLLIE BENTHALL'S FAMILY: SCOTTISH CONNECTIONS

Mollie Benthall played a crucial role in managing Benthall Hall after it was taken over by the National Trust and when she and Paul moved to live there in 1962. There are several portraits of her ancestors and relatives in the Benthall Hall collection.

Mollie was baptised Mary Lucy Pringle in 1905, the second of three daughters of John Archibald Pringle, a mining engineer, and his wife, Edith. Their eldest daughter, Betty, was born while John Archibald was working in South Africa; Mollie was born two years later at Leamington Spa, Warwickshire. He then obtained a post in Brazil, where the third daughter, Nancy, was born in 1907. A few years after that, he obtained a position at the Kolar Gold Fields, near Mysore, in South India, southwest of Bangalore, where the whole family moved. They were in England on home leave at the start of the First World War, but returned to India and stayed there until 1920, when Mollie and her sisters were sent back to an English boarding school. Mollie visited India again in 1924, but then took a three-year teacher training course at the Froebel Educational Institute, London, and became a primary school teacher. Her sister Nancy married Peter Godfrey-Faussett, who was in the Ceylon Forest Service, and it was on her return

from a visit to see them in 1832 that Mollie met Warren Sparkes, Ruth Cable's cousin (see previous chapter), and through him met Paul.

John Archibald Pringle, Mollie's father, was a member of one branch of the widespread Pringle clan, another branch of which is now well known for its clothing business. Mollie's branch of the clan traces its descent from Robert Hoppringle, the builder of Smailholm Tower in the Scottish Borders. (Smailholm is today one of eight sites in Scotland awarded five stars as a tourist attraction by the Scottish tourism office).[354] There are miniatures at Benthall Hall of several members of the Pringle family, as well as of other ancestors of Mollie's, and the chart in Figure 38.1 explains their relationships to each other.

John Archibald was the eleventh out of 12 children of the Rev. Alexander David Pringle (1828–1908), vicar of Blakeney, in Gloucestershire. Before settling down back in England, Alexander David had spent several years in the town of Hope, British Columbia, where he commissioned the first church to be built on that province's mainland. His eldest children were born there, in a parsonage made of logs.

John Archibald's mother was Mary Louisa Mackenzie, whose father was the Rev. Charles

Mackenzie. Charles was born at Torridon, a village in a remote part of the Scottish Highlands, but became prebendary of St Paul's Cathedral, London. Charles's father, John (not shown in Figure 38.1), married Ann Isabella van Dam, whose great grandfather was Rip van Dam, acting governor of New York Province from 1731 to 1732, and who has many illustrious American descendants. Rip's son Isaac lived in New Jersey, and his grandson, another Isaac (Ann Isabella's father), was a wealthy merchant based on the Caribbean island of St Eustatius who bought gunpowder in France and sold it to the revolutionaries during the American War of Independence.

Mollie's great-grandfather, Alexander's father, David, and his grandfather, another Alexander, were in the East India Company's civil service, as were David's three elder brothers, John Alexander, William and Robert (who are not shown in the above pedigree).[355]

David Pringle had the misfortune to be a passenger on the East Indiaman *Kent* when, on 1 March 1825, it caught fire in a storm in the Bay of Biscay with 641 people aboard. Remarkably, other ships in the area came to the rescue, and before the Kent finally exploded 547 survivors had been pulled from the water, including David.

There is a fine miniature of David's brother John Alexander and a watercolour of John Alexander's wife, Christina Ann Dirom, at Benthall Hall (see Figure 38.2). They married in 1828. John Alexander's portrait was painted at about that time, and is attributed to Andrew Plimer. The portrait of Christina Ann is listed as "Italian School, c. 1825." Sadly, she died in Calcutta two years after their marriage.

The father of David Pringle and his three brothers was Alexander Pringle, 8th Laird of Whytbank and Yair (two estates on the banks

Figure 38.2: John Alexander Pringle (1792–1839) and his wife, Christina Ann

Figure 38.3: Mrs and Mr Alexander Pringle

of the River Tweed, not far from Melrose in the Scottish Borders). His father, the 7th Laird, also Alexander, had supported the Jacobite rising of 1745 when Charles Edward Stuart, grandson of King James II of England and VII of Scotland, landed in the far northwest of Scotland from his exile in France. The British Army was then busily deployed in Europe as part of the War of the Austrian Succession, and a grand plan had been hatched by the French and Spanish to restore a Catholic monarchy in Britain. The plan involved an insurrection in Scotland, led by "Bonnie Prince Charlie," and a French invasion on the southern coast of England. Charles raised an army, marched south, captured Carlisle and Manchester, and then got as far as Derby, Nottinghamshire. At that point there was no sign of a French invasion, and the cities they had captured did not produce many recruits to their cause. Reality intervened, and the insurgents decided that they were outnumbered and

at risk of being cut off, so decided to turn back and consolidate their position in Scotland. They were defeated, decisively and brutally, in 1746 at the Battle of Culloden by a redcoat army representing the incumbent House of Hanover.

In the aftermath, Alexander, like Charles's other supporters, was heavily fined and had to sell the Yair estate, but his son went to India and made enough money to buy it back.[356] This Alexander built a new mansion, raised his family there, became a Member of Parliament and was a friend of Sir Walter Scott, who also lived nearby and who described the young Pringle brothers as: "*Those sportive boys, companions of my mountain joys, just at the age 'twixt boy and youth, when thought is speech, and speech is truth.*"[357] There are portraits of Alexander junior and of Mary Dick, his wife, at Benthall Hall (see Figure 38.3).

The miniature portrait of Mary Dick, Mrs Alexander Pringle, was painted by Richard Cosway RA in about 1780. The miniature of

Alexander was painted 15 years later by George Engleheart, but deliberately in the style of the earlier one to provide a matched pair.

Figure 38.4: Robert Murray Fraser

We turn now to Mollie's maternal ancestry. There are also portraits of two of her other great-great-grandparents at Benthall Hall: Robert Murray Fraser and Mary Goodman, Mrs Henry Simonds. Mollie's mother was baptised Edith Margaret Holme Woodcock, the daughter and granddaughter of men both named Edward Holme Woodcock. Edith's mother was born Emily Pears, the daughter of Abijah Pears (1799–1895) and his wife Elizabeth (née Bray). Abijah was a ribbon manufacturer in Coventry who became mayor of that city in 1842.[358] Abijah and Elizabeth became close friends with their next-door neighbour Marian Evans, better known today as the novelist George Eliot. Elizabeth was the sister of Charles Bray, also a ribbon manufacturer, author and enthusiastic social reformer. George Eliot in turn was

deeply influenced by Charles Bray, and after her father's death in 1849 she travelled with the Brays on a visit to Europe. It was another eight years before her literary career took off, but historians cite her connection to the Brays, through the Pears family, as deeply formative.[359]

Edith's paternal grandmother was Margaret Fraser, daughter of Robert Murray Fraser (1764–1844), who was of Scottish descent but became a successful businessman in Dublin. Robert's portrait at Benthall Hall dates from 1785, and was painted by Jeremiah Meyer RA (see Figure 38.4).

Mollie's great-grandfather, Charles Mackenzie, was a prebendary at St Paul's Cathedral, London. He married Henrietta Simonds, whose mother was Mary Simmonds (née Goodman) (1790–1858). Mary's portrait at Benthall Hall is attributed to the "Italian School" and dates from about 1830 (see Figure 38.5).

Figure 38.5: Mary Goodman, Mrs Henry Simonds

## Chapter 39

# A LIFE IN THEATRE:
# MICHAEL BENTHALL AND HIS FRIENDS

The last member of the family to be covered in this study is Michael (the son of Tom and Ruth Benthall ), who also became a major benefactor of the National Trust. At Benthall Hall there are two portraits of him as a child, as well as a studio photograph dating from the 1960s (see Figure 39.1).

Michael was an "oppidan" (town boy – see Chapter 14) at Eton College and then went up to Christ Church, Oxford. In 1938 the Australian ballet dancer Robert Helpmann came to perform there, met Michael, and the two formed a romantic and professional partnership that would last almost until Michael's death in 1974.

Robert Helpmann, known to his friends as Bobby, was born at Mount Gambier, South Australia, in 1909. He started his dance career as part of Anna Pavlova's touring dance company, before being taken up by Ninette de Valois to join her Sadler's Wells Company. He would become famous during the 1940s, when he was both dancing with Margot Fonteyn and acting at the Royal Shakespeare Theatre, under Michael Benthall's direction. After he retired from ballet, his career continued as a stage and screen actor, choreographer and director, and he died in 1986 as Sir Robert Helpmann CBE.[360]

Michael, having decided at first to be an actor, gained a small role in a play in London

Figure 39.1: Michael Benthall

in 1938, but his aspirations were interrupted by the Second World War, in which he served in the Royal Artillery and was "*mentioned in dispatches*."[361] He participated in the Normandy Invasion in June 1944, and a transcript of the letters he wrote from there survives. He left the army with the rank of major.[362]

Between his military deployments Michael was able to collaborate with Bobby Helpmann, and in 1943 he came up with an idea for a ballet named *Miracle in the Gorbals*, to be choreographed by Bobby. They arranged for the sets and costumes to be designed by the artist Edward Burra, and for the music by to be composed by Arthur Bliss. The plot, devised by Michael, was loosely based on a short story by Jerome K. Jerome, entitled "The Passing of the Third Floor Back," but relocated to a Glasgow slum. The first performance was given in October 1944 by the Sadler's Wells Ballet, and the piece continued to be in the repertoire of the Royal Ballet (as Ninette de Valois' company subsequently became known) for many years. In 2014 the ballet was revived and performed once again at Sadler's Wells Theatre.[363]

After the war Michael and Bobby continued to work together in theatre. In 1947 Michael directed a performance at the Duchess Theatre in London of John Webster's tragedy *The White Devil*, with Bobby, Claire Bloom (then aged 16) and a young Hugh Griffiths in the cast.[364] With the Royal Opera in London, he directed productions of *Turandot* in 1947 and *Aida* in 1948. He also worked with the Royal Shakespeare Theatre at Stratford-upon-Avon, where in 1948 he directed a production of *Hamlet* performed in Victorian dress; Paul Scofield and Bobby alternated in the main role, while Claire Bloom, now 17, played Ophelia.[365] A page on the BBC website gives this description:[366]

*Benthall took the radical step of casting two Hamlets (Paul Scofield and Robert Helpmann) for his production. Audiences could compare the actors' performances on different nights, seeing how an actor's individual personality and presence can change the atmosphere of a production. Robert Helpmann was a famed ballet dancer, and when he was not performing Hamlet in Stratford he would return to London to perform as a dancer. Reviewers commented on Helpmann's elegance of movement; when he talked about catching the conscience of the king Helpmann pinched out the candles one by one.*

At that time the management of the Royal Shakespeare Theatre was in some disarray. The chairman of its board of governors, Fordham Flower, had appointed a new artistic director named Harry Jackson in 1947, and it was he who brought in Michael and Bobby. But by the end of 1948 it was clear that Flower and Jackson could not work together, and Jackson was forced out. Michael Benthall was considered to be the likely candidate to succeed him, but the job was given to Anthony Quayle, who was younger and less experienced, but had played Othello at Stratford-upon-Avon that year.[367]

In 1950 Michael was approached by a friend of Katharine Hepburn, who was considering trying her hand at Shakespeare, specifically as Rosalind in *As You Like It*, but needed a good director.[368] Michael travelled to the United States to meet her, and a deal was arranged. The play was staged first in New York, where it ran for 180 performances before going on tour. Hepburn then went off to film *The African Queen* with Humphrey Bogart, but once that difficult shoot was completed, a year or so later, she was persuaded to go to London and star in another play, Bernard Shaw's *The*

*Millionairess.* Michael directed, Bobby played the leading male role, and Pierre Balmain designed her costumes. The reviews were not great, but *The African Queen* had opened at the same time in the cinemas and the play proved very popular. The production moved to New York, where it was equally successful with the public, though equally unsuccessful with the critics.

In between, Michael directed Vivien Leigh and Laurence Olivier in two plays that were performed in repertory on alternating nights: Shaw's *Caesar and Cleopatra*, and Shakespeare's *Antony and Cleopatra*. Leigh was Cleopatra in both, while Olivier played Caesar in the first and Anthony in the second. Bobby likewise appeared in both productions, which were first performed in London and then in New York, to rave reviews.[369]

Michael's last production for the Royal Shakespeare Theatre was in 1951: *The Tempest*, with Michael Redgrave as Prospero, Hugh Griffith as Caliban and Richard Burton as Ferdinand.

In 1953 Michael signed a five-year contract as artistic director of the Old Vic theatre, in London. He decided to produce the complete "First Folio" – i.e., the first 36 of Shakespeare's plays – in repertory. His contract was then extended for four more years, during which a broader range of plays were staged,[370] including fine productions of Shaw's *St. Joan* and Oscar Wilde's *The Importance of Being Ernest*. At any one time, the company of actors and actresses would be performing three or four different plays on different evenings. When the project started, the company contained Richard Burton, Claire

Bloom and Michael Hordern.[371] Several other of its members would later become famous – Judi Dench, for example, who in 1957 made her professional debut with the company, and in due course played in a memorable production there of *Romeo and Juliet*, directed by Franco Zeffirelli.

During these honeymoon years of Michael's directorship, the Old Vic company was frequently also on tour worldwide. In 1955 Katharine Hepburn and Bobby appeared in three of Shakespeare's plays on an Australian tour.[372]

In 1960 Michael was awarded a CBE. However, by the early 1960s the theatrical world had become dominated by the "Angry Young Men," and the plays they wrote were not particularly suited to Michael's classical style. Furthermore, he had also by then started to become an alcoholic. He left the Old Vic in 1962.

In 1969 Katharine Hepburn starred in a musical named *Coco*, based on the life of Coco Chanel, and she asked Michael to direct it. He went to New York to take up the role, but by some accounts he was no longer capable of effective work, and Hepburn and the choreographer, Michael Bennett, basically managed the entire production.[373] Nonetheless, all three were nominated for Tony awards.

By 1970 Michael was a very sick man, and he eventually died in September 1974. Before then Bobby had moved to Australia, where he was co-director of the Australian Ballet. But when Hepburn heard that Michael was dying, she travelled to London and was there to support him during the last few weeks of his life.

## DIGRESSION: MIMI FOGT

In Chapter 35 it was noted that Michael's mother, Ruth, spent much of her time in the 1950s in the south of France, as the guest of Maurice Fogt, who had a daughter named Mimi. Mimi was an artist, married it seems in 1941 to another artist named Sven Blomberg, while both were students in Birmingham. Her mother travelled the USA in 1951, in the company of a couple named Garland, who lived in Buzzards Bay, Massachusetts. Mimi went to visit her in 1955, and then obtained an introduction to Marcel Duchamp, the artist who helped redefine the concept of art at that time. In 1956, she moved to New York and stayed for several months with Marcel Duchamp and his wife, and painted his portrait. She also met other luminaries such as Salvador Dali. In 1957 she met a Mexican named Alberto Ramirez Capmany, encouraged him to paint, then moved to Mexico City to be with him. Eventually he became more of a sculptor than a painter and they moved to Portugal, built a house and where many of their works are on display in a small gallery, named the "*Casa-Museu Passos Canavarro*". In 2008 a set of letters addressed to Mimi were sold at auction in London by Christie's.[374] The lot description read:

> *Maurice Chevalier, Robert Helpmann And Michael Benthall*
>
> *A collection of correspondence addressed to artist Mimi Fogt including:*
> *— a series of four autograph letters from Maurice Chevalier, signed and an autograph postcard, signed, correspondence addressed Chére Mimi, from various addresses in Beverly Hills, Denver and France, August 1959–October 1967, altogether five pages in autograph, all written in French, four with corresponding envelopes;*
> *— a series of six autograph letters from Robert Helpmann, signed and two typescript letters, signed, the correspondence variously addressed from various hotels and residences in Australia, London and Rome, January 1968–September 1975, approximately 10 pages in autograph, two pages typed, a number with corresponding envelopes; and*
> *— a series of five autograph letters from Michael Benthall, signed and three autograph postcards, signed, the correspondence variously addressed (Dearest Adulterous Cannibals, Ma chére Madame Impudences et Cannibellette and Chére Cannibals foux) majority sent from Eaton Square,[375] London, January 1970–September 1973, altogether approximately 19 pages in autograph, a few with corresponding envelopes.*

Although the 'Maurice Chevalier' referred to here is accepted as being the famous French singer and actor, there is just a small possibility that this was a pen name used by her father, also Maurice, and a Chevalier.

The strange jokes within Michael's greetings may seem somewhat mysterious now; but to an artist closely associated with such irreverent figures as Duchamp and Dali, they were presumably funny and then either uncontroversial, or deliberately so.

# PART VI.
# AFTERTHOUGHTS

Readers who has made their way to this point in the book have demonstrated considerable fortitude, in the face of a great amount of detailed information about over 300 relatives of the two patriarchs, William Bentall and Dr William Marshall, as well as descriptions of the many family portraits that have accumulated at Benthall Hall, either as part of the National Trust collection or in the family archives that are also stored there. The main goal of this book has been to tie together the stories of the people in those portraits, for the benefit of their many living descendants and other visitors to the house. There are many difficult historical issues that I am not qualified to evaluate, other than to report the results of my research – especially the involvement of the British merchant class in the institution of slavery and in the colonial expansion of the British Empire. But this last part of the book attempts to address some more modest social issues that were mentioned in the introduction and touched upon in earlier chapters.

## Chapter 41

# WHAT DEFINES A GENTLEMAN?

The rather difficult question posed in this chapter's title has had many answers over the years, rarely much in agreement. But whatever the definition, the pursuit of the honorific "gentleman" was long considered to be of utmost importance to those who thought they were entitled to it, especially when they were not sure if everyone else agreed. The great 19th-century English novelists – Austen, Eliot, Dickens, Thackeray, Trollope, and others – built much of their reputations by finding ways to illuminate this problem, which not surprisingly exercised many members of the Benthall and Marshall families.

Throughout the 19th century it was generally accepted that an English gentleman: was educated, with some mastery of the classical languages (certainly Latin, possibly also some Ancient Greek); spoke, both grammatically and in pronunciation, the socially accepted version of the dialect known as the King's (or Queen's, depending on the reign) English; and understood and practised "manners" – that is, a social etiquette that could pass muster in high society.

But for those at the top of the heap, there was a subtle difference between being a "gentleman" and a member of the "gentry." The nobility and the "landed gentry" (owners of a rural estate, but without a hereditary title to go with it) tended to think that to be a gentleman,

it was necessary to live off rents or other unearned income and not to have to hold down a job, except possibly as a clergyman or as an army or naval officer.[376] If not ennobled, it was certainly helpful to be entitled to use a family coat of arms, as a symbol of being part of the aristocracy.[377]

That left the urban classes in an uncertain position. In urban trade directories published in the first half of the 19th century, it was normal for them to start by listing the "*Nobility, Gentry and Clergy*" who lived there, before proceeding with more useful persons such as innkeepers, lawyers and merchants. They might be very rich and have a coat of arms, and be indistinguishable in education and manners from those rural landowners, but they were still not fully accepted by them as equals. The term "bourgeois" was not in common use in England until popularised by Karl Marx in the second half of the 19th century, but it is generally accepted that there was an acknowledged distinction before then between the wealthy merchants based in towns and cities and the wealthy rural landowners. There was also a distinction between the "high bourgeois," corresponding to the educated merchant and professional classes, and the "petty bourgeois," made up of less educated tradesmen. The Benthalls, Marshalls and other relatives considered themselves to be part of the well-educated merchant classes – i.e., high bourgeois – and there are numerous examples in this book of how this sense of family pride affected their lives. Here are three that are worth reviewing.

## William and Francis Benthall

These two sons of William Searle Bentall (see Chapters 15 and 21) provide an intriguing contrast. In 1830 a Totnes directory listed William Searle and his brother Thornton, along with several other relatives, in the section entitled *"Nobility, Gentry and Clergy"* as well as in the *"Trades"* section, as bankers.

By contrast, the younger William Bentall, eldest son of William Searle and educated at Westminster and Cambridge, was not listed in that section in a Totnes directory published in 1848. He was listed as engaged in various trades – e.g., *"Insurance Agent," "Wine Merchant,"* and *"Coal Merchant"* – but not under *"Gentry, Clergy &c."* Whether that was his choice, or that of the compiler, is uncertain. It may be that it cost money to be listed in the directory, and he chose not to pay for the additional entry. On the other hand, it may also be that whereas William Searle and Thornton Bentall, being joint owners of an estate in Buckfastleigh, could have been deemed "landed" in 1830, in 1848 the younger William merely owned a house and various businesses in Totnes. In any event, on a day-to-day basis he was clearly regarded by the townsfolk as a "gentleman" (for example, when entertaining Charles Babbage – see Chapter 15), so it probably mattered little to him whether he was officially part of the "gentry."

William's younger brother Francis was a successful solicitor based in London, and a passionate antiquarian. It was he who arranged for the Totnes Bentalls to reinsert the lost "h" into the family name, after paying a fee to the College of Arms. When Francis became the owner of Buckfast Abbey, he also laid a somewhat doubtful claim to have thereby become the "Lord of the Manor of Buckfast," and referred to his family as the "Benthalls of Buckfast" as if they had lived there for generations. And he took the trouble to have a footnote to this effect included in *The Baronial Halls and Picturesque Edifices of England*.

In contrast to his elder brother, Francis was clearly insecure about his social position, and intent on establishing his claim to being not only a gentleman, but also a member of the gentry. He must have found it very frustrating when some of his siblings, namely Henry, Alfred and Thornton, were so clearly not behaving like gentlemen – i.e., going to jail, producing illegitimate children and fleeing the country to avoid arrest, respectively. Looking back on this 170 years later, it is hard to know if claiming to be "Lord of the Manor of Buckfast" made much difference to his happiness, or the respect that he was accorded later in life.

## Lord Palmerston and William Henry Drake

This condescending distinction between "gentry" and "gentility," based on land ownership, came into strong relief during the Crimean War, in an exchange between William Henry Drake and the recently appointed prime minister, Henry John Temple, 3rd Viscount Palmerston. Drake is a peripheral figure in this book, whose career as a member of the Commissariat was told in Chapter 3. (A great-nephew of Dorothy Marshall, he was also the father-in-law of Charles Henry Marshall [see Chapter 26].)

By early 1855 public criticisms had been made about the conduct of the Crimean War – namely, that the army was failing because it was run by aristocrats who had bought their commissions but who otherwise had no claim to competence. In February of that year, an MP named Charles Newdegate responded with a speech defending the gentry and proposing an alternative reason for the army's problems. The prime minister, Lord Palmerston, supported Newdegate's argument in a subsequent speech:

*I must say that there was great truth and great force in the observations which fell from the hon. member for North Warwickshire [Newdegate], in answer to the attacks which have been made upon the aristocracy, along with whom I suppose we must include the gentry of the country, for I believe the term 'aristocracy' includes the two.*

*In reply to the charges that our army has not been successful, as it ought to have been, in consequence of the great number of gentlemen who are officers in it, I think the hon. member made the most triumphant answer, by showing that where your system has broken down–that where evil has arisen from want of capacity, of energy, of intelligence, or of accurate and zealous performance of duty– it was not that the gentry, not that the aristocracy, not that the noblemen in the army were at fault, but persons belonging to other classes of the community.*

*It is the medical department, the commissariat department, and the transport department, which nobody contends are filled with the sons of the aristocracy or the gentry, – it is there that your system has broken down, it*

*is there that the service has failed, and that it is that has been the main cause of the suffering of which we are all complaining.*[378]

The report of this speech arrived in Balaclava early in March 1855. Henry Drake, who was a Deputy Commissary-General there, was incensed and wrote of his outrage both in his journal and in letters home to his wife. He was quite aware that although Lord Palmerston was descended from a wealthy Irish family (the Temples) that qualified as part of the Irish aristocracy – the prime minister's great-grandfather had been granted a large estate in western Ireland – his mother, Mary Mee, was in fact the daughter of a London merchant, not an aristocrat. Drake wrote to his wife: "*I claim to belong to the Gentry of England as much as any Temple that ever lived & certainly as much so as the offspring of Miss Mee who I should fancy was not a very aristocratic personage by birth.*"

Drake organised a letter of protest, signed by all 34 commissaries posted in Balaclava, which was published in *The Times* that April. The letter gave the text of Palmerston's speech, as quoted above, and then continued:

*We can hardly imagine that Lord Palmerston could have meant that the officers of the commissariat do not belong to the class of society called 'gentlemen;' but the expressions made use of by his Lordship certainly convey that meaning. ... We are invidiously designated as not belonging to the class of society usually termed 'gentlemen,' but as belonging to other classes of the community. While we conduct ourselves honourably it matters little with what families we are connected; but we contend that the officers of the commissariat, as a body, do belong to the class termed 'gentry,' and that we are as well educated, as well informed, and as honourable and upright in every respect as any other body of officers in the army. Our duties are of a most responsible nature, and there are no officers in the service in whom such an amount of trust is placed, which should surely entitle us to be classed in the highest ranks of the public service.*

## Alfred and William Marshall, and their biographers

The respective biographies of Alfred Marshall published by the economists Coase and Groenewegen discussed at length the issue of gentility in his family. They stated, correctly, that Alfred's father, William, gave his occupation on his marriage certificate as "*gentleman*" and that his bride, Rebecca, was the daughter of a butcher. But Groenewegen further asserted that the Bentalls and Marshalls boycotted the wedding because of Rebecca's parentage. Both biographers dwelt upon William's efforts to "*regain for himself the trappings of the status of 'gentleman' he had claimed for himself on his marriage certificate,*"[379] as well as the "*concealment through falsehood*"[380] that they claimed permeated the stories told about Alfred's upbringing, in order to claim for him greater "gentility" than was actually deserved.

As noted before, Stevens has repudiated these allegations, reclaiming William as a cantankerous but not particularly unusual member of the high bourgeois class he grew up in, and opined that Coase, who had a very much less privileged upbringing, "*might have wanted his own struggle against class, and for a good education, to mirror that which he portrayed for Alfred Marshall.*"[381] William's career and his family's gradual moves to increasingly expensive neighbourhoods, while paying for the best education available for his children, seem very familiar to those of similar backgrounds in the 20th century.

# Chapter 42

# "INCEST & INFLUENCE"

In the introduction a reference was made to Adam Kuper's book *Incest & Influence: The Private Life of Bourgeois England*, which studies the 19th-century English phenomenon of family intermarriage, common among the merchant class and royalty but rare among the aristocracy and rural gentry. Kuper argues that these merchant clans were:

> *...impelled by their own characteristic interests, informed by a distinctive pattern of family sentiment, governed by their own standards of decorum and morality. The consequences were profound. Marriages between relatives sustained networks of kin. ... These webs of relationships delivered enormous collateral benefits, shaping vocations, generating patronage, yielding information, and giving access to capital.*[382] *... Marriage within the family – between cousins or between in-laws – was a characteristic strategy of the new bourgeoisie, and...it had a great deal to do with the success of some of the most important Victorian clans. ... The leading bourgeois clans played a great role in the history of this industrial and imperial Britain. The marriage patterns of the English bourgeoisie therefore played a significant part in making the nineteenth-century world.*[383]

Such prominent "incestuous" networks included the Rothschilds, the Wedgewood–Darwin–Allen clan, the interrelated Wilberforce and Thornton families (see Chapter 5), and the Bloomsbury Group. The Adams–Bentall–Marshall clan was less prominent and lesser known, but bourgeois they certainly were, and their marriage preferences support Kuper's argument.

The Catholic Church regarded marriages between first or second cousins as null unless the Pope granted a dispensation. But in Anglican England there were no such restrictions. Charles Darwin, for example, married his first cousin Emma Wedgewood, whose brother Joe was already married to Darwin's sister Caroline. A son of Charles and Emma, George Darwin, together with Francis Galton, half-cousin to Charles and an early statistician who coined the term "eugenics," studied the genetic implications of inbreeding, but they concluded that *"cousin marriages caused no harm in the best families."*[384]

Indeed, in 19th-century England the question of whether a man should be allowed to marry his deceased wife's sister was a much more contentious issue than whether he could marry his first cousin. Anglican doctrine taught that, once married, a couple became "one flesh," and therefore one's spouse's siblings were seen as one's own. Whereas in the United States, several states began to pass laws prohibiting marriages between first cousins (not to mention between races), in Britain it was not until the early 20th century that a law was passed to permit marriage to a deceased wife's sister, and by then a growing understanding of genetics – in particular, the activation of recessive genes – had changed attitudes towards first-cousin marriages. In 1940, when Paul Benthall wrote a letter intended to be read by his sons when they were old enough, his first specific words of advice were: "*Don't marry your cousins.*"

The first marital connection between the Adams, Bentall and Marshall families was made when Dr William Marshall married Dorothy Chadder in 1771, thereby becoming the brother-in-law of Dr William Adams (see Chapter 3). The next connection was made in January 1800, when Elizabeth Bentall married Samuel Adams, the son of Dr Adams and nephew of Dr Marshall (see Chapters 3, 6 & 7). Two of Samuel's elder sisters had already married two brothers named Welsford, who were business partners with his elder brother, the future William Adams MP. Just under two years later, in December 1801, William Searle Bentall (Elizabeth's brother) married Mary Ann Marshall, daughter of Dr Marshall and thus Samuel's first cousin. In 1805 William Searle's brother Thornton married Margaret Eleanora Admonition Marshall, Mary Ann's sister. (see Chapter 9). So far, these were marriages between clans, not between cousins.

Two other convenient intermarriages were those of William Dacres (W.D.) Adams and Thomas Peregrine Courtenay to two sisters, the daughters of Mayow Wynell Mayow, in 1804 and 1805 respectively (see Chapters 7 & 10). The two men had become friends a few

years earlier, and their marriages cemented that friendship, so that when the older William Adams, W.D.'s father, decided to retire from Parliament and was looking for a successor, Courtenay was an easy choice. According to the principle of "one flesh," through marriage Courtenay had become a brother of W.D. Adams, and by extension also a brother of Samuel and Elizabeth Adams (née Bentall) and, therefore, various other Bentalls and Marshalls. To some extent that explains the familiarity with which Courtenay could write from Essex to Thornton Bentall and talk about "*our*" coat of arms (see Chapter 10).

In 1810 Louisa Bentall – sister to Elizabeth, William Searle and Thornton – married William Marshall, first cousin of Mary Ann and Margaret (see Chapter 13). As a new "brother," Courtenay arranged for William to be appointed to the position of the Assistant Paymaster General in the Cape Colony.

So far, so good! These intermarriages helped build a new, strong mercantile and political alliance, but without the genetic implications of an intra-family (i.e. cousin-to-cousin) marriage. The close connections maintained between the Adams, Bentall and Marshall families in the next generation meant that they helped each other out in India, Australia and elsewhere when they could, and even though they did not command a business empire, they played their part in "*making the nineteenth-century world.*"[385]

The next generation became more complicated, however. Two sets of first cousins married: first Edward Benthall and Clementina Marshall, and then William Marshall and Mary Benthall. There were no obvious signs of adverse effects, although out of William and Mary's nine children, only four lived to adulthood and only one of those married and produced descendants.

Among the next generation yet, there were more such marriages. Various intermarriages between the Wardale, Waterfield, Gay and Benthall families included two between first cousins (see Chapter 16), both of which produced several children with living, healthy descendants today.

More worryingly, Edith Benthall, the eldest daughter of Edward and Clementina (first cousins themselves), married her first cousin William Henry Benthall. Paul Benthall wrote that this *"double in-breeding resulted in poor cousin Willy, who has been in an asylum for years."* Subsequently, two of the grandchildren of Samuel and Elizabeth Adams (George Henry and Ellen Harriet Adams) became yet another family example of a first-cousin wedding, although at ages when they could not expect to have children (see Chapter 7).

The last cousin marriage (so far!) on the Benthall side was between Mary Clementina Benthall and Floyer Dale (see Chapter 32). She refused to marry him until she was past child-bearing age. It is not entirely clear whether this was because by then the risks of in-breeding were better understood, or because she was well aware that there was a strong streak of mental instability in Floyer's family that she did not want to risk passing on. Probably it was a combination of both.

By then the marriage patterns of the merchant class had changed. Businesses were sustained by becoming limited companies, rather than as partnerships between close kin, and young men and women looked further afield for prospective marriage partners, beyond simply the families of their uncles and aunts.

## *Chapter 43*

# HOW ROTTEN WAS OUR BOROUGH?

With "incest," in theory, came "influence." References were made in Chapter 10 to several allegations of corruption relating to the Adams–Benthall–Marshall interest at Totnes. Now that the lives all the individuals concerned have been described, it is time to look at those allegations in more detail to make some assessment of their validity. Just how rotten was the borough of Totnes? How corrupt were the people who controlled its parliamentary elections between 1801 and 1832, and how much of the public criticism was justified? These are questions of some historical interest, not to mention family pride.

The allegations covered at least three different types of behaviour that had, in fact, long been considered commonplace and acceptable, and which only began to be seen as corrupt during the first two decades of the 19th century. The first was the practice of buying a seat as an MP in the House of Commons. The second was the practice of rewarding political support with stipends attached to official positions that had trivial or non-existent responsibilities – i.e., sinecures. The third was nepotism: using political connections to find jobs for one's relatives or friends.

Certainly, to a modern sensibility there is an odour of rot in the idea that a small group of closely related men such as the Adams–Bentall–Marshall clan, living in a small provincial town, could team up with a couple of ambitious and powerful politicians in London, namely W.D. Adams and T.P. Courtenay, ensure the re-election of their preferred candidate to Parliament over a 20-year period, and use these connections to find jobs and financial perks for the family.

At that time, the issue of corruption had been central to much of the debate about reform. In about 1820 a journalist named John Wade published a serialised book initially entitled *The Black Book, or Corruption Unmasked! Being an Account of Persons, Places, and Sinecures*. By the standards of the day it was a best seller, and a new edition was published in 1831, then reprinted in 1832 and 1835, under a more elaborate title page, as shown in Figure 43.1.[386]

This polemical book explained in great detail the inner workings of the British system of patronage, and named many of the beneficiaries. In its opening arguments it averred, with reference to Machiavelli, that "*the policy of governing nations by enlightening the few and hoodwinking the many is of very old standing.*"

First in *The Extraordinary Black Book's* sights was the Church of England:

*It is the inefficiency of the clergy as public teachers, the hurtful influence they have*

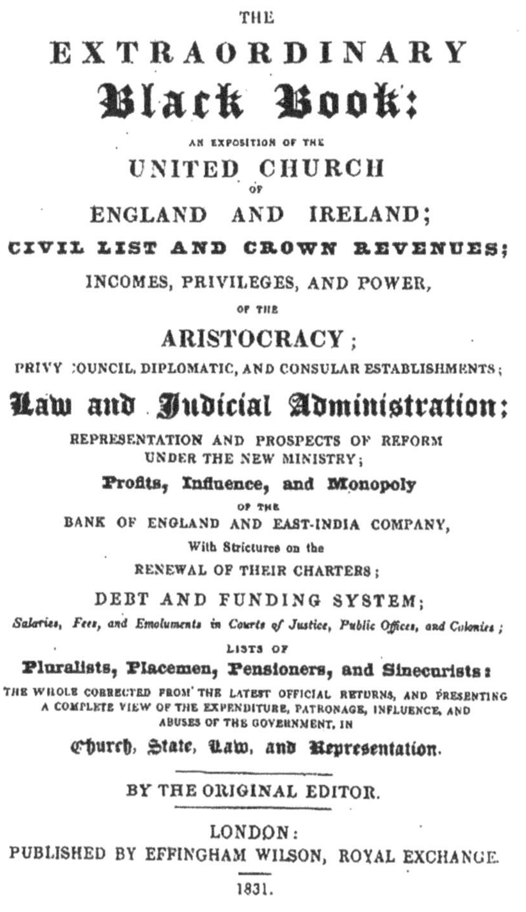

THE

# EXTRAORDINARY
## 𝕭𝖑𝖆𝖈𝖐 𝕭𝖔𝖔𝖐:

AN EXPOSITION OF THE

### UNITED CHURCH
OF

### ENGLAND AND IRELAND;

**CIVIL LIST AND CROWN REVENUES;**

INCOMES, PRIVILEGES, AND POWER,

OF THE

### ARISTOCRACY;

PRIVY COUNCIL, DIPLOMATIC, AND CONSULAR ESTABLISHMENTS;

### 𝕷𝖆𝖜 𝖆𝖓𝖉 𝕵𝖚𝖉𝖎𝖈𝖎𝖆𝖑 𝕬𝖉𝖒𝖎𝖓𝖎𝖘𝖙𝖗𝖆𝖙𝖎𝖔𝖓;

REPRESENTATION AND PROSPECTS OF REFORM
UNDER THE NEW MINISTRY;

**Profits, Influence, and Monopoly**

OF THE

BANK OF ENGLAND AND EAST-INDIA COMPANY,

With Strictures on the

RENEWAL OF THEIR CHARTERS;

### DEBT AND FUNDING SYSTEM;

*Salaries, Fees, and Emoluments in Courts of Justice, Public Offices, and Colonies;*

LISTS OF

**Pluralists, Placemen, Pensioners, and Sinecurists:**

THE WHOLE CORRECTED FROM THE LATEST OFFICIAL RETURNS, AND PRESENTING
A COMPLETE VIEW OF THE EXPENDITURE, PATRONAGE, INFLUENCE, AND
ABUSES OF THE GOVERNMENT, IN

𝕮𝖍𝖚𝖗𝖈𝖍, 𝕾𝖙𝖆𝖙𝖊, 𝕷𝖆𝖜, 𝖆𝖓𝖉 𝕽𝖊𝖕𝖗𝖊𝖘𝖊𝖓𝖙𝖆𝖙𝖎𝖔𝖓.

### BY THE ORIGINAL EDITOR.

LONDON:
PUBLISHED BY EFFINGHAM WILSON, ROYAL EXCHANGE.

1831.

Figure 43.1: The Extraordinary Black Book

*exerted on national affairs, and their inert-*
*ness in the promotion of measures of gen-*
*eral utility, that induce men to begrudge the*
*immense revenue expended in their support,*
*and dispose them to a reform in our ecclesi-*
*astical establishment.*

Furthermore, it decried the "*measureless*
*rapacity that directs the disposal of church-pre-*
*ferment,*" as reflected in many clergymen being
nominally in charge of multiple parishes and
being rewarded with multiple stipends, out of
which they could cheaply hire surrogates to perform their duties.

After tackling that relatively easy target, the
book then moved on to the more difficult task

of explaining corruption in secular governance.
Much of the revenue that sustained the government actually came from the rents paid by
tenants on Crown lands, along with other taxes
such as the "droits of Admiralty" that nominally
were paid to the sovereign. Since the restoration
of the monarchy in 1660 after the English Civil
War, each new sovereign surrendered most of
his or her income from these sources to the government, in return for a fixed annuity known
as the "Civil List." This was used to support
the "Royal Household," which included a large
number of sinecures; for example, one duke
was "*master of the hawks*" with an annual
salary of £1,372, while another nobleman was
"*master of the dogs*" with an annual salary of
£2,000. (Multiply by about 100 to convert to
current spending power.) The Civil List also
funded various pensions – for "*servants of the*
*household, favourites of royalty and superannu-*
*ated diplomatists*" – and disbursements. Thus,
although *The Extraordinary Black Book* pre-
dated the decision to send Alfred Bentall's ship
to Turkey with a gift of horses for the Sultan
(see Chapter 18), it is likely that the associated
expenses were claimed from this fund.

There was little oversight of how government ministers chose to spend the funds of the
Civil List. Even less oversight was given to
how they used Crown lands and disposed of
the surplus income from rents and taxes. For
example, the government bought the allegiance
of the nobility by leasing out to them, at low
rates, huge tracts of land nominally owned by
the Crown, in the expectation that the noblemen
would use the profits from their estates to buy
the election of the government's preferred candidates. Those revenues all flowed through the
Office of Woods and Forests, managed in part
by William Dacres Adams and his relatives.

*The Extraordinary Black Book* ran to almost 600 pages, of which about 80 comprised an itemised list naming the "*placemen, pensioners, sinecurists and grantees.*" Several of the subjects of this book appear on that list, including T.P. Courtenay (and his wife and three daughters), W.D. Adams and Edward Marshall.

By 1831 the inflammatory book had been widely circulated, providing grist to the mill for radical politicians and journalists who were intent on reform, even long after the passage of the Great Reform Act in 1832.

This chapter attempts to assess the extent to which the situation in Totnes fitted into the bigger picture in two parts: first, by examining historical electoral corruption in Totnes (in this respect, the Adams–Bentall–Marshall interest gets a relatively clean bill of health); and second, by exploring the issue of sinecures and nepotism. Courtenay had strong views on these matters and when he decided not to stand again for election to Parliament after passage of the Great Reform Act of 1832, he gave a long speech to his constituents, which he then published.[387] His defence of his career was cogent, and some of his more pessimistic predictions came to pass.

## Election-rigging

Was Totnes as rotten as most other small boroughs? In fact, the evidence shows that before and during the heyday of the Adams–Bentall–Marshall interest, the town was remarkably free from financial inducements to rig elections.

In Chapter 10 it was noted that during the 1770 parliamentary election, an attempt was made by one party to sway the election by offering a bribe of £150 to any freeman who would switch his vote, but none accepted. Likewise, in subsequent years there was plenty of negotiating and conspiring to challenge the sitting members, but no evidence that money changed hands.

Consider William Adams MP, who obtained his first parliamentary seat at Plympton Erle and his second at Totnes. In contrast to Totnes, two local landowning families dominated the Plympton Erle corporation, and controlled the appointment of freemen, most of whom were non-resident. Each family nominated and arranged for the election of one MP (without any formal vote by the freemen), and both sold this honour to the highest bidder, provided that the candidate pledged allegiance to the government of the day.

In Courtenay's farewell address he predicted that under the new rules "*the holders of all sorts of Property will continue to have power, since the expenses of Elections will be great, and there is even a more extensive field for bribery.*" Post-Reform Act novels by Charles Dickens (*The Pickwick Papers*), Anthony Trollope (*Doctor Thorne*) and others include memorable scenes that document the ongoing tradition of buying elections with cash and beer.

Thirty-five years later, the issue of electoral corruption came up again. More Parliamentary commissions went to work, and Totnes was again the target of special attention. A fresh report documented corrupt practices that had by then become standard to the Totnes election process – in other words, Courtenay was proved right. A resolution presented in the House of Commons by Sir Lawrence Palk on 9 April 1867 provides a summary of that report. From Palk's speech, it is clear that from 1839 on, the Seymour family, who had to some extent been side-lined when the Adams–Bentall–Marshall interest was in power, became increasingly influential. Following the Great Reform Act, a householder living on a property valued at £10 or above became eligible to vote, and this made it possible for the Seymours to stack the voting lists. Palk argued that:

*Previously to the Reform Act Totnes had been a free borough, **untainted with bribery and corruption** [my emphasis]; but, after the passing of that Act the boundaries of the borough of Totnes were much enlarged.*

*The power of creating votes was largely increased by the quantity of meadow land brought within the limits of the borough at the Reform Bill. Sheds of a better and more expensive character than had hitherto existed were erected on the different fields, and a manufactured qualification of £10 for "buildings with land' was thus obtained. This system of creating qualifications, though adopted by both sides, has added a large number of votes to the Liberal interest, and is now only available to any extent to that party.*[388]

However, a tenant of such a property was effectively constrained in voting choice, since to vote against one's landlord could result in eviction. The speech went on to give examples of how bribery had become commonplace:

*The Earl of Gifford died in January, 1863, and, immediately Mr. Alfred Seymour and Mr. Dent presented themselves as candidates. Mr. Seymour sent to Totnes the sum of £1,000, which was paid into the account of the Messrs. Michelmore with the National Provincial Bank*

*The only way by which the Conservative candidate could win the election was by the purchase of a number of votes in Bridgetown, tenants of small holdings under the Duke, who might, by the temptation of very large sums, be induced to brave the penalty of certain eviction from their holdings. Fifteen of these people were thus bought at prices varying from £60 to £150 a head, but they were not enough to turn the scale in Mr. Dent's favour.*

The consequence of this investigation was that the borough of Totnes was disenfranchised – i.e., stripped of the right to elect its own Members of Parliament.

## Sinecures and Nepotism

The *Extraordinary Black Book* was a bestseller, influential in energising the reform movement and providing a treasure trove of detail for aspiring politicians and journalists to exploit. Two subsequent documents, targeted specifically at the Adams–Bentall–Marshall interest, built upon its polemics in attempting to catalogue the alleged "*Tory reign of plunder*"[389] in Totnes during the period 1800–1832. The first was the report of a Parliamentary commission in 1834, and the second was a newspaper article published in 1839, when the local press were concerned that there might be a rekindling of enthusiasm for the old guard. These two documents are summarised below, so that the specific allegations can be evaluated.

By contrast, in T.P. Courtenay's 1832 retirement speech the outgoing MP covered every significant political position that he had taken during career and explained his reasons for having voted the way he did. He vigorously defended his philosophy and stance relating to "improper influence," and argued that most of the excesses exposed by the original publication of the *Black Book* had anyway already been addressed by the time of the Great Reform Act. His comments serve as a yardstick against which to measure the validity of the other two documents' allegations.

After providing extracts from these primary sources, the remainder of this chapter attempts to evaluate the criticisms in light of Courtenay's defence of his own career and of the progress that had been made during his time in office, as well as the histories of the individuals named in the allegations and described in the early parts of this book. My conclusions are that whereas the allegations against those families supposedly benefitting from sinecures are thin in the extreme, the allegations of nepotism certainly have a stronger case. However, while it is certainly true that some of the most important government departments – the India Office, the War Office and the Office of Woods, Forests and Land Revenues – were well staffed by the Marshall, Waterfield and Adams families respectively, since there was no organised mechanism at that time to find and recruit people for such positions except by word of mouth and family connections, it is a stretch to describe nepotism in this context as "corrupt." I believe that Courtenay's analysis was, in the main, accurate, and I hope that readers will agree.

## Parliamentary Commission of 1834

After the election of 1832, conducted under the new rules defined by that year's Great Reform Act, a Parliamentary commission was set up in 1834 to inquire into the municipal corporations of England and Wales. The commission's report on Totnes, which was finally published in March 1835, delivered a scathing indictment of the fiscal irresponsibility of the borough's governing body.[390]

The report started by summarising the organisation of the Totnes Corporation and the roles of the aldermen and burgesses. It listed the aldermen by name and elucidated their family connections:

*Many of the masters are related. The Bentells [sic] are brothers, as are likewise the Marshalls. Mr. Adams and Sir George Adams are uncle and nephew. Mr. Farwell the town clerk is brother to Mr. Christopher, and uncle to Mr. Charles Farwell. The families of the Marshalls, Bentells and Adams are connected by marriage. Dr. Marshall was also connected by marriage to the town clerk. Many of the masters are also nearly related to many of the burgesses. ... Twenty-four of the burgesses are connected, either by blood or marriage, with the family of Mr. Adams, and 12 others of the burgesses are connected in the same manner, either amongst themselves or with the masters and counselors.*

Apart from the lazy spelling, the details above are all accurate, as have been documented at length in this book. There follows a long explanation of the town's finances, which were touched upon in Chapter 10:

*The debts of the corporation are considerable. In or before 1804, the local church was struck by lightning, and a local builder was hired to fix it. In 1834 he was still owed £661, including 5% interest. £320 was owed to "Mr. William Bentill [sic]" ... "W.D. Adams holds a bond for £100" ... "The town clerk's bill amounts to £918" [etc.] ... Formerly the accounts... were kept in one book, but for the past 30 or 40 years this system has been discontinued.*

*This has been very imperfectly done, and for the past three or four years the accounts have not been made up, in consequence, as it has been stated, of the arrears of rent not having been received. ….. In the present state of their finances, the corporation are quite unable to meet the demands upon them.*

After providing much more substance to support this, the report concludes:

*There is little to distinguish the corporation of Totnes from that of other boroughs in the West of England, unless it be a more striking negligence in the management of their affairs, and a greater disregard of municipal duties. The constitution differs indeed in some degree from that of many of the neighbouring corporations, the freemen having voices in the election of the mayor, and of the masters and the counselors; but as the freemen themselves are elected by the masters and the counselors, the select body in fact possesses the entire power of the corporation. That power has been used to forward the interests of a particular family, whose political influence has, in return, been made subservient to the private advantage of individual members of the corporation. Of their own affairs, as a body, the corporation have been grossly negligent, and have continued to contract debts long after they knew themselves to be unable to meet their existing engagements. Great apathy also appears to prevail on the subject of their debts…[that] they had not…made any effort to discharge.*

*Henry Roscoe, Henry Rushton. London, Jan 17, 1834.*

## Article in the *Western Morning News*, 3 August 1839

A by-election was held in Totnes on 26 July 1839, after the retirement of Jasper Parrott, who had been one of the two elected MPs since the election of 1832. The vote was a tie: a "double return" took place and both of the candidates – one Conservative, the other a Whig – were deemed elected for the single seat in question. This meant that neither could participate in Parliament until that institution decided who should prevail. A week later, the *Western Morning News*, a local newspaper, published a scathing article listing 25 people whom it thought had benefited from corruption in previous years, all of whose lives have been described at least briefly in this book. Parts of that article are reproduced below:

*From want of time to reply to the ravings of the Tories on the Totnes contest and the old constitution, we publish the following list of good things enjoyed by the Tory leaders of the borough, under the Tory reign of plunder, and which will account for their opposition to Mr. Blount. They want Totnes to be "free"–the freedom of the hungry dog in a larder. These are the men, as they stood connected to the old corporation: –*

*Alderman William Searle Bentall, Banker, Wool Stapler, and Serge Manufacturer.*
*Alderman Richard Marshall, Doctor of Medicine and Barrack Master.*
*Alderman George Farwell, Solicitor, expelled Town Clerk, and Agent to the Lord Darlington.*
*Alderman Chris. Farwell, Banker & a retired Colonel in the Army.*

*Alderman George Pownal Adams, a Major General in the Army.*

*John Robert Wise, Esq., nephew of Archdeacon Froade [sic],[391] &c.*

*The Right Honourable Thomas Peregrine Courtenay, late M.P. for Totnes, late Secretary of the Board of Control and Vice-President of the Board of Trade, a Freeman of the Borough, and though out of office, retains the valuable appointment of Agent for the Cape of Good Hope. Mr. Courtenay has a son, a Clerk in the Treasury, and his brother, the present Earl of Devon, lately filled the lucrative office of Clerk-Assistant of the Parliaments in the House of Lords. When Mr. Courtenay accepted the office of Vice-President of the Board of Trade, he stated openly in his place in parliament that his mind was as ignorant of its duties as a sheet of white paper.*

*William Searle Bentall Esq., Alderman of the Borough and Father of the old Corporation, holds the sinecure places of Tide and Landing Waiter of Totnes; which town, however, is not, and never was a port.*

*John Bentall, Wine Merchant and Stock Broker, Angel Court, Throgmorton Street, London, a non-resident Freeman of the Borough, and brother of the above Wm. Searle Bentall; has for a great number of years filled the lucrative sinecure place of Clerk of the Petty Bag in the Court of Chancery.*

*John Bentall, second son of the above Wm Searle Bentall, non-resident Freeman of the Borough; one of the Masters in Westminster School.*

*Edward Bentall, third son of the above Wm. Searle Bentall, a Writership in Bengal.*

*Henry Bentall, fourth son of the above Wm. Searle Bentall, a Clerkship in one of the Public Offices.*

*Alfred Bentall, fifth son of the above Wm. Searle Bentall, a Midshipman the Royal Navy.*

*Thomas Nelson Waterfield, son-in-law of the above Wm. Searle Bentall, and a non-resident Freeman of the Borough; an Assistant Clerk in the Office of the Board of Control.*

*George Pownal Adams, an Alderman of the Borough; a Major General in the Army, which exalted status the gallant knight has attained by means of the family borough, his country having yet to learn that he ever distinguished himself by his services in any one of the ranks of his military career through which he so rapidly passed.*

*William Dacres Adams, brother of the above G.P. Adams, and a non-resident Freeman of the Borough; one of his Majesty's Commissioners of Woods, Forests and Land Revenue, and receiving a large Pension for having formerly filled the sinecure position of a Commissioner of the Lottery.*

*William Pitt Adams, son of the above Wm. Dacres Adams, and a non-resident Freeman of the Borough; a Clerk in the Secretary of State's Office for Foreign Affairs.*

*Mayow William Adams, another son of the above Wm. Dacres Adams; a Clerk in the Office of Woods and Forests.*

*Richard Dacres, uncle of the above Wm. Dacres Adams, and a non-resident Freeman of the Borough; a Vice-Admiral of the White.*

*William Adams Welsford, another relative of the above Wm. Dacres Adams, and a non-resident Freeman of the Borough; Distributor of Stamps at Plymouth.*

*Samuel Adams, uncle of the above Wm. Dacres Adams, and brother-in-law of the foregoing Wm. Searle Bentall, a non-resident Alderman of the Borough; formerly Barrack*

*Master at Berryhead, now a double Barrack Master at Hounslow.*

*William Adams, son of the above Samuel Adams, and a non-resident Freeman of the Borough; a Clerk in the Office of Woods and Forests.*

*Edward Adams, second son of the above Samuel Adams, and a non-resident Freeman of the Borough; has received £40 a year from his infancy till old enough to take a Commission in the Engineers.*

*Henry Bentall Adams, third son of the above Samuel Adams, and a non-resident Freeman of the Borough; a Clerk in the Office of Woods and Forests.*

*George Adams, fourth son of the above Samuel Adams; a Writership in India.*

*Frederick Adams, fifth son of the above Samuel Adams; a Cavalry Cadetship in India.*

That the newspaper was regurgitating these ten-year-old allegations in 1839 tells us something about how deeply they had divided the electorate. The rhetorical style is seductive, but the substance should be treated with caution.

## Courtenay's Farewell Address

Thomas Peregrine Courtenay is, of course, a central figure in this book. If there was undue patronage or corruption, it would have been primarily exercised through him. An account of his life was provided in Chapter 10, and his personal involvement in the family affairs relating to the Marshall orphans was described in several previous chapters elsewhere.

His farewell address to his constituents – briefly quoted from above where it predicted, post-Great Reform Act, a *growth* in electoral corruption – included a vigorous defence of his political philosophy and stance relating to "improper influence." Courtenay was particularly pessimistic about the impact of the Act, which he thought would unduly expand the remit of government:

*On the whole I am persuaded that the Parliament will have every imputed vice of the old system, excepting perhaps, (and even this is doubtful) that of direct nomination;[392] there will flourish the influence of Government, the influence of money, the influence of delusion; and it will not more effectually ensure compliance with the sober wishes and opinions of intelligent men. It will bring into more favourable and rapid operation the demands of those who are not intelligent, and if for that reason only, I would have opposed the Bill.*

He addressed this topic explicitly later in his address:

*Objections are made to the public expenditure, not only as it increases taxes, but as it facilitates corruption. I fearlessly assert that the influence of Government has been, during the whole period [preceding 1832], progressively on the decline; and that more and more regard has been had to merit and sufficiency, in appointments of all kinds. Among the measures for the reduction of patronage, sinecures, being the object of not unnatural jealousy, were long ago, abolished; and it is one of the many instances of injustice done, towards Tory Ministers, that the call for the abolition of these offices, continues as loud, as when the government successfully resisted it!*

239

And later, with an argument that remains pertinent to this day:

*They have probably obtained some popularity by this measure, partly through the erroneous supposition that most of those salaries had been augmented during the war. I refused to concur in this reduction. Its operation on the finances is imperceptible; and it has in common with other suggestions of the present day, this injurious tendency: – it tends to give a monopoly of public office to persons born to hereditary wealth, a result as little conducive to efficient service, as it is inconsistent with justice, with the philosophy which teaches that the hope of reward stimulates to exertion, or with the desire, now so loudly pretended, of calling forth the intellect of the people at large.*

Then later again:

*It is very well to abolish sinecures, and to reduce any salaries which may be found enormous, but though such retrenchments may be right in principle, they must be small in amount. I say boldly, in opposition to a popular cry, that the reduction in efficient civil offices, has already gone too far for the public good. This rage for the limitation of salaries is indeed one of the most curious forms of "liberality". I am clearly for abolishing useless offices; but I contend for such a remuneration for the active, and laborious, and responsible public servant, as may maintain him in his due class in society, while actively employed, and in his old age; and in the case of political functionaries, liable to loss of office upon Ministerial changes, I argue for such a rate and condition of allowance, as may tempt various talents into them, and enable those who are not born rich to preserve an independence of character.*

In other words, Courtenay thought it important to find the most talented people to run the government, rather than to depend just on those with hereditary wealth but no guarantee of talent, and that in order to do this, public servants needed to be offered appropriate remuneration.

**Assessment**

In modern parlance, the term "political patronage" is used in more than one way. Courtenay had a "patron" in Charles Long (an associate and supporter of William Pitt the Younger), who spotted an ambitious, intelligent and impecunious young clerk, hired him as his private secretary, and used him to conduct a "pamphlet war" with the government of the day. When returned to power, Courtenay continued to be given bigger and better jobs, even after Long retired. That type of patronage – networking and mentoring – was, and continues to be, a mainstay of both government and industry. But there was also a long tradition of rewarding political loyalty by appointing people to positions that were either sinecures, or required little competence to fulfil.[393] So the question to be answered is whether, case by case, this type of "improper influence" was evident – i.e., that as a result of political loyalty, a beneficiary was found an appointment that paid too much for doing too little.

I interpret Courtenay's remarks, quoted above, to indicate that he was interested in attracting talented and honest people into public service. In today's terminology, this was a matter of "networking." Many of the sons of the Adams, Bentall, Marshall and Waterfield families were helped into jobs based on recommendations from Courtenay and other influential friends. But Courtenay was a champion of "efficient civil offices," and would have argued that their appointments were based on merit. The principle described by Kuper – the historical importance of close family connections in the development of private enterprise – extended over into efficient government.

The question to be addressed now is whether the influence that helped find careers for the Adams, Bentall and Marshall offspring was improper. The following paragraphs consider the individuals mentioned in the "Report of the Commissioners" from 1834, and in the *Western Morning News* article of 1839.

### "*Barrack Masters*": Samuel Adams and Richard Marshall

Two of the allegedly corrupt freemen became barrack-masters: Samuel Adams, first at Berry Head, then Hounslow; and Richard Marshall, first at Chatham, then Maidstone. There was a huge effort during that period to professionalise the management of military bases. Until 1792, there were very few barracks – i.e., purpose-built buildings designed to house troops when not on active duty – in Britain. That year, with a war in the offing, a building program was started to provide bases initially for cavalry, and then infantry regiments. In 1795 the management of the growing number of barracks was placed under the control of a "Barrack Master General." The building frenzy prompted a *"warm debate"*[394] in the House of Commons, about the costs, patronage opportunities and even the constitutional morality of

placing permanent troops in buildings whose primary purpose was to house soldiers collectively, in strategic locations for policing within the realm rather than for defence of the realm around the coast. By 1796 the construction costs had risen to £1,400,000 (a vast sum in those days), and a total of 46 barrack-masters had been employed.[395] There were not yet 46 working barracks, so questions were raised in Parliament about why these men were needed. Furthermore, there were three instances reported where a barrack-master had been appointed without there even being any intention of erecting barracks. One instance was apparently a reward for some small political favour, so there may have been a residual suspicion that all of these appointments were in fact just "jobs for the boys."

But by the time Samuel Adams and Richard Marshall were appointed barrack-masters, at least several years later, some of the controversy had died down. Samuel started locally at Berry Head, and was then moved to Hounslow. The Hounslow Cavalry Barracks was one of the first to have been built, with construction starting in 1793. (Several of the original buildings are today listed for conservation.) Based on the birth and baptism records of Samuel's children, his family did not move to Hounslow until around 1820 – all but the youngest of the children, born in 1821, were baptised at Totnes – but he may have been appointed to that position much earlier. He was barrack-master there until he died in 1842. Richard Marshall was appointed as an assistant barrack-master at Chatham in 1805, and in 1839 became the barrack-master at Maidstone, with an annual salary of £182 10s.[396] This was another cavalry barracks, which became the Cavalry Riding Establishment in 1835.[397]

Richard's appointment was made while the younger William Adams was MP for Totnes. Samuel's may have been made before, but he was mayor of Totnes in 1809, and was living at Buckfast Abbey until around 1828 (see Chapter 11) so the timing is not clear. However, the job of barrack-master required a degree of competence and was certainly not a sinecure – not, at least, once the barrack had been built and occupied. William Adams might have pulled some strings to get jobs for his kid brother and his cousin, but even if he did, they were accountable, once appointed, for maintaining a good reputation for their families. Nor do I think they can be criticised for keeping their voting rights as freemen in Totnes while no longer resident, since that was the practice of the time.

## Two Brothers: William Searle and John Bentall

I see very little evidence that these brothers depended much, if at all, on *"rewards for political loyalty"*.

William Searle inherited a set of businesses from his father, and for most of his life ran them successfully. It was nugatory to suggest that his apparent position as *"Tide and Landing Waiter of Totnes"* was egregious, since he actually owned a significant section of the riverfront, and the town, although not at that time an international port, handled substantial coastal traffic. It would be interesting to know whether the associated stipend amounted to much.

John became a stockbroker and a clerk of the Petty Bag, but if there was patronage involved, then it was almost certainly through his uncle, Thomas Mendham, who had held that office previously. That said, it is likely that for some years the clerkship was precisely the type

of sinecure that the *Extraordinary Black Book* (legitimately) targeted. When the government decided to address the issue and make changes in the conduct of the Court of Chancery (see Chapter 5), this forced John to work harder and together with the two other clerks produce written reports,[398] but the pension he eventually received was possibly still overgenerous.

It looks as though the brothers all made a lot of money by investing in real estate, and as such were not overly beholden to either William Adams MP or Courtenay. In fact, Courtenay is on record as saying that he was grateful to William Searle Bentall for his help in providing the evidence to justify his brother's inheritance of a title and an estate (see Chapter 10).

## William Dacres (W.D.) Adams, and General Sir George Pownall (G.P.) Adams KCH

W.D. Adams was to some extent a mentor to Courtenay (see Chapter 10). They married sisters, and W.D. Adams, in consultation with his father, William Adams MP, decided to recommend Courtenay to the Totnes clan as his father's successor. If there was improper influence in the appointment of W.D. Adams to positions in government, it might have been because his mother had been wet nurse to Princess Amelia, but Pitt would not have picked W.D. as his private secretary (who would have been at his beck and call every day, and who ultimately was at his bedside when he died) merely because he owed something to his mother or father.

George Pownall Adams, brother of W.D. Adams, was a cavalry officer and fought in India. Although his superiors in India thought he did a good job, his promotions between 1813 and 1831 could have been encouraged by Courtenay. In the absence of more information, this allegation cannot be ruled out, despite Courtenay's general statements in defence of his professional conduct.

## Other Bentall, Marshall, Waterfield and Adams Appointments

There are several Bentall relatives mentioned specifically in the *Western Morning News* article, plus about ten descendants of William and Samuel Adams (and one Welsford, their nephew). William Bentall, the eldest son of William Searle Bentall and grandson of the original patriarch, was conspicuously absent from the list, as were other Marshalls, in particular Edward (of the War Office – see Chapter 12) and John (then a banker in Cape Town – see also Chapter 12). Edward was named in the *Black Book*, and John's appointment was very clearly the work of Courtenay. Can we assume that these two were so conspicuously competent in their professions that their names were omitted from the *Western Morning News* list?

In fact, the most important service that Courtenay provided to the Adams and Bentall families was to encourage and help their children to access the very best education facilities available, according to their individual capabilities. This is consistent with Courtenay's professed interest in finding the best talent to run his area of government. Courtenay did arrange a recommendation from another MP for Edward Bentall to attend Haileybury in 1825, in preparation Edward's subsequent career in the Indian Civil Service – presumably Courtenay did not want his name on that recommendation, because of his known connections with the family. It is also possible that he pulled strings to help Alfred and later Octavius Bentall into naval school, but when they became adults,

they were expected to fend for themselves. Both brothers assumed substantial responsibilities early in life, distinguished themselves in different ways, and died trying.

A cynical view and that of the *Western Morning News* is that the family just divided up the spoils: Courtenay pulled strings to find jobs for his family at the Board of Control; W.D. Adams put his relatives into positions at the Office of Woods, Forests and Land Revenues; Edward Marshall provided jobs for his nephews at the War Office. Yet Courtenay was very clear that he believed in a meritocracy and a system of remuneration that would adequately compensate an "*active, and laborious, and responsible public servant,*"[399] so that the exercise of government was not dependent upon people with wealth but limited talent. Efforts were made to find jobs in the bureaucracy for Courtenay's many children after he died, but those were not necessarily well-paid.

The conclusion I take from this rather discursive account of these families is that there was a strong governing belief, based on the experience of being urban merchants – part of the rising bourgeoisie rather than the landed gentry – that the preservation of the family's status in society was dependent primarily upon education. Great efforts were made to guide each boy into productive careers that matched their talents. That sounds very modern.

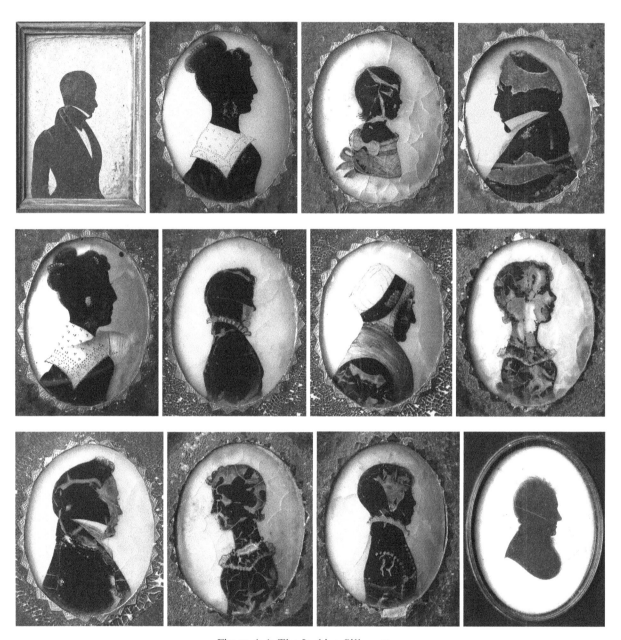

Figure A.1: The Jenkins Silhouettes

*Appendices*

# APPENDIX A: THE JENKINS FAMILY

The collection of miniatures at Benthall Hall contains 12 silhouette portraits known to be of members of the Jenkins family (see Chapter 31).[i] These include portraits of Jane Price's mother, grandfather and miscellaneous relatives, dating from around 1820. One or two are in fair condition, but most are severely damaged (see Figure A.1).

The subjects' names are written on the backs of their portraits as follows (the dates are taken from the National Trust Collections website):

Top row (l–r): *Elias Jenkins* (1840); *Rachel Jenkins* (1820); *John Borlase Jenkins as an Infant* (1810); *John Borlase Jenkins* (c. 1830).

Middle row: *Mary Borlase Jenkins* (c. 1820); *Richard 'Dick' Jenkins* (c. 1820), *Mrs. Jenkins* (c. 1820); *Rebecca Jenkins* (c. 1820).

Bottom row: *Thomas Jenkins* (c. 1820);[ii] *Mary Jenkins* (c. 1820); *Elias Jenkins* (1835)*; Mrs. Morgan* (1820).

Only for the first and last of these is anything known about the artist. The first portrait of Elias Jenkins is attributed to the Hubard Gallery; however, this Elias died on 30 December 1834, aged just 18,[400] so the dating of that portrait and of the third one in the bottom row are questionable. The portrait of Mrs Morgan is attributed to John Miers, one of the leading silhouette painters of his age.

From various websites; a hand-written family tree created by Mary Clementina Benthall (see Chapter 31) that is now in the West Glamorgan Archives, Swansea; and a number of other documents listed in that archive's catalogue, as well as in the National Library of Wales; it is possible to piece together a simple family tree and make some sense of the family's fortunes and misfortunes.

The father of this family was Elias Jenkins (1779–1850), "*gentleman*," of Kilvey House, Llansamlet, Swansea. He is not one of the people shown above, but he may be the subject of one of the unnamed silhouettes. Elias senior was in the copper smelting business, for 50 years the manager of the White Rock Copper Works, on the east bank of the River Tawe a few miles north of Swansea, and he was a property owner and civic leader in Swansea itself. In 1830 he was elected as one of two "Trustees of the Harbour of Swansea." He married Mary Rogers

---

[i]  There are also six unnamed silhouette portraits in the collection; they are in very similar frames, and so probably depict members of the same family.

[ii]  The subjects of the other portraits here can be identified with a high degree of certainty, but Thomas is something of a mystery.

(probably the "*Mrs. Jenkins*" in the second row of Figure A.1) and they had five children.

The eldest, Mary (1811–1892), married William Price. Their portraits can be seen in Figure 31.2. Their daughter then married Ernest Benthall, eventually making Mary the grandmother of Mary Clementina (Molly) Benthall. The second silhouette in the bottom row is of her.

The next, Rebecca (1814–1876), married the Rev. Ebenezer Stead Hart. Her silhouette is in the middle row, on the right and her sister Elizabeth (1815–1908) married Richard White Beor and had eight children, including Elias Jenkins Beor (born 1847). She is not identified as the subject of any of the silhouettes. The next was Elias (1818–1834) who, as noted above, died young. He is the subject of the Hubard Gallery portrait (top row, left) and also of the third portrait in the bottom row. Then there was Sarah (1824–1875) who died in Bristol, unmarried. She is not identified as the subject of any of the silhouettes.

Going back a generation further, the father of Elias Jenkins senior was named Richard. He was likewise in the copper smelting business and owned the Middle Bank Copper Works, situated on the same side of the River Tawe upstream from the White Rock works. He was married twice, the second time to Mary Borlase. Elias was their eldest son and there were three more, named Thomas, Samuel and John Borlase, all of whom had families. John Borlase Jenkins (1791–1850) married Rachel Morgan in 1809 and had about eight children, including Mary Borlase Jenkins (1811–1900),[401] Rachel Jenkins (b. 1815), Richard Jenkins (b. 1818) and another John Borlase Jenkins (1823–c.1881).

The silhouette on the far right in the top row of Figure A.1 is of John Borlase Jenkins senior.[402] The handwritten note on the back of

it reads: "*John Borlase Jenkins m. 1. Rachel Morgan, 2. somebody horrid Aunt Mary's step.*" Who wrote that is a mystery, and exactly what step-relation was intended is also unknown. The silhouette to his left is of his youngest son, also John Borlase Jenkins, as an infant, and the one to the left of that is of his daughter Rachel. The silhouette on the far left in the middle row is of Mary Borlase, next to her is son Richard, and the "*Mrs. Morgan*" on the far right in the bottom row is probably John senior's mother-in-law.[403] (The Morgan family owned and ran an iron works and also a tin works.)

Richard Jenkins, the father of Elias senior, had brothers named Lewis, Llewellyn and Samuel, and daughters named Margaret and Catherine. The description of a document in the West Glamorgan Archives reads:

*Probate of Will of Richard Jenkins of Middlebank Copper Works, Llansamlet, gent., devising and bequeathing to his son John Jenkins his eight day clock and portable writing desk; to his grandson David Morgan Jenkins son of John Jenkins, his small metal watch which belonged to his son Daniel; the rest of his household furniture and effects to his wife Mary Jenkins, with the leasehold estate which he holds from Lord Vernon in Llansamlet, which is to go to his son John Jenkins after her decease, also his right to 3a of land in Aberavon, as a burgess of Aberavon, to his wife; also to his sons Elias, Samuel and John and to Mary Jenkins, widow of his son John, £5 each; to his wife the profits from the sloop Albion in Cardigan, for her life, and then to Elias and John after her decease; the rest of his estate to be divided into quarters, between Elias Jenkins, John Jenkins, Samuel Jenkins and the children of his deceased son*

*Thomas Jenkins. made 24 June 1817, proved*
*23 Sept. 1818.*[404]

The father of this Richard Jenkins was
another Elias Jenkins, described in a lease
agreement in 1735 as a *"yeoman of Llantwit-*
*Juxta-Neath."* Another gentleman of that name
was a prominent lawyer in Swansea and was
under-sheriff of Glamorgan in 1763, but it is not
clear whether they were closely related.

# APPENDIX B.
## FROM THE *TAUNTON COURIER*, 19 AUGUST 1903

Articles appeared in several regional newspapers in the days after the death of Edward Robert Dale (see Chapter 32). This version appeared in the Taunton Courier on 19 August 1903

### DEATH OF MR. E. R. DALE
### AT SALISBURY
### EXTRAORDINARY SUICIDE
### HEAD SMASHED WITH AN AXE

*Early in the morning of Saturday week Mr. Edward Robert Dale, a native of Glanvilles Wootton, who for some years had been acting as an electrical engineer at Salisbury, was found lying terribly injured in a pool of blood at his workshop in Windsor-street, Fisherton. His skull had been fractured by blows from a sharp instrument, there being about 20 cuts on the top of the head. An axe, covered in blood, was found in the middle of the room. The head of the axe was away from the handle, and it seems the deceased must have struck himself repeatedly with the loose head. When discovered he was lying with his head on a cloth which had been placed on a box, and a bucket full of water and blood was just beside him. After the wounds had been dressed, Mr. Dale was removed to the Infirmary, where he* *died on Wednesday without having recovered full consciousness.*

*Mr. Dale was the son of the late Mr. James Charles Dale, of Wootton Glanville, who was High Sheriff of Dorset in 1843, and is a brother to Mr. C. W. Dale, now residing at the Manor House in that village. Formerly deceased lived at Long-street, Sherborne, in the house now occupied by Mr. Williams, and afterwards on Greenhill. Eventually he removed to Salisbury. It seems that Mr. Dale's interest in electrical matters was inspired by scientific rather than commercial motives, and that he carried on his experiments with the help of an allowance from his family. Mr. Dale married a daughter of Dr. Benthall, but his wife died some years ago. He leaves a son and daughter, with whom much sympathy is felt in their sorrow.*

### THE INQUEST

*was held at the Infirmary on Wednesday afternoon by the City Coroner (Mr. S. Buchanan Smith). Mr. A. C. Huxtable, of the firm of Messrs. Andrews, Son, & Huxtable, of Dorchester represented the relatives of the deceased. Mr. J. Saunders was chosen foreman of the jury.*

*Miss C. M. Hurdle of Mill-road, Fisherton, deposed that deceased was about 50 years old and had lodged with her for about fifteen years. On Friday evening, August 7th, she was talking to him about financial and other matters. He then went out, and witness saw him no more that night. On arising on Saturday morning she discovered that he had not been in the house all night, and aroused her brother. Together they went to deceased's workshop in Windsor-street, and opened the door–which was not locked–and stepped in. She saw Mr. Dale lying on some boxes in a pool of blood, and then her brother pulled her back. Witness said that her last words to Mr. Dale on the Friday night were a suggestion that he should go for a long walk to Durnford. He said he thought he would, and did not say anything about not coming back. He had a latch-key, but witness waited up for him until 1.30 on Saturday morning. She had never heard him threaten to take his life. He worked at electrical engineering as a hobby. Witness added that Mr. Dale had stopped out all night before, but he generally mentioned it when he was going to do so. He was rather excitable, but she did not think he had any deep quarrel with anyone, and she did not know of anyone who owed him a grudge.*

*Mr. H. L. E. Wilks, medical practitioner at Salisbury, stated that he was called to Windsor-street about eight a.m. on Saturday. He went to a shed at the back of the house, and found a man lying at the further end with a fractured skull and his brain protruding. In the middle of the room there was a pool of blood and a hatchet, the head of which was separate from the haft. There was also blood at the entrance of the shed. The fracture of the skull was caused by a series of blows in parallel lines with a sharp and long instrument. There were several "tentative" cuts on the head, which had only just penetrated the skin. The injuries could have been self-inflicted if the axe-head alone had been used, but if the haft had been in the head it could not have been.*

*The Coroner: If the wounds had been caused by another person, would there have been so many small cuts? Witness: No. My own opinion is that the injuries were inflicted by the deceased.*

*Witness, continuing, said that when he saw Mr. Dale he was alive, but unconscious. He dressed the wounds, and had him removed to the Infirmary. In answer to the jury, witness said that the injuries could not have been caused through deceased falling on the axe, as there were some 20 cuts on the skull. Deceased was in such a position that it looked as if he had lain down after putting the bucket to catch the blood. It was quite possible for Mr. Dale to inflict all the cuts on himself.*

*The house surgeon at the Infirmary (Mr. C. A. Badcock) said that the deceased was brought there about nine o'clock on Saturday morning. He never properly recovered consciousness, and died on Wednesday. The injuries were sufficient to cause death.*

*The Coroner summed up, and said there were three verdicts the jury could return, namely, that deceased was accidentally killed, but the doctor had said that was impossible; that Mr. Dale was killed by some other person, but there was no evidence in support of that; or they might return a verdict of suicide. All of them knew Mr. Dale, and knew that he was rather eccentric, but there was no evidence as to the state of his mind.*

*The Foreman observed that it was only a surmise that the wounds were self-inflicted, and said that he thought they ought to return an open verdict.*

*The Coroner said that the jury might like to hear something about Mr. Dale's financial position.*

*Mr. Huxtable then said he had had the privilege of transmitting funds to Mr. Dale for many years. Occasionally Mr. Dale, in his electrical business, ran a little short of money, and when he was pressed advances were made to him, although the relatives had tried by all the means in their power to induce him to give up the business. Mr. Dale was in receipt of a monthly allowance of £16 13s 4d, or £200 a year. Whenever he wanted money he was allowed more than that. His allowance for this month had been sent only a day or two before his death, so Mr. Dale was not in any particular financial trouble. He (Mr. Huxtable) could think of no motive for this rash act.*

*A juryman asked if the axe belonged to the deceased?*

*The Coroner said it was impossible to find out. All enquiries had been made, but nothing further could be discovered.*

*Sergeant Whitbread stated that deceased had money and a watch and chain on him when found.*

*The jury, after discussing the facts in private, returned a verdict of 'Suicide whilst of unsound mind'*

# NOTES

## Preface, Introduction and Part 1

1   http://www.genealogistsforum.co.uk (retrieved April 2019).

2   A publication of Duke University Press, see Stevens (2020).

3   http://www.ravestijn.org/ (retrieved April 2019).

4   Kuper (2009) page 27. See the bibliography for the full citation.

5   See Note 2.

6   https://en.wikipedia.org/wiki/Totnes_Castle (retrieved April 2019).

7   English Heritage (2010) "Advice Report: Swallowfield Weir, River Dart, Totnes".

8   Windeatt (1891).

9   Russell (1984) page 64.

10   Keynes (1924).

11   Their great grandson, Richard Michell, was the first Principal of the second foundation of Hertford College, Oxford, see https://en.wikipedia.org/wiki/Richard_Michell (retrieved April 2019).

12   A note by Laura Benthall states that "*Joanna Southcott was [John Marshall's] cook in her earlier years before her imaginary visions and prophecies began, which for a time made her so notorious in London.*" Joanna Southcott became famous as a religious prophetess who for a time had thousands of followers (see https://en.wikipedia.org/wiki/Joanna_Southcott). I have not yet found anything to corroborate this connection, except that John Marshall may have been the rector of Musbury before moving to Exeter, and she started her career there as a cook and house servant.

13   At that time, election of the King's scholars at Eton College "*had become a mere farce, preference being given to the sons of Fellows or Masters or other persons nearly connected with the College, so that the whole Foundation became a private preserve ... The King's scholars, moreover, proceeded to King's College, Cambridge by seniority in regular rotation, and not by competition.*" Cust (1899) pp. 183–184.

14   Hawtrey (1903). This book contains extensive information about several generations of the Hawtrey family, and in its preface the author makes special reference to her cousin "*Miss Marshall*" (Louisa Maria Marshall, the daughter of William and Louisa–see Chapter 25).

15 https://janeaustensworld.wordpress.com/2013/04/22/sidmouth-where-jane-austen-found-love/ (retrieved April 2019).

16 http://discovery.nationalarchives.gov.uk/details/rd/adce677c-47d2-46a2-8621-28b0decd52b7 (retrieved April 2019). The document also refers to "*Richard Marshall, clerk,*" and "*Edward Marshall, clerk,*" who were two of Elizabeth's brothers mentioned above. There are also papers in the Eton College collections dealing with the lease of some college property to "*the Reverend Thomas Baker, D.D. of Loventor, in Berry Pomeroy, Co. Devon.*"

17 Cited by Coase (1994) and Groenewegen (1995).

18 The National Archives: PROB 11/100.

19 The Honourable East India Company (HEIC) was one of the first joint-stock (i.e., shareholder-owned) companies, founded in 1600 to trade with the Far East. It came to rule most of the Indian subcontinent, with a huge private army, navy, merchant marine organisation and civil service.

20 The original portrait of Sarah Chadder belonged to the Jackson family, descendants of Sir William Henry Drake's second marriage, to Elizabeth Lucy Wood, but its current location is unknown.

21 http://www.xroyvision.com.au/drake/surnames/surnames24.html (retrieved April 2019).

22 Stevens wrote her Master's thesis on the topic *William Henry Drake and the Commissariat in the Crimean War.* See https://downrabbitholes.com.au/wp-content/uploads/2018/04/stevens-civilians-at-war.pdf. The information here about him and his father comes from her.

23 Stevens has made new transcripts of all these, with extensive annotations, and as of April 2019 they are available at http://cwrs.russianwar.co.uk/cwrs-R-mstevens-drake-letters.html.

24 The history of the early Benthall family has been extensively documented (e.g., Wagner, 1975).

25 https://en.wikipedia.org/wiki/Robert_Burnell (retrieved April 2019).

26 http://www.british-history.ac.uk/vch/salop/vol10/pp247-257 (retrieved April 2019).

27 Lawrence Benthall (1590–1652), 12 generations in descent from John Burnell, attended Oriel College, Oxford, and then entered the Inner Temple, one of London's four Inns of Court, in 1611. He lived at Benthall Hall and added the staircase and the overmantle in the main hall, whose carvings include wyverns from his wife's family coat of arms. He inherited the estate from his father John Benthall, the youngest of 11 sons (and four daughters) of his grandfather, Richard. His uncle George was employed by the Earl of Shrewsbury, and was his 'gentleman porter' responsible for a team of 40 armed men in charge of the house arrest of Mary Queen of Scots at Chatsworth House, until Queen Elizabeth expressed "*a very hard opinion of*" George, and he was moved to London. See Leader (1880) pages 236, 538, and 605–606.

28 The legal issues in this lawsuit were eventually described, extensively analysed and then reported in Atkyns (1767), pages 195–205.

29 In August 1572, at the Assizes held in Colchester, Agnes Steadman, a "*common witch,*" was found guilty of bewitching "*Sibel Bentall, wife of Thomas Bentall yeoman there, so that for the space of 12 days she was violently ill and despaired of her life*" (Essex Records Office: reference T/A 418/20/38).

30  https://en.wikipedia.org/wiki/John_Riley_(painter) (retrieved April 2019) based on an entry in the Dictionary of National Biography.

31  A 'draper' was a cloth merchant. At that time York was the centre of a very prosperous woollen industry. Also, see Hunter – ed. Clay (1899).

32  Yorkshire, Archbishop of York Marriage Licences index, 1613–1839, transcribed and made available through www.findmypast.co.uk as are the other dates in this section.

33  Walker (1714), quoted in Thornton (1912).

34  http://www.mylearning.org/history-around-hull/p-223/ (retrieved April 2019).

35  National Archive PROB 11/648-34.

36  Forster (1956), page 21. Robert Thornton moved to Clapham in 1735. In 1733, a partnership of Robert, Godfrey and William Thornton (other brothers), William Wilberforce (brother-in-law), and two other merchants founded a sugar refinery on Lime Street, Hull, which remained partially owned by the family for 100 years – see http://www.mawer.clara.net/loc-hull.html (retrieved April 2019).

37  Francis (1848).

38  Numerous sources, including Forster (1956, p. 21), Kuper (2009) page 239, and the *History of Parliament Online* claim that John Thornton (Robert's son and Henry's father) was a director of the Bank of England, but his name does not appear on the list of directors published by Francis (1848), nor in the original *Director Annual Lists 1694–1908* in the Bank of England archives see https://www.bankofengland.co.uk/-/media/boe/files/archive/directors-annual-lists/1694–1908-book1.pdf (retrieved April 2019).

39  Kuper (2009), page 140.

40  Ibid.

41  https://en.wikipedia.org/wiki/Henry_Thornton_(reformer) (retrieved April 2019).

42  There is a record of a marriage at Colchester between John Thornton and Letitia Cock (a widow) in 1728, and before that a marriage in 1720 in London between Daniel Cock and Letitia Lane, both "*of Colchester*." There is no independent corroboration that this was the same John Thornton, but the Colchester connection makes it plausible. However, this John's age on his marriage license is given as 24, while another source states that Elizabeth's brother was baptised in 1700. The quotes here are from Laura's *Annals*, as are those that follow.

43  Urban (1833), page 474.

44  Dickens (1853). *Bleak House*: chapter 1: "*There is the registrar below the judge, in wig and gown; and there are two or three maces, or petty-bags, or privy-purses, or whatever they may be, in legal court suits.*"

45  Great Britain, House of Commons (1816).

46  These letters were kept by family members, and are in an archive at Benthall Hall. In the 1920s a transcript was made by Mary Clementina Benthall, which makes their content easier to read, and the quotation here is from that transcript.

47  John Thornton died in 1769, followed by his wife Leticcia (or Letitia) in 1771. They were both buried at Ashprington. The record of his will was stored at the Exeter Probate Registry, and was destroyed when that building was bombed in 1942.

48  Laura Benthall *Annals*.

49  Cherry, Bridget and Pevsner, Nicholas (1989): page 875.

50  Henry Thornton's relationship to William's mother was outlined in chapter 5.

51  Windeatt (1904) p. 504.

52  Several generations of the Searle family were buried at Dartington. The church used to be situated next to Dartington Hall, but early in the last century it was moved, stone by stone, to a site a mile or so away. The original graveyard remains, but with little attempt at upkeep.

53  Thorne (1986) page 38. At around that time, William Bentall, in one of his letters to Thomlinson, mentioned that he was sending barley to Liverpool rather than London, because the prices there were better. It is interesting to speculate that young William Adams might have been the source of that commercial information, as well as William Bentall's contact in Liverpool.

54  https://www.thegazette.co.uk/London/issue/12459/page/3 (retrieved April 2019). Historians seem to be confused about who Adams partnered with, and associate him with John Parr Welsford, rather than Giles, but I have found no evidence to corroborate that theory.

55  Fryer & Dracott (1998) p. 219.

56  One of them, Vice-Admiral James Richard Dacres, was married in 1777 at Totnes. The other was Vice-Admiral Sir Richard Dacres KCH, whose children were born at Totnes. Since both brothers were at sea for most of their lives, their wives may have lived in Totnes to be close to their sister-in-law—see https://en.wikipedia.org/wiki/James_Richard_Dacres_(Royal_Navy_officer,_born_1749) and https://en.wikipedia.org/wiki/Richard_Dacres_(Royal_Navy_officer) (both retrieved April 2019). There was a John Dacres who was admitted as a freeman of Totnes in 1784, but his relationship, if any, to the others is unknown.

57  https://www.kentarchaeology.org.uk/Research/Libr/MIs/MIsSydenham/01.htm (retrieved April 2019).

58  His replacement at Plympton Erle received a bill for £400 after he was elected in a by-election, according to The History of Parliament Online, see http://www.historyofparliamentonline.org/volume/1790–1820/constituencies/plympton-erle (retrieved April 2019). See also Chapter 43: *How Rotten Was our Borough?*

59  Bray (1833), page 199.

60  The Lawrence painting can be seen at http://www.historicalportraits.com/Gallery.asp?Page=Item&ItemID=235 (retrieved April 2019).

61  Urban (1856) page 118 has his obituary.

62  McConville (1995) page 112.

63  Wines (1873) page 137.

64  https://en.wikipedia.org/wiki/Great_Fulford (retrieved April 2019).

65  According to the marriage list in *The Asiatic Journal and Monthly Register for British and Foreign India, China and Australasia*, Vol. XIII, January–April 1834: "*At Mymunsing, George Adams, Esq, civil service, to Miss Emilia Read, daughter of the late Capt. James Read, of the Bengal N.I.*" (This town is now Mymensingh, also known as Nasirabad, about 70 miles north of Dakha in Bangladesh). In the *Bengal Obituary Booklet* (1851) there is a record of a memorial at Kedgeree: "*Sacred to the Memory of Captain James Read, of the 1ˢᵗ Regt. B. N. I., who departed this life on the 23ʳᵈ Sept. 1826, aged 36 years. Forget me not.*" (Kedgeree is now known as Khichri, a town about 200 miles west of Kolkata, formerly Calcutta. However, there was another small town on the river approach to Calcutta that was also known to the British as Kedgeree, so the location of this memorial may be in doubt.) The 1ˢᵗ Regiment, Bengal Native Infantry was the earliest of the infantry regiments in the Bengal Army, and was given that name in 1824. It mutinied at Cawnpore in 1857..

66  https://www.thegazette.co.uk/London/issue/15660/page/1826 (retrieved April 2019).

67  From Laura Benthall's *Annals*.

## Part II

68  Stott (2012) described this engraving but said she could not reproduce it "*for copyright reasons.*" This copy is in the possession of the Benthall family.

69  Anonymous (1794). This first full account of the story was published in 1794, written by a lawyer who was "*one of the Counsel*" (either Erskine, Fielding, Mills, or Dawes), but it is not clear which one.

70  Stott (2012), pages 92–96, and articles posted by Naomi Clifford at http://www.naomiclifford.com/the-bristol-elopement/2/ (retrieved April 2019).

71  Paul's account names Westmoreland as the location of the encounter, whereas the trial transcript says it was in Cumberland. However, 60 miles south of Gretna would have indeed put the couple close in Westmoreland, close to the town of Windermere.

72  This is also from Paul's account. The original quote from the record of the trial was (in the original orthography): "*On ſeeing Miſs Clerke, ſhe called out, Miſs Clerke, for God's ſake Miſs Clerke let me ſpeak to you; when Mr. Perry put himſelf out of his coach window and ſaid no ſuch perſon is here. Mrs. Perry is here if you pleaſe — drive on boys.*"

73  Paul was able to compare and contrast the penmanship of Clementina – "*a copybook hand, very easy to read*" – with Richard's, "*written in the terrible hand that might be expected of an 18th century surgeon accustomed to writing illegible prescriptions.*"

74  Horace Walpole, the famous writer and politician, wrote in a letter to his protégé Mary Berry in 1791:

> *Good Hannah More is killing herself by a new fit of benevolence about a young girl with a great fortune, who has been taken from school at Bristol to Gretna Green, and cannot be discovered, nor the apothecary who stole her. Mrs Garrick, who suspects as I do, that Miss Europa is not very angry with Mr Jupiter, had very warm words a few nights ago at the Bishop of London's with Lady Beaumont; but I diverted the quarrel by starting the stale story of the Gunning. You know Lady B.'s eagerness – she is ready to hang the apothecary with her own hands, and he certainly is criminal enough.*

75  Paul's version is that she was accompanied by "*a distant relative of the Ogilvies called Leslie*," while Stott's account says that she was accompanied by Mary's brother James. Their accounts of the events in Ghent differ, but both agree that the attempt to arrest the fugitives failed, and that further pursuit was abandoned afterwards.

76  Anonymous (1794) page iv.

77  Whereas, even according to the same catalogue, an inscription on the back reads "*painted by Engleheart MEA Marshall m. 1805 Thornton Benthall*." George Engleheart was a famous and celebrated miniaturist, and John Cox Dillman Engleheart was his nephew and student. However, the inscription was evidently added much later, since it was not until 1843 that the "h" was added back to the family name, so it cannot be relied upon.

78  National Archives PROB 11/1598/59. The executor, the Rev. William Marshall, was married to Isabella (see later in Chapter 8), Sarah Marshall was one of his sisters, and Thornton Bentall was married to another of his sisters (see Chapter 9).

79  Robertson, David; Bligh, Richard; Wilson, James; Maclean, Charles Hope; Bell, Sir Sydney Smith; Macqueen, Jon Fraser (1898). *The Scots Revised Reports: House of Lords series. 1821 – 1827* (W. Green & Sons), pages 829–838.

80  This account is based on a report in "*The Monthly Repository of Theology and General Literature, Volume 20, January to December, 1825*", pages 695 – 697.

81  Alexander Johnstone Ross was a character: he started out as a Presbyterian minister, but eventually found himself unable to be reconciled with their doctrines and switched to the Church of England. He was awarded a Doctor of Divinity degree in honour of his writings.

82  According to Wikipedia (https://en.wikipedia.org/wiki/Francis_David_Morice, retrieved April 2019), the Reverend Francis David Morice was a noted theologian, linguist and Classical scholar. Educated at Winchester, from which he went up in 1866 to New College, Oxford, he gained high distinction as a Classical scholar, and in 1874 was appointed a master at Rugby under Dr Jex-Blake. There he remained for 20 years, retiring ultimately in 1894 to Woking, where he took a house next to his great friend Edward Saunders, and devoted himself to entomological research.

83  Amy Clementina died on 15 June 1926 at Westhampnett, Sussex. Her executor was her brother the Rev. Francis David Morice, who himself died on 21 September the same year.

84  Cuthbert Morice was an officer in the Royal Engineers. He married Alice Letitia Steward in Bombay in 1892. She died in 1928, and he lived until 1942. Their son Reginald Francis Morice, Commander RN CBE, was born at Poona in 1894. He was commander of the Second World War destroyer *HMS Wanderer*, retired in 1944, and appears to have died in 1971.

85  https://archive.org/details/b29146719_0001 page 45 (retrieved April 2019).

86  Henry Edward was a solicitor. He was also an executor of the will of Thomas Hayter Lewis, the husband of Elizabeth Bentall Adams (see Chapter 7).

87  Simister (2015) Chapter 3.

88  Hardy (1811). There is much confusion over ships named *Ann*. Wikipedia is aware of two, neither of which appears to be this one, which, based on a hardly legible appendix in this book, seems to have been built at the Randall & Brent Shipyards in 1801.

89  http://www.nationaltrustcollections.org.uk/object/509522 (retrieved April 2019).

90  Devon Heritage Centre: reference number 1262M/0/O/LD/85/43.

91  Pigot & Co.'s Devonshire (1830).

92  House of Commons (1843), and T.B (1844) – page 52.

93  In 1840 John Bentall was named as an executor in a will, and his address was then given as Angel Court, Throgmorton Street, London.

94  http://www.1879zuluwar.com/t2807-captain-bethall (retrieved April 2019).

95  https://en.wikipedia.org/wiki/Joseph_d%27Aguilar_Samuda (retrieved April 2019).

96  https://www.jewisheastend.com/samudabrothers.html (retrieved April 2019).

97  There are two primary sources for the information in this chapter. One is a series of articles written by Edward Windeatt under the general title of *Totnes: Its Mayors and Mayoralties*, and published over the period 1890–1905 in various journals. The other is the *History of Parliament Online* website, which contains numerous articles originally published in book form by the History of Parliament Trust. This quote is from that website's article at: http://www.historyofparliamentonline.org/volume/1715–1754/constituencies/totnes (retrieved April 2019).

98  http://www.historyofparliamentonline.org/volume/1754–1790/constituencies/totnes (retrieved April 2019).

99  These details and those that follow come from Windeatt (1904).

100  Russell (1984) and *Appendix to the First Report of the Commissioners appointed to inquire into the Municipal Corporations of England and Wales, Part I. Midland, Western and South-Western Circuits, Ordered to be printed 30ᵗʰ March 1835*, pages 639–646.

101  Thorne ed. (1986), also http://www.historyofparliamentonline.org/volume/1790–1820/member/courtenay-thomas-peregrine–1782–1841 (retrieved April 2019); Fisher ed. (2009), and http://www.historyofparliamentonline.org/volume/1820–1832/member/courtenay-thomas–1782–1841 (retrieved April 2019).

102  This detail is included in a memoir by J.P. Waterfield, available online at http://www.tamburlane.co.uk/resources/Some%20memories%20for%20my%20grandchildren.pdf (retrieved April 2019).

103  See also Thorne (1986).

104  Windeatt (1905).

105  This and the other quotations that follow are from Fisher, Ed. (2009) see note 101 above.

106  For more details see https://www.historic-uk.com/HistoryUK/HistoryofBritain/Queen-Caroline/ (retrieved April 2019).

107  Fisher, Ed. (2009).

108 The election of 1830 had not provided a secure Parliamentary majority, and the Tory government led by the Duke of Wellington soon fell, to be replaced by a Whig government under Lord Grey, whose primary goal was to reform the electoral system. When he found that his proposed bill could not pass, he prevailed upon King William IV to dissolve Parliament and call an early election.

109 Fisher, Ed (2009).

110 https://books.google.com/books?id=qT5cAAAAcAAJ (retrieved April 2019).

111 Fisher, Ed (2009).

112 Ibid.

113 Baines (1822) page cxl.

114 Up until 1818, Thornton's banking partners were Walter Prideaux and George Farwell, but Farwell retired from the partnership that year.

115 The first abbey at Buckfast was Benedictine, founded in 1018, but this was "small and unprosperous." A new one was established by Savigniac monks in around 1134, then became Cistercian in 1147. See https://en.wikipedia.org/wiki/Buckfast_Abbey (retrieved April 2019).

116 Emery (2006) quoted also at https://en.wikipedia.org/wiki/Buckfast_Abbey (retrieved April 2019).

117 In the Devon Heritage Centre there is a document, reference number Z2/9, described as: *Plan "Buckfast Abbey Estate in the parish of Buckfastleigh, Devon. The property of William Searle Bentall and Thornton Bentall, Esqs." Field names and acreage of land given. Surveyor: Thomas Richards, Totnes 23" 25?".* *Pasted on stiff card. Scale: 1" to 2 chns.* 1815.

118 http://www.oldashburton.co.uk/the-berry-family.php (retrieved April 2019).

119 White (1830).

120 Both titles are suspect. In 1828, the name was still spelled 'Bentall', and the house was owned by the two brothers. The engraving, a copy of a picture painted in 1828, was used in a book entitled *The History of Devonshire from the Earliest Period to the Present*, compiled by the Rev. Thomas Moore.

121 Justice of the Peace and Local Government Review, vol 35. Page 812: https://books.google.com/books?id=UwQ5AQAAMAAI

122 In 1720 the "Bubble Act" established two marine insurance companies, but more importantly it also prohibited the foundation of new companies except by Royal Charter or a Private Act of Parliament. In those days most business ventures were established as partnerships, including the various syndicates of Lloyd's underwriters. Until 1824, the subjects of the Bubble Act were the only joint-stock firms allowed to write marine insurance. But in that year Parliament started to approve new companies, and the Act was repealed in 1825. Nonetheless, until 1844 a Private Act was still the only way to establish a new joint-stock company, with limited liability for shareholders.

123 e.g.: *Arnold on the Law of Marine Insurance*; Beal's *The Law of Bailments, embracing Deposits, Mandate, Loans for use, Pledges, Hires, Innkeepers and Carriers*; Merkin's *Marine Insurance Legislation* and *Insurance and the Law of Obligations*; Selwyn's *An Abridgment of the Law of Nisi Prius*.

124 e.g.: *Liability for Damages arising in the navigation of Vessels: Hearing before the Committee on Commerce, United States Senate, 62ⁿᵈ Congress, 3ʳᵈ session, 1913.*

125 *Pigot & Co.'s Devonshire* (1830), also at https://www.genuki.org.uk/big/eng/DEV/Totnes/Totnes1830 (retrieved April 2019).

126 Turner (2017) p. 70.

127 Walter Prideaux, who for a few years was the Recorder of Totnes, was a partner in a bank in Kingsbridge that failed in 1825, see https://en.wikipedia.org/wiki/Devon_and_Cornwall_Bank (retrieved April 2019).

128 *The London Gazette*, Part 3: 1842, page 2458.

129 *The London Gazette*, Part 4: 1843, page 4451–4452.

130 Cherry, Bridget and Pevsner, Nicholas (1989).

131 A document now in the Devon Record Office, prepared 20 years later when a rail line was being planned to serve the river front, listed the owner of the underlying lease on those properties as John Benthall. However, he was dead by then, and William Bentall (the eldest son of William Searle) was the occupier and almost certainly the owner of the underlying 2,000-year lease. That document has been summarised and supplied to me by William Bellchambers, a Totnes historian.

132 Also the brother of Lady Teignmouth, who, with Thornton and Margaret Bentall, dined with Henry Thornton (see Chapter 9).

133 Presumably a relative, but the Searle family tree is not well documented.

134 As reported in a diary maintained by Clementina Benthall (see Chapter 17).

135 Presumably, since Anne Gowan Marshall was baptised on 5 January 1785.

136 Referred to in some sources as "*an Officer in the Indian Navy.*"

137 Transcript provided by Virginia Denton, a descendant of Richard's daughter Mary Ann Edgcumbe.

138 I am grateful to Len Barnett, who provided some of this information, and a lot more about the career of nephew William (see Chapter 13).

139 John and Jane's descendant, Ralph Ravestijn, has tried to trace her family so far without success. He has considered two theories. The first comes from the fact that on John and Jane's return voyage from Calcutta there were two other passengers, a Captain Alexander Campbell and his four-year-old daughter, Catharine. His wife had died a year or so before and one suggestion is that Jane was his relative, possibly his sister, and had travelled out to Calcutta to help look after the child. Alexander Campbell does appear to have had a sister named Janet, baptised in 1787. The second theory is that she was the Jane Campbell born at Fort Marlborough on the island of Java, and baptised there in 1785, the daughter of a senior civil official in the Honourable East India Company. However, the notice of Jane Marshall's death in the *Morning Post* recorded that she died in April 1868, aged 78. If that notice was correct, then both these possibilities are ruled out.

140 W.C. Ord was a private merchant in Bengal and a subscriber to the Bank of Bengal when it opened in 1809. Several years later, in 1815, John Marshall stood as bondsman to W.C. Ord when the latter needed a

financial guarantee of £500 for his application to reside permanently in Bengal. Ord died at sea on his return voyage to Bengal later that year. (This information was also provided to me by Ralph Ravestijn.)

141  Reid (1850).

142  Quotes here are from http://www.victorianweb.org/history/empire/india/37.htm (retrieved July 2019).

143  The Cape Colony was originally Dutch, then taken over by the British in 1795, and returned in 1802 by the Peace of Amiens. It was re-occupied by the British in 1806, and eventually ceded formally by the Dutch in 1814.

144  http://www.s2a3.org.za/bio/Biograph_final.php?serial=1850 (retrieved April 2019).

145  *The Atheneum* (1839), page 925.

146  Hazlitt (1912) page 52.

147  Hendley (2012) page 67.

148  www.ravestijn.org (retrieved April 2019)..

149  Martens, P.J.C., and Ravestijn, Ralph (2019), *Een Engelsman op Java: Francis Ord Marshall en zijn voor- en nagelschlift*. Indische Genealogische Verenignig, 's–Gravenhage.

150  *Reports from Committees of the House of Commons Vol XIII, Finance Reports XXIII to XXXVI 1798*, page 684.

151  Mr. Merry held the position of Chief Examiner of Army Accounts from 1809 until 1826. Edward was certainly in that position by 1833. Palmerston's biographer, David Brown (2010) thinks that he held that position under Palmerston – i.e. taking over from Mr. Merry in 1826, but I have not found independent confirmation of this.

152  http://www.historyofparliamentonline.org/volume/1820–1832/constituencies/totnes (retrieved April 2019).

153  Ibid.

154  Philip (1981).

155  https://en.wikipedia.org/wiki/Van_Diemen's_Land_Company (retrieved April 2019).

156  Boyd (1871).

157  Hansard: *The Parliamentary Debates – New Series Volume VI*, page 1217.

158  In the *Royal Kalendar, and Court and City Register for England, Scotland and Ireland* of 1841, the officials at the War Office are listed. They included the Secretary at War –(Rt. Hon. Thos. Babington Macaulay, a son of Zachary Macaulay and Selina Mills) his Deputy (Laurence Sulivan, Esq.); the Chief Examiner of Army Accounts (Edward Marshall, Esq.) ; the First Clerk (Chas. Chamier Raper, Esq.); followed by 8 Clerks, 1st Class, 17 Clerks, 2nd Class, 24 Clerks, 3rd Class. There was also the Private Secretary to the Secretary at War (C.Z. Macaulay Esq. younger brother of Thomas), a Private Secretary to the Deputy, a Law-Clerk, a Compiler of Military Statistics, a Head Messenger, 13 Messengers, and a Housekeeper. The 3rd class clerks included two of Edward's nephews: William Marshall, son of Richard, and William Ord Marshall, son of Captain John Marshall.

159  I am grateful to Len Barnett for his research at the British Library that provided these details and those on John Marshall from the following sources: Anthony Farrington: *A Biographical Index of East India Company Maritime Service Officers 1600–1834* (London: The British Library, 1999): page 521; India Office Records: L/MAR/C/659 – Commanders and Mates. Descriptions, &c. 1804-06: page 277; India Office Records: L/MAR/C/660 – Commanders and Mates. Descriptions, &c. 1807-09: page 263.

160  It is useful to place this career in the Maritime Service in the context of the state of the world at the time. Between 1793 and 1815, with one short period of peace in 1802–1803, Britain was fighting a continuous naval war with France and Holland. The East India Company convoys represented commercial targets. The ships were not armed like a naval warship, but the ones that William served on were about 150 feet in length, 40 feet wide, and with a 17-foot draft. They had two decks and were equipped with 36 guns, to deter enemy warships and pirates. Their captains were generally provided with "letters of marque," which entitled them to attack and capture enemy vessels.

161  Respectively, Louisa Bentall's father, sister, their friend William Adams MP, brother and nephew (the eldest son of William Searle Bentall).

162  Hunt (2014), page 177.

163  An Afrikaans term for a plot of land, commonly about half an acre in size. http://www.merriam-webster.com/dictionary/erf (retrieved April 2019).

164  Coase (1994) pp. 132 – 134, based on records in the National Archives – see next note.

165  National Archives CO 167/45.

166  There is no indication of what type of trade he engaged in. It is possible that his cousins at Totnes were expanding their wine business, and possibly he was charged with arranging a supply of wine bottles from the Leith Glass Company, one of the leading manufacturers at the time.

167  https://en.wikipedia.org/wiki/1817%E2%80%9324_cholera_pandemic (retrieved April 2019).

168  As of September 2016, this letter was in the possession of Richard Benthall.

169  The Asiatic Journal and Monthly Register vol. 18, July–December 1824, page 96.

170  According to Coase, William Marshall wrote in one of his books: "*Boys in Scotland in my schooldays used to be chastised by leather thongs called 'taws'.*"

171  Stevens quotes this from the journal of Charles' wife, Charlotte.

172  These details are of importance because Alfred Marshall's biographers confused two different individuals in those directories named William Marshall and treated them as evidence for William's weak character.

173  Quoted by Coase and confirmed by Megan Stevens based on an email from a local historian in Leith.

174  The documents are in the National Archives at Kew, catalogue no. PROB 31/1254, and thanks are again due to Len Barnett for locating them. The logistics involved in collecting those signatures on one sheet of paper, so that they could be presented to the probate court, must have been quite tricky.

175  Groenewegen (1995) page 32.

176  Marshall (1883).

177  The administrators at http://www.genealogistsforum.co.uk/ were very helpful finding these details. Our conversation is available at http://www.genealogistsforum.co.uk/forum/showthread.php?t=25186 (retrieved April 2019).

# Part III

178  The "scholars" at those schools were and still are limited in number, selected nowadays by competitive examination but then by more obscure means, and educated then for free, but now means-tested.

179  Spending a year or two at university was considered useful, but even in 1920, when Paul Benthall went up to Oxford, there was a sense that staying for a full three years in order to graduate was not necessary if one planned to go into business rather than embark on a professional career.

180  *The Elizabethan*, Volume 22, number 4, (July 1937) page 79, in an article entitled "Westminster Families".

181  The Rev. Thomas Cleave was appointed the master of the Totnes Grammar School in 1820. As a boarder William lived at the home of the master, and was subject to school discipline 24 hours a day.

182  It was the custom for boys to be dressed in frocks until they were 'breeched', i.e. dressed in trousers, often at around the age of seven. See https://en.wikipedia.org/wiki/Breeching_(boys) (retrieved April 2019).

183  Miss Coombes was one of the witnesses at Dorothy Marshall's 80th birthday party.

184  This letter now in the possession of descendants of Helen Davidson's father, who provided a copy, plus a transcript, to the Totnes Museum.

185  Benthall (2000).

186  http://wc.rootsweb.ancestry.com/cgi-bin/igm.cgi?op=GET&db=sandberg&id=I14976 (retrieved April 2019).

187  Hunt & Co. (1848).

188  Pemberton (1986) page 12.

189  Pengelly (1885). The story is also told in Simister (2015), but that version's description of "William Bentall" is not quite accurate.

190  *The Exeter Flying Post*, 25 January 1860.

191  Ibid. The sum mentioned is equivalent to about £200,000 today.

192  Wills (1863).

193  *The Justice of the Peace, December 23, 1871*, p. 812.

194  https://en.wikipedia.org/wiki/Buckfastleigh,_Totnes_and_South_Devon_Railway (Retrieved April 2019).

195  Essentially the same obituary was printed on p. 239 in Urban (1863) and on p. 410 in *The Annual Register, or a View of the History and Politics of the year 1862*, published the same year. The now unfamiliar ways in

which the names of Indian campaigns are spelled are the same in both publications. The original version in Urban is effusive about his personal character: "*His Christianity, like his charity, was genuine and unostentatious. Among his shining qualities, not the least conspicuous were his modest estimate of himself, and his readiness, however busy himself, to help anyone who stood in need of help.*"

196 Waterfield, John Percival (1998) *Some Memories, for my Grandchildren* – published electronically at http://www.tamburlane.co.uk. This memoir, written by T.N. Waterfield's great-grandson, states that Courtenay found jobs for both T.N. and his father.

197 The Waterfield family was deeply tied up with the Indian Army, and in the same memoir it says that "*a Waterfield was the first and another the last officer to be killed in the Indian Mutiny.*"

198 Letter from Charles Henry Marshall to Mary Ann Benthall, transcript provided by Megan Stevens.

199 As reported in the *Stinchcombe Parish Magazine* of 1870.

200 i.e., seventh place in the final mathematics exam.

201 Wainewright (1907), page 445.

202 Welch (updated 1852). The name of the editor of this revision of Welch's original list is not obvious, but must have been well known to his contemporaries. In his preface he thanks T.N. Waterfield for his "*constant and valuable aid.*"

203 Chapman (1984).

204 https://en.wikipedia.org/wiki/Henry_Waterfield (retrieved April 2019).

205 Wardale (1922) and (1935).

206 Lewis (1966). The reference is to Alfred the Great, who unified the southern Anglo-Saxon kingdom of Wessex in around 886 AD and created the first English navy.

207 Sixth Junior Optime, equivalent to a third-class degree.

208 *Boyle's Court Guide for January 1860*, page 103.

209 Account of the Celebration of the Jubilee of the Uniform Inland Penny Postage (1891) page 39.

210 Hall (1983).

211 I am not sure how many of the other characters were named after Post Office officials, but it might be interesting to check.

212 The account was written by committee and published in 1891 by Richard Clay & Sons.

213 http://www.westminster-abbey.org/our-history/people/harriett-benthall (retrieved April 2019).

214 The exact location and distance between John's house and that of his Waterfield brother-in-law is somewhat uncertain.

215 Sargeaunt (1898). In 1818 there were 324 pupils enrolled at the school, but by 1841 the number had dropped to 67. The school was not separately endowed with property and the cost of educating the scholars and

maintaining its buildings was covered by a grant from the Abbey next door. This grant did not keep up with inflation. Living conditions deteriorated and parents pursued other options.

216   A short history of John's life and that of his surviving son, William Henry, has been published on the internet, and can be accessed at the following pages (retrieved April 2019). There are a number of minor inaccuracies in the content, but the overall account given is a good one.
http://clutch.open.ac.uk/schools/willen99/w_employment/Benthall/JBintro/JBintro.html
http://clutch.open.ac.uk/schools/willen99/w_employment/Benthall/JBtrag/JBtrag.html
http://clutch.open.ac.uk/schools/willen99/w_employment/Benthall/JBlate/JBlate.html
http://clutch.open.ac.uk/schools/willen99/w_employment/Benthall/JBson/JBson.html.

217   At that time, it seems that aunts were referred to by the same conventions that applied to their husbands. Within the household the eldest son, William Searle, would be referred to as "Mr. Benthall," and his younger brothers as "Mr. Thornton," "Mr. John," etc. Thus "Aunt Benthall" referred to Mary Ann, the wife of William Searle, while "Aunt Thornton" referred to Margaret, the wife of Thornton Benthall.

218   Brendon (2005).

219   Forshall (1884).

220   Benthall (2000), based on papers at the Centre for East Asian Studies and elsewhere.

221   Charles Bathurst, as one of the commissioners of the India Board of Control, was technically one of Courtenay's bosses, and his recommendations would have been taken seriously.

222   At that time titles were important. Until 1836 his title was either an 'Assistant to' or a 'Joint', 'Deputy' or 'Officiating' Magistrate or Tax Collector.

223   Brendon (2005) made use of Clementina's diaries and letters for her book, and notes that the transcriber redacted some comments, including a sentence written in 1845 referring to the gambling and bankruptcy of Edward's younger brother Thornton.

224   Benthall (2000).

225   Brendon (2005).

226   Newham, ed. Coltman (1984).

227   https://www.oldbaileyonline.org/browse.jsp?div=t18410301-944 (retrieved April 2019).

228   The author has a similar set of mother-of-pearl counters.

229   Exactly how Henry Bentall was able to recommend James William Newham for this job is mysterious. Newham, "Mr. William Palmer, solicitor *(agent for the Sheriff of Kent) for whom he had done some important work, had asked him if he knew anyone who would like the appointment.*"

230   http://www.migration.amdigital.co.uk/Documents/Details/Australian-and-General-Emigration-Company—Registered-Between–1844-and–1856—and-Either-Dissolved/TNA_BT_41_34_192 (retrieved April 2019).

231   The Register Insurance Directory, 1856, published by William Tweedie, page 56. See https://books.google.com/books?id=XCIOAAAAQAAJ (retrieved April 2019).

232  http://nla.gov.au/nla.obj-398763147 (retrieved April 2019).

233  *The Sydney Morning Herald*, Wednesday 4 January 1882.

234  Henry was very involved in this venture. The North Wales Chronicle, Saturday January 14, 1865, reported that in the village of Edeyrn, following a party for local schoolchildren, "*Tea being over, Mr. Benthall, Port Nant Granite Quarry, amused the juveniles for the remainder of the evening, by exhibiting beautiful pictures with his magic lantern.*"

235  Rossetti (1895).

236  Hunt (1932), Fyfe (2014).

237  http://www.tate.org.uk/art/artworks/boyce-blackfriars-bridge-moonlight-sketch-t05011 (retrieved April 2019).

238  The settlement was quoted at some length in a case, *Rutty v. Benthall*, at the Court of Common Pleas in April 1867, as documented in *The Law Times Reports*, Volume XVI., New Series, from March to August 1867, page 287.

239  As of April 2019 they may be viewed at a web site devoted to the memory of Lizzie Siddall: http://lizziesiddal.com/portal/photograph-of-chatham-place/ and http://lizziesiddal.com/portal/another-photograph-of-chatham-place/.

240  These quotations come from a review of Rothwell & Ternstrom (2008) in the *Journal of the Lundy Field Society*, 2, 2010.

241  https://archiveshub.jisc.ac.uk/search/archives/ee682343-7c97-3b56-8c28-f344423d05b7 (retrieved April 2019).

242  As part of a memorial in St Mary's Church, Totnes.

243  https://en.wikipedia.org/wiki/HMS_Galatea_(1810) (retrieved April 2019).

244  *The Nautical Magazine for 1833, vol 2*: pages 45 and 46.

245  These details come from various Royal Naval 'Ship's Muster books', stored at The National Archives and transcribed there by Len Barnett.

246  The leading auctioneer of race horses in London at the time, and still today.

247  https://en.wikipedia.org/wiki/Treaty_of_H%C3%BCnk%C3%A2r_%C4%B0skelesi#European_reaction (retrieved April 2019).

248  These dates come from issues of *The Asiatic Journal and Monthly Register* for the relevant years.

249  There is a baptismal record for an Elizabeth Ann Ackland, dated 14 Aug 1818, at Totnes, Devon, with a father named Joseph whose occupation is listed as "*servant.*" Joseph's wife was Martha Dyer. Joseph died and was buried at Totnes in 1823, and Martha married again in 1826 (at Totnes) to John Salter. She signed her name and John "made his mark."

250  *Western Times, Devon*: 25 January 1840.

251 Elizabeth Ann's sister, Jane, was married to Thomas Caddy, a labourer, and gave birth in July 1839 to a son named William Dyer Caddy, whose birth certificate states that he was born at 67 Chapel Street, Devonport, with a relative Ann Dyer in attendance. That ties in with the baptism record at Totnes, that gives the name of Elizabeth's mother as Martha Dyer. Why Elizabeth in her Will gave her residence as Hoddesdon is also a mystery.

252 There is a hand-written addendum to the probate record for Alfred's will that states *"This grant revoked by Interlocutory Decree and Admon granted May 1842."* That plea was filed by Francis Bentall, and is preserved in the National Archives, box reference PROB 31/1417, statements 1081 and 1082. The reason for this was that by producing a posthumous legitimate heir (the son Alfred, who was not born when the original Will was proved) the original Will was no longer valid, even though Alfred died within months. The effect was for Francis to become the responsible executor and to relieve Henry and Thornton of any further role. However, it provides no clue as to Ellen's whereabouts.

253 Moon (1858).

254 *The Illustrated London News*, July 12, 1845, page 27.

255 This Arthur Cornish was probably the son of Charles Cornish, who was another brother of James Cornish, the MP for Totnes, and also of Thornton's uncle William Floyer Cornish, (see Chapter 12) and Hubert, Thornton's sister-in-law's father (see Chapter 15).

256 Elizabeth Adams (see Chapter 7) ended up living at Mitcham, near Croydon, and invested £5,000 with young Thornton, which she lost when he fled the country.

257 At that time it was generally not necessary to have a passport to leave England or to travel in Europe, other than to France and Belgium. So, once accepted by this Danish family, and having furthermore established some credentials under his new name, it must have been easy to get a job in Christiania without other papers.

258 According to Norwegian sources, the playwright Henrik Ibsen was one of Thomas Bennett's students.

259 Morrell (2014), page 479.

260 As recorded in a Bennett family album, compiled by Thomas Bennett's grandson.

261 As noted in the acknowledgments, I became interested in this family story as a result of an enquiry from Philip Morrell, who wrote a chapter about Thomas Bennett in his autobiography. Much of the information here about Thomas comes from him.

262 The senior partner was Thomas Hilton Bothamley (1805–1874), the son of Joseph Bothamley, a London merchant. His sister Catherine was an accomplished watercolourist, praised by William Wordsworth. Clementina's journal indicates that there were friendly relations between the Bentalls and Bothamleys in 1835.

263 Francis' father, William Searle Bentall, was also living at 14 York Street, Portman Square, in 1844 when he purchased the vault at Highgate Cemetery for brother Thornton (see Chapter 9).

264 According to an email from an assistant librarian at the Lincoln's Inn Library, *"a 'parliamentary agent was a solicitor licensed by Parliament to draft, promote and oppose Private Bills and so their busiest time was at time of railway expansion since railways were created through this type of parliamentary bill"*.

265 These photographs from the Benthall Hall archives do not name the subject, but the papers with which they are stored relate to Buckfast, and Francis was the only family member who lived anywhere near Luton, where the photographs were apparently taken.

266 Hall (1848).

267 *Transactions of the Shropshire Archaeological Society*, Part I, vol XI, October 1887.

268 An unsolved mystery is why she was given the middle name "Blayds." The name is that of a family of merchants and bankers in Leeds, Yorkshire, and a ship of that name was built in 1777 at Liverpool for use in the transatlantic slave trade, but I have found no connection between any Bentall or Marshall and anyone named Blayds.

269 Their nephew, Francis Younghusband, was commissioned as a subaltern in the 1ˢᵗ King's Dragoon Guards in 1882 (the same year that John Matthew Benthall retired from the same regiment—see below). In 1903–1904 he led an invasion of Tibet (by exceeding his instructions from London).

270 *The Genealogist Volume 2*, (1878), edited by George W. Marshall, page 60: Notes on the family of Younghusband.

271 *Allen's Indian Mail – November 1865* reports: "*at Nusseerabad*", the birth on October 11 and the death on October 18 of Ellen Edith, then in the next issue, the death on October 29 of Ellen Blayds, wife of Brigadier-General Younghusband, C.B.

272 See Chapter 12, and note 158.

273 Drake's journal mentions an exchange of visits with Edward Marshall, of the War Office, and then dining many times with William and Mary Marshall.

274 Devon Heritage Centre. Reference numbers 1863A/1/PF/6 and 1863A/1/PF/7. There is no longer any street named Church Lane in Totnes.

275 This was a large house on the top of the hill at the south end of Dawlish which later became the Rockstone Hotel. Louisa Marshall was staying at that house in 1884 while acting as executor of Charles Marshall's estate http://trove.nla.gov.au/newspaper/article/225589545 (retrieved April 2019). It seems that by then her cousin Laura had acquired Rockstone, making Louisa one of the first guests.

276 It is not entirely clear when the old house on The Plains was sold. A typed version of Laura's *Annals* reads: "*In one of the windows of the house there is still (Sept. 14ᵗʰ, 1875) a pane of glass with 'John Clarke, 1737', scratched on it. (Dec. 1876. The house being sold to Mr Tucker, who was making many alterations, L.B. went over for a last look at it and obtained this pane from the glazier, paying him for a new one, and gave it to W.H.B.)*" This looks as though it was added by the typist (who may have been William Henry Benthall), and implies that the house was sold before William died, but that somehow Ann Dart stayed on. But the sale to Mr. Tucker may have fallen through; it could be that the house was still Laura's until after 1881.

277 Keynes (1924).

278 Coase (1994) page 128.

279 As noted in Chapter 7, W.D. Adams was then one of the three Commissioners of Woods, Forests and Land Revenues, and Henry was his nephew. The witnesses signed the document in their office at Whitehall Place.

280 A currier is a specialist in the techniques of dressing, finishing and colouring to the tanned hide to make it strong, flexible and waterproof. The leather is stretched and burnished to produce a uniform thickness and suppleness, and dyeing and other chemical finishes give the leather its desired colour. See https://en.wikipedia.org/wiki/Currier (retrieved April 2019).

281 "*(1) Use mathematics as shorthand language, rather than as an engine of inquiry. (2) Keep to them till you have done. (3) Translate into English. (4) Then illustrate by examples that are important in real life. (5) Burn the mathematics. (6) If you can't succeed in 4, burn 3. This I do often.*" (Letter from Alfred Marshall to Arthur Bowden, 1906). Quoted in Thornton (2014).

282 Coase and Groenewegen made a big deal about how William and Rebecca moved from Bermondsey, known for its tanneries, to the more genteel neighbourhood of Clapham. Coase wrote: "*The signs of upward mobility in the Marshall family reflected in their successive moves from Bermondsey to Sydenham to Clapham to Clapham Common … may indicate little more than his Father's attempts to regain for himself the formal trappings of the status of 'gentleman' that he had claimed for himself on his marriage certificate.*"

283 Groenewegen (1995) on p. 26 notes that "*his final months were made easier by the stay in South Africa his father probably financed, perhaps with assistance from his sons.*" However, this was more probably arranged by his aunt Charlotte. Her father, William Henry Drake, was posted to Grahamstown in 1859, and moved there with his wife, who died there in 1862, after which Drake remarried a year later to Elizabeth Lucy Wood. Susannah Ayliff was Elizabeth Lucy's elder sister.

284 Groenewegen (1995) page 23.

285 Keynes stated that his publications included one named *Man's Rights and Woman's Duties*, but no copies are known to exist.

286 Coase (1994) page 123.

287 Groenewegen (1995) page 29.

288 Ibid, page 23.

289 Scott (2005).

290 Coase (1994) page 125.

291 Ibid, page 135.

292 House of Commons (1845).

293 There is a family connection here. James Richard Dacres died in Mozambique in 1848. James's father and grandfather were also named James Richard Dacres; both were admirals, and the grandfather was the brother of Anna Maria Adams, wet nurse to Princess Amelia (see Chapter 7) and mother of William Dacres Adams, who witnessed William Marshall's acceptance of John Bentall as his legal guardian (see Chapter 13). See https://en.wikipedia.org/wiki/James_Richard_Dacres_(Royal_Navy_officer,_born_1788) (retrieved April 2019).

294 This quote, and those that follow, are from Clowes (1901) pages 369–371.

295 Colburn's United Service Magazine: 1856 Part III page 472. Also see https://en.wikisource.org/wiki/Darien_Exploring_Expedition_(1854) (retrieved April 2019).

296 Clowes (1901) pp 429–432.

297 If Coase was right and this is also correct, he must have been born in the last six weeks of 1816.

298 Clementina wrote in September 1838 from Shaldon (in a letter in the Benthall Hall archives): "*On the 21st Louisa Bentall, Louisa Marshall and Aunt Sally were driven here by Thornton Bentall. He and my Aunt returned the same evening and the next day he came down again with Uncle and Aunt Thornton.*"

299 Although by name a cottage, this house had been called the "High House" and regained that name after Eliza's death. It is still there and is a listed building https://historicengland.org.uk/listing/the-list/list-entry/1306511 (retrieved April 2019).

300 Keynes (1924) reported that Alfred Marshall's "*zeal directed itself at times towards the field of Foreign Missions.*" That sounds like Louisa's influence.

301 Hawtrey (1903).

302 Groenewegen (1995) page 29.

303 Most of the information here covering Marshalls and other relatives in Australia has been provided by Stevens.

304 This account of his career in Australia is taken from Wikipedia: https://en.wikipedia.org/wiki/Glengallan_Homestead (retrieved April 2019).

305 In Edinburgh they visited Leith to see the house where Charles had lived as a boy, and visited the grave of his father.

306 In May 1882 Charlotte Louisa became engaged to Edward Shearburn Marshall, grandson of the Edward Marshall who was a director of the Van Diemen's Land Company and who argued with Palmerston. She broke off the engagement in August, and three years later married Horace Ayliff in South Africa.

307 Alfred (see Chapter 23) had attended Merchant Taylors School and, being academically successful, was entitled to a scholarship at Oxford, which would have been the first step towards ordination and the career that his father wanted for him. But Alfred was dead against a "*continued servitude to the Classics*" and wanted to read Mathematics at Cambridge, in opposition to his father's wishes.

308 The story is told in Summerscale (2012).

309 Charlotte inherited their share of the partnership, which continued until the property was sold in 1904.

310 Groenewegen (1995) page 29.

311 From a letter sent by Charlotte Marshall to her Australian business partner in 1881, quoted by Stevens. See also: https://en.wikipedia.org/wiki/Thomas_Hughes (retrieved April 2019).

312 *An Early Victorian New Zealand Diary*, published in two articles in The Whakatane and District Historical Society's "*Historical Review*" in May and November 1968.

313 *The Elizabethan* Volume 22, number 4, (July 1937) page 79, in an article entitled "*Westminster Families*".

314 In the 1841 census he was listed (aged 19) as residing at Southwark as a pupil in the surgeon's house.

315 Thornton Marshall's descendants were aware that he had spent some of his youth at Totnes, and believed that he had attended Blundell's School, Tiverton, before going up to Cambridge and later completing his medical training at Guy's Hospital. Blundell's published in 1904 a complete register of its pupils from 1770 to 1882, and his name does not appear there. Nor is there a record of his attending Cambridge University, but there is a clear record that he attended Westminster School.

## Part IV

316 Benthall (2000).

317 Brendon (2005).

318 Clementina's diary, and the copious family correspondence, are archived at the Centre of South Asian Studies, Cambridge.

319 http://www.marlboroughcollege.org/about/place/college-history/ (retrieved April 2019).

320 Forshall (1884) page 361.

321 A full account of his cricketing career is available at http://www.espncricinfo.com/england/content/player/9702.html (retrieved April 2019).

322 A number of genealogical web sites provide data from the *Bethlem Hospital patient admission registers and casebooks 1683–1932*.

323 Makepeace, Margaret (2011) *The relationship between the East India Company and its London warehouse labourers, 1800–1858*, Economic History Society Conference April 2011.

324 William Price's mother, Dorothy Penderel, was descended from one Richard Penderel, a farmer in Shropshire who helped Charles II escape from the Parliamentarian New Model Army after his defeat at the Battle of Worcester in 1852. There is a plaque at Benthall Hall commemorating that bizarre episode in British history.

325 https://en.wikipedia.org/wiki/Ystalyfera (retrieved April 2019). A tinplate works there was reputed to be the largest in the world in 1863.

326 Two volumes catalogued as "Life of Elias Jenkins of Tir-gwl, 1777 – 1850, my grandfather", by M.C. Benthall c. 1850" are in the West Glamorgan Archives. However, Elias was her great grandfather, not her grandfather, and the date is certainly suspect. It is more likely that this was written originally by her mother, Jane Benthall, and transcribed by Molly.

327 Trew (2012). The author has kindly sent me copies of the photographs that he published in that book and has given me permission to include them here.

328 https://en.wikipedia.org/wiki/James_Charles_Dale (retrieved April 2019).

329 Great Britain, Patent Office (1878).

330 *English Mechanic and World of Science: Volume 28* page 185.

331  Family records spell her name Madeleine, but census records spell it Madeline. She was known as Minnie.

332  Tachella (1902).

333  https://en.wikipedia.org/wiki/Derby_School (retrieved April 2019).

334  *Journal of the Institute of Electrical Engineers*, Vol. 32, 1902 – 1903, page 541.

335  *Manchester University Roll of Service* (Longman Green & Co., 1922).

336  The church at Cofton had been built as a chapel and was in ruins until 1839, when the parish of Cofton was carved out from the parish of Dawlish and a new church was built by William Courtenay, Earl of Devon, whose younger brother Thomas Peregrine Courtenay had, with the help of William Searle Bentall, arranged for him to inherit the title and the estate of Powderham Castle, nearby. It was not unreasonable that a Benthall should be given the job.

337  The Royal Pioneer Corps was a unit in the British Army that was used for "light engineering tasks." It was the only British military unit in which "enemy aliens" could serve. See https://en.wikipedia.org/wiki/Royal_Pioneer_Corps (retrieved April 2019).

338  In Chapter 4 it was noted that Benthall Hall had been sold in 1844 by the last descendants of its original builders to Lord Forester, who owned much of the farmland in neighbouring parishes. Forester and his descendants leased out the house. The first notable tenant was George Maw, owner of a very successful business nearby manufacturing decorative tiles and also a notable botanist, with a particular passion for crocuses. Another was Robert Bateman, a distinguished artist, architect and horticulturalist, who was the last to occupy Benthall Hall before Charles Francis took his lease.

# Part V

339  Gilbert's correspondence related to this event is in the Shropshire Archives, in Shrewsbury.

340  In the Shropshire Archives.

341  Ernest's father was George Cable and his mother was Emily Maria Pickersgill, who came from an artistic family. There are four Pickersgill portraits at Benthall Hall, and these are discussed in Chapter 36.

342  From Tom Benthall's papers in Centre of Indian and African Studies, Cambridge: *Reflections on Mahatma Gandhi*.

343  https://api.parliament.uk/historic-hansard/written-answers/1953/nov/10/middle-east-mission (retrieved April 2019).

344  Georges obtained a visa to visit Brazil in 1953, and gave those names on his application.

345  Letter from Ruth Benthall to Doreen Morton, dated 30th November 1940, transcribed by Doreen's son.

346  The information here is from Miller (2019).

347  The same Samuel Carter Hall who was immortalised as "Seth Pecksniff" by Charles Dickens, and who published books about the 'Baronial Halls of England' – see Chapter 21.

348  Miller (2019) page 23.

349  Ibid, page 134.

350  In addition to his legitimate children with his wife, Frances, Jerdan fathered many other children out of wed-lock, including a third with Letitia in 1829. They were placed with foster parents, but he kept in touch with them. When Ella emigrated to Australia at age 25, her father wrote to wish her well (ibid., page 82). Letitia herself became addicted to laudanum, married George Maclean, the governor of Cape Coast Castle, a slave-trading outpost in West Africa (now in Ghana), and, soon after arriving there in 1838, died from an overdose of prussic acid (then in use as a narcotic that could replace or supplement laudanum).

351  Bell's palsy is a rather vague term used to describe a failure of the nerve that controls facial muscles. It describes a symptom, and there are many possible causes. Usually it is temporary, but in Paul's case it was not. Today, it is recognized that it can be triggered by the same virus that causes chickenpox and shingles.

352  In Burma (now Myanmar).

353  https://en.wikipedia.org/wiki/Battle_of_Kohima (retrieved April 2019).

354  https://en.wikipedia.org/wiki/Smailholm_Tower (retrieved April 2019).

355  The family played a substantial role in the setting up the East India College (where Edward Benthall trained—see Chapter 17). The Pringle family crest is a winged heart, and the College's coat of arms contains three winged hearts, as well as the motto "Sursum Corda," echoing the Pringle motto "Sursum."

356  Hughes (1904) page 280, see also https://www.historyofparliamentonline.org/volume/1820–1832/member/pringle-alexander–1791–1857 (retrieved April 2019).

357  Scott, W. (1808). Marmion, introduction to Canto Second.

358  Abijah Pears inherited his ribbon manufacturing business from his father, who "*employed some 60 engine looms on narrow ribbons, and at least 300 single hand looms on wider ribbons*": Plummer (1972) page 333.

359  https://www.ucm.es/data/cont/docs/119-2014-02–19-George%20Eliot.pdf (retrieved April 2019).

360  The CBE came first, in 1964; in 1968 Robert Helpmann was awarded a KB. In 2009 an exhibition at the Royal Opera House was held to celebrate the centenary of his birth and was summarised at: http://www.telegraph.co.uk/journalists/rupert-christiansen/5229257/Cute-as-a-monkey-quick-as-a-squirrel.html (retrieved April 2019).

361  From a letter at Benthall Hall written by Dr Sara Serpell in 1996, quoting from *Who Was Who*.

362  Michael Benthall's obituary in the New York Times provides some of the details for this account, and can be found at: https://www.nytimes.com/1974/09/09/archives/michael-benthall-is-dead-at-55-directed-the-old-vic-for-9-years.html?_r=0 (retrieved April 2019).

363  A video documenting the process of recreating Miracle in the Gorbals can be found at https://www.youtube.com/watch?v=Kvv6qmUlr50 (retrieved April 2019).

364  http://www.imdb.com/name/nm0341518/otherworks (retrieved April 2019).

365  https://www.rsc.org.uk/hamlet/past-productions/staging-hamlet-at-the-rsc (retrieved April 2019).

366 http://www.bbc.co.uk/hamlet/past_productions/rsc_stage_1948.shtml (retrieved April 2019).

367 A description of this episode is provided in the letter at Benthall Hall written by Dr Sara Serpell in 1996 mentioned in Note 361.

> *But it was Quayle who was appointed, and he has said that Benthall never showed any sign of resenting this. In fact, he went on working for the company under Quayle. Another reason for the failure of Jackson and Flower to get on seems to have been the fact that Flower disliked homosexuals, and was aware that both Jackson and Benthall were of this inclination. Quayle, who was very much the military ex-army 'chap', and very heterosexual, was more to his liking. (Everyone seems to have overlooked Benthall's military record).*

368 A detailed account of this episode in Hepburn's life is told in Edwards (1985).

369 See *Shakespeare Conquers Broadway: The Olivier Antony and Cleopatra*, by Alice Venezky: Shakespeare Quarterly, Vol. 3, No. 2 (Apr., 1952), pages 121–124, Published by Oxford University Press.

370 See Rowell (1993) for a history of this period.

371 An interesting note on the way this all worked is at http://www.janenightwork.com/robert-gillespie/recollections/hamlet-the-old-vic–1954-assembly-hall-edinburgh-festival/ (retrieved April 2019).

372 https://crystalkalyana.wordpress.com/2016/05/12/katharine-hepburn-in-australia/ (retrieved April 2019).

373 Higham (1975), Carter (2016).

374 The letters are now at the National Library of Australia: https://catalogue.nla.gov.au/Record/4650064 (retrieved April 2019).

375 Michael Benthall, Robert Helpmann and a number of other theatrical people lived for many years in a very fancy block of apartments on Eaton Square. Vivien Leigh was at number 54, Bobby and Michael in adjoining basement apartments separated by a small garden at number 72, and Rex Harrison at number 75.


## Part VI and Appendices

376 Traditionally, owning land was a prerequisite for the right to ride in a fox hunt. See Jenkins (1983) page 197.

377 Titles, and usually also any land, passed to the eldest son. The right to a coat of arms passed to all sons, so younger brothers who found ways to acquire their own rural estates had a small advantage in this regard.

378 As quoted in the letter discussed later in the chapter, published in *The Times* on 10 April 1855.

379 Groenewegen (1995) page 26.

380 Coase (1994) page 144.

381 Stevens (2020) page 2.

382 Kuper (2009) page 24.

383  Ibid. page 27.

384  Ibid. page 99.

385  Ibid. page 27.

386  Wade (1831). Available online through Google Books and various other sources. See https://books.google. co.uk/books/about/The_Extraordinary_Black_Book.html?id=pZTSAAAAMAAJ&redir_esc=y (retrieved April 2019).

387  Courtenay (1832).

388  Hansard's Parliamentary Debates: VOL. CLXXXVI, page 1357.

389  *Western Morning News*, 3 August 1839.

390  *Appendix to the First Report of the Commissioners appointed to inquire into the Municipal Corporations of England and Wales, Part I. Midland, Western and South-Western Circuits. Ordered to be printed 30th March 1835*, pages 639–646.

391  Actually Froude, not Froade. His son, James Anthony Froude, started his education at Buckfastleigh Grammar School and was another Scholar at Westminster. In later life he wrote a poignant memoir about his childhood.

392  Courtenay also said: "*The only alleged evil of the old system, which the New Act removes, is direct Nomination. This has long ceased to exist at Totnes; but it is rather curious, that one of your new Candidates appears to contemplate it among the new constituency.*" At that time, about 267 MPs were returned without a formal vote, based on the nomination of the appropriate patron—as was William Adams when he became M.P. for Plympton Erle.

393  As there is today, in the United States, especially as far as ambassadorial appointments are concerned.

394  Sir Sibbald David Scott Bart (1880) *The British Army: its Origin, Progress and Equipment Vol. III*, page 398.

395  *Hansard's Parliamentary Debates. Vol. XXXII* page 929.

396  *Accounts and Papers of the House of Commons: A return of the barrack Masters ...*, ordered by the House of Commons to be printed 7 March 1856.

397  https://www.hamhigh.co.uk/news/heritage/king-s-troop-the-early-beginnings-of-the-st-john-s-wood-bar-racks–1–1205400 (retrieved April 2019).

398  House of Commons (1840) pages 25–27.

399  Courtenay (1832) page 28.

400  West Glamorgan Archive Service: D/D Je 199.

401  Ernest Benthall was named the executor of Mary Borlase Jenkins' will.

402  The younger John Borlase Jenkins became a lieutenant in the 6th Glamorgan Rifle Volunteers in 1861.

403   It appears that the elder John Borlase Jenkins was bankrupted in 1836, when he was described as a "*lime burner*," but eventually he succeeded his father as manager of the Middle Bank Copper Works..

404   West Glamorgan Archive Service: D/D Je 120.

# ILLUSTRATION SOURCES

## Maps

Map 1: The United Kingdom. Map data © 2018 GeoBasis-DE/BKG (©2009), Google.

Map 2: The South Hams, Devon. Map data © 2018 Google.

Map 3: The River Exe Estuary. Map data © 2018 Google.

## Introduction

Figure 1: Dr William Marshall and William Bentall. (i) © National Trust Images (reference CMS_PCF_509845) (ii) © National Trust (reference CMS_PCF_509816)[i]

Figure 2: Bentall and Marshall Intermarriages. Diagram by the author.

## Part I

Figure 1.1: Borough of Totnes, mayors 1686–1967. Photograph by Alun Stevens (detail).[ii]

Figure 2.1: Dr William Marshall © National Trust / Catriona Hughes (reference CMS_BHH421) (detail).

Figure 2.2: The Rev. William Marshall and some of his descendants. Diagram by the author.

Figure 2.3: Elizabeth Marshall, Mrs. Thomas Baker. © National Trust / Catriona Hughes (reference CMS_BHH422).

Figure 3.1: Dorothy Chadder, Mrs. William Marshall. (i) © National Trust / Catriona Hughes (reference CMS_BHH423), (ii) © National Trust Images (reference CMS_PCF_509842) (detail).

Figure 3.2: Dorothy Chadder's family and ancestry. Diagram by the author.

Figure 3.3: Christopher Wise. Photo credit: Totnes Elizabethan House Museum (accession no. TOTEH1963.128).

Figure 3.4: Dorothy Marshall's birthday party register, 29 August 1822. Photograph by the author.

Figure 3.5: Sarah Chadder. Photograph provided by Megan Stevens.

Figure 4.1: William Bentall ca. 1782. © National Trust (reference CMS_PCF_509838).

Figure 4.2: William Bentall's connections to the Benthall family in Shropshire. Diagram by the author

Figure 4.3: Benthall Hall, built around 1580. Photograph by the author.

---

[i]  References to images reproduced by permission are tagged with the owner's image reference.

[ii]  The reference here and on other images to 'detail' indicates that I have cropped the image to provide a clearer picture within the space constraints of the printed page.

Figure 5.1: Abigail Thornton (née Bulwer) and her daughter Elizabeth Thornton, Mrs John Bentall. (i) ©National Trust Images/John Hammond (reference 98119) (ii) © National Trust (reference CMS_PCF_509819).

Figure 5.2: Elizabeth Thornton's extended family. Diagram by the author.

Figure 5.3: John and Henry Thornton. (i) Public domain. Photograph by Google Cultural Institute, original at SCAD Museum of Art, (ii) © National Portrait Gallery, London (Reference D14768), by permission.

Figure 5.4: Portraits of the Rev. Claude Carter's relatives by Thomas Gainsborough. (i) © Tate, London 2017 Image released under Creative Commons CC-BY-NC-ND (3.0 Unported), (reference T12609), (ii) © The National Gallery, London (reference NG6301), by permission.

Figure 6.1: Grace Searle, Mrs. William Bentall (i) © National Trust Images (reference CMS_PCF_509848), (ii) © National Trust (reference CMS_PCF_509835).

Figure 6.2: Christopher and John Searle. (i) © National Trust / Catriona Hughes (reference CMS_BHH432), (ii) © National Trust / Catriona Hughes (reference CMS_BHH446).

Figure 6.3: Totnes Waterside diagram. Photograph by Philip Morrell.

Figure 6.4: Symon's Passage façade in 2019. Photograph by Edward Benthall.

Figure 6.5: William and Grace Bentall's children. Diagram by the author.

## Part II

Figure 7.1: The Adams waistcoat © 2019 Royal Albert Memorial Museum & Art Gallery, Exeter City Council (reference 108/1952/2); see https://rammcollections.org.uk/object/108–1952-2/ (retrieved April 2019).

Figure 7.2: The Adams Family. Diagram by the author.

Figure 7.3: Portrait of William Dacres Adams after a drawing by Lawrence (Garlick 1964, p.211.1) © The Trustees of the British Museum (reference AN1024012001), licensed under a Creative Commons Attribution-NonCommercial-ShareAlike 4.0 International (CC BY-NC-SA 4.0) license.

Figure 7.4: William Searle and Elizabeth Bentall, as children, © National Trust (reference CMS_PCF_509836).

Figure 7.5: Thomas Welch © National Trust (reference CMS_PCF_509837).

Figure 8.1: Elopement from Bristol. Photograph by the author.

Figure 8.2: The Ogilvie, Perry and Marshall Families. Diagram by the author.

Figure 8.3: George and Barbara Ogilvie. (i) © National Trust / Catriona Hughes (reference CMS_BHH145), (ii) © National Trust Images (reference CMS_PCF_509836).

Figure 8.4: French Passports: 1790. Photographs by the author.

Figure 8.5: Richard, Clementina and Isabella Perry Ogilvie. (i) and (ii) Photographs by the author, (iii) © National Trust / Catriona Hughes (reference CMS_BHH143), (iv) © National Trust / Catriona Hughes (reference CMS_BHH152), (v) © National Trust / Catriona Hughes (reference CMS_BHH146).

Figure 9.1: William Searle, Thornton and John Bentall and their families. Diagram by the author.

Figure 9.2: Mary Ann Marshall and William Searle Benthall. (i) © National Trust (reference CMS_PCF_509836), (ii) © National Trust / Catriona Hughes (reference CMS_BHH429) detail, (iii) © National Trust / Catriona Hughes (reference CMS_BHH435) detail, (iv) photograph by the author.

Figure 9.3: William Searle and Mary Ann Benthall (née Marshall), by Laura Benthall. (i) © National Trust / Catriona Hughes (reference CMS_BHH084) detail, (ii) © National Trust / Catriona Hughes (reference CMS_ BHH083) detail, (iii) photograph by the author.

Figure 9.4: Thornton's armorial tea set. © National Trust / Catriona Hughes (references CMS_BHH529 and CMS_BHH530).

Figure 9.5: Thornton and Margaret Bentall (née Marshall). © National Trust / Catriona Hughes (references CMS_ BHH527, CMS_BHH425 and CMS_BHH530).

Figure 10.1: Thomas Peregrine Courtenay (1782–1841) © National Portrait Gallery, London (reference D34169).

Figure 11.1: Buckfast Abbey. Photograph provided by Alun Stevens.

Figure 12.1: Rev. William Floyer Cornish, and Elizabeth Marshall. (i) © National Trust / Catriona Hughes (reference CMS_BHH379) detail, (ii) photograph by the author.

Figure 12.2: Vestal and Wildfire in a Race Match, 1857. Image © 2017 University of Missouri, licensed under a Creative Commons Attribution 4.0 International License.

Figure 12.3: Ellen and Thomas Marshall. Photographs provided by Ralph Ravestijn.

Figure 12.4: Mary and Alexander Marshall. © National Trust / Catriona Hughes (references CMS_BHH439 and CMS_BHH437) detail.

Figure 13.1: William and Louisa Marshall. Photographs provided by Megan Stevens.

Figure 13.2: William and Louisa Marshall's children. Diagram by the author.

## Part III

Figure 15.1: William and Elizabeth Bentall. (i) Photograph by the author, (ii) © National Trust Images (reference CMS_PCF_509843) detail.

Figure 16.1: Wardales, Waterfields, Gays and Benthalls. Diagram by the author.

Figure 17.1: John and Edward Benthall, and their children. Diagram by the author.

Figure 17.2: John Benthall, his first wife and children. © National Trust / Catriona Hughes (references CMS_ BHH386 and CMS_BHH388 and CMS_BHH100) (details).

Figure 17.3: Fanny Levi. Photograph by the author.

Figure 17.4: Edward and Clementina Benthall (c. 1840). (i) © National Trust / Catriona Hughes (reference CMS_ BHH065), (ii) © National Trust Images/John Hammond (reference 98121).

Figure 17.5: The House at Jessore. © National Trust / Catriona Hughes (reference CMS_BHH456).

Figure 17.6: Edward and Clementina Benthall in retirement (i) Photograph by the author, (ii) © National Trust / Catriona Hughes (reference CMS_BHH512) (detail).

Figure 18.1: Sarah Ellen and Henry Benthall © National Trust / Catriona Hughes (references CMS_BHH448 and CMS_BHH460) (details).

Figure 18.2: Blackfriars Bridge. Publisher Tombleson & Company 1834, copied from Dennett (1998).

Figure 19.1: Octavius Benthall © National Trust / Catriona Hughes (references CMS_BHH433 and CMS_ BHH426) (detail).

Figure 20.1: Thomas Bennett (a.k.a. Thornton Bentall or Benthall). Photographs provided by Philip Morrell.

Figure 21.1: Francis (Frank) Benthall. Photograph by the author.

Figure 22.1: Louisa and Ellen Blayds Benthall. Details from a photograph by the author.

Figure 22.2: Willen Vicarage. Original, property of the Centre for Buckinghamshire Studies, and reproduced by permission, reference PR/231/3/3.

Figure 22.3: Laura Benthall. (i) Photograph provided by Philip Morrell, (ii) Photograph by the author.

Figure 22.4: Laura Benthall's portrait collection. Photograph by the author.

Figure 23.1: Alfred Marshall. Photograph from The Economic Journal, September 1924.

Figure 26.1: Charles Henry Marshall. Photograph provided by Megan Stevens.

Figure 18.1: Thornton and Fannie Marshall. Photograph copied from The Whakatane and District Historical Society's Historical Review, published May 1968.

## Part IV

Figure 29.1: Clement Edward Benthall: Photographs by the author.

Figure 29.2: Bertha Benthall: Photographs by the author.

Figure 30.1: Edith Benthall, wife of William Henry Benthall, © National Trust / Catriona Hughes (references CMS_BHH392, CMS_BHH147 and CMS_BHH394) (details).

Figure 30.2: Henry (Harry) Everett and William Louis Benthall © National Trust / Catriona Hughes (references CMS_BHH364 and CMS_BHH445) (details).

Figure 31.1: Ernest and Jane Benthall (and her sister) © National Trust / Catriona Hughes (references CMS_BHH381 and CMS_BHH393) (details).

Figure 31.2: William and Mary Price. Photographs by the author.

Figure 31.3: Benthall Mugs. © Michael Trew, reproduced by permission.

Figure 31.4: Mary Clementina (Molly) Benthall. Photographs by the author.

Figure 32.1: Madeleine Benthall and Edward Robert Dale. Photographs by the author.

Figure 32.2 Mary Clementina Benthall and James Floyer Dale. Photograph by the author.

Figure 33.1: The Rev. Charles Francis Benthall. (i) Photograph by the author, (ii) © National Trust (reference CMS_PCF_509822).

Figure 33.2: Anne Benthall. (i)–(iii) Photographs by the author, (iv) © National Trust / Catriona Hughes (reference CMS_BHH095).

Figure 33.3: The family of Charles and Anne Benthall. Diagram by the author.

Figure 33.4: Paul and Mick Benthall. Photograph by the author.

## Part V

Figure 35.1: Ruth and Tom Benthall. © National Trust (references CMS_PCF_509820 and CMS_PCF509824).

Figure 36.1: Pickersgill and Cable Family Tree. Diagram by the author.

Figure 36.2: Henry William Pickersgill Paintings. © National Trust Images (references CMS_PCF_509855 and CMS_PCF_509856).

Figure 36.3: Frederick Richard Pickersgill: Lady in a Persian Dress and Samson Betrayed. (i) © National Trust (reference CMS_PCF_509828), (ii) © National Trust Images (reference CMS_PCF_509854.)

## Part VI

## Appendices

# BIBLIOGRAPHY

Atkyns, J. T. (1754). *Reports of Cases Argued and Determined in the High Court of Chancery in the Time of Lord Chancellor Hardwicke* (Vol. 2). London: A. Strahan & W. Woodfall, Law-Printers to the King.

Baines, E. (1822). *History, Directory and Gazetteer of the County of York, with select lists of the Merchants and Traders of London*. Leeds: Edward Baines.

Benthall, A.P. (1946) *The Trees of Calcutta and its Neighbourhood*. Calcutta: Thacker, Spink & Company.

Benthall, J. (2000). *Families in India*. Unpublished typescript.

Benthall, Mrs. C. (1911). *When I Was*. London: Guy & Hancock.

Boyd, M. (1871). *Reminiscences of Fifty Years*. London: Longmans, Green & Co.

Bray, A. E. K. (1838). *Traditions, Legends, Superstitions and Sketches of Devonshire* (Vol. 3). London: John Murray.

Brendon, V. (2005). *Children of the Raj*. London: Weidenfeld & Nicholson.

Brown, D. (2010). *Palmerston: A Biography*. New Haven and London: Yale University Press.

Carter, G. M. (2016). *Katharine Hepburn*. Retrieved from https://www.kobo.com/us/en/ebook/katharine-hepburn-4.

Chapman, R. A. (2011). *Leadership in the British Civil Service: A Study of Sir Percival Waterfield and the Civil Service Selection Board*. Abingdon-on-Thames: Routledge. (Original work published 1984).

Cherry, B., & Pevsner, N. (1989). *Devon*. Pevsner Architectural Guides: The Buildings of England. New Haven and London: Yale University Press.

Clowes, W. L., & Markham, C. R. (1901). *The Royal Navy: A History from the Earliest Times to the Present* (Vol. 6). London: Sampson Low, Marston & Co.

Coase, R. H. (1984). Alfred Marshall's Mother and Father. *History of Political Economy, 16*, 519–527.

Coase, R. H. (1990). Alfred Marshall's Family and Ancestry. In R. M. Tullberg (Ed.), *Alfred Marshall in Retrospect* (pp. 9–27). Cheltenham: Edward Elgar Publishing.

Coase, R. H. (1994). *Essays on Economics and Economists*. Chicago and London: Chicago University Press.

Courtenay, T. P. (1832). *A Farewell Address to his Constituents at Totnes*. London: Caulkin & Budd.

Cust, L. (1899). *A History of Eton College*. London: Duckworth & Co.

Dennett, L. (1998). *A Sense of Security: 150 Years of Prudential*. Cambridge, UK: Granta Editions.

Dickens, C. (1853). *Bleak House*. London: Chapman & Hall.

Dunlap, J. A. (Ed.). (1844). *Reports of Cases in Chancery Argued and Determined in the Rolls Court During the Time of Lord Langdale, Master of the Rolls* (Vol. 17). New York: Gould, Banks & Co.

Edwards, A. (1985). *Katharine Hepburn: A Remarkable Woman*. New York: Macmillan.

Emery, A. (2006). *Greater Medieval Houses of England and Wales, 1300–1500* (Vol. 3). Cambridge, UK: Cambridge University Press.

Fisher, D. R. (Ed.). (2009). *The History of Parliament: The House of Commons 1820–1832*. Cambridge, UK: Cambridge University Press.

Forshall, F. H. (1884). *Westminster School, Past and Present*. London: Wyman & Sons.

Forster, E. M. (1956). *Marianne Thornton*. London: Butler & Tanner.

Foster, J. (1889). *The Register of Admissions to Gray's Inn, 1521–1889*. London: The Hansard Publishing Union.

Francis, J. (1848). *History of the Bank of England, Its Times and Traditions* (Vol. II). London: Willoughby & Co.

Fryer, M. B., & Dracott, C. (1998). *John Graves Simcoe, 1752–1806: A Biography*. Toronto: Dundurn Press.

Fyfe, P. (2014). *Accidental Death: Lizzie Siddal and the Poetics of the Coroner's Inquest*. Victorian Review, 40(2), 17–22.

Green, M. A. E. (Ed.). (1889). *Calendar of the Proceedings of the Committee for Compounding, etc. 1643–1660, Preserved in the State Paper Department of Her Majesty's Public Record Office* (*Vol 3: Cases, 1647–June, 1650*). London: Eyre & Spottiswoode for Her Majesty's Stationary Office.

Groenewegen, P. D. (1995). *A Soaring Eagle: Alfred Marshall 1842–1924*. Cheltenham: Edward Elgar Publishing.

Hall, N. J. (Ed.). (1983). *The Letters of Anthony Trollope*. Stanford, CA: Stanford University Press.

Hall, S. C. (1848). *The Baronial Halls and Picturesque Edifices of England*. London: Chapman & Hall.

Hardy, C. (1811). *A Register of Ships Employed in the Service of the Honourable the United East India Company from the Year 1760 to 1810*. London: Black, Parry & Kingsbury.

Harrison, G. (1956). *Bird and Company of Calcutta: A History Produced to Mark the Firm's Centenary 1864–1964*. Calcutta: Bird & Co.

Hawtrey, F. M. (1903). *The History of the Hawtrey Family*. London: George Allen.

Hazlitt, W. C. (1912). *The Hazlitts, Part the Second; A Narrative of the Later Fortunes of the Family*. Edinburgh: Ballantyne, Hanson & Co.

Hendley, M. C. (2012). *Organized Patriotism and the Crucible of War*. Montreal: McGill-Queen's University Press.

Higham, C. (1975). *Kate: The Life of Katharine Hepburn*. New York: W. W. Norton & Co.

Houghton, W. E. (1957). *The Victorian Frame of Mind, 1830–1870*. New Haven and London: Yale University Press.

House of Commons. (1816). *Report of the Commissioners for Examining into the Duties, Salaries and Emoluments, of the Officers, Clerks and Ministers, of the Several Courts of Justice, in England, Wales and Berwick-upon-Tweed; as to the Court of Chancery: Dated 9th April 1816*. London: H.M. Stationery Office.

House of Commons. (1840). *First Report of the Deputy Keeper of the Public Records*. London: H.M. Stationery Office.

House of Commons. (1843). *Return of the State of Several Funds Standing in the Name of the Accountant-General of the Court of Chancery, and the Charges upon the Same Dated 28 February 1843*. London: H.M. Stationery Office.

House of Commons. (1845). *Correspondence with the British Commissioners … relating to the slave trade, from January 1 to December 31, 1844 inclusive*. London: H.M. Stationery Office.

Hughes, M. A. W., & Hutchinson, H. G. (Ed.). (1904). *Letters and Recollections of Sir Walter Scott*. London: Smith, Elder & Co.

*Hunt & Co.'s Directory and Topography for the cities of Exeter and Bristol* etc. (1848). London: E. Hunt & Co.

Hunt, T. (2014). *Cities of Empire: the British Colonies and the Creation of the Urban World*. New York: Metropolitan Books.

Hunt, V. (1932). *The Wife of Rossetti: Her Life and Death*. London: John Lane, Bodley Head.

Hunter, J., & Clay, J. W. (Ed.). (1894). *Familiae Minorum Gentium* (Vol. 1). London: Harleian Society.

Jenkins, P. (1983). *The Making of a Ruling Class: The Glamorgan Gentry 1640–1790*. Cambridge, UK: Cambridge University Press.

Keynes, J. M. (1924). Alfred Marshall, 1842–1924. *The Economic Journal, 34*(135), 311–372.

Kuper, A. (2009). *Incest & Influence: The Private Life of Bourgeois England*. Cambridge, MA, and London: Harvard University Press.

Landes, D. S. (1998). *The Wealth and Poverty of Nations: Why Some Are So Rich and Some So Poor*. New York: W. W. Norton & Co.

Leader, J.D. (1880). *Mary Queen of Scots in Captivity*. London, George Bell & Sons.

Lewis, C. S., & Lewis, W. H. (Ed.). (1966). *Letters of C. S. Lewis*. New York: Harcourt Brace.

McConville, S. (1995). *English Local Prisons, 1860–1900: Next Only to Death*. London: Routledge.

Miller, L. (2019). *L.E.L.: The Lost Life and Scandalous Death of Letitia Elizabeth Landon, the Celebrated "Female Byron."* New York: Knopf.

Moon, H. (1858). *An Account of the Wreck of H. M. Sloop "Osprey"; with the Encampment of Her Crew, and Their March Across the Island of New Zealand: Blended with Moral and Scriptural Illustrations*. Landport: Annett & Robinson.

Morrell, P. (2014). *Return Ticket Home: The Boy from Barnardo's Who Floated the Queen*. London: Magna Carta S. C.

Morris, N., & Rothman, D. J. (Eds.). (1998). *The Oxford History of the Prison: The Practice of Punishment in Western Society*. Oxford: Oxford University Press.

Newham, J. W. & Coltman, P. (Ed.). (1984). *The Diary of a Prison Governor: James William Newham, 1825–1890*. Maidstone: Kent County Council.

O'Byrne, W. R. (1849). *A Naval Biographical Dictionary: Comprising the Life and Services of Every Living Officer in Her Majesty's Navy, from the Rank of Admiral of the Fleet to that of Lieutenant, Inclusive*. London: John Murray.

Pemberton, P.A. (1986). *Pure Merinos and Others: The "Shipping Lists" of the Australian Agricultural Company*. Canberra: Australian National University.

Pengelly, W. (1885). *W. Prince's "Worthies of Devon" and the Dictionary of National Biography, Part I*. Transactions of the Devonshire Association, 17, 199–214.

Philip, P. (1981). *British Residents at the Cape, 1795–1819*. Cape Town: David Philip.

Plummer, A. (1972). *The London Weavers' Company 1600–1970*. London: Routledge & Kegan Paul.

Poole, E. (1886). *The Illustrated History and Biography of Brecknockshire from the Earliest Times to the Present Day*. Brecon: Author.

Reid, Lieut.-Colonel W. (1838). *An Attempt to Develop the Law of Storms by Means of Facts, Arranged According to Place and Time…* London: John Weale.

Rossetti, D. G., & Rossetti, W. M. (1895). *Dante Gabriel Rossetti: His Family Letters, with a Memoir by William Michael Rossetti*. London: Ellis & Elvey.

Rothwell, P., & Ternstrom, M. (2008). *The Lundy Granite Company: An Industrial Adventure*. Marwood, Devon: Westwell Publishing.

Rowell, G. (1993). *The Old Vic Company: A History*. Cambridge, UK: Cambridge University Press.

Russell, P., & Masson Philips, E. N. (1984). *The Good Town of Totnes*. Exeter: The Devonshire Association.

Sargeaunt, J. (1898). *Annals of Westminster School*. London: Methuen & Co.

Sellers, C. (1899). *Oporto, Old and New. Being a Historical Record of the Port Wine Trade, and a Tribute to British Commercial Enterprize in the North of Portugal*. London: Herbert E. Harper (*The Wine and Spirit Gazette*).

Simister, L. (2015). *Charles Babbage from the Beginning*. Retrieved from https://www.kobo.com/us/en/ebook/charles-babbage-from-the-beginning-2.

Scott, G. R. (2005). *The History of Corporal Punishment: A Survey of Flagellation in its Historical, Anthropological and Sociological Aspects*. Abingdon-on-Thames: Routledge. (Original work published 1938).

Scott, W. (1808). *Marmion: A Tale of Flodden Field*. Edinburgh: Archibald Constable & Co.

Stevens, M. (2020). *The Wrong Marshall*. History of Political Economy.

Stott, A. (2012). *Wilberforce: Family and Friends*. Oxford: Oxford University Press.

Summerscale, K. (2012). *Mrs. Robinson's Disgrace: The Private Diary of a Victorian Lady*. London: Bloomsbury.

Tachella, B. (Ed.). (1902) *The Derby School Register, 1570–1901*. London: Bemrose & Sons.

T. B. (1844). *A Few Words of Friendly Caution to the Tories in the Two Houses of Parliament*. London: Painter.

Thorne, R. G. (Ed.). (1986). *The House of Commons, 1790–1820*. The History of Parliament. London: Secker & Warburg for the History of Parliament Trust.

Thornton, P. M. (1912). *Some Things We Have Remembered: Samuel Thornton, Admiral, 1797–1859; Percy Melville Thornton, 1841–1911*. London: Longmans, Green & Co.

Thornton, P. (2014). *The Great Economists: Ten Economists Whose Thinking Changed the Way We Live*. London: FT Publishing International.

Trew, M. (2012). *Ynysmeudwy and the Williamses*. Burry Port: Author.

*The Trial of Richard Vining Perry, Esq. for Forcible Abduction, or Stealing an Heiress, from the Boarding-School of Miss Mills, in the City of Bristol* (1794). Bristol.

Turner, J. D. (2014). *Banking in Crisis: The Rise and Fall of British Banking Stability, 1800 to the Present*. Cambridge, UK: Cambridge University Press.

Urban, S. (Ed.). (1833). *The Gentleman's Magazine and Historical Chronicle*. (Volume CIII) London: E. Cave.

Urban, S. (Ed.). (1856). *The Gentleman's Magazine and Historical Review*. (Volume I, New Series) London: John Henry and James Parker.

Urban, S. (Ed.). (1863). *The Gentleman's Magazine and Historical Review* (Volume XIV, New Series) London: John Henry and James Parker.

Vivian, J. L. (1895). *The Visitations of the County of Devon, Comprising the Herald's Visitations of 1531, 1564, & 1620*. Exeter: Henry S. Eland for the Author.

Wade, J. (Ed.). (1832): *The Extraordinary Black Book: An Exposition of Abuses in Church and State...* London: Effingham Wilson, Royal Exchange.

Wagner, A. (1976). *Pedigree and Progress: Essays in the Genealogical Interpretation of History*. London: Phillimore & Co.

Walker, J. (1714). *Sufferings of the Clergy Part II* page 385. London.

Wardale, E. E. (1922). *An Old English Grammar*. New York: E. P. Dutton & Co.

Wardale, E. E. (1935). *Chapters on Old English Literature*. London: K. Paul, Trench, Trubner & Co.

Welch, J. (1852). *The List of the Queen's Scholars of St. Peter's College, Westminster...* London: G. W. Ginger.

White, T. (1830). *Naval Researches; or, a Candid Inquiry into the Conduct of Admirals Byron, Graves, Hood, and Rodney, in the Actions off Grenada, Chesapeake, St. Christopher's, and of the Ninth and Twelfth of April, 1782...* London: Whittaker, Treacher & Arnott.

Wills, W. J., & Wills, W (Ed.). (1863). *Successful Exploration Through the Interior of Australia, from Melbourne to the Gulf of Carpentaria*. London: Richard Bentley.

Wilson, B. (2007). *The Making of Victorian Values: Decency & Dissent in Britain: 1789–1837*. New York: Penguin Press.

Windeatt, E. (1891). Totnes: Its Mayors and Mayoralties – continued. *The Western Antiquary, 10*, (W.H.K. Wright, Editor)

Windeatt, E. (1904). Totnes: Its Mayors and Mayoralties, 1751–1800. *Transactions of the Devonshire Association, 36*, 487–505.

Windeatt, E. (1905) Totnes: Its Mayors and Mayoralties. Part V. *Transactions of the Devonshire Association, 37*, 398–410.

Windeatt, E. (1908). The Constitution of the Merchants' Company in Totnes, 1579–1593. *Transactions of the Devonshire Association, 40*, 148–171.

Wood, J. C. (Ed.). (1993). *Alfred Marshall: Critical Assessments*. London: Routledge.

# INDEX

14 Chatham Place, 130–133

Adams, Amelia, née Read (1815–1884) 40, 46, 255n65

Adams, Anna Maria, née Dacres (c.1751–1830), 11, 40, 42

Adams, Arthur (1852–1926), 45

Adams, Edward (1804–1892), 40, 45, 239

Adams, Elizabeth, née Bentall (1779–1848), xix, 37, 40–41, 44–45, 64, 71, 80, 230

Adams, Elizabeth, née Wynell-Mayow (c.1791–1814) 40, 73

Adams, Ellen Harriet, née Adams (1840–1908), 46, 231

Adams, Frederick (1814–1892), 40, 46, 239

Adams, George (1808–1892), 40, 46, 239

Adams, George Henry (1835–1915), 46, 231

Adams, George Pownall (1778–1856), 40, 42–44, 66, 72, 74, 107, 238, 242

Adams, Harriet, née Bickham (1805–1885), 40, 45

Adams, Henry Bentall (1806–1901), 40, 45, 102, 156, 239

Adams, Horace Reid (1849–1911), 45

Adams, Lewisa Sawyer (1783–1867), 40, 42

Adams, Louisa, née Sanford (1830–1929), 40, 46

Adams, Mary, née Chadder (1733–1797), 14, 40–41

Adams, Mary Josepha, née Reid (1813–1901), 40, 45

Adams, Mayow Wynell (1808–1896), 44, 238

Adams, Dacres (1806–1871), 44, 131

Adams, Samuel (1770–1842): barrack master at Hounslow, 101–102, 123, 238–239, 241; children, 40, 44–46;

marriage to Elizabeth Bentall, xviii–xix, 13, 36–37, 41, 45, 64, 71, 230–231; Totnes freeman and mayor, 44, 72

Adams, William (doctor) (1723–1789), xix, 13–14, 40–42, 230

Adams, William (MP) (1752–1811), 11, 13–14, 40–44, 47, 66, 70–72, 97-98, 230, 232, 234, 236

Adams, William (Office of Woods and Forests) (1802–1868), 40, 45, 126, 239

Adams, William Dacres (1775–1862), 13, 40–45, 72–74, 102, 155, 230, 233, 238, 242, 267n279, 268n293

Adams, William Pitt (1804–1852), 44, 108, 238

Amelia, Princess, 11, 42, 242, 268n293

Armstrong, Arthur Henry (1893–1972), 190–191

Armstrong, Monica Clare (Mick), née Benthall (1891–1969), 190–192

Ashprington, 7–8, 254n47

Aunt Thornton. *See* Benthall, Margaret Eleanora Admonition, née Marshall (1787–1860)

Austen, Jane, 10, 161, 225, 252n15

Ayliff, Charlotte Louisa, née Marshall (1859–1937), 164, 269n306


Babbage, Charles, 112, 226

Baker, Elizabeth, née Marshall (1735–1825), 9–11, 15

Baker, Thomas (1727–1803), 9, 11, 42

Bank of England, 27, 79, 156, 253n38

Baring-Gould, Edward, 159

Baring-Gould, Sabine (1834–1906), 159